# A Procedural Framework for Transboundary Water Management in the Mekong River Basin

# International Water Law Series



VOLUME 1

The titles published in this series are listed at *brill.com/iwl*

# A Procedural Framework for Transboundary Water Management in the Mekong River Basin

*Shared Mekong for a Common Future*

*By*

Qi Gao

BRILL
NIJHOFF

LEIDEN | BOSTON

Library of Congress Cataloging-in-Publication Data

Gao, Qi , author.
A procedural framework for transboundary water management in the Mekong River basin : shared Mekong for a common future / by Qi Gao.
pages cm. — (International water law series ; volume 1)
Originally issued as author's thesis (Ph. D.)—University of Western Sydney, 2013.
Includes bibliographical references and index.
ISBN 978-90-04-26678-0 (hardback : alk. paper) — ISBN 978-90-04-26679-7 (e-book) 1. Water resources development—Law and legislation—Mekong River Watershed 2. Mekong River Watershed—International status. I. Title.

KNC660.M45G36 2014
341.4'420959—dc23

2013049069

This publication has been typeset in the multilingual 'Brill' typeface. With over 5,100 characters covering Latin, IPA, Greek, and Cyrillic, this typeface is especially suitable for use in the humanities.
For more information, please see brill.com/brill-typeface.

ISSN 2351-9606
ISBN 978 90 04 26678 0 (hardback)
ISBN 978 90 04 26679 7 (e-book)



This book is printed on acid-free paper.

MIX
Paper from responsible sources
FSC® C109576
www.fsc.org

Printed by Printforce, the Netherlands

*To my beloved parents,*
*Shenghong Gao and Jie Xin,*
*my dear husband Lei Duan*
*and*
*In memory of*
*Professor Michael Jeffery, QC*

# Contents

# Preface

This book marks the culmination of my past six years of research in the area of transboundary water management. My academic journey was first guided by Professor Ke Jian from the Wuhan University, who aroused my interests on transboundary water management and the associated legal and political theories. I spent two years focusing on the management of transboundary water pollution within China, which led me to rethink the prevalent theory of integrated water resources management in the context of developing countries like China.

Further down this road, I shifted my attention to transboundary water management issues at the regional level, bearing in mind of the questions I had since my previous research. In particular, I was puzzled, yet, deeply attracted by the increasingly polycentric nature of transboundary cooperation, the various stages of domestic reforms and complicated geopolitical situation in the Mekong region. I therefore conducted around four years of research on the Mekong water governance in Australia at the University of Western Sydney (UWS) with financial support from both the Chinese Scholarship Council and the UWS. I wish to express my sincere gratitude to all those people who have given me their generous help and warm encouragement during the preparation of this book.

I am deeply grateful for Professor Michael Jeffery, QC who went beyond the call of duty to ensure that I was not only academically well supervised but also that my stay in Australia was an enjoyable and memorable one. I am also very grateful to Professor Donna Craig, for her generosity and kindness and for her influence on me as a successful female academic who managed to find a good balance between work and life. I was truly shocked and saddened to learn about the passing of Professor Jeffery in July 2013. Publishing this book is my way of remembering him and offering my condolences to his family.

For the past four years, Professor Ke Jian from Wuhan University has kindly made many valuable suggestions to me. Thanks to him, I was introduced to the Mekong Legal Network in Thailand, which has been very beneficial to my research. I would therefore like to thank Daniel King and all of the other friends I made through this great network. I have also interacted with academics and students from the Mekong Research Group (previously known as the Australian Mekong Resource Centre). I would like to thank everyone there who, in their different ways, gave support and helped me carry out my research, especially Professor Philip Hirsh, Professor Bernard Boer, Visiting Professor Lu Xing, Dong Xing, Yumiko Yasuda and Oulavanh Keovilignavong.

My academic life at the UWS, School of Law was greatly enriched by my dear colleagues. Dr. Xiaobo Zhao, Dr. Xiaoyi Jiang and Dr. Hem Aitken who helped a lot when

I first started my study there and have since shared their valuable research and life experiences. I am also grateful for numerous interesting discussions with Manzoor Rashid, Elizabeth Gachenga, Xiangbai He and Ying Shen.

I would like to thank Professor Wang Xi and the KoGuan Law School of the Shanghai Jiao Tong University for the great support I received during the process of finalizing this book. I am also deeply appreciative of the efficient and skilful help from Marie Sheldon, Lisa Hanson and the rest of the team at Brills.

Finally, the successful completion of this book would not have been possible without the enormous support and sacrifice of my family. I owe a large debt of gratitude to my loving parents for being so supportive of their daughter's choice even if that meant their only child rarely came home for the past four years. My deep apologies and gratitude also extend to my dear husband, Lei Duan, who is currently a PhD candidate in the University of Tokyo, Japan and has been my soul mate and best friend for over eight years. I would like to thank my relatives and friends in China and Japan for their generous support and help, not only to myself, but also to my parents and husband.

# Abstract

The Mekong River is "both a uniting and dividing force" for China and Southeast Asia.[1] The initial focus of the study will identify the major environmental challenges on the Mekong River ecosystem and the status quo of water resources management in the Mekong region, focusing on the existing water-related legal arrangements and mechanisms at both domestic and regional levels. It will discuss the ongoing difficulties and as well as aspirations for reform of the water management regime. The capacity of governments and inter-governmental organisations with regard to implementation and legal regulation will also be analysed, as well as the role of non-state actors on decision-making processes concerning development activities in the region. It is obvious that, despite attempts to reshape the management of Mekong water resources into a more integrated regime, the current frameworks at both domestic and regional levels remain fragmented.

Under these circumstances, this book attempts to explore procedural implications of integrated water resources management and its application in the Mekong region. The increasingly polycentric nature of transboundary cooperation must be borne in mind, with the emergence of newly recognised stakeholders who represent a broader range of interests than has been the case in the past. The following major procedural requirements can be identified in the proposed procedural framework: information exchange and data collection on a regular basis (chapter three); notification and consultation (chapter four); the public's right of access to information and participation (chapter five) and environmental impact assessment, strategic environmental assessment, and their applications in the transboundary context (chapter six).

In order to tailor and better understand the procedural requirements in the context of the Mekong region, both the ideal and practical scenarios are considered, combined with selected case studies. Existing legislation and practice concerning the use and application of procedural mechanisms in the Mekong region will be analysed. The discussion on procedural mechanisms will also consider how to improve their implementation in light of the ongoing tradition and strong preference for soft law approaches to transboundary cooperation. The relationship between legally-binding agreements and the capacity for compliance in the context of the Mekong region will be discussed. In addition, the relationship between the procedural and substantial elements of integrated river basin management will be re-examined in the final chapter. The final chapter will outline the conclusions and suggest possible areas for future research.

1 Philip Hirsch et al., 'National Interests and Transboundary Water Governance in the Mekong' (Report, University of Sydney, 2006) iii.

## List of Abbreviations

| | |
|---|---|
| ACFTA | Association of Southeast Asian Nations—China Free Trade Area |
| ADB | Asian Development Bank |
| ANZ | Australia and New Zealand Banking Group Limited |
| ASEAN | Association of Southeast Asian Nations |
| BDP | Basin Development Plan Programme |
| BNP Paribas | Banque Nationale de Paris Paribas |
| CEO | Chief Executive Officer |
| CHR | Commission for the Hydrology of the Rhine Basin |
| EGAT | Electricity Generating Authority of Thailand |
| EIA | environmental impact assessment |
| EU | European Union |
| GDP | gross domestic product |
| GEF | Global Environmental Facility |
| GMS | Greater Mekong Subregion |
| GTI | Greater Tumen Initiative |
| IBWC | International Boundary and Water Commission |
| ICEM | International Centre for Environmental Management |
| ICJ | International Court of Justice |
| ICPR | International Commission for the Protection of the Rhine |
| IEE | initial environmental examination |
| IKMP | Information and Knowledge Management Programme |
| IPCC | Intergovernmental Panel on Climate Change |
| IUCN | International Union for Conservation of Nature |
| IWRM | integrated water resources management |
| KBS | Kredietbank ABB Insurance CERA Bank |
| MEP | Ministry of Environmental Protection |
| MOU | memorandum of understanding |
| MOX | mixed oxide |
| MRC | Mekong River Commission |
| MWR | Ministry of Water Resources |
| NAFTA | North American Free Trade Agreement |
| NEQA | Enhancement and Conservation of National Environmental Quality Act |
| NGO | non-governmental organisation |
| NMC | National Mekong Committee |
| NWRC | National Water Resources Committee |
| PM | particulate matter |

| | |
|---|---|
| SEA | strategic environmental assessment |
| UN | United Nations |
| UNCLOS | United Nations Convention on the Law of the Sea |
| UNDP | United Nations Development Programme |
| UNECE | United Nations Economic Commission for Europe |
| UNEP | United Nations Environment Programme |
| WTO | World Trade Organisation |

# List of Figures

CHAPTER 1

# Introduction

## I The Mighty Mekong: A River at Risk

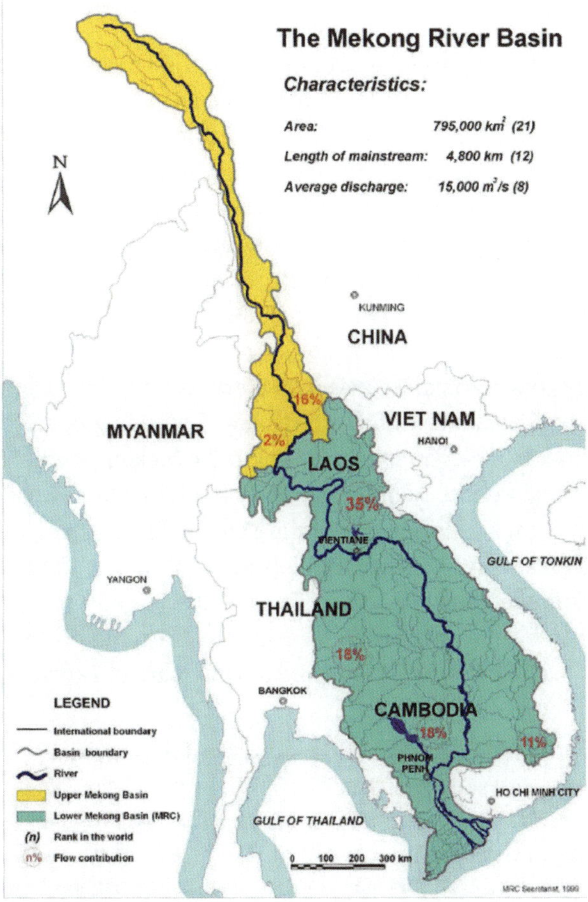


FIGURE 1 *Hydrographic map of the Mekong Basin, with indication of the Mekong River and the main tributaries and flow contribution by country*
SOURCE: WORLD BANK AND ASIAN DEVELOPMENT BANK, 'WB/ADB JOINT WORKING PAPER ON FUTURE DIRECTIONS FOR WATER RESOURCES MANAGEMENT IN THE MEKONG RIVER BASIN: MEKONG WATER RESOURCES ASSISTANCE STRATEGY' (WORKING PAPER, WORLD BANK AND ASIAN DEVELOPMENT BANK, 2006) 13.

 | DOI 10.1163/9789004266797_002

The Mekong River is "both a uniting and dividing force" for China and Southeast Asia.[1] It originates from Qinghai Province in China. Known as the Dza Chu River in Qinghai and Tibet, it integrates with the Angqu River in Chamdo, Tibet. Only after this point, it became known as the Lancang River. It then flows southeast through the Yunnan Province and enters into Southeast Asia. The Mekong River basin (henceforth referred to as the Mekong region), with a total land area of 795 000 square kilometres, includes parts of China, Myanmar and Vietnam, about one third of Thailand and most of Cambodia and Laos.[2]

Not only has the river supported one of the world's most diverse wildlife, second only to the Amazon River,[3] it also has been of major cultural, traditional, social and economic significance to the dense population living in this region.[4] All riparian states of Mekong are developing countries and most inhabitants are relevantly poor. The strong need for economic growth has tightened competition over water resources and aroused serious environmental concerns and disputes. The environmental discourses are also "intricately bound up in a wider world of geopolitics, which include China's emerging relations with regional neighbours".[5]

One highly controversial issue is dam construction. Driven by rapid industrialisation, export-led economic growth and expanding domestic consumer markets, demand for electricity is growing in the Mekong region.[6] The governments in this region have seen a great potential for hydropower development on the mainstream and tributaries of the Mekong River.

The mainstream hydropower development initially started on the upper Mekong in Yunnan Province, China from 1980s. Based on the most recent data, there has been a cascade of 16 dams (half located on the upstream of Lancang and half on the midstream and downstream of Lancang) planned on

---

1 Philip Hirsch et al., 'National Interests and Transboundary Water Governance in the Mekong' (Report, University of Sydney, 2006) iii.

2 Mekong River Commission, *About Mekong—the Land & its Resources* <http://nsl.mrcmekong.org/about_mekong/about_mekong.htm>.

3 World Wildlife Fund, *Greater Mekong* <http://wwf.panda.org/what_we_do/where_we_work/greatermekong/>.

4 Mekong River Commission, *People* <http://www.mrcmekong.org/topics/people/>.

5 Philip Hirsch, *Cascade Effect* (8 February 2011) China Dialogue <http://www.chinadialogue.net/article/show/single/en/4093-Cascade-effect>.

6 But the magnitude of this growth is contested between government agencies and civil society groups. See Carl Middleton, Jelson Garcia and Tira Foran, 'Old and New Hydropower Players in the Mekong Region: Agendas and Strategies in François Molle, Tira Foran and Mira Käkönen (eds), *Contested Waterscapes in the Mekong Region* (Earthscan, 2009) 23, 24.

the mainstream of Lancang River in Yunnan.[7] Among them, two projects have already been cancelled by 2007 due to environmental reasons.[8] In particular, the second eight-dam cascade located on the midstream and downstream of Lancang has attracted most of the attention. At the time of writing, six of them are already completed and one is in the final stage of getting formal approval.[9] It was not until more recently, has the hydropower development on the upstream of Lancang and in the Dza Chu River begun to raise more attention domestically and internationally. Combined with another 14 dams planned in the Dza Chu River in Tibet and Qinghai Province,[10] there are in fact 28 dams in total planned (eight of them are already completed) on the mainstream of Mekong in China.

Despite the benefits argued by Chinese officials, the ongoing dam construction has created serious concerns about its potential negative impact on the ecosystem. In 2010, a severe drought in Southwest China remarkably decreased the water level in the Mekong River and exacerbated tensions between China and neighbouring countries.[11] Whether China's management of a series of hydroelectric projects on the upper reaches of Mekong River has aggravated the crisis was under fierce dispute. This situation is further complicated by eleven mainstream dam proposals on the lower Mekong River, which might have a huge negative impact on the passage and breeding capacities of the Mekong's many migratory fish species.[12] The rapid hydropower expansion on the Mekong tributaries (both in China and the four lower Mekong countries) should be noted as well.[13] Moreover, developments like the expansion

---

7 中国河流网 [China River],《水电地图》[Hydropower Map] <http://www.river.org.cn/map.aspx>.

8 They are the Guonian Dam and the Mengsong Dam, the second and the last project of the cascade respectively. This will be further discussed in chapter two.

9 Detailed information on these dams is available in chapter two. See《中国在湄公河的水电开发将承受更大国际压力》[China's Dam Construction on the Upper Mekong Faces Increasing International Pressure], 中国经营网 [China Business] (21 April 2011) <http://www.cb.com.cn/economy/2011_0421/201694.html>.

10 International Rivers, *Spreadsheet of Major Dams in China* (23 May 2013) <http://www.internationalrivers.org/resources/spreadsheet-of-major-dams-in-china-7743>.

11 See Richard Stone, 'Severe Drought Puts Spotlight on Chinese Dams' (2010) 327(5971) *Science* 1311, 1311.

12 Milton Osborne, 'The Mekong: River under Threat' (Working Paper No 27, Lowy Institute, 2009) 17, 19.

13 For tributary dams in the lower Mekong region, see generally Philip Hirsch, 'The Changing Political Dynamics of Dam Building on the Mekong' (2010) 3(2) *Water Alternatives* 312. Tributary dams in the upper Mekong in China are less high-profile. But there are at least

of agriculture, the growth of factories and the discovery of oil in the Mekong region also raise concerns about pollution.[14] River clearances, which aim to increase navigation, could affect the health of the Mekong River by changing its deep reaches and rapids.[15]

The Mekong region not only suffers from traditional environmental concerns,[16] it is also under the global threat of climate change. The glaciers located on the Tibetan Plateau which feed the Mekong during periods of snow melt are steadily retreating, due to increased temperatures and an accompanying lower rate of precipitation.[17] Although its long term effects and scenarios remain contested,[18] the possible variations will influence the ecological system of Mekong River at all levels.

Interestingly, instead of the upstream dam construction, the Chinese government and scholars argue that the severe draught in 2010 should be blamed on climate change. The arguments on hydropower as a promising approach to mitigate climate change impact further add to the uncertainty and intricacy of the high-profile hydropower dispute.[19] Meanwhile, sea-level rise is another issue raised by climate change, which may be the cause for salt water encroachments into the Mekong Delta in recent years.[20] Climate change mitigation and adaptation is crucial to the Mekong region for the countries of the region are among the most vulnerable to climate change in the world.[21] But most development processes are currently planned and implemented without due con-

---

15 tributary dams planned on the Yangbi River and Xier River. See generally 中国河流网 [China River], 《水电地图》 [Hydropower Map] <http://www.river.org.cn/map.aspx>.

14 Milton Osborne, 'River at Risk: The Mekong and the Water Politics of China and Southeast Asia' (Working Paper No 2, Lowy Institute, 2004) 18–9.

15 Ibid. 25–30.

16 The major traditional environmental hazards often refer to various kinds of pollution or natural resources damage that only have a local or regional impact and mainly call for the application of the preventive principle due to its relatively low level of scientific uncertainty. Other environmental issues like ozone depletion, biodiversity conservation and climate change have notable global significance and often involve a much higher degree of scientific uncertainty, thus requiring the application of the precaution principle.

17 Osborne, above n 12, 43–4.

18 Osborne, above n 14, 44.

19 Philip Hirsch and Rosalia Sciortino, 'Climate Change and the Resource Politics of the Greater Mekong Subregion' in Kobkun Rayanakorn (ed), *Climate Change Challenges in the Mekong Region* (Chiang Mai University Press, 2011) 223, 243.

20 Osborne, above n 14, 44.

21 Mekong River Commission, *Climate* <http://www.mrcmekong.org/the-mekong-basin/climate/>.

sideration of climate change risks.[22] Even if it was taken into account, there is a high risk of the discourse being selectively used as a pretext for "pre-existing resource politics aiming at exploiting the commons for macroeconomic purposes and corporate profit".[23]

Environmental threats are not respectful of national borders and thus any one country may be effectively unable to protect its own environment.[24] This is especially true with respect to transboundary river basin management. The ecological integrity of the Mekong region calls for cooperation among all riparian states. So far, some mechanisms in this region could be used to facilitate such cooperation, including the Mekong River Commission (MRC),[25] the Greater Mekong Subregion Program (the GMS Program),[26] and the Association of Southeast Asian Nations (ASEAN)[27] and its dialogue relationship with China.

But in reality, these cooperative mechanisms still suffers from many problems which can be briefly concluded as follows: China and Myanmar are not the formal members of the MRC; the increasing marginalisation of the MRC; the prevailing culture of "ASEAN Way" that relies on consensus-building and cooperative programs instead of legally binding treaties or strong regional bureaucracy; the loose structure of the GMS; not enough integration of environmental concerns into trade, investment and exploitation of natural resources, etc. As will be analysed in chapter two, despite the attempt of further integration, the current regional cooperation remains highly polycentric.

---

22 Masao Imamura, 'Introduction: Water Governance in the Mekong Region' in Louis Lebel et al. (eds), *Democratizing Water Governance in the Mekong* (Mekong Press, 2007) 1, 4.

23 Hirsch and Sciortino, above n 19, 227.

24 *Transport, Health and Environment Pan-European Programme (THE PEP) and Environmental Aspects of Transport: Strengthening of Environmental and Health Aspects of Transportation*, UN ESCOR, ITC, 70th sess, UN Doc ECE/TRANS/2008/4 (2007) 2; Roger W. Findley and Daniel A. Farber, *Environmental Law in a Nutshell* (West Publishing, 2000) 53.

25 The MRC member states include Cambodia, Thailand, Laos and Vietnam. Two upstream states, China and Myanmar, only participate as dialogue partners, instead of formal members of the MRC.

26 The GMS is made up of Cambodia, China (specifically Yunnan Province and Guangxi Zhuang Autonomous Region), Laos, Myanmar, Thailand and Vietnam. In 1992, with assistance from the Asian Development Bank, all six Mekong countries jointly launched a program of subregional economic cooperation (the GMS Program) to enhance their economic relations, building on their shared histories and cultures, covering nine priority sectors, which also include environment. Asian Development Bank, *Greater Mekong Subregion* (22 July 2011) <http://www.adb.org/gms/>.

27 All the Mekong riparian states, except China, are formal members of ASEAN. China maintains a strategic partnership with ASEAN.

## II Challenge-Response: The Rationale for a Procedural Perspective

In response to the above problems and challenges, this study takes a procedural perspective to promote sustainability in the Mekong region, mindful of its relationship with the (equally important) substantive counterparts and the fact that the distinction between procedural and substantive elements could be obscure in some cases. This choice is based on a practical consideration of the cooperation background in the Mekong region and underscores the values of procedure.

Procedure can be treated as an end in itself or as a means to an end.[28] Procedure is desirable as an end per se because of its valuable nature, such as openness, transparency, participation, accountability and predictability, which themselves constitute as important characteristics of good governance. Meanwhile, it is a means to improve the governance of shared water resources. The development of procedural framework is a more practical and constructive choice, for the substantial elements of good water governance and the substantive resolution of the multi-fold environmental challenges have been proved to be more sensitive or controversial to be reached on consensus across the Mekong region. Detailed analysis in this respect is provided in chapter two. At the international level, good governance relies on cooperation in goodwill and a more democratic atmosphere. A well-designed procedural framework could help direct the riparian states in the Mekong region to work more cooperatively towards sustainable water governance.

Although the procedural arrangements may not be quite as conspicuous as the substantive principles and targets established at the international level, it is observed that a large percentage of international efforts on tackling environmental challenges have in fact concentrated on procedural reforms.[29] This can be easily identified in many multilateral environmental treaties, which usually "contain a few material principles of great generality while more detailed provisions address procedural issues".[30] The latter often includes a combination of the following (though not necessarily covers all of them): information exchange and data collection, prior notification and consultation, public

28 Durwood Zaelke, Matthew Stilwell and Oran Young, 'What Reason Demands: Making Law Work for Sustainable Development' in Durwood Zaelke, Donald Kaniaru and Eva Kružíková (eds), *Making Law Work: Environmental Compliance and Sustainable Development* (Cameron May Ltd, International Law Publishers, 2005) vol. 1, 29, 42.

29 Martti Koskenniemi, 'Peaceful Settlement of Environmental Disputes' (1991) 60 *Nordic Journal of International Law* 73, 73.

30 Ibid.

participation, transboundary environmental impact assessment (EIA) and strategic environmental assessment (SEA), non-compliance mechanism and other institutionalised cooperation between the member states.

The provisions on information exchange, prior notification or consultation through international organisations could be found in numerous international treaties, such as the *UN Convention on the Law of the Sea* (UNCLOS), the *London Dumping Convention*, the *Basel Convention*, the *Convention on Long-range Transboundary Air Pollution*, the *1994 Danube Convention* and the United Nations Economic Commission for Europe's (UNECE) *Water Convention*. Moreover, specific procedural conventions, such as the *Espoo Convention* and its SEA *Protocol*, together with the *Aarhus Convention*, represent the most advanced examples in the international procedural rules so far, particularly with regard to EIA, SEA, access to information and public participation. Several EU Directives in the above aspects are quite important as well. International judicial and arbitral cases, such as the *Lake Lanoux Arbitration*, the *Icelandic Fisheries Case*, the *North Sea Continental Shelf Case*, the *Gabčíkovo-Nagymaros Case*, the *MOX Plant Case* and the *Pulp Mills Case*, also support and address procedural aspect of problem-solving. Non-binding documents, including but are not limited to the *1997 UN Watercourses Convention* (not yet in force), the Rio Declaration and 2001 Draft Articles on Prevention of Transboundary Damage from Hazardous Activities, also have significant reference values in terms of procedural mechanisms.

The above documents will be further referred to or analysed during the discussions on each procedural mechanism. However, it should be noticed that there are examples which not only imply procedural requirements but also able to achieve more precise targets on pollution reduction or regulatory measures.[31] In addition, the effectiveness of the more procedural-focused conventions is not shield from criticism. Relevant debates further raise the issue of the relationship between procedural and substantive requirements. Bearing in mind this question, the values of procedure should not be denied or over-exaggerated.

The theoretical rationale for developing procedural requirements to govern transboundary water resources lies in the very concept of sustainable development, the theory of integrated water resources management (IWRM) and the international water law, all of which provide the basis for developing the legal and institutional framework for sustainable governance of Mekong, with an emphasis on procedural aspects. Through the analysis below, it is more theoretically evident that the procedural perspective should at least be highlighted

31 See ibid. 79.

as one of the priority issues in the Mekong region. Not only does the due process reflect the requirements of procedural justice, it is also a valuable approach to promote the improvement of substantive requirements, to evaluate and secure a more sustainable outcome.

### A *Sustainable Development*

As developing countries, economic and social development is one of the highest priority concerns of the Mekong countries. This leads to fierce controversies between development and environmental protection in this area. In many cases, the former takes priority over the latter. While increasing emphasis and claims on the right to development in this region should be fully recognised, the growth-driven deterioration of environment and disputes raised by competitive water usage and exploitation of natural resources has generated lots of tension and instability in the Mekong region. Meanwhile, environmental protection also relies on further economic and social development to provide enough financial and technical support to build capacity and raise public awareness on environmental protection. Therefore, how to promote sustainable governance of water resources in this area is a key issue.

Although sustainable development is viewed as a core concept of international environmental policy, its legal status remains highly controversial, especially with regard to its concrete meaning in a specific context. As different governments and international organisations pursue their own priorities and make their own value judgment,[32] the diversified, conflicting claims and interpretations about the concept's specific normative implications seems to abound, triggering disputes which are often exceedingly difficult to resolve.[33]

Having acknowledged the potential controversies, it is argued that even if there is no legal obligation to develop sustainably, there may nevertheless be law "in the field of sustainable development" and a more realistic suggestion is to focus on its components, rather than on the concept itself.[34] Among the elements that have been identified,[35] the integration of environmental protection

---

32 Patricia Birnie, Alan Boyle and Catherine Redgwell, *International Law and the Environment* (Oxford University Press, 3rd ed, 2009) 54.

33 Gunther Handl, 'Environmental Security and Global Change: The Challenge to International Law' (1990) 1 *Yearbook of International Environmental Law* 3, 25.

34 Birnie, Boyle and Redgwell, above n 32, 127.

35 This includes, but is not limited to, the integration of environmental protection and economic development, the right to development, the sustainable utilisation of natural resources, the equitable allocation of resources both within the present generation and between present and future generation, public participation, access to information and environmental impact assessment.

and economic development is one of the key criteria and has been explicitly articulated by Principle 4 of the Rio Declaration.[36] In practice, however, substantive reconciliation of interests is still largely left to the discretion of administrative authorities and often varies according to the specific contexts. In general, courts are reluctant to make a judgment on whether the outcome of a development decision is sustainable. The potential tension between environmental protection and development is illustrated in the *Gabčíkovo-Nagymaros Case*. In order to settle the disputes arising out of a hydroelectric project situated on a shared river border, the International Court of Justice (ICJ) recognised the need to reconcile economic development with protection of the environment.[37] Instead of ruling on whether the national action falls short of a standard of "sustainable development", however, the court held that parties should negotiate to reach a resolution.[38] Here, it seems that the court viewed sustainable development as a value or objective that should be considered by parties during the decision-making process.[39]

Following the logic of this judgment, although international law may not require development to be sustainable, it does appear to require development decisions to be the outcome of a process which promotes sustainability.[40] The primary criterion of this test would be whether the normative elements of sustainable development are introduced into this process. The substantive elements of sustainability, ranging from the integration of environmental protection and economic development to inter-generational and intra-generational equity, should certainly be taken into account while making a decision. Meanwhile, the procedural elements should be viewed as an integral part of sustainability itself. They also can be used to further secure the consideration of the substantive elements and contribute to a more sustainable outcome.[41] The connection between sustainable development and procedural requirements has been recognised by several important procedural conventions, which affirm the need to ensure sustainable development in the preambles.[42] For lawyers, the key point to grasp is that sustainable governance

---

36 *Report of the United Nations Conference on Environment and Development*, UN Doc. A/CONF.151/26 (vol. I) (28 September 1992).

37 *Gabčíkovo-Nagymaros Project (Hungary/Slovakia) (Judgment)* [1997] ICJ Rep 7, 78.

38 Ibid. 83; Birnie, Boyle and Redgwell, above n 32, 126.

39 Alan Boyle, 'The Gabcikovo-Nagymaros Case: New Law in Old Bottles' (1997) 8 *Yearbook of International Environmental Law* 13, 18.

40 Birnie, Boyle and Redgwell, above n 32, 127.

41 See ibid. 116.

42 See *Convention on Environmental Impact Assessment in a Transboundary Context*, opened for signature 25 February 1991, 1989 UNTS 309 (entered into force 10 September 1997);

is "as much about processes as about outcomes".[43] As further demonstrated below, procedural elements are fundamental in the cooperation among riparian states, while some substantive elements have proved to be more difficult to gain normative contents in the specific context of shared water resources management.

### B *Integrated Water Resources Management (IWRM)*

The concept of IWRM has been viewed as a paradigm shift in society's approach to water.[44] According to Global Water Partnership, integrated water resources management is:

> a process that enables the coordinated management of water, land and related resources within the limits of a basin so as to optimise and equitably share the resulting socioeconomic well-being without compromising the long-term health of vital ecosystems.[45]

As a highly comprehensive approach, IWRM reflects a cross-sectoral and cross-jurisdictional concern towards sustainability of water resources. It is viewed as a promising solution to deliver sustainability in the governance of shared water resources. The significance of IWRM is also highlighted as an effective response to climate change. According to the IPCC's Fourth Assessment Report, the connection between climate change and sustainable development is explicitly established and integrated strategy should be an instrument to explore adaptation measures to climate change.[46]

With a sense of bioregionalism, IWRM entails a holistic consideration of the hydrological cycle and relevant natural resources and ecosystems; natural and human issues; environmental concerns and development needs. It also represents a fundamental transformation of the decision-making process towards a

---

*Convention on Access to Information, Public Participation in Decision-making and Access to Justice in Environmental Matters*, opened for signature 25 June 1998, 2161 UNTS 447 (entered into force 10 September 1997).

43 Birnie, Boyle and Redgwell, above n 32, 57.

44 Fiona Miller and Philip Hirsch, 'Civil Society and Internationalized River Basin Management' (Working Paper No. 7, Australian Mekong Resource Centre, 2003) 6.

45 Global Water Partnership and International Network of Basin Organizations, *Handbook for IWRM in Basins* (Handbook, Global Water Partnership, 2009) 18.

46 M.L. Parry et al. (eds), 'Climate Change 2007: Impacts, Adaptation and Vulnerability. Contribution of Working Group II to the Fourth Assessment Report of the Intergovernmental Panel on Climate Change' (Fourth Assessment Report, IPCC, 2007) 196, 200.

more cooperative and participatory approach of water management. In particular, it aims at reconciling water-related interests of both upstream and downstream, and integrating all stakeholders in the planning and decision process.[47] While the idea of integration per se cannot guarantee an optimal outcome, the integrated decision-making process certainly leads to changes in this direction.

Even though the idea of IWRM has been accepted and applied in various basin contexts,[48] it is not obligatory as a matter of general international law and its application often differs in many detailed aspects, which in most cases has not yet been sufficiently comprehensive or effective.[49] As a desirable principle, however, it certainly does give international water law a broader ecological perspective and represents the future trend of water management.[50] Since there is no blueprint valid for all cases, it is further argued that a fully integrated approach is not always needed for successful IWRM. Instead, the appropriate scale for integration will depend on the extent to which it facilitates effective action in response to specific needs.[51] In order to develop more specific arrangements, some important elements of IWRM should be adjusted and strengthened according to unique circumstances, including an enabling environment, the institutional roles and functions, and the management instruments.[52]

The effectiveness of IWRM is strongly influenced by many factors, including but not limited to regional, national, or local water-related policies; substantive obligations and objectives; liability and accountability; standards and technology; and the roles and functions of various administrative levels. This involves a multitude of controversial issues, which have been dealt with numerous difficulties at both domestic and regional levels. For example, China's existing river basin management frameworks are criticised for flawed

---

47 Anil Agarwal et al., 'Integrated Water Resources Management' (TAC Background Papers No 4, Global Water Partnership Technical Advisory Committee, 2000) 25, 28.

48 Numerous river basin management institutions have been established at the domestic and regional levels to promote IWRM, such as the Murray-Darling Basin Authority, the Tennessee Valley Authority, the Yangtze River Water Resources Committee, the US-Canadian International Joint Commission, the Permanent Joint Technical Commission for Nile Waters, the Zambezi Intergovernmental Monitoring and Coordinating Committee, the Amazonian Cooperation Council, the Danube River Protection Commission and the International Commission for Protection of the Rhine.

49 Birnie, Boyle and Redgwell, above n 32, 546, 581.

50 Ibid. 536, 546.

51 Marcus Moench et al., 'The Fluid Mosaic: Water Governance in the Context of Variability, Uncertainty and Change' (Paper, Nepal Water Conservation Foundation, 2003) 9.

52 Agarwal et al., above n 47, 30.

demarcation of responsibilities, poor coordination among various levels of administrative authorities and varied expertise in water management issues.[53] These deficiencies result in gaps or overlaps in management, intensify and further stir conflicts over water-related interests among governments and lead to low-efficient water management. This situation is further complicated by the following disadvantages: problematic compliance of existing environmental obligations and responsibilities; low-efficiency of management instruments; and a lack of proper dispute settlement mechanisms and the difficulty of providing timely and sufficient judicial remedies. How to shift the current water management system into actually embracing the idea of IWRM is one of the most challenging environmental issues in China.

The regional application of IWRM has been proved to be even more troublesome. There are some commendable examples like the case of the Rhine River, though one should not forget that it took the Rhine states more than half a century to build up its current water management regime which is comparatively favourable but still facing its own difficulties and challenges.[54] Since

53 For more information, see section II(A), chapter two.

54 The history of transboundary water cooperation among the Rhine states can be dated back to the 1950s. The development of vast industrial complexes along the river, such as the Ruhr, has led to serious chemical, salt and thermal pollution since the mid-twentieth century. The canalisation of the Rhine and the construction of numerous dams and weirs also raise concerns on the ecological health of the river system. Moreover, due to the impact of climate change, severe floods and droughts are expected to occur more often in the Rhine basin. Cooperation before the 1987 has proved to be less effective. Only after the occurrence of the severe 1986 Sandoz accident that countries began to take more effective cooperative actions on the protection of the Rhine. The following elements have served as important contributing factors to this process: (1) representative democratic system; (2) general respect for the rule of law; (3) the rise of participatory or deliberative democracy since 1960s; (4) the overall situation of IWRM at domestic level; (5) the European integration process; (6) emerging international and domestic environmental law; and (7) a strong need to facilitate cooperation on transboundary environmental matters. In particular, the regional water cooperation in the Rhine basin also indicates an increasing emphasis and demanding efforts on ensuring due process. See generally Tom Raadgever, 'Transboundary River Basin Management Regimes: The Rhine Basin Case Study' (Background Report of the NeWater Project, Centre for River Basin Management, Delft University of Technology, August 2005); Ine D. Frijters and Jan Leentvaar, 'Rhine Case Study' (PCCP Series 17, UNESCO-IHP, 2003); J. G. Lammers, *Pollution of International Watercourses* (Martinus Nijhoff, 1984); Marco Verweij, 'A Watershed on the Rhine: Changing Approaches to International Environmental Cooperation' (1999) 47 *GeoJournal* 453; Mita Patel and Jan H. Stel (eds), 'Public Participation in River Basin Management in Europe: A National Approach and Background Study Synthesising Experiences

IWRM has dealt with numerous difficulties in more developed regions, it will not be any easier in the context of the Mekong region. In fact, many substantive elements of IWRM seem too controversial to be find consensus or to be properly implemented in the near future. This can be mainly attributed to the underdeveloped economy and the fierce competition over water resources in the region; the multi-fold environmental challenges and considerable scientific uncertainty; the immaturity of general political and legal systems at the regional, national and local levels; and the polycentric status of the existing domestic and regional transboundary cooperative mechanisms.

Moreover, procedural values like openness, transparency, information abundance and effective stakeholder participation are inherent in the idea of IWRM itself. In practice, they are a part of the enabling environment for the development and functioning of IWRM and are generally viewed as an essential component to: (1) cultivate good will cooperation, (2) to catalyse consensus-building on specific IWRM arrangements, (3) to regulate water-related institutions, (4) to justify the legitimacy of development decisions, (5) to help settle disputes and (6) to better secure a more sustainable outcome in the long run. Since there might be huge difficulties for the Mekong countries to agree on many substantive elements of IWRM, a more realistic and constructive approach could be to include the procedural framework as one of the priority issues to be addressed in the Mekong region. This may help avoid the political deadlock.

The procedural requirements are highly related to the substantive aspect of IWRM, but it does not directly address the distribution of sensitive interests or impose any substantive obligations on riparian states. Through the increasing acceptance of due process as a notion across the region and a gradual development of more detailed procedural arrangements, the essence of IWRM and its substantive implications can be reflected and spread among riparian states in a more subtle way, which would ultimately contribute to the overall enhancement of sustainable water governance in the region. It should be noticed, however, that highlighting the procedural components of IWRM does not mean we could overlook or deny the importance of its substantive counterparts. The substantive obligations and objectives could have a notable

of 9 European Countries' (Workpackage 4, HarmoniCOP Project, 2004); M. Grant, 'Implementation of the EC Directive on Environmental Impact Assessment' (1989) 4 *Connecticut Journal of International Law* 463; Pierre Maurel, 'Public Participation and the European Water Framework Directive: Role of Information and Communication Tools' (WorkPackage 3 Report, HarmoniCoP Project, 2003).

impact on the compliance and efficacy of relevant procedural requirements, not to mention that the substantive obligations also constitute a part of the theoretical rationale for due process.

This section only focuses on the concept of the IWRM and a brief explanation on why procedural elements of the IWRM should be considered as a priority compared to substantive counterparts. In chapter two, deeper research is done in the context of the Mekong region regarding the criticisms and misunderstandings on IWRM itself and the prospects of improving the status quo via procedural approaches. As observed by Miller and Hirsch, one of the most contested dimensions of IWRM is how the diverse perspectives, values and objectives held by a wide range of stakeholders can be negotiated, accommodated and reflected in the processes and institutions for river basin management.[55] Relevant discussions will be based on two sets of fundamental tensions: one is between the theory of IWRM and polycentric water management reality in the Mekong region; and the other is between the centralised and decentralised approaches of the IWRM.

### C *International Watercourse Law*

While the domestic implementation of the IWRM will have influences on its application at the regional level, it is also necessary to consider the background and foundation built by international law regarding water management. Despite the incipient and controversial nature of the international water law on environmental protection and sustainable use, the support for due process can be identified.

Historically, the international water law has mainly focused on allocating water supply in international watercourses between upstream and downstream states and only incidentally addresses environmental or sustainability issues.[56] Along with its development, most modern commentators have dismissed absolute sovereignty over water within their territory.[57] Instead, equitable utilisation became the most widely accepted theory of water allocation and utilisation. The requirements of conservation and sustainable use are of increasing importance as well. Then, having recognised the logical combination of the natural integrity of river basin and the significance of integrating the environmental, social and economic objectives, the idea of IWRM

55 Miller and Hirsch, above n 44, 7.

56 Information in this paragraph is derived from: Birnie, Boyle and Redgwell, above n 32, 536, 540–1, 544, 580.

57 More specific analysis on the Harmon Doctrine is available in chapter three.

is increasingly endorsed as a community-of-interest approach which goes beyond the allocation of equitable rights.

While embracing IWRM as a promising institutional machinery to improve cooperation on sustainable development, numerous disputes remain under the international water law, such as the relationship between equitable utilisation and the obligation to prevent harm to other riparian states, which not only is a fundamental theoretical issue, but also reflects a huge political divergence between upstream states and downstream states.[58] Moreover, the ecological perspective brought in by IWRM further raises challenges on how to incorporate ecosystem protection into international water law.[59] As argued by Birnie, Boyle and Redgwell, although now it "can be asserted with some confidence that countries are no longer free to pollute or otherwise destroy the ecology of a shared watercourse to the detriment of their neighbours", definitive conclusions are difficult to draw from a legal perspective.[60] However, the idea that the obligation to prevent harm "works in tandem with the principle of equitable utilisation" does reflect some sort of integration.[61]

Despite the existing ambiguity and controversy, evidence can be found in international water law which is in favour of promoting procedural requirements. To begin with, it is generally agreed that the obligation to prevent harm is an obligation of performance rather than an obligation of result.[62] Namely, it requires "avoidance of harm in a way and to an extent that is reasonable under the circumstances".[63] While the main advantage of due diligence is its

---

58 During the negotiations, the upstream states were generally in favour of equitable utilisation as the controlling principle. However, as McCaffrey points out, the apparent conflict between these principles is unreal and often based on a misunderstanding of the obligation to prevent harm in international law. It is further argued that equitable balancing is applicable to pollution and environmental protection of international watercourses in two situations only: when the harm is less than "significant", or where it is significant but unavoidable by the exercise of due diligence. See Birnie, Boyle and Redgwell, above n 32, 549–52; Stephen C. McCaffrey, *The Law of International Watercourses* (Oxford University Press, 2007) 436–446.

59 It is argued that "comprehensive ecosystem protection remains an underdeveloped concept in general international law, and it is not yet possible to conclude that states have a general duty to protect and preserve ecosystems in all areas under their sovereignty". See Birnie, Boyle and Redgwell, above n 32, 557–61.

60 Ibid. 580–1.

61 McCaffrey, above n 58, 445.

62 See *Pulp Mills on the River Uruguay (Argentina v Uruguay) (Judgment)* [2010] ICJ Rep 14, para 192.

63 McCaffrey, above n 58, 407.

flexibility and responsiveness to circumstances, one often accused flaw is that it provides "limited guidance on what legislation or technology are required in specific cases".[64] However, the obligation of diligent prevention does entail some procedure requirements and the due process could be used as a useful criterion to decide whether a state has acted properly. Therefore, exploring its procedural implications can give more content to the notion of due diligence.[65] For example, in the *Pulp Mills Case*, the International Court of Justice rules that:

> due diligence, and the duty of vigilance and prevention which it implies, would not be considered to have been exercised, if a party planning works liable to affect the régime of the river or the quality of its waters did not undertake an environmental impact assessment on the potential effects of such works.[66]

In addition, there is a general obligation to cooperate in good faith between states sharing the watercourse.[67] Sufficient cooperation and communication is fundamental to IWRM in terms of trust building; increasing transparency and abundance of water-related information; involving stakeholders at all levels; providing a platform to substantively integrate numerous considerations and interests on water-related issues; to settle relevant disputes and to maximise mutual benefits. Good neighbourliness and the duty to cooperate calls for the application of due process and at least some minimum procedural standards as concrete forms of meaningful cooperation. Although there is a high risk that

---

64 Birnie, Boyle and Redgwell, above n 32, 149.

65 Of course, procedural implications are not the only aspect of due diligence requirement. In the *Pulp Mills Case*, the Court defines the obligation to act with due diligence as:

> "an obligation which entails not only the adoption of appropriate rules and measures, but also a certain level of vigilance in their enforcement and the exercise of administrative control applicable to public and private operators, such as the monitoring of activities undertaken by such operators, to safeguard the rights of the other party".

*Pulp Mills on the River Uruguay* (*Argentina v Uruguay*) (*Judgment*) [2010] ICJ Rep 14, para 197.

66 Ibid. para 204.

67 McCaffrey, above n 58, 465. The general obligation to cooperate has been supported by numerous non-binding documents, treaties and international judicial decisions. See Philippe Sands, *Principles of International Environmental Law* (Cambridge University Press, 2nd ed, 2003) 249–51.

the effectiveness of the procedural requirements can be significantly weakened without well-defined substantive obligations, the lack of the latter does not necessarily invalidate the values of due process itself and its positive impact on cultivating and deepening goodwill cooperation and contributing to consensus-building on more complicated substantive requirements. Moreover, even if substantive obligations can be explicitly endorsed by riparian states, procedure is still required to attach a degree of normative significance to them and to operationalise and evaluate their compliance.

## III Overview

Although the Mekong countries have generally claimed to embrace the concept of sustainable development, deep-rooted controversies still exist on how to integrate the strong needs for economic development with environmental protection and how to reconcile different interests represented by multiple stakeholders. In many cases, there are doubts on what the right development direction is and whether "pollute first, clean up later" is really avoidable at the early stage of industrialisation. Meanwhile, the ecological system of the Mekong River is currently under threats from both the traditional environmental problems and global threats like climate change, the combination of which generates huge pressure and scientific uncertainty on environmental policy-making. This is further complicated by the intricately intertwined geopolitical interests and immature legal and political systems in the region. Such triple-layered dilemma makes it very difficult to even identify where and how to start solving the problems. Under such circumstances, the comprehensiveness of the study and the unique procedural perspective will add to the existing literature on what the future direction of water reform in the region should be and how to facilitate the introduction and improvement of necessary procedural mechanisms. Moreover, the discussions on the theory and application of integrated water resources management, procedural justice, soft law and hard law, domestic and international compliance theories will contribute to the scholarship on international water law and policy in general.

The initial focus of this research will identify the major environmental challenges of the Mekong ecosystem and the status quo of water resources management in the Mekong region, focusing on the existing water-related legal arrangements and mechanisms at both domestic and regional levels. It will discuss both the ongoing difficulties and as well as aspirations for reform of the water management regime. The legal analysis of the status quo will be comprehensive. It covers all Mekong states, considers water governance at both regional and domestic levels and canvasses the legal rights and responsibilities of both governments as well as other actors, including investment banks, enterprises, local communities and NGOs. This can offer a more profound legal understanding for governmental policy makers, researchers in various disciplines, local communities and legal advocates in the region.

Despite the values of procedural mechanisms, insufficient attention has been placed on procedural implications of IWRM and their applications in the context of the Mekong region. In light of the above theoretical rationale, this book will focus on the procedural aspect of problem-solving. The increasingly polycentric nature of transboundary cooperation must be considered, with newly recognised stakeholders emerging who represent a broader range of interests than has been the case in the past. At least five major procedural requirements can be identified in the proposed procedural framework. They are: information exchange and data collection on a regular basis; notification and consultation; public's right of access to information and participation; and environmental impact assessment (EIA), strategic environmental assessment (SEA), and their applications in the transboundary context.

Data collection and information exchange among riparian states on a regular basis is considered to be an initial and essential step of cooperation. Notification requires states "planning an activity to transmit to potentially affected states all necessary information sufficiently in advance so that the latter can prevent damage to its territory, and, if necessary, enter into consultation with the acting state".[68] Consultation then obliges "states to allow potentially affected [s]tates an opportunity to review and discuss a planned activity that may have potentially damaging effects".[69] The right to access information mainly relies on domestic application and relevant information exchange and notification at the regional level. It also serves as a prerequisite for effective participation. Public participation, as another principle enumerated in the Rio Declaration, is democratic in nature and justified as a means toward improving the quality of environmental decision-making and more generally as a way to mitigate the environmental impact.[70] Transboundary EIA or SEA provide two legal procedures to get the public and other riparian states involved in evaluating and discussing the likely transboundary impact of a proposed activity, plan

68 David Hunter, James Salzman and Durwood Zaelke, *International Environmental Law and Policy* (Foundation Press, 3rd ed, 2007) 526.

69 Ibid. 527.

70 Neil Craik, *The International Law of Environmental Impact Assessment* (Cambridge University Press, 2008) 147.

or program. These procedural mechanisms are interrelated to each other and should be considered in a holistic way.

A major challenge of this study is how to tailor and comprehend the procedural requirements in the context of the Mekong region. To this end, it is suggested that both the ideal and practical scenarios should be considered, combined with selected case studies in the field. The existing legislation and practice regarding the procedural mechanisms in the Mekong region will be analysed. The discussion on procedural mechanisms in the Mekong region will also consider how to improve the implementation in light of the ongoing tradition of strong preference for soft law documents and approaches. More studies will be done on the relationship between legally-binding agreements and the capacity for compliance in the context of the Mekong region.

Although this study is focused on the procedural aspect of problem-solving, it does recognise the limit of this approach. The substantive aspect of IWRM should not be overlooked. Therefore, the research will also be based on the knowledge of substantive issues on environmental protection of water resources that has proved to be controversial but progressive. Meanwhile, the study is on the alert to the other extreme scenario of procedures, which could result in ritualism, reduced flexibility and increased bureaucracy. It should be borne in mind that there is a real danger that the procedural requirements may end up as a mere formality to go through to justify decisions already made and to defuse political opposition. Therefore, how to improve the compliance of these procedural requirements to secure a more sustainable outcome will be paid special attention to in this book.

This research would involve a comprehensive legal analysis concerning: (1) relevant domestic legislation and international agreements on water management and procedural mechanisms; (2) institutional design of both domestic water governance regimes and regional water-related cooperation platforms. In addition, through case studies, further study will be done to evaluate the implementation and compliance of soft/hard law documents and the functioning of the current institutional design in the field. Moreover, comparative studies will be carried out regarding the consistencies and discrepancies among the Mekong states' domestic legal arrangements and practices, as well as experiences and lessons provided by other transboundary water management practices occurred outside of the Mekong region.

Several key questions of the study will be addressed as follows:

(1) What legislation, soft law/guidelines, policies and institutional arrangement exist for water resources management in the Mekong countries? What capacity do the Mekong countries have to implement their own laws and regulations? What are the bottlenecks to effective regulation?

(2) What roles do the MRC, GMS, ASEAN-China dialogue relationship play in the current governance? What are the deficiencies and strengths of the current cooperation regarding transboundary water governance?
(3) What adjustments should be made regarding the approaches of promoting water reform in the Mekong region? What water-related legal responses should be emphasised as priorities in this region?
(4) What is the current status of legislation and practice regarding the procedural mechanisms? How can they be enhanced in the context of the Mekong region? What are the limitations of procedural approaches?
(5) What is the relationship between legally-binding agreements and the capacity for compliance in the context of the Mekong region? How should implementation be improved in light of the ongoing tradition of strong preference for soft law documents and approaches?

CHAPTER 2

# Towards Sustainable Development: A Multidimensional Debate in the Mekong Context

Water governance has been characterised as a highly complex and multidimensional issue. Whilst integrated water resources management (IWRM) is an appealing concept, to what extent its ambitious principles can be applied in practice remains an open question.[1] Although many efforts have been made to promote the application of IWRM in the Mekong context, the multifaceted environmental dilemma and the existing decision-making arrangements in the region certainly pose huge challenges and risks on its actual implementation.

The following discussion will begin by examining the major environmental threats to the Mekong region and discussing the consistency and controversy in multiple claims on aqua-environmental protection and climate change. In the respect of the tangled nature of environmental challenges in this region, attention will then be paid to the existing multilevel governance of water resources in the region and the diverse players that are shaping the governance of the Mekong River. Questions will then be raised on the current approaches used to promote IWRM in the region, in light of the huge difficulties of tipping the scales in this direction and the fact that even if countries managed to transform relevant legislation and institutions, in many cases the reform could only end up as no more than another window-dressing exercise. In the end, this chapter will try to develop an answer to the question of how to configure hydrological boundaries into existing political boundaries in the Mekong region.

## I Development and Environment: Multifaceted Dilemma

Mainland Southeast Asia is one of the fastest growing regional economies in the world and water resources development has assumed a central role for the

1 Doubts have been raised by Asit K. Biswas, who argued that "in the real world, the concept of IWRM will be exceedingly difficult to be made operational". See Asit K. Biswas, 'Integrated Water Resources Management: A Reassessment' (2004) 29(2) *Water International* 248.

 DOI 10.1163/9789004266797_003

region's economic growth.[2] In the meantime, tense competition over water resources has resulted in increasing disputes at both domestic and regional levels concerning the major potential impact on the Mekong ecosystems and the livelihoods of local communities. Although in principle, the Mekong states seem to have embraced the concept of sustainable development, the painstaking struggle towards balancing development imperatives with environmental protection in the region has proved to be a highly complicated process filled with confusing and even frustrating twists and turns. This can be discerned from two of the most high-profile environmental challenges in this area.

### A *Hydropower Expansion*

The increasing momentum for hydropower development on the mainstream and tributaries of Mekong is one of the most troubling issues in this region. As observed by Hirsh, over the past half century, hydropower development in the Mekong region has "ebbed and flowed with broader events and ideologies", particularly the region's "shifting, and often fractured, geopolitical landscape".[3] During the Cold War period, most of the work of the Mekong Committee[4] focused on planning a cascade of large dams on the mainstream, but none of them materialised at the time mainly due to a variety of political obstacles.[5] From the late 1980s onwards, demand for natural resources including energy has grown rapidly but the dam proposals were set within very different eco-political milieus.[6]

Deeply embedded driving forces for the hydropower expansion mainly include: rapidly escalating globalisation, urbanisation and industrialisation, domestic and foreign investment, energy demand and restructuring, agricultural irrigation, trade and security concerns.[7] The construction and planning

---

2 Maso Imamura, 'Introduction: Water Governance in the Mekong Region' in Louis Lebel et al. (eds), *Democratizing Water Governance in the Mekong* (Mekong Press, 2007) 1, 2.

3 Philip Hirsch, 'The Changing Political Dynamics of Dam Building on the Mekong' (2010) 3(2) *Water Alternatives* 312, 313.

4 The Mekong Committee, with the membership of four lower Mekong countries, was established with the auspices of the United Nations but under the de facto hegemony of the United States early during the Cold War period. Ibid.; Jeffrey W. Jacobs, 'Mekong Committee History and Lessons for River Basin Development' (1995) 161(2) *Geographical Journal* 135.

5 Hirsch, above n 3.

6 Ibid. 314.

7 See generally John Dore, Yu Xiaogang and Kevin Yuk-shing Li, 'China's Energy Reforms and Hydropower Expansion in Yunnan' in Louis Lebel et al. (eds), *Democratizing Water Governance in the Mekong* (Mekong Press, 2007) 55, 60–7; Chris Greacen and Apsara Palettu, 'Electricity Sector Planning and Hydropower' in Louis Lebel et al. (eds), *Democratizing Water Governance in the Mekong* (Mekong Press, 2007) 93.

of numerous hydropower dams, river-linking and diversion schemes unavoidably raise significant concerns with respect to their negative environmental effects.

### 1 Tributary Dams

Against the backdrop of increasing global concern over the social and environmental impact of large dams and a strong environmental movement within Thailand,[8] Thailand started to expand its natural resource exploitation across its national borders. Meanwhile, Laos, in its bid to become "the battery of Southeast Asia", sought to enhance its income by exploiting and exporting its natural resources.[9] Vietnam has also looked to its neighbours to secure its electricity supply while the large hydropower dams within its own territory have often been criticised for causing serious social upheaval and high environmental costs.[10]

Although Cambodia has taken a more negative position on hydropower development due to its downstream location and its dependence on wild capture fisheries,[11] it is also on the "threshold of an extensive domestic hydropower development programme to improve its rudimentary electricity infrastructure", supported mainly by Chinese developers and financiers.[12] The Mekong only passes through a small part of Myanmar where settlement is sparse, but the plans for extensive hydropower development on other river systems within Myanmar should be taken into account as well.[13]

By 2010, most Mekong tributaries have cascades of dams in place or planned, among which approximately 71 projects are expected to be operational by 2030.[14] Several Mekong tributaries themselves are transboundary rivers and

---

8 The successful opposition to the Nam Choan Dam in the mid-to late-1980s is a good example here. Philip Hirsch, 'Water Governance Reform and Catchment Management in the Mekong Region' (2006) 15(2) *Journal of Environment and Development* 184, 188. For more detailed discussion on the environmental movement in Thailand, see section II in this chapter.

9 Hirsch, above n 3.

10 Carl Middleton, Jelson Garcia and Tira Foran, 'Old and New Hydropower Players in the Mekong Region: Agendas and Strategies' in François Molle, Tira Foran and Mira Käkönen (eds), *Contested Waterscapes in the Mekong Region: Hydropower, Livelihoods and Governance* (Earthscan, 2009) 23, 37.

11 Hirsch, above n 8, 189.

12 Middleton, Garcia and Foran, above n 10, 38.

13 Ibid. 39.

14 International Centre for Environmental Management, 'Mekong River Commission Strategic Environmental Assessment of Hydropower on the Mekong Mainstream' (Report, ICEM, 2010) 8.

the dam construction has caused disputes among their riparian states. Moreover, the rapid expansion of hydropower projects on the tributaries may ultimately have a cumulative impact on the mainstream. Some of the most controversial cases include the Pak Mum Dam in Thailand, the Yali Falls Dam in Vietnam, the Theum-Hinboun Dam, Nam Ngum 3 and the Nam Theun 2 Dam in Laos, and the Sesan 2 Dam and the Kamchay Dam in Cambodia. The decision-making processes of some high-profile tributaries projects will be used as case studies in the future chapters to gain more empirical information on the problems of current water governance in the region and shed light on how to promote the development of appropriate procedural mechanisms.

Meanwhile, Mekong tributary hydropower development in China has been much less high-profile. The tributaries of Dza Chu and Lancang are generally considered to have great potential for hydropower development.[15] Along with the rapid expansion of hydropower in the southwest of China, the Mekong tributary dam construction in China seems very unlikely to be avoidable. But since all the tributaries of Dza Chu and Lancang are located within China, tributary dams are less likely to raise regional disputes compared to the mainstream dam proposals. Instead, they could become the source of transboundary disputes between different riparian provinces or cities inside China. This study, however, will focus more on Mekong mainstream dams and tributary dams in the lower Mekong region.

## 2 Mainstream Dams

### (a) *Upstream*

With respect to mainstream hydropower development, China's construction and operation of the Lancang cascade in Yunnan Province exemplified the tension between upstream and downstream states regarding the utilisation and protection of international rivers. To date, the only mainstream dams on the Mekong River exist in China. As mentioned earlier, there has been a cascade of 16 dams (half of them on the upstream of Lancang and half of them on the midstream and downstream of Lancang) planed on the mainstream of Lancang River.[16]

In particular, the eight-dam cascade on the midstream and downstream of the Lancang River has attracted most of the attention. The first of these, the Manwan Dam, was completed in 1994, followed by Dachaoshan, Jinghong and

15 Such as the Angqu River, the Yangbi River and the Xier River.

16 中国河流网 [China River], 《水电地图》 [Hydropower Map] <http://www.river.org.cn/map.aspx>.

Nuozhadu.[17] In March 2010, the Xiaowan Dam was completed as the highest arch dam in the world.[18] And the Gongguoqiao Dam started operating at the end of 2012. The Ganlanba Dam is in the final stage of getting formal approval. The Mengsong Dam, as the lowest of the eight dams on the cascade, was cancelled in 2007 in order to allow fish passage up a significant tributary to compensate for the obstructed passage past Jinghong (and the Ganlanba Dam in the future).[19]

Along with the implementation of the Western Region Development Strategy,[20] and the ongoing energy restructuring in China to reduce greenhouse gas emissions and secure energy production, boosting production of "clean green" hydropower is seen as a strategically vital sunrise industry.[21] The proponents of the Lancang dam cascade allege that they could also benefit the downstream in terms of irrigation, navigation, power generation and flooding control.[22] But the ongoing dam construction and operation in the upper Mekong has raised concern and tension regarding its potential negative impact on the ecosystem.

To some extent, the doubt and mistrust could be attributed to the lack of transparency during the decision-making process, which was conducted solely by the Chinese government without proper transparency and domestic public participation procedure and was kept outside of any general awareness by the other Mekong states until the mid-1990s.[23] Along with the deepening of cooperation between China and downstream states, an agreement on the provision of hydrological information on the Mekong River was signed in 2002 and China promised to provide water level data in the flood season.[24] Talks are under way to expand this data sharing agreement to include dry season levels. Relevant development will be further discussed in chapter three.

Attention should also be paid to the first half of the Lancang dam cascade. On the upstream of Lancang, five dams are already under construction and two

---

17 Hirsch, above n 3, 317.

18 *Xiaowan Hydropower Station Easing Electricity Demand in YN* (16 March 2011) InKunming <http://en.kunming.cn/index/content/2011-03/16/content_2448960.htm>.

19 Hirsch, above n 3, 319.

20 This policy aims at reducing the economic gap between eastern and western parts of China.

21 See Dore, Yu and Li, above n 7, 56.

22 Ibid. 77.

23 Milton Osborne, 'River at Risk: The Mekong and the Water Politics of China and Southeast Asia' (Working Paper No 2, Lowy Institute, 2004) 11.

24 Mekong River Commission, *Upstream Partners* <http://www.mrcmekong.org/about-the-mrc/upstream-partners-2/>.

are planned to be built. The Guonian Dam, initially planned as the second of the Lancang cascade, was later cancelled due to its potential impact on glacier melting in the Three Rivers Headwaters National Nature Reserve.[25] Recently, scandal came out that the construction of the Huangdeng Dam, the sixth of the cascade, has begun without getting approval from the government.[26] Despite controversies surrounding China's dam construction on the upper Mekong at the international level, the decision-making process of the Huangdeng Dam further reveals challenges for relevant domestic law-making and implementation inside China. This case will be further discussed in chapter six.

Meanwhile, China's hydropower development on the Mekong mainstream in Tibet and Qinghai Province (known as the Dza Chu River) should not be overlooked. The smallest dam on the Mekong mainstream is the Longqingxia Dam in Zadoi, Qinghai Province. Completed in 2006, it is the first dam that the Mekong mainstream encounters on its way to the mouth. Before then, Zadoi was the only county in the Qinghai Province that did not have electricity supply.[27] In addition, a six-dam cascade is planned on the Dza Chu River in Tibet, which constitutes a part of a broader plan to develop hydropower in Tibet. Electricity generated by these dams in the future will be transmitted to inland China.[28] In the next decade, the rapid hydropower development in China will likely to expand from Yunnan and Sichuan Provinces to Tibet. The decision-making regarding dam plans in Tibet can be more politically sensitive and is placed in a different geopolitical environment compared to hydropower development in Yunnan Province. To date, information on these dam plans remains limited.

---

25 北极星电力网 [Polestar Electricity Website],《华能澜沧江水电一个月2项目获批》[TwoHuanengProjectsApprovedwithinoneMonth](20March2013)<http://news.bjx.com.cn/html/20130320/423733.shtml>.

26 Shane Worrell, *Dam Firm Violated Law* (05 June 2013) <http://www.phnompenhpost.com/2013060566083/National/dam-firm-violated-law.html>; 中华人民共和国审计署 [National Audit Office of the People's Republic of China],《2013年第3号公告：中国华能集团公司2011年度财务收支审计结果》[No.3 Notification in 2013: The Audit Result of Financial Revenue and Expenditure of the China Huaneng Group in 2011] (10 May 2013) <http://www.audit.gov.cn/n1992130/n1992150/n1992500/3277991.html>.

27 青海新闻网 [Qinghai News],《龙青峡水电站试运行发电 杂多县将结束无电历史》[Test Run of the Longqingxia Dam has begun and the History of No Electricity in Zadoi will Come to an End] (23 November 2006) <http://www.qhnews.com/newscenter/system/2006/11/23/000025460.shtml>.

28 华能集团 [China Huaneng Group],《华能澜沧江上游水电有限公司》[Huaneng Upstream Lancang River Hydropower Co., LTD] (17 October 2010) <http://www.chng.com.cn/n93521/n93834/c95347/content.html>.

### (b) *Downstream*

The lower Mekong mainstream is threatened by eleven downstream dam proposals, two in Cambodia and the rest in Laos (two of them are on the Lao-Thailand reaches of the mainstream).[29] Among all the proposals, the furthest advanced projects are the Xayaburi Dam in north-central Laos and the Don Sahong hydropower scheme in southern Laos near the Cambodia border.[30] Damming the lower Mekong mainstream is extremely controversial due to the possibility of a significant negative impact on the passage and breeding capacities of the Mekong's many migratory fish species.[31] The escalating momentum for mainstream dams in the lower Mekong region presents a real test for the inchoate regional environmental cooperation regime.

Under the 1995 *Agreement on Cooperation for the Sustainable Development of the Mekong River Basin (the Mekong Agreement)*, the Mekong River Commission (MRC) have taken some measures to facilitate regional cooperation and communication on the lower Mekong mainstream hydropower development. This is represented by the MRC programs on IWRM, basin development plan, information and knowledge management, fishery, environment and hydropower; the MRC procedural documents on information exchange and prior notification and consultation; and some internal strategies and policies on how to improve information transparency of the MRC and involve different stakeholders.

Several recent developments under the MRC have particularly addressed the mainstream hydropower issues: commissioning a transboundary strategic environmental assessment (SEA) research on all proposed lower Mekong mainstream hydropower project which later recommended a 10-year deferral for mainstream hydropower development due to many of its remaining uncertainties and serious risks;[32] holding prior consultations on the Xayaburi Dam Project; and reaching consensus on commissioning another transboundary

29 The Don Sahong project, near the Khone Falls in Laos, only involves partial damming (one channel of the mainstream, but it is the only channel that is known to provide a year-round route for migrating fish). Other than the eleven dam projects, there is another lower Mekong mainstream hydropower proposal called Thakho, which located in Laos. But different from all the others, it is a river diversion project rather than a dam. International Centre for Environmental Management, above n 14, 8, 31, 94.

30 Hirsch, above n 3, 318.

31 The Stung Treng and Sambor dams in Cambodia are two of the largest possible dams in the lower Mekong region and could be the most potentially destructive ones in terms of the area flooded and the impact on fisheries. Ibid.; Milton Osborne, 'The Mekong: River under Threat' (Working Paper No 27, Lowy Institute, 2009) 17, 19, 41.

32 International Centre for Environmental Management, above n 14, 138.

environmental impact assessment (EIA) research on the proposed Xayaburi Dam. Despite the above efforts, the MRC remains largely ineffective in resolving the mainstream hydropower disputes, let alone the existence of several other cooperative mechanisms in the region which are highly involved in regional development. Relevant issues will be discussed in detail in Section II.

### B Climate Change

As another major environmental concern, climate change is expected to result in higher temperatures, increased extreme weather events, rising sea levels, changes in runoff patterns and more intensified monsoonal climate in this area.[33] Although concerns about the accuracy of the hypothesised impact and the effectiveness of the proposed approaches still exist, it is safe to conclude that the Mekong region, particularly the lower Mekong area, may be more severely affected than many other parts of the world due to its great reliance on water resources.[34] It is also argued that the effects of climate change will further intensify the competition to exploit the still abundant, but increasingly stressed water resources in the Mekong region.[35]

On the positive side, the impact of climate change and the need for mitigation and adaptation have begun to attract more attention from the decision-makers in the Mekong countries and there is a slowly increasing awareness of the necessity to integrate this issue into broader policy-making and basin development plans.[36] For instance, the lower Mekong countries have agreed on a Climate Change and Adaptation Initiative to promote basin-wide harmonisation of effective strategies and plans at various levels.[37] The MRC supports relevant progress with technical advice and dialogue-based forums.[38] But it is also pointed out that this MRC initiative tends to avoid explicit connections to the dams and most of its work focuses scenario analysis based on the MRC's

33 Philip Hirsch and Rosalia Sciortino, 'Climate Change and the Resource Politics of the Greater Mekong Subregion' in Kobkun Rayanakorn (ed), *Climate Change Challenges in the Mekong Region* (Chiang Mai University Press, 2011) 223, 225.

34 Ibid. 224–5.

35 Richard P. Cronin and Timothy Hamlin, 'Mekong Tipping Point: Hydropower Dams, Human Security and Regional Stability' (Report, Henry L. Stimson Centre, 2010) 1.

36 Mekong River Commission, *Climate Change* <http://www.mrcmekong.org/topics/climate-change/>.

37 Mekong River Commission, *Climate Change and Adaptation Initiative* <http://www.mrcmekong.org/about-the-mrc/programmes/climate-change-and-adaptation-initiative/>.

38 Mekong River Commission, above n 36.

modelling capacity.[39] Here, the scope of the climate change issue seems to be carefully narrowed to reduce controversy.

Meanwhile, China, being the world's biggest $CO_2$ emitter,[40] is also very vulnerable to climate change itself. At the international level, the Chinese government refuses to accept any mandatory emission reduction target before 2020, whereas it shows more willingness to take domestic measures to cope with climate change. In 2007, China became the first developing country to formulate and implement a national program to address climate change. Two years later, China put forward the goal of action to reduce the per-unit GDP greenhouse gas emission in 2020 by 40 to 45 percent as compared to that of 2005.[41] In December 2011, the Minister of Environmental Protection signed agreements with 31 provincial-level governments and eight state-owned enterprises, which specify mandatory emission reduction targets and pollution control targets for these local governments and enterprises, respectively, within the 12th Five-Year Plan period (2011–2015).[42] This includes Yunnan Province and major energy enterprises in China, such as Huaneng—the main corporate player involved in the hydropower development on the upper Mekong in China.[43]

The cooperation on climate change between China and other Mekong countries is slowly progressing. Responding to climate change and addressing its impact has been recognised as one of the ten priority areas of environmental cooperation between China and the Association of Southeast Asian Nations (ASEAN).[44] Currently, the collaborative practice is mainly limited to less controversial areas like public education and awareness raising, climate change

---

39 Hirsch and Sciortino, above n 33, 232.

40 International Energy Agency, '$CO_2$ Emissions from Fuel Combustion: Highlights (2011 edition)' (Report, IEA, 2011) 9.

41 State Council Information Office of the People's Republic of China, *China's Policies and Actions for Addressing Climate Change* (22 November 2011) Xinhua News Agency <http://news.xinhuanet.com/english2010/china/2011-11/22/c_131262368.htm>.

42 Xinhua News Agency, *China Assigns Mandatory Emission Reduction Tasks to Local Gov'ts, State-owned Enterprises* (20 December 2011) <http://news.xinhuanet.com/english/china/2011-12/20/c_131317697.htm>.

43 John Dore and Yu Xiaogang, 'Yunnan Hydropower Expansion: Update on China's Energy Industry Reforms & the Nu, Lancang & Jinsha Hydropower Dams' (Working Paper, Chiang Mai University's Unit for Social and Environmental Research and Green Watershed, 2004) ii.

44 China-ASEAN Environmental Cooperation Centre, *China-ASEAN Strategy on International Environmental Cooperation* <http://www.chinaaseanenv.org/english/events/271416.shtml>.

research,[45] renewable energy and cleaner production. The ongoing cooperative measures fall short of interest and political will in developing institutional arrangements to integrate climate change considerations during the decision-making process. This is not surprising, however, given the general immature status of transboundary environmental cooperation in the Mekong region which in many cases does not have cooperative decision-making arrangements. In addition, the lack of domestic legislation and pragmatic political arrangements on climate change often undermines the possibility of effective implementation in practice and results in a high risk of the discourse being used to justify the decisions on hydropower development.

The possible tensions between responses to climate change concerns and pursuance of other environmental goals add another level of complexity and uncertainty to sustainable governance of Mekong water resources.[46] Hydropower development is often viewed as a climate change-friendly option for large-scale energy production,[47] despite some existing science-based challenges to this idea.[48] And dams are considered as a basic agriculture infrastructure to improve irrigation and limit the threat of aggravated flooding, hence contributing to climate change adaptation.[49] Thus, the issue of climate change somehow finds itself caught on the horns of a multifaceted dilemma in the Mekong region.

While the impact of climate change can further escalate tensions over water resources, the attempt to deal with it also risks a real danger that the discourse will be used as a convenient excuse for not taking action against entrenched economic interests. As viewed by Hirsch and Sciortino, "approaches to climate change effects and their impacts are deeply value-bound and do not occur in a neutral political space".[50] Under such circumstances, the key that may break the deadlock does not mainly lie in science or technology; rather, it depends

45 Research cooperation and communication on climate change has been carried out in areas like biodiversity, forestry, transboundary rivers and underground water.

46 Hirsch and Sciortino, above n 33, 224–5.

47 Ibid. 231. Efforts have been made to achieve subsidies for dams through the Clean Development Mechanism (CDM) and the Xeset 2 Dam in Laos has become the first Mekong hydropower project to apply for carbon credit support through CDM.

48 Some scientific studies of existing hydropower projects in tropical areas suggest that large dams in these climates are considerable emitters of many greenhouse gases. See International Rivers, *Dirty Hydro: Dams and Greenhouse Gas Emissions* (November 2008) <http://www.internationalrivers.org/resources/dirty-hydro-dams-and-greenhouse-gas-emissions-2648>.

49 State Council Information Office of the People's Republic of China, above n 41.

50 Hirsch and Sciortino, above n 33, 227.

on an improvement of the decision-making processes. With increasing transparency, improved governmental cooperation, better secured public participation and necessary environmental assessment and monitoring process, there is a better chance to lower the possibility of bad climate change policy and gain legitimacy for the decision despite the existence of a certain degree of uncertainty.

## II Existing Decision-making Landscapes: Polycentric Governance and Diverse Actors

Before exploring approaches that can encourage more integrated water governance, it is necessary to understand how the development decisions in the Mekong region are made in practice. As will be further illustrated, the current water governance in the Mekong region is still fragmented and poorly coordinated among the different levels/sections of government and regional intergovernmental organisations, which result in low efficiency, extensive conflicts and bureaucratic infighting.

Apart from the governments, many other actors also played an important role in shaping the water governance in the Mekong region, such as foreign donors, investment banks, private and state-owned enterprises and even powerful local families. Despite the significant impact of many development decisions on local communities, their opportunity and ability to participate in the decision-making process is still very much limited and there is often a lack of political opportunities for NGOs to help raise their voice. Even if they were able to participate, it would be really difficult, if not impossible, for them to have a real impact on the outcome of the process. Understanding the interplay between and among these actors under the current governance regime can shed light on how to improve the decision-making process in order to better integrate multiple stakeholders and their interests.

### A *Domestic Perspective: Water Governance Bureaucracies and the Legal Environment*

Transboundary water governance is not solely based on regional organisations and agreements. It is also related to water governance bureaucracies and the legal environment in each riparian state. The Mekong region has been deeply beset by instability and security issues. Currently, it remains very immature in terms of democracy and rule of law. The domestic development of water governance certainly places another layer of uncertainty in promoting transboundary water cooperation. The Mekong countries are currently undergoing water reforms at different speeds and with varied priorities. The struggles and hope reflected in this process can add to the discussion on how to promote IWRM in the context of Mekong and give valuable reference to policy makers. In particular, the following discussion will cite China, Thailand, Laos and Cambodia as typical examples.[51]

## 1 China

China embraced the concept of IWRM at the legislation level through the revision of *Water Law* in 2002, which stipulates that: "[the] state shall, with respect to water resources, adopt a system that organises the administration by watersheds as well as by administrative areas".[52] The duel track system which highlights both river basin management and jurisdictional management reflects

51 Myanmar is not discussed in detail partly for the fact that the Mekong River only briefly touches its territory and its contribution to the Mekong watershed is relatively small. Another reason is that water governance remains very much underdeveloped in this country, even compared to other Mekong countries. But along with the ongoing political transition in Myanmar, it seems possible to expect more improvements in its water-related policy, legislation and governance regime. Vietnam is currently going through institutional reform in order to shift the major responsibilities for water resources management from the Ministry of Agriculture and Rural Development to the Ministry of Natural Resources and Environment. Despite the bureaucratic infighting and deficiencies of these ministries, the water management in Vietnam also suffers from problems such as a lack of awareness, incomplete legal systems for water management, a lack of specific mechanisms and policies, low transparency, insufficient and inaccurate information and public involvement. The case of Vietnam is not analysed in detail to avoid unnecessary repetition, although the degree of these common problems varies across the Mekong region. For more information on water management in Vietnam and Myanmar, see generally François Molle and Chu Thai Hoanh, 'Implementing Integrated River Basin Management: Lessons from the Red River Basin, Vietnam' (Report, International Water Management Institute, 2009); Carl Middleton and Gary Lee, 'Mekong Water Resources Assistance Strategy: Justifying Large Water Infrastructure with Transboundary Impacts' (2006) 12(1) *Watershed* 10; Nguyen Thai Lai, 'Viet Nam: National Water Resources Council' (Paper presented at the Regional Meeting of National Water Sector Apex Bodies, Hanoi, 18–21 May 2004); Cronin and Hamlin, above n 35, 24–5; Global Water Partnership, 'Evaluation of the Status of IWRM Implementation in Southeast Asia 2000–2010 in Respect to Policy, Legal and Institutional Aspects' (Report, Global Water Partnership, 2011).

52 François Molle, 'Irrigation and Water Policies: Trends and Challenges' in Louis Lebel et al. (eds), *Democratizing Water Governance in the Mekong* (Mekong Press, 2007) 9, 24; 《中华人民共和国水法》 [Water Law of the People's Republic of China] (People's Republic of China) National People's Congress Standing Committee, Order No 61, 21 January 1988, art 9, as amended by 《中华人民共和国水法》 [Water Law of the People's Republic

reconciliation between the new theory of IWRM and China's entrenched water governance landscape.

In practice, however, the water governance in China remains highly fragmented by administrative boundaries. Before the amendment of the *Water Law*, seven river basin authorities have been established based on seven major watershed areas, among which, the Changjiang (Yangtze) Water Resources Commission exercises water administrative functions in the Yangtze River basin and other river basins of South Western China (west to and inclusive of the Lancang River).[53]

All river basin authorities are under the supervision of the Ministry of Water Resources (the MWR), the leading administrative authority responsible for water governance in China. Therefore, this setting can do little to overcome the barriers to cross-sectoral management of water and may only partly address the fragmentation created by administrative boundaries.[54]

For example, with respect to water resources protection, water pollution prevention and control, the river basin water resources protection bureaus of the commissions are supposed to be under the co-leadership of both the MWR and the State Environmental Protection Agency (upgraded to the Ministry of Environmental Protection in 2008).[55] Yet in reality, such integration is highly restricted due to the unresolved issues among two ministries regarding the funding sources and powers of appointments.[56] This problem can then be traced back to the flawed demarcation of responsibilities between the MWR and the Ministry of Environmental Protection (MEP). In general, the MWR is responsible for water resources protection,[57] while the MEP is in charge of

---

of China] (People's Republic of China) National People's Congress Standing Committee, Order No 74, 29 August 2002, arts 12, 14.

53 长江水利委员会 [Changjiang Water Resources Commission],《单位简介》 [Introduction of CWRC] <http://node.cjw.com.cn/cjwintro/cjw.asp>.

54 The CWRC is responsible for water conserving, allocation and protection, basin planning, flood control and drought relief, river course management, key hydraulic project construction and management, river sand extraction management, soil conservation, hydrology, scientific research as well as operation and stewardship of State owned assets.

55 Dajun Shen, 'River Basin Water Resources Management in China: A Legal and Institutional Assessment' (2009) 34(4) *Water International* 484, 492.

56 Ibid. 495.

57 This mainly includes drafting water resource protection plans, water function zoning in major rivers and lakes and supervising their implementation; reviewing and verifying the capacity of pollutant load of water bodies; making proposals on the limit of total wastewater discharge; providing guidance on the protection of drinking water sources, exploitation and use of groundwater as well as management and protection of groundwater

water quality protection and water pollution prevention.[58] But there are considerable overlaps in their responsibilities and sectoral interests. The lack of mechanisms for cross-sectoral cooperation, coordination and dispute settlements often results in excessive bureaucracies and conflicts in practice.

These commissions have also been criticised for being narrowly focused on more centralised water governance without paying enough attention to promoting cooperation and participation among different stakeholders and local governments.[59] Moreover, these organisations have been allocated responsibilities that go beyond the particular river basin concerned. Therefore, they in fact look more like regional offices of the MWR rather than integrated river basin management agencies.[60] Such awkward design of river basin organisations indeed creates further conflicts between river basin management bureaucracies and jurisdictional agencies. Combined with the strong local protectionism that exists in water resources governance in China, their real influence on water resources management and utilisation is indeed restricted in the field.[61]

Therefore, the existing river basin organisations in fact create more problems than it resolves, adding another level of confusion to the pre-existing flawed distribution of responsibilities among different administrative sectors. The traditional Chinese idiom "nine dragons ruling water" is often referred to

---

resources in the planned areas of cities. See Ministry of Water Resources of the People's Republic of China, *About the Ministry of Water Resources* <http://www.mwr.gov.cn/english/aboutmwr.html>.

58 This mainly includes drawing up policies, programs, laws, administrative regulations, rules, standards and criteria for water pollution prevention and control; dividing special environmental function zones for water and drafting plans accordingly; drafting plans to prevent and control pollution of important drinking water sources, watersheds and underground water and supervising their implementation; establishing and implementing systems for water quality evaluation; environmental protection of headwater catchments and water quality monitoring and information disclosure. See Ministry of Environmental Protection of People's Republic of China, *Major Responsibilities of the Department of Pollution Prevention and Control* <http://english.mep.gov.cn/About_SEPA/Internal_Departments/200910/t20091015_162419.htm>.

59 There is no commission board or board of directors in the commissions and the provincial governments have no role in their governance. See Shen, above n 55, 492, 494–5.

60 Ibid. 491.

61 纪逗 [Ji Dou],《水资源市场配置管理体制障碍的法律分析》[A Legal Analysis of the Institutional Obstacles on Market Allocation of Water Resources] (16 September 2003) 武汉大学环境法研究所 [Research Institute of Environmental Law of Wuhan University] <http://www.riel.whu.edu.cn/article.asp?id=25668>.

as a vivid image of the fragmentation among agencies.[62] Moreover, the application of IWRM in China is facing challenges brought by the unclear separation of the regulator, manager and provider functions.[63]

In light of the enormous challenges and resistance against the institutional restructuring, recent years have witnessed increasing attention on improving cross-boundary and cross-sectoral cooperation and coordination. Riparian governments are encouraged to sign cooperation agreement with each other regarding water issues and to resolve water-related disputes through consultation. If the consultation was unsuccessful, the issue in dispute will be subject to ruling by the government at the next level up. While this ground rule has been vaguely set forth by current *Water Law* and the *Law on the Prevention and Control of Water Pollution*,[64] there is no clearer guidance or stipulation under the existing administrative law or environmental protection law. The current water legislation in China also falls short of requirements on information disclosure and public participation. With the implementation of the Regulations on Government Information Disclosure in 2008 and the gradually increasing requirements on public participation in administrative law and environmental law, there seems to be a tendency towards a more transparent and participatory water related decision-making process. But the current practice in this area is still far from satisfactory and more detailed arrangements should be made to better secure participation on water issues.

## 2 Thailand

In Thailand, although the concept of IWRM has been incorporated into several national policies and water has been declared as one of key national agendas, the legislation to implement it remains inadequate.[65] For example, Thailand still does not have a comprehensive water law in place. This is in contrast

62 These agencies include, but are not limited to: the Ministry of Water Resources, the Ministry of Environmental Protection, the Ministry of Transport, the Ministry of Construction, the Ministry of Agriculture, the State Forestry Administration, the Ministry of Health, the Ministry of Land and Resources, the National Tourism Administration, the State Electricity Regulatory Commission.

63 Molle, above n 52. This is particularly obvious in the electricity sector.

64 《中华人民共和国水法》 [Water Law of the People's Republic of China] (People's Republic of China) National People's Congress Standing Committee, Order No 74, 29 August 2002, art 56; 《中华人民共和国水污染防治法》 [Law of the People's Republic of China on the Prevention and Control of Water Pollution] (People's Republic of China) National People's Congress Standing Committee, Order No 87, 2 February 2008, art 28.

65 World Bank, 'Thailand Environment Monitor: Integrated Water Resources Management—A Way Forward' (Report, World Bank, 2011) 39.

with Laos, Vietnam, and Cambodia, which passed such laws in 1996, 1998 and 2007 respectively.[66] Separate pieces of legislation were put in place regarding groundwater, irrigation and water quality in Thailand, but in a fragmented and overlapping way and fall short of a coherent framework.[67] Instead of viewing water resources management holistically,[68] the existing regulations were developed in accordance with a subsector planning and budgeting approach, which suits varied sectoral purposes.

In order to promote cooperation and coordination on water governance, the National Water Resources Committee (NWRC) was established in 1996 to: (1) suggest water policies to the cabinet, (2) comment on budget allocation to water projects, (3) assign water rights to river basins, (4) issue water permits for large-scale water use, (5) supervise river basin organisations and resolve conflicts between river basins.[69] It is chaired by a deputy prime minister and comprises representatives from state agencies, local government, river basin committees, NGOs and experts, which do reflect a higher degree of integration.[70] The Director General of the Department of Water Resources heads the secretariat of NWRC. But it is doubtful whether the NWRC is equipped with enough power to actually overcome the sectoral and administrative boundaries, since there is still no clear national direction on the relationship among river basin committees, national agencies and local authorities.[71] The NWRC is also criticised for its restricted scope to debate issues due to the fact that key decisions are in fact already made prior to committee meetings.[72] In addition, the NWRC suffers from a limited budget, insufficient expertise and

66 Hirsh, above n 8, 190. It should be noted that the quality of water law in these countries is questionable, especially for Laos and Vietnam. With regard to the latter, see generally Philip Hirsch et al., 'National Interests and Transboundary Water Governance in the Mekong' (Report, University of Sydney, 2006) 36.

67 Hirsch et al., above n 66, 35.

68 World Bank, above n 65.

69 Southeast Asian Water Utilities Network, *Water Organizations in Southeast Asia* <http://seawun.org/index.php?page=water-links-regional-and-local>.

70 Mekong River Commission, 'Stakeholder Analysis for the MRC Basin Development Plan Programme Phase 2 (BDP2)' (Report, Mekong River Commission, 2010) 72; World Bank, above n 65, 42–3.

71 World Bank, above n 65, 53.

72 Hirsch et al., above n 66.

the lack of coordination between the newly established Department of Water Resources and the traditionally powerful agency Royal Irrigation Department.[73]

Despite the existence of 76 provinces, river basin committees have been established in each of Thailand's 25 river basins promoted under Thailand's Seventh National Plan (1992–1996).[74] Currently, these committees are under the supervision of the Department of Water Resources which is established as a part of the Ministry of Natural Resources and Environment.[75] Each committee includes 35 representatives from government and key stakeholders.[76] But these committees often fall short of necessary decision-making power, technical capacity, clearly defined roles and operational procedures.[77] They are also claimed to be infrastructure emphasised in practice and public participation still needs to be improved.[78]

It should be acknowledged that the current governance structure does open the door in theory for multi-stakeholder participation and consultation. Combined with the ongoing strong environmental movement within Thailand, Thailand seems to have more ability to deliver a better form of IWRM in reality. In fact, it is argued that an important reason for Thailand's tardiness in passing its water law is that:

> civil society has had the opportunity to challenge some of the underlying principles of the proposed water law and has taken exception to issues such as water pricing and what is perceived as entrenchment of state agency control over what NGOs and community actors see as local resources.[79]

Nevertheless, this domestic enlightenment does not necessarily lead to the conclusion that Thailand would be more willing to participate in transboundary

---

73 Ibid. 35–6; Sacha Sethaputra et al., 'Thailand's Water Vision: A Case Study' in Le Huu Ti and Thierry Facon (eds), *A Synthesis of Experiences in Southeast Asia* (RAP Publication, 2001) 71, 86.

74 Carl Middleton and Gary Lee, 'Mekong Water Resources Assistance Strategy: Justifying Large Water Infrastructure with Transboundary Impacts' (2006) 12(1) *Watershed* 10, 18.

75 Hirsh, above n 8, 195.

76 World Bank, above n 65, 43.

77 Ibid. 53; Hirsh, above n 8, 196.

78 Hirsh, above n 8, 195. Some pilot programs at Bang Pakong and other basins continue to search for more innovative ways to bring basin stakeholders into decision-making through committees.

79 Ibid. 190.

cooperation and consultation at the regional level. Many dam plans in the Mekong region are designed to provide electricity for Thailand because its domestic environmental movement has made it much more difficult to build dam within its own territory. It is also interesting to note some efforts to help villagers from eight Mekong provinces in Thailand to bring an Administrative Court complaint against the Thailand agencies. They claim that the decision on purchasing electricity from Xayaburi Dam which is planned to be built on the Mekong mainstream river in Laos is in violation of procedural requirements on public participation under Thailand's domestic law.[80] While this case will be analysed in detail in chapter five, it can be concluded here that it represents an attempt to explore possible solutions or at least raise more attention with respect to dam issues through the domestic legal regime.

## 3 Laos

As a country in which most of its territory lies within the Mekong region, the major river basins in Laos are all tributaries of the Mekong River.[81] The *Law on Water and Water Resources* in 1996 provides a legal foundation for water management. But it was not implemented until 2001 when the Prime Minister's Decree on Implementation of the Law on Water and Water Resources was issued.[82] This act only vaguely states the roles and responsibilities of various water-related sectors and many detailed arrangements are still yet to be made.[83] Among the existing water sectors, it is currently the irrigation and hydropower departments that remain the most important in terms of investment.[84] The goal to develop hydropower in Laos can also be found in Article 25 of the *Law on Water and Water Resources*, which states that:

80 Email from Daniel King to Qi Gao, 21 February 2011.

81 Sengmanichanh Somchanmavong, 'The Challenge of Water Resources Management in Laos' (Speech delivered at the Commonwealth Scientific and Industrial Research Organisation Land and Water Seminar, Perth, 28 June 2007) <http://www.clw.csiro.au/division/perth/seminars/2007/documents/Somchanmavong_July2007.pdf>.

82 Global Water Partnership, above n 51, 38.

83 See Phonechaleun Nonthaxay, *Water Resources Management in Lao PDR* (2004) Network of Asian River Basin Organizations <http://www.narbo.jp/data/01_events/materials/tc01_cr_laopdr01.pdf>. According to Article 19, "water and water resources shall be centrally managed, and management [responsibilities] shall be allocated according to the size and [type of] water use right" and "administration and inspection of such use are assigned to relevant divisions and local administrative authorities for execution". *Law on Water and Water Resources* 1996 (Lao People's Democratic Republic) art 19.

84 Nonthaxay, above n 83.

> the government promotes the development and use of water resources in the production of large, medium and small-scale electrical power at water sources where there are suitable conditions for the production of electrical power.[85]

According to the Law, hydropower projects should be developed "with due concern for environmental protection, flood protection, water supply, irrigation, navigation, fisheries and others".[86] And there are several other provisions devoted to water and water resources protection and the control of harmful effects.[87] But the legislation falls short of proper legal arrangements and mechanisms to actually consider environmental needs during the hydropower development.

Efforts have been made that reflect some features of the IWRM, such as the development of the National Water Sector Strategy and Action Plan, the establishment of the Water Resources Coordination Committee under the Prime Minister's Office, and the establishment Nam Ngum River Basin Committee. But these changes are more like window-dressing and do not have much real impact in reality, especially with regard to hydropower decision-making. For example, the Water Resources Coordination Committee has been chaired by the Water Resources and Environment Administration[88] since 2007 with representatives from five ministries and other organisations.[89] But the Lao National Committee for Energy at the time, which was later replaced by the Department of Energy Promotion and Development under the Ministry of Energy and Mines in 2006, was not included in the Committee. This administrative setting raises concern of how much influence the Committee will actually have on hydropower development in this country. Despite the continuing

---

85 *Law on Water and Water Resources* (Lao People's Democratic Republic) National Assembly, 11 October 1996, art 25.

86 Ibid. art 25.

87 Ibid. arts 22, 29–32, 39–43.

88 The Water Resources and Environment Administration was created within the Office of the Prime Minister and absorbs the responsibilities of the Science Technology and Environment Agency, the Water Resources Coordination Committee Secretariat and the Lao National Mekong Committee Secretariat. See Global Water Partnership, above n 51, 46.

89 They are Ministry of Agriculture and Forestry (Vice Chairman), Ministry of Industry and Handicrafts, Ministry of Communications, Transport, Post and Construction, Ministry of Public Health, Ministry of Justice, Lao National Mekong Committee, Lao Front for National Construction and Lao Women Union.

high fragmentation at the agency level, the Committee is also criticised for minimal representation of civil society.[90]

## 4 Cambodia

Cambodia has about 86 percent of its land within the Mekong catchments area[91] and the Tonle Sap Great Lake is said to be one of the most productive inland waters in the world and also acts as a buffer for the Mekong River system in flood and the source of beneficial dry-season flows.[92]

Cambodia is undergoing rapid reforms in water management under the influence of various donors and organisations. For example, several water-related sectoral laws have been issued since 2000.[93] In particular, the *Law on Water Resources Management* was finally approved in 2007, which clearly endorse the principle of IWRM.[94] Under this law, the Ministry of Water Resources and Meteorology (officially established in 1999) continues to take a leading role in water-related activities. But it is required to collaborate with other agencies and local authorities in many cases. Guided by the concept of IWRM, this legislation strongly supports and encourages the collaboration with and participation of the relevant agencies and other stakeholders. It also includes provisions on information disclosure, participation of water users and their associations in the sustainable development of water resources.[95]

Nonetheless, this rather advanced legislation seems a bit detached from the water management status quo in Cambodia and many of its provisions either resemble political statements or lack specific support from other legislation, regulation, or the existing administrative structures. Institutional reform in the water sector faces numerous challenges as well. While the establishment of several new institutions reflect the endeavours to promote wider cooperation and integration, such as the Tonle Sap Authority, the current institutional structures and arrangements in Cambodia remain highly compartmentalised

---

90 Hirsch et al., above n 66, 40.

91 Department of Natural Resources Assessment and Environmental Data Management, 'Cambodia Environment Outlook' (Report, Ministry of Environment, Kingdom of Cambodia, 2009) 9.

92 Ngo Bunthan, *The Review of Current Situation of Water Resources Management and the Role of Agricultural Education in Cambodia* (2005) University of Tsukuba <http://www.nourin.tsukuba.ac.jp/~tasae/2005/Cambodia.pdf>.

93 Including the *Land Law* (2001), the *Forestry Law* (2002), the *Fishery Law* (2002) and the *Inland Water Navigation Law* (2010). Global Water Partnership, above n 51, 35.

94 *Law on Water Resources Management* (Kingdom of Cambodia) National Assembly, 29 June 2007, art 4.

95 Ibid. arts 1, 7, 8, 19.

and often fall short of necessary capacity to carry out their responsibilities.[96] In addition, Cambodia's institutional performance has never been strong as this country has been through a very unstable and turbulence period in recent history.[97] Further, the idea of information transparency and public participation is still fairly new to this country.

Cambodia represents a classic illustration of the difficulties in applying the ideologies of IWRM in the context of an entrenched water regime, to which more attention should be paid during the policy-making process. How to tailor the concept of IWRM and develop suitable strategies to improve the current system requires a more comprehensive and pragmatic approach at different governance levels and should take into consideration the roles played by various actors.

### B *Regional Perspective: Polycentric Governance of Transboundary Water Resources and the Influence of Non-state Actors*

Whilst water reform at the domestic level has proved to be difficult and less effective in the Mekong countries, regional cooperation in the governance of Mekong water resources is also struggling to move forward in the existing complex and dynamic transnational arena. As will be further illustrated below, although there is a river basin organisation set up in the Mekong region, its design and functionality is quite limited to play its role in practice. Rather, the Mekong River is currently governed in a more polycentric way, with increasing influence of the GMS program and ASEAN-China Dialogue relations. The following discussion will begin by discussing the deficiencies and strengths of three intergovernmental platforms on transboundary water governance and environmental cooperation.

In addition, attention will also be paid to the roles of various donors, investment banks, enterprises, NGOs and local communities in shaping the governance of Mekong. While some of them are quite influential as non-state drivers of water-related development and governance, the impact of NGOs and local communities on decision-making process remain very much limited. Through the discussion on these non-state actors, it is becoming more evident that transboundary water governance in the Mekong region is not just about riparian states. The interaction and counteraction among states, intergovernmental

96 See Chem Phalla et al., 'Framing Research on Water Resources Management and Governance in Cambodia: A Literature Review' (Working Paper 37, Cambodia Development Resource Institute, 2008) 33–7.

97 Ibid. 36.

organisations and non-state factors could provide more insight into the problem of how to deliver sustainability in the Mekong context.

## 1 Mekong River Commission (MRC)

### (a) *Introduction*

The history of cooperation on the Mekong River can be traced back to the end of 1940s, when a Mekong Consultative Committee was first created by Vietnam, Cambodia and Laos under the influence of France.[98] However, it was not until 1954 when a Provisional Mekong Committee was finally able to be established after the First Indochina War. As one of the earliest international river basin management institutions in the developing world, the focus of the Committee was to promote free navigation on the river,[99] which was later proved to be infeasible at the time due to the weak design of the committee, an insufficient level of technology, unstable political conditions and a lack of urgent necessity.

Along with the legacy of decolonialism in Indochina and subsequent geopolitical developments, the Mekong Committee was created among all four lower Mekong countries in 1957 under the "auspices of the United Nations but under the de facto hegemony of the United States early during the Cold War period".[100] Most of the work of the Committee until 1975 focused on planning a cascade of large dams on the mainstream of Mekong, which it was not able to carry out due to the Second Indochina War and Cambodia's withdrawal from the Committee in 1975.[101] An Interim Mekong Committee was thus formed in 1978, which mainly devoted itself to studies, data collection and implementation of small-scale projects.[102] This weakened organisation remained in place until the early 1990s, which exemplified the political impasse that had existed in this region for almost two decades.[103]

Different from the purely development-oriented setting, the creation of the MRC through the adoption of the *Mekong Agreement* in 1995 was set within

---

98 Unless otherwise indicated, information in this paragraph is derived from: Thi Dieu Nguyen, *The Mekong River and the Struggle for Indochina: Water, War and Peace* (Praeger Publishers, 1999) 35–6.

99 Blake D. Ratner, 'The Politics of Regional Governance in the Mekong River Basin' (2003) 15(1) *Global Change, Peace and Security* 59, 65.

100 Hirsch, above n 3; Jeffrey W. Jacobs, 'The United States and the Mekong Project' (2000) 1(6) *Water Policy* 587.

101 Hirsch, above n 3.

102 Mikiyasu Nakayama, 'International Collaboration on Water Systems in Asia and the Pacific: A Case of Transition' (2002) 3(2) *International Review for Environmental Strategies* 274, 277.

103 Ibid.

a very different eco-political circumstance.[104] The Agreement was also influenced to some extent by the work of the International Law Commission on drafting the *Convention on the Law of the Non-navigational Uses of International Watercourses* (the *UN Watercourses Convention*), which was adopted by the General Assembly of the United Nations in 1997. For example, the Agreement embraces some important principles in transboundary water governance, namely the general obligation to cooperate, the principle of equitable and reasonable utilisation and the obligation not to cause significant harm (the term used in the text is "substantial damage").[105] It should be noted though, the Convention has not yet entered into force and no Mekong country has actually signed it.[106]

According to the Agreement, the four downstream states also aim to promote and cooperate "in the development of the *full potential* of sustainable benefits to all riparian states and the prevention of wasteful use of Mekong waters".[107] Against the backdrop of this strong intention, the *Mekong Agreement* has faced criticism for being too "soft" to actually promote sustainability in the region.[108] Most parts of the document are drafted in "hortatory" language,[109] thus unable to be enforced due to the lack of legal teeth.[110] In addition, studies also show that the *Mekong Agreement* has not succeeded in being implemented in national legislation of member states.[111]

In addition, the MRC established under this Agreement has also been subjected to criticism for its problematic functioning in practice. According to the

---

104 Hirsch, above n 3, 314.

105 *Agreement on the Cooperation for the Sustainable Development of the Mekong River Basin*, opened for signature 5 April 1995, 2069 UNTS I-35844 (entered into force 5 April 1995) arts 1, 5, 7.

106 Fleur Johns et al., 'Law and the Mekong River Basin: A Socio-Legal Research Agenda on the Role of Hard and Soft Law in Regulating Transboundary Water Resources' (2010) 11(1) *Melbourne Journal of International Law* 154, 158.

107 *Agreement on the Cooperation for the Sustainable Development of the Mekong River Basin*, opened for signature 5 April 1995, 2069 UNTS I-35844 (entered into force 5 April 1995) art 2 (emphasis added).

108 Johns et al., above n 106.

109 For example, there is an explicit mandatory commitment "to protect the environment from pollution and other harmful effects resulting from development plans and uses of water-related resources". *Agreement on the Cooperation for the Sustainable Development of the Mekong River Basin*, opened for signature 5 April 1995, 2069 UNTS I-35844 (entered into force 5 April 1995) art 3.

110 Hirsch et al., above n 66, 26–7.

111 See ibid. 33–42.

Agreement, the MRC consists of three permanent bodies: the Council, the Joint Committee and the Secretariat. Their roles and functions have been concluded as follows:

> The Ministerial Council, which meets once per year, is the political body and comprises one ministerial representative from each member country. The Joint Committee is the bureaucratic management body that meets twice annually and comprises one permanent secretary-level representative from the most relevant ministry in each country. The MRC Secretariat manages the day-to-day affairs of the MRC, with a headquarters currently based in the Lao capital, Vientiane. This is also the technical arm of the MRC and is responsible for core programs including the Basin Development Plan, Water Utilisation Program, Environment Program, and Flood Mitigation and Management Program... A further element of the MRC governance structure that sits parallel to the above is the National Mekong Committee (NMC) system. Each riparian state has an NMC that is supposed to act as a conduit between the MRC and basin-relevant matters internal to the respective countries. The technical and political strengths of the NMCs vary from one riparian state to another.[112]

(b) *Limitations*

The MRC is currently caught in a multifaceted dilemma, which has significantly weakened and impaired its roles and functions in transboundary water governance. For one thing, there are notable tensions between the MRC as a donor-driven organisation and one owned by riparian states.[113] The funding of the MRC now relies primarily on Australia (Australia is currently the largest donor),[114] European donors (governments of Denmark, Sweden, Finland, Netherlands, Belgium, Germany and France) and the World Bank.[115] Their

---

112 Hirsh, above n 8, 192.

113 Ibid. 194.

114 Australian Government Aid Program, GMS *Ministerial Conference Statement—Australia—20 August 2010* (2010) <http://www.adb.org/documents/events/2010/16th-gms-ministerial-conference/16th-MC-statement-AusAID.pdf>.

115 These donors share common characteristics in the way they perceive the MRC as the organisational means to promote their ideas of development in the region (notes from International Donor Meeting in Vientiane, 19 June 2009). Diana Suhardiman, Mark Giordano and François Molle, 'Scalar Disconnect: The Logic of Transboundary Water Governance in the Mekong' (2011) 0 *Society & Natural Resources: An International Journal* 1, 5 <http://www.tandfonline.com/doi/abs/10.1080/08941920.2011.604398>.

changing perceptions toward the role of the MRC in promoting regional development often have a significant impact on the MRC's work.[116] As a region where "foreign interests, experts and donors have always played an important and at times dominant role",[117] recent years have witnessed an attempt to increase the member states' ownership of the MRC. The former MRC Chief Executive Officer (CEO) used to mention the riparianisation of all management positions in the Secretariat by 2011, including the CEO position.[118] Yet the official timeframe for this transition towards full ownership status was later set at 2030.[119]

This process is accompanied by many unresolved questions and doubts of the transition towards more ownership by the riparian states. Not only about how a CEO from four member states will be chosen, but also regarding this CEO's ability to "navigate the varied interests and drivers of mainstream hydropower development", since a Mekong national serving as CEO "could be more susceptible to various influences that would constrain the independence of the MRC Secretariat and impact its research agenda".[120] Thus, the MRC found itself caught in a dilemma of its own making. The dominance of the Secretariat by the donors provides a platform for them to have more control over the use of donor funds and express their ideologies about how to promote more sustainable and integrated water governance in the Mekong region. Yet this donor-driven pattern does create a sense of alienation of the MRC to its member states and in turn raise the risk of MRC being marginalised or bypassed in reality.

This issue is also complicated by the ambiguous leadership of the CEO in practice. It seems that "the CEO of the MRC Secretariat often presents himself as, and is often perceived by others to be, the CEO of the MRC itself", which also compromises the Secretariat's independent role of providing "informed, impartial and bold support for making decisions",[121] and further raise tension

---

116 This can be discerned in the MRC's changing position on hydropower development in the region over the last two decades. See Hirsch, above n 3, 314–7.

117 Hirsch et al., above n 66, xxi.

118 Mekong River Commission, *The Four 'R's for Mekong Cooperation Ministers and Diplomats Welcome New MRC CEO* (9 April 2008) <http://www.mrcmekong.org/news-and-events/news/the-four-r-s-for-mekong-cooperation-ministers-and-diplomats-welcome-new-mrc-ceo/>.

119 Mekong River Commission, *The 17th Meeting of the MRC Council, Joint Meeting with the MRC Donor Consultative Group* (26 January 2011) <http://www.mrcmekong.org/news-and-events/speeches/the-17th-meeting-of-the-mrc-council-joint-meeting-with-the-mrc-donor-consultative-group-2/>.

120 Cronin and Hamlin, above n 35, 24.

121 Hirsch et al., above n 66, 114.

between riparian states and donors. This role assumption further attracts lots of misplaced criticisms on the MRC Secretariat for the current situation of transboundary water governance, while in fact the MRC is not a supranational body.[122]

Moreover, although it is commendable that donors have changed their assumption of the MRC from a development agent to a regional body that promotes sustainable development through the application of IWRM, its implementation up till now still seems far from satisfactory. This could at least be partly attributed to the approach donors have used to impose the concept of IWRM, which is disconnected with member states and most river basin users' experience and this external pressure and rationale often fails to be internalised into state behaviour. With the ongoing hydropower expansion in this region, the political struggle between donors and member states seems to become increasingly critical under the framework of the MRC.

Ironically, studies also suggest that the MRC and member states

> can proceed with their conflicting development plans and reproduce the current disconnect between the national and regional-level decision-making landscape, without displaying this tension in public... The former is tolerated because it does some window dressing on participatory and IWRM rhetoric. The latter can proceed because the MRC lacks power to direct transboundary water governance issues in the region.[123]

This is related to another long-standing tension between the MRC's institutional culture and the dominant Southeast Asian political culture, which is illustrated to a large extent by the concept of the "ASEAN Way".[124] As a collaborative approach, it is "derived from global principles and the local, social-cultural and political milieu in Southeast Asia".[125] It relies on "consensus building and cooperative programs rather than legally binding treaties" and shows a "preference to national implementation of programs rather than reliance on a strong region-wide bureaucracy".[126] For example, the MRC Joint Committee "has the authority to prepare legally binding rules for water utili-

122 Osborne, above n 31, 50.

123 Suhardiman, Giordano and Molle, above n 115, 11–2.

124 Hirsch et al., above n 66, xx.

125 Paruedee Nguitragool, *Environmental Cooperation in Southeast Asia: ASEAN's Regime for Transboundary Haze Pollution* (Routledge, 2011) 28.

126 Koh Kheng-Lian and Nicholas A. Robinson, 'Regional Environmental Governance: Examining the Association of Southeast Asian Nations (ASEAN) Model' in Daniel C. Esty

sation and inter-basin diversions, pursuant to Article 5 and Article 26 of the *Mekong Agreement*", yet no such rules have been presented by the MRC.[127] To date, the *Mekong Agreement* "largely relies on informal procedures approved by member states",[128] and their application cannot be secured in practice.[129]

Thus, in many ways the MRC suffers from the fact that "national interests often ultimately triumph over concerns for policies that might be implemented in relation to the river as a whole".[130] Despite the donor-driven character of the Secretariat, the MRC itself cannot act on its own "in any fashion that has not been approved by the member states".[131] Having recognised that, it is the question on how to promote the change of policy by riparian states that is the real challenge. Obviously, reform in the water sector is "part of much wider social, economic, and political reform processes".[132] At least, it is doubtful that the current impasse or confrontation between donors and riparian states could lead to changes in this direction under the framework of the MRC. Many externally-driven efforts seem to be made in a different frequency with the entrenched political settings, which cannot create much real resonance with the riparian states. The reality calls for the MRC to better adjust and acknowledge the political culture while promoting "mutual self-interest" among the riparian states with regard to the Mekong water resources. If it is not impossible, at least it will be a very gradual process.

Facing the rather immediate issues like hydropower expansion, however, it is understandable that people would want a more direct and instant resolution. Yet there is little chance of finding a long term resolution to the Mekong issues without addressing more fundamental and time-consuming issues by means of building trust, facilitating goodwill cooperation and communication, and promoting a greater sense of joint ownership of the Mekong among riparian states. Immediate environmental challenges do not necessarily require instant solutions. Instead, simply prolonging the decision-making process by introducing more prudent procedural requirements could to a large extent

and Maria H. Ivanova (eds), *Global Environmental Governance: Options and Opportunities* (Yale School of Forestry and Environmental Studies, 2002) 1, 4.

127 Johns et al., above n 106.

128 For example, the Procedures for Notification, Prior Consultation and Agreement, Procedures for Water Use Monitoring and Procedures for the Maintenance of Flow on the Mainstream. See Mekong River Commission, *Policies, Procedures and Guidelines* <http://www.mrcmekong.org/publications/policies-procedures-and-guidelines/>.

129 Hirsch et al., above n 66, 30–1.

130 Osborne, above n 31, 48.

131 Osborne, above n 23, 9.

132 Hirsh, above n 8, 184.

increase the opportunity for more sustainable outcomes. Although this choice is indeed not that "simple" in the Mekong context, as will be further analysed in later chapters, it could be a relatively more feasible and less controversial approach in light of the existing multifaceted dilemma.

The disconnection and tension between the MRC and national decision-making landscapes is also reflected in the problematic setting and functioning of the NMC at the domestic level. Although the NMC is designed to link the MRC's regional programs with sectoral ministries' development plans and policies at the national level, in reality it is not consistent with the national decision-making regimes.[133] For instance, the NMC secretariat often found it very difficult to arrange national consultation meetings as an inter-ministerial decision-making forum. This is because donor's efforts on implementing IWRM through programs are often in conflict with sectoral ministries' development interests and the bureaucratic competition among diverse water sectors remains fierce, especially between planning authorities and environmental authorities.[134] In addition to the lack of power to promote real coordination between the MRC and the NMC or among participating ministries, the NMC suffers from shortages in human and financial resources, and not surprisingly, remain distant from civil society.[135] The composition, capacity and effectiveness of the NMC also vary considerably from one country to another.[136] The differences can be attributed to varied status quo of domestic water governance and reform in each country, not to mention the fact that the NMC is established by domestic legislation and there is a lack of guidance at the regional level. It is foreseeable that the awkward existence of the NMC will generate more debates and uncertainties on its future role in relation to water reform in this region.

Another obvious structural limitation is that all the MRC formal members are downstream states, while two upstream states, China and Myanmar, merely maintain dialogue relations. So far, the only outcome from this dialogue partnership is an agreement on the provision of hydrological information on the Mekong River, under which China promises to provide water level data in the flood season.[137] Talks are under way to expand this data sharing agreement to include dry season levels. During the severe drought in 2010, China has agreed

133 Suhardiman, Giordano and Molle, above n 115, 4.

134 Ibid. 4, 6, 9.

135 Nathan Badenoch, 'Transboundary Environmental Governance: Principles and Practice in Mainland Southeast Asia' (Report, World Resources Institute, 2002) 17; Hirsch et al., above n 66, 54, 121.

136 Hirsch et al., above n 66, 21.

137 Mekong River Commission, above n 24.

to provide water level data from two dams in Yunnan province until the end of the drought.[138] Despite the increasing engagement of China as a dialogue partner, it is unlikely for China to fully accept the *Mekong Agreement* which only reflects the consensus among downstream states under external influences, not to mention the highly controversial nature of transboundary water management and China's negative position on the *UN Watercourses Convention*. Combined with the existing tension over control of the MRC between donors and riparian states, it is no surprise that China is much less motivated to join the organisation that is more donor-driven than state-owned.

China shares borders with 14 countries and has many international rivers.[139] In most cases, China is an upstream state. Over the past number of years, several international disputes have been associated with international rivers, such as the Mekong dam construction and the Songhua River pollution accident.[140] Considering China's national interests in hydropower and navigation, one may well argue that it "would have everything to lose and little to gain from the constraints of riparian regulation".[141] Yet, it is suggested that downstream states could raise the incentives for cooperation by enhancing their ability to "deploy the resources that they do have in ways that affect the interests of other more powerful riparian states".[142] Politically, China's leaders have, on different occasions, declared that China would be a large country with international responsibility.[143] Combined with its diversified interests in Southeast Asia, this political gesture may open a door for more constructive cooperation with

138 Bangkok Post, *China to Provide Water Data on Dams* (2010) <http://bangkokpost.newspaperdirect.com/epaper/viewer.aspx>.

139 See China Briefing, *China's Borders* <http://www.china-briefing.com/news/specialreport/chinas-borders>.

140 The Songhua River pollution accident will be further discussed in chapter four. See generally Zou Keyuan, 'Transnational Cooperation for Managing the Control of Environmental Disputes in East Asia' (2004) 16 *Journal of Environmental Law* 341, 347; L. Waldron Davis, 'Reversing the Flow: International Law and Chinese Hydropower Development on the Headwaters of the Mekong River' (2006) 19 *New York International Law Review* 1, 2–16; Wang Xiangwei, 'Mainland's Environmental Chief Sacked over Toxic Chemical Spill', *South China Morning Post* (Hong Kong), 3 December 2005, 1.

141 Hirsch et al., above n 66, 46.

142 Ratner, above n 99, 70.

143 For example, such statement is reaffirmed by Yang Jiechi, the former and the tenth Foreign Minister of PRC. 杨洁篪 [Yang Jiechi], 《维护世界和平，促进共同发展：纪念新中国外交60周年》 [Maintaining World Peace and Promoting Common Development: Commemoration of the 60th Anniversary of the New China's Diplomacy] (13 October 2009) <http://www.china-embassy.org/chn/zmgx/t619945.htm>.

other Mekong states. However, it has to be noted that China's participation in transboundary water governance has just started and remains very incipient in many ways with respect to environmental protection.[144]

With the development of ASEAN-China dialogue relationships, the increasing cooperation under the GMS Program and the emerging importance of development banks, construction firms and other private companies, the MRC is facing an increasing risk of being marginalised or bypassed in decision-making processes.[145] As will be further discussed later, the growing polycentric nature of water governance at the regional level provides more choices for all Mekong riparian states and developers outside the framework of the MRC. The competitiveness among these frameworks and a lack of communication and coordination among these intergovernmental organisations certainly deepens the problems existing in regional governance over Mekong water resources.

## 2 Greater Mekong Subregion (GMS) Program

In 1992, with assistance from the Asian Development Bank (ADB), all riparian states of Mekong entered into a program of subregional economic cooperation, which set a path towards regional economic integration. The GMS program does not have a formal organisation, instead, it holds

> a cycle of ministerial meetings and a biennial prime ministerial summit, which they all attend (at the most senior political level and in large numbers) and use to mark their "ownership" of this emerging regional institution.[146]

Functioning as a loosely structured forum, it adopts a flexible, results-oriented and activity-based approach,[147] which again in some parts reflects the political culture of the "ASEAN Way". Nine areas of cooperation have been highlighted under the GMS, including agriculture, energy, environment, human

144 Currently, China is enhancing cooperation on transboundary water issues with neighbouring countries (e.g. Russia, Kazakhstan, North Korea, Mongolia, India, Thailand and other Mekong countries) at both bilateral and multi-lateral levels. Details will be discussed in the following chapters.

145 Suhardiman, Giordano and Molle, above n 115, 10.

146 Hirsch et al., above n 66, 69.

147 Asian Development Bank, 'Midterm Review of the Greater Mekong Subregion Strategic Framework (2002–2012)' (Report, Asian Development Bank, 2007) 2.

resource development, telecommunications, transport, tourism, trade and investment.[148]

To date, most of the GMS activities have targeted improving physical interconnectivity of the region and around ten billion (US) dollars' worth of priority infrastructure projects have either been completed or are being implemented.[149] This includes transnational highways, railways, hydropower projects, regional electricity transmission lines and programs that encourage cross-border trade and the integration of markets.[150] The rapid infrastructure developments under the GMS have been subjected to criticisms on their potential environmental impact. In particular, through the GMS, the ADB has co-financed some of the hydropower dams in the Mekong region, such as the controversial Theum-Hinboun Dam[151] and Nam Theun 2 Dam in Laos.[152] In addition, the ADB is also involved in the construction of a few individual dams in the Mekong countries (i.e., Song Bung 4 in Vietnam[153] and Nam Ngum 3 in Laos[154]). Moreover, the ADB has funded the Sekong-Sesan and Nam Theun river basins hydropower development study that prioritised six dams for further development within the three river basins shared by Cambodia, Laos and Vietnam.[155]

In addition, with a goal of establishing a power grid, more than 20 hydro energy-related projects in the GMS involve the construction of transmission lines to transfer power from dams in China, Myanmar, Laos and Cambodia to

148 Ibid.

149 Asian Development Bank, *Greater Mekong Subregion: Overview* <http://beta.adb.org/countries/gms/overview>.

150 François Molle, Tira Foran and Philippe Floch, 'Introduction: Changing Waterscapes in the Mekong Region-Historical Background and Context' in François Molle, Tira Foran and Mira Käkönen (eds), *Contested Waterscapes in the Mekong Region* (Earthscan, 2009) 1, 10.

151 See generally Philip Hirsch, 'Globalisation, Regionalisation and Local Voices: The Asian Development Bank and Re-scaled Politics of Environment in the Mekong Region' (2001) 22(3) *Singapore Journal of Tropical Geography* 237, 242–4.

152 See generally Middleton, Garcia and Foran, above n 10, 32; Shannon Lawrence, 'The Nam Theun 2 Controversy and Its Lessons for Laos' in François Molle, Tira Foran and Mira Käkönen (eds), *Contested Waterscapes in the Mekong Region: Hydropower, Livelihoods and Governance* (Earthscan, 2009) 81–112.

153 See generally Middleton, Garcia and Foran, above n 10, 38.

154 Both ENDs, *The ADB-GMS Support for Hydropower Dams and Power Grid:* ADB *and the Greater Mekong Subregion Program* <http://www.bothends.org/uploaded_files/document/hydropower-FINAL-1.pdf>; Asian Development Bank, *Project Database* <http://www.adb.org/Projects/summaries.asp?query=&browse=1&mode=1&ctry=LAO&sctr=3200&sctr=3800&year=ALL>.

155 Both ENDs, above n 154.

Thailand and Vietnam.[156] The relationship between the construction of transmission lines and hydropower development in the region has been described as follows:

> If the ADB does not build the high-voltage transmission lines, then certainly some of the dams will not be built at all. At the same time, in order for transmission lines to be financially viable, dams must be constructed. The ADB claims that dams (that would supply power to the transmission lines) will meet the ADB environmental and social safeguards. For many of the dams, there are no real requirements to meet ADB's safeguards policy, since the Bank has no direct involvement in their development. In recent years, there has been an increase in the volume of investment from private investors and export credit agencies from Vietnam, China, Thailand, Malaysia and Russia who are all interested to finance [sic] hydropower development.[157]

Although people should "avoid confusing or conflating ADB-funded water initiatives with GMS initiatives",[158] it is clear that either way the MRC has little impact on their decision-making processes, especially considering the increasing of private investments in GMS projects. The marginalisation of the MRC is obvious in the Upper Mekong Navigation Improvement Project under the GMS program which focuses on river clearance and facility upgrading to improve navigation on the Mekong River.[159]

---

156 Such as the transmission lines to connect Thailand to the Jinghong and Nuozhadu dams on the Lancang River and dams on the Salween River in Myanmar; and the transmission lines to connect Thailand and Vietnam to the controversial Nam Theun 2 dam in Laos. See Hirsch et al., above n 66, 70; Xiaojiang Yu, 'Regional Cooperation and Energy Development in the Greater Mekong Sub-region' (2003) 31 *Energy Policy* 1221, 1227.

157 Both ENDs, above n 154.

158 Hirsch et al., above n 66, 69. The GMS aims more broadly at economic development of the region, while the ADB focuses on financing particular projects. Katri Mehtonen, Marko Keskinen and Olli Varis, 'The Mekong: IWRM and Institutions' in Olli Varis, Cecilia Tortajada and Asit K. Biswas (eds), *Management of Transboundary Rivers and Lakes* (Springer, 2008) 207, 212.

159 Plans for the Mekong navigation improvement project were conceived in the early 1990s and finalised and approved by the governments of China, Myanmar, Laos and Thailand in early 2002. Details regarding its decision-making process, particularly the joint EIA study, are available in chapter six.

The GMS itself does not have any regulatory functions regarding the Mekong River water management.[160] But as a program of subregional economic integration, recent years have also witnessed a gradual awareness of the need to incorporate environment considerations into decision-making process. A Working Group on Environment was established in 1995 which initially focused on capacity building and establishing environmental information systems.[161] Since 2005, the Meeting of the GMS Environment Ministers has been held every three years and the Core Environment Program was endorsed at the first meeting to promote a poverty-free and ecologically rich GMS, with the Biodiversity Conservation Corridors Initiative set as a key component of the program.[162] It is notable that China has committed significant funding (20 million US dollars at least) to environmental cooperation under the GMS.[163] While the environmental initiative focuses mainly on land ecosystems, a corridor for the Mekong Headwaters and one for the Tonle Sap Inundation Zone are included, hence raising another concern of functional demarcation between the MRC and the GMS.[164]

The second phase of the program (2012–2016) starts to pay more attention to the development of climate-related and environmental management measures. Efforts are geared towards integrating environmental considerations in investment decisions of key economic sectors (i.e. energy) and in the development of economic corridors across the GMS.[165] In particular, since 2007, the SEA has been promoted as a possible planning support tool in economic corridor and sector development processes in the GMS.[166] While chapter six will revisit the SEA under the GMS Program, it can concluded here that it is still suffering from the immaturity of and inconsistency among the existing domestic

160 Osborne, above n 23, 6.

161 *Meeting of the GMS Environment Ministers: Joint Ministerial Statement* (25 May 2005) <http://www.wwfchina.org/english/downloads/GMSstatement.pdf>.

162 Ibid.

163 Hirsch et al., above n 66, 64.

164 Ibid. 69.

165 Greater Mekong Subregion Environment Operations Centre, *3rd GMS Environment Ministers Meeting, 27–28 July 2011* (18 November 2011)<http://www.gms-eoc.org/events/3rd-gms-environment-ministers-meeting-phnom-penh-cambodia->.

166 Greater Mekong Subregion Environment Operations Centre, 'The Core Environment Program and Biodiversity Conservation Corridors Initiative Progress Report for the Period April–September 2011' (Report, Greater Mekong Subregion Economic Cooperation Program, 2011) 4.

SEA policies and legislation, and the lack of support from other environmental mechanisms at domestic and regional levels.

Although there is an increasing tendency towards more integration of environmental considerations during economic cooperation under the GMS program, the progress is still scattered to a large extent and falls short of more specific arrangements to pursue the achievement of environmental goals. Along with the burgeoning economic growth in this region, whether the environmental cooperation under the GMS can shift from rhetoric to reality remains to be seen.

The GMS is perceived by some as a competitor to the MRC, due to the fact that the GMS is the only regional mechanism that includes all six riparian states, it is rapidly developing a much higher profile and is stronger than the MRC in terms of power, influence, ownership and funding.[167] Currently, the GMS is "becoming increasingly Asian and less 'ADB-driven'," with strong ownership by the Mekong countries, particularly China.[168] The GMS is also viewed to be "strongly aligned with the prevailing regional sentiment that is driving ASEAN-China relations and regional integration",[169] which again raises the issue of the effectiveness of the "ASEAN Way" and soft law. This chapter will briefly address this question but it will always be subjected to rethinking during more detailed discussion on specific procedural mechanisms and a final conclusion will be drawn in the end of the book.

In fact, despite the competitiveness between the MRC and the GMS in terms of regional influence, they do not have much direct contradiction in the area of water governance.[170] Even if they both dealing with somewhat similar issues, the GMS and MRC play their roles in very different approaches. While the MRC's perspective is to view the Mekong River chiefly as a natural resource to govern, the GMS program seems to "consider the river more as a symbol that defines the region in which they are promoting economic growth and cooperation".[171] The latter perspective is at least partly responsible for the ignorance of the Mekong River and aquatic biodiversity aspects during the ongoing environmental cooperation under GMS. But as a regional economic coopera-

167 Hirsch et al., above n 66, 69.

168 Ibid. 106; Evelyn Goh, 'China in the Mekong River Basin: The Regional Security Implications of Resource Development on the Lancang Jiang' (Working Paper, Institute of Defense and Strategic Studies, 2004) 8.

169 Hirsch et al., above n 66, 70.

170 Ibid. 69.

171 Marko Keskinen, *Bring Back the Common Sense? Integrated Approaches in Water Management: Lessons Learnt from the Mekong* (PhD Thesis, Aalto University, 2010) 86.

tion mechanism, the GMS could approach environmental problems in a way that is more directly linked to power trade and the decision-making process of specific development projects and has the potential to serve as a regional environmental platform which could better incorporate and comprehend the roles of non-state factors such as financiers and investors.

Therefore, given the increasing concerns on the impact of energy infrastructure development on hydropower expansion, it is necessary to enhance environmental cooperation and develop specific environmental mechanisms under the GMS program. Meanwhile, even if the GMS have a more extended role in the governance of Mekong water resources, the relationship between the GMS and the MRC could be more complementary than it is presently the case. In light of the increasingly polycentric nature of transboundary cooperation on water governance in the region, a closer relationship between the MRC and the GMS based on "comparative advantages and distinct functional roles would have a number of benefits, not least if the GMS institute a water investment program in the region".[172]

Under the partnership arrangement between the ADB and the MRC signed in March 2000, both parties agreed to take measures to better and more effectively coordinate activities covering the GMS program.[173] The cooperation so far seems to focus on climate change adaptation (particularly in flood and drought management) and the MRC mainly supports the member states through empirical and technical knowledge production to improve the sustainability of their projects.[174] Nevertheless, it is uncertain to what extent the MRC can "project its scientific knowledge to influence the politicised decision-making process".[175]

In order to promote the implementation of the GMS's environmental protection policies and enhance its cooperation and collaboration with MRC, more specific institutional mechanisms are needed. Particularly, the development of procedural instruments can contribute to the environmental goals of both frameworks and some preliminary progress towards this direction has been made at these two levels. While the MRC may be more focused on the

---

172 Hirsch et al., above n 66, xxii.

173 Asian Development Bank, above n 147, 35.

174 Mekong River Commission, *Statement to the GMS Ministerial Conference by the Mekong River Commission* (31 August 2011) <http://www.scribd.com/doc/63622096/17th-GMS-MC-MRC-Secretariat-Statement>; Greater Mekong Subregion Economic Cooperation Program, *17th GMS Ministerial Conference Meeting Summary* (4 August 2011) <http://beta.adb.org/sites/default/files/17th-MC-SOP-Ministerial-Meeting.pdf>.

175 Middleton, Garcia and Foran, above n 10, 47.

application of procedural requirements on transboundary water governance, the GMS could serve as a platform to foster and facilitate negotiations regarding the procedural requirements on the decision-making process of numerous development projects and strategies. However, as will be further analysed in future chapters, promoting procedural arrangements under the GMS can be even more challenging than relevant developments under the MRC, due to the loose structure of the GMS itself and its strong economic orientation.

## 3 Association of Southeast Asian Nations (ASEAN) and ASEAN-China Dialogue Relations

While the MRC serves as a unique platform for transboundary water governance and the GMS opens the door for considering the environmental impact during the process of promoting integrative economic links among the riparian states, ASEAN is also involved in the Mekong regional issues. In June 1996, a Basic Framework of ASEAN-Mekong Basin Development Cooperation was adopted by the ASEAN countries and China to strengthen economic linkages among relevant countries and encourage dialogue on and identification of economic projects in the region.[176] ASEAN's interest in the Mekong region has been driven by Singapore and Malaysia. Funding has been a headache issue for projects under this regime since the beginning, due to the disagreement among the ASEAN countries and the difficulties to bring other foreign investors and non-Asian countries already with commitments to other Mekong projects into participation in ASEAN's program.[177] As of 9 July 2009, there were 46 projects at various stages of implementation and a total of 14 projects still requiring funding worth 44.5 million US dollars.[178]

Although the ASEAN-Mekong Basin Development Cooperation does not seem to be as vigorous as it is under the GMS program, ASEAN has played an important role in energy development in the Mekong region.[179] The ASEAN Power Grid Program consists of 16 bilateral and multilateral electricity interconnection projects that cover many areas in the Mekong region and could

176 ASEAN, *Basic Framework of ASEAN-Mekong Basin Development Cooperation* (17 June 1996) <http://www.asean.org/communities/asean-economic-community/category/overview-16>.

177 Donald E. Weatherbee, 'Cooperation and Conflict in the Mekong River Basin' (1997) 20(2) *Studies in Conflict and Terrorism* 167, 174, 181.

178 ASEAN, *Joint Media Statement of the 11th Ministerial Meeting of the ASEAN-Mekong Basin Development Cooperation* (16 August 2009) <http://www.asean.org/news/asean-statement-communiques/item/joint-media-statement-of-the-11th-ministerial-meeting-of-the-asean-mekong-basin-development-cooperation-ambdc-bangkok-16-august-2009>.

179 Yu, above n 156, 1228.

pave the way to enhance intra-regional electricity trade in the region.[180] In particular, the following projects are planned to be commissioned within next two decades: Thailand–Laos, Laos–Cambodia, Thailand–Myanmar, Vietnam–Cambodia, Laos–Vietnam and Thailand–Cambodia.[181]

Considering the increasing economic cooperation under ASEAN and its important role in political and social regional stability, it as a broader regional economic and political cooperation regime can have a notable impact on the Mekong region. In particular, the political culture reflected in this regime and the comprehensive platform provided for negotiation on various interests should be better understood. Transboundary water governance is also highly relevant to the overall environmental awareness and arrangements at regional level. Therefore, the following discussion will briefly address the environmental cooperation under ASEAN and the ASEAN-China Dialogue Relations which can provide another dimension of eco-politics in the region.

Understandably, environmental management was not expressly recognised as a concern when ASEAN was established in 1967.[182] But increased population, rapid economic growth and existing and region-wide social inequities among the ASEAN countries has put increasing pressures on the natural resources of the region and brought to light various common or transboundary environmental issues.[183] Environmental cooperation among the ASEAN countries can be traced to 1977, and the years since have witnessed the development of

> an increasingly complex but for the most part non-formal web of soft-law declarations, resolutions, plans of action and issue-specific programs that together define the administrative, institutional and normative contours of regional environmental governance.[184]

After more than three decades of development, the ASEAN environmental cooperation now covers areas including nature conservation and biodiversity; transboundary pollution; water resources management; animal and human

---

180 Ibid. The number of projects listed in this paper is 14, while according to the more recent data, two more projects have been proposed. See Bambang Hermawanto, *Report of the 8th Mekong of APGCC* (23 June 2011) <http://www.hapuasecretariat.org/doc2011/Report%208_APGCC.pdf>.

181 Hermawanto, above n 180.

182 Koh and Robinson, above n 126.

183 ASEAN Environment, *An Overview on ASEAN Environmental Cooperation* <http://environment.asean.org/about-us-2/>.

184 Lorraine Elliott, 'ASEAN and Environmental Cooperation: Norms, Interests and Identity' (2003) 16(1) *Pacific Review* 29, 36.

health; and energy and climate change.[185] Meanwhile, it aims at harmonising environmental policies and databases, and prioritises the development of environmental education, public participation and environmentally sound technology.[186] Every three years, the ASEAN Ministerial Meeting is held, which functions as the overall decision-making body. Since 1994, annual informal meetings have also been organised in between the formal meetings.[187] The ASEAN Senior Officials on the Environment and its subsidiary working groups have the responsibility for policy recommendations and the promoting of regional cooperation.[188]

Environmental cooperation has also been gradually developed under the ASEAN-China Dialogue Relations. Currently, the environmental cooperation is guided by the ASEAN-China Environmental Protection Strategy 2009–2015. It specified six priority areas, including raising public awareness on environmental protection and enhancing environmental education; promoting environmentally sound technology and eco-label program; biodiversity conservation; environmental management capacity building; global environmental concerns; and environmental protection industry and relevant programs.[189] To implement this Strategy, the ASEAN-China Environmental Cooperation Centre was established by the Chinese government in 2010. Other than the priority areas, ASEAN and China are also seeking cooperation on transboundary water issues.[190] In addition, one latest development of the relationship between ASEAN and China is the implementation of the ASEAN-China Free Trade Area (ACFTA) in 2010. Guided by the concept of sustainable development, many free trade areas around the world are under the process of combining environmental concerns with regional economic cooperation. Along with the future

185 Koh Kheng-Lian (ed), *ASEAN Environmental Law, Policy and Governance: Selected Documents (Volume I)* (World Scientific, 2009) xxi.

186 ASEAN Environment, above n 183. The evolution of environmental cooperation under ASEAN has been concluded by Lorraine Elliott. See generally Elliott, above n 184, 38–44.

187 Elliott, above n 184.

188 Ibid.

189 《中国-东盟注重云南生态，搭建环保合作平台》[China and ASEAN Set up Platform for Environmental Cooperation: Attention Paid to the Ecosystem in Yunnan Province], 新华社 [Xinhua News Agency] (11 June 2010) <http://www.yn.xinhuanet.com/newscenter/2010-06/11/content_20043796.htm>.

190 《中国-东盟环保合作中心组建》[The Establishment of the ASEAN-China Environmental Cooperation Centre], 中华人民共和国环境保护部 [Ministry of Environmental Protection of the People's Republic of China] (19 March 2010) <http://www.zhb.gov.cn/zhxx/hjyw/201003/t20100319_187059.htm>.

development of the ACFTA, it is suggested that member states[191] should further communicate and cooperate on environmental relations.

In the face of increasing regional environmental challenges and transboundary disputes, environmental cooperation under ASEAN is sandwiched between and influenced by both the global best practices and the regional political traditions.[192] The latter, often referred to as the "ASEAN Way", is a "distinctive approach to dispute-settlement and regional cooperation developed by the members of ASEAN with a view to ensuring regional peace and stability",[193] and it also has a profound influence on the ASEAN-China Dialogue Relations. With regard to how to comprehend this concept, the following analysis is quite incisive:

> The 'ASEAN way' consists of a code for inter-state behaviour as well as a decision-making process based on consultations and consensus. The code of conduct incorporates a set of well-known principles, e.g. non-interference in the domestic affairs of each other, non-use of force, pacific settlement of disputes, respect for the sovereignty and territorial integrity of member states, that can be found in the Charter of the United Nations as well as regional political and security organizations elsewhere in the world. To this extent, the 'ASEAN way' is not an unusual construct.[194] But where it can claim a certain amount of uniqueness is the manner in which these norms are operationalized into a framework of regional interaction. In this respect, the "ASEAN way" is not so much about the substance or structure of multilateral interactions, but a claim about the *process* through which such interactions are carried out. This approach involves a high degree of discreetness, informality, pragmatism, expediency, consensus-building, and non-confrontational bargaining styles which are often contrasted with the adversarial

191 At the time of writing, the ACFTA entered into force for ASEAN 6 (Brunei Darussalam, Indonesia, Malaysia, Philippines, Singapore and Thailand) and China, and will be further extended to the newer ASEAN member states by 2015.

192 Elliott, above n 184, 38.

193 Amitav Acharya, 'Ideas, Identity, and Institution-building: From the "ASEAN Way" to the "Asia-Pacific" Way' (1997) 10(3) *Pacific Review* 319, 328.

194 However, it should be noted that these internationally agreed principles are not shielded from disputes, such as the boundaries of non-interference and issue of absolute sovereignty, which also has an impact on countries' responses to transboundary environmental issues.

> posturing and legalistic decision-making procedures in Western multilateral negotiations.[195]

It is interesting to notice Acharya's emphasis on process as the key difference between the "ASEAN Way" and Western multilateral negotiations. While the "ASEAN Way" claims to follow the principles of international law, it is the way they are implemented in the context of Southeast Asia that is the real subject of discussion. ASEAN countries' preference for personal contacts and informality rather than the strength of formal institutions during cooperation are further elaborated as follows:

> The ASEAN dialogue process is 'unstructured, with no clear format for decision-making or implementation' and 'often lacks a formal agenda, issues are negotiated on an ad hoc basis as and when they arise'... consultations tend to be open-ended rather than being tied to a specific timetable... If institutions and procedures are to be devised at all, then they tend to be ad hoc, rather than permanent... institution-building is about developing a regular but flexible framework of coordination and cooperation by national governments without delegating state sovereignty to a regional authority.[196]

The "ASEAN Way" is strongly characterised by heavy reliance on consensus-building.[197] Although it is in fact the most common approach of addressing international and regional issues, this term in the ASEAN context is also originated from a particular decision-making style within the Javanese village society that highlights the non-hostile psychological setting, informal and flexible decision-making environment, and avoidance of open and public disagreement in order to raise the so-called "comfort level"—an important precondition for successful consultations and negotiations.[198] Therefore, even when the ASEAN members find it impossible to arrive at a common position, they often "speak and act as though a certain level of unity has been achieved on that particular issue" and "a great deal of care is always taken not to isolate or embarrass any individual ASEAN member in international fora".[199] This attempt, however, is now increasingly challenged in reality, represented by the unprecedented

195 Acharya, above n 193, 328–9 (emphasis added).

196 Ibid. 329–30.

197 Koh and Robinson, above n 126.

198 Acharya, above n 193, 329–31.

199 Ibid. 331.

failure in the ASEAN history to issue a joint statement at the end of the Foreign Ministers' Meeting due to disagreements over the South China Sea.[200]

The influence of the "ASEAN Way" on ASEAN's successes and failures is a controversial issue. While participants may cultivate enough goodwill by "stressing the positives" and "sweeping controversial issues under the carpet", it is argued that the current ASEAN bureaucratic setting and the "ASEAN Way" is only capable of dealing with "issues where members' interests converge than problems where members have opposing interests" and is also ill equipped to deal with urgent events.[201] Instead of legally-binding agreements and strong region-wide bureaucracy, the preference and reliance on consensus-building, consultation, non-confrontation, domestic implementation and private and personal diplomacy has raised doubts regarding the extent of member states' commitment to and compliance with shared norms and the depth of their collective identity.[202]

Thus the environmental principles and values developed so far have been characterised as more of a "thin, declaratory form of normative community".[203] In reality, the environmental objectives of ASEAN are often surpassed by various narrow self-interests represented by the member states and the weakness of the "ASEAN Way" has been demonstrated in attempts to solve the Indonesia haze problem.[204] Moreover, even if member states managed to reach consensus on a specific issue, any implementation largely relies on member states and ASEAN seems to be lack of measures and legal teeth to secure an effective compliance, for there is a lack of strong central ASEAN bureaucracy and most consensus is reflected in the form of soft laws.[205]

Recent years have witnessed a gradual shift away from an absolute application of the "ASEAN Way", especially in the area of environment cooperation. For example, serving as a basic legal document for ASEAN, the *ASEAN Charter* finally entered into force in 2008 and the future of ASEAN was characterised as "a rules-based and people-oriented organisation with its own legal

---

200 Saifulbahri Ismail, *ASEAN Summit Fails to Agree on Concluding Joint Statement* (13 July 2012) Channelnewsasia.com <http://www.channelnewsasia.com/stories/southeastasia/view/1213369/1/.html>.

201 Koh and Robinson, above n 126, 15; Acharya, above n 193, 332.

202 Koh and Robinson, above n 126; Elliott, above n 184, 37.

203 Elliott, above n 184, 37.

204 Koh Kheng-Lian, 'ASEAN Environmental Protection in Natural Resources and Sustainable Development: Convergence versus Divergence' (2007) 4 *Macquarie Journal of International and Comparative Environmental Law* 43, 46.

205 Ibid. 45.

personality".[206] While the term of "rules-based" seems to open a door for more hard law documents, the idea of "people-oriented" also reflects an attempt to break away from absolute sovereignty or non-interference principle and an increasing recognition of the important role of "people" (public participation) and other non-state actors in shaping the notion of sustainable development.[207] But it is still unclear at this moment the extent to which ASEAN is prepared to go the "hard" way.[208] Despite the unusual success of putting a hard law (the *ASEAN Agreement on Transboundary Haze Pollution*)[209] in place to tackle the transboundary haze pollution in 2002, the Agreement has not yet been ratified by Indonesia, who caused the forest fires.[210] Moreover, the only hard law agreement directly targeting natural resources—the *1985 ASEAN Agreement on the Conservation of Nature and Natural Resources*—has still not entered into force and the draft *ASEAN Framework Agreement on Access to Biological and Genetic Resources* (2000) has not yet been adopted by the member states.[211]

With regard to environmental cooperation, ASEAN has been increasingly influenced by internationally accepted environmental law principles, best practices and exposed to external and internal pressures.[212] This is also incorporated into the general process of gradually improving democracy, civil society and rule of law. In the context of the entrenched political traditions, environmental cooperation among the ASEAN countries is struggling to find a way to move forward. While it is gradually recognised that more hard law should be put in place to give more legal teeth to tackle environmental problems, the process of forming hard law documents still relies on consensus-building to a large extent. More importantly, simple adoption of legally-binding treaties does not necessarily mean better chances of compliance. Despite the obvious

---

206 ASEAN, *ASEAN Charter Enters into Force Next Month* (15 November 2008) <http://www.asean.org/news/item/asean-charter-enters-into-force-next-month-bangkok-15-november-2008>.

207 Koh, above n 204, 46, 48.

208 Ibid. 68.

209 See generally Paruedee Nguitragool, 'Negotiating the Haze Treaty' (2011) 3(51) *Asian Survey* 356; Alan Khee-Jin Tan, 'The ASEAN Agreement on Transboundary Haze Pollution: Prospects for Compliance and Effectiveness in Post-Suharto Indonesia' (2005) 13 *New York University Environmental Law Journal* 647.

210 Koh, above n 204, 49. Notably, in March 2011, a deputy environment minister in Indonesia said that Indonesia will eventually ratify the Agreement. Antara News, *Indonesia to Ratify ASEAN Agreement on Trans-boundary Haze Pollution* (7 March 2011) <http://www.antaranews.com/en/news/68888/indonesia-to-ratify-asean-agreement-on-trans-boundary-haze-pollution>.

211 Koh, above n 204, 50.

212 Elliott, above n 184, 38.

weaknesses, it is argued that over the longer term, the flexibility of the "ASEAN Way" may, in fact, help ASEAN to build a stronger basis for regional action and effective policy-making regarding the environment.[213] In many ways, ASEAN and the MRC are facing similar challenges on how to tailor and promote the acceptance of modern environmental theories and practices in the regional context. While it has proved to be unlikely or less effective to impose environmental norms in a way that is disconnected to the traditional political culture and regime, people in the field have to learn how to work with the entrenched system, rather than trying to completely abandon or ignore it. This is necessary in order to promote not only the transformation of the existing system itself, but also progressive changes towards sustainable development.

Through the discussion on the "ASEAN Way", it is interesting to notice the significance of process or procedures during environmental cooperation. Nevertheless, the emphasis on procedural implications of sustainable development is facing at least three-fold challenges. For one thing, the procedural perspective is confronted with the long-ingrained legal tradition in the Mekong countries which tends to overlook due process. Meanwhile, it is necessary to be aware of the risk of formality in the "ASEAN Way" and limits of procedural mechanisms without proper commitments to substantive obligations. Despite the general reluctance to enter into substantive commitments on regional environmental cooperation, the preference for soft law approaches rather than hard law also raise concerns on how to secure the implementation of procedural requirements. Therefore, how to integrate the considerations of both the realistic need to adapt to the entrenched political and legal system and the constructive objective to improve and reshape the existing regime is indeed a pivotal dilemma facing the development of procedural arrangements in this region.

## 4 Other Actors

In addition to riparian states, regional organisations and foreign donors, Mekong water governance is also subject to influences from other players ranging from investment banks (international, foreign and domestic), major UN organisations, private and state-own enterprises, and powerful local families. Local communities, however, generally have the fewest opportunities, capacities and resources to influence the decision-making process and their voices are all too often drowned out by other players.[214] Meanwhile, NGOs in most parts of the region suffer from restricted political freedom to operate.

---

213 Koh and Robinson, above n 126, 17.

214 Cronin and Hamlin, above n 35, 8.

With regard to investment banks, despite the controversial role of the ADB in hydropower expansion in the region (as illustrated in the discussion of the GMS program), it also served as an important external force to promote and support the development of national water policies, legislation and bureaucratic reforms.[215] But as mentioned before, these reform measures have proved to be less effective in practice. Meanwhile, although the ADB recognises "accountability, participation, predictability and transparency as key elements in good governance",[216] procedural arrangements to promote these core values are still very much undeveloped in the region.

The World Bank also plays a contested role through its support for specific dams, infrastructure projects and its specific environment-targeted programs via the Global Environment Facility and other means.[217] In particular, the ambitions of the World Bank in the region have been reflected in its Mekong Water Resources Assistance Strategy,[218] which is targeted at three controversial subregions in the Mekong area[219] and has been criticised for its lack of transparency and consultation during the preparing process and its controversial vision for Mekong development scenarios, mitigation arrangements and water governance reforms.[220] There is a concern that the Mekong region may become "oversaturated" with initiatives and the World Bank's new strategy "may be just one too many", especially considering its additional institutional and governance proposals that lie outside the existing arrangements.[221]

Foreign banks, including but not limited to the Australia and New Zealand Banking Group Limited (ANZ), the Banque Nationale de Paris (BNP) Paribas,

215 Pieter M. Smidt, 'Creating Synergy and ADB's Water Policy' (Paper presented at the International Water Conference, Hanoi, 14–16 October) 1; Hirsch, above n 8, 190.

216 Hirsch et al., above n 66, 160.

217 Philip Hirsch, 'Beyond the Nation State: Natural Resource Conflict and National Interest in Mekong Hydropower Development' (1999) 29 *Golden Gate University Law Review* 399, 409.

218 Although the Bank has repeatedly stated that the MWRAS is a joint initiative with the ADB, the latter keeps a very low profile. Hirsch et al., above n 66, 102.

219 Typical examples include: the area shared by northeast Thailand and Laos, where large-scale trans-basin diversions are proposed; the Sesan, Srepok and Sekong river basins where the interests of Cambodia, Vietnam and Laos collide due to the extensive hydropower development plans; and the Mekong Delta shared by Cambodia and Vietnam where flood, navigation, agriculture and wetlands associated projects are proposed. Middleton and Lee, above n 74, 12.

220 See ibid. 18; Hirsch et al., above n 66, 100–5.

221 Hirsch et al., above n 66, 105.

the Kredietbank ABB Insurance CERA Bank (KBS) and the Bank of Tokyo Mitsubishi UFJ, are also financing the hydropower development in the region, such as the controversial Theun-Hinboun Dam.[222] In particular, the ANZ has outlined a new regionally-based strategy to accelerate its progress toward becoming the leading foreign bank in the region.[223]

In order to govern the participation of international and foreign banks in the development of the Mekong region, efforts have been made from the aspect of corporate social responsibility, particularly the Equator Principles.[224] Despite the adoption of the Equator Principles by most, if not all, international and foreign banks, they are still criticised for lack of accountability and transparency in their implementation of these principles.[225] Even if they could comply with relevant requirements which would make the decision-making process burdensome, time-consuming and costly, governments may seek their alternative sources of finance and investment from the new generation of hydropower developers from their own countries, especially the state-owned enterprises from China and Thailand, such as the China Southern Power Grid, the Sinohydro Corporation and the Electricity Generating Authority of Thailand (EGAT).[226] The increasing competitiveness and lack of supervision in Mekong's hydropower marketplace certainly add to the momentum of hydropower expansion. Hence, other than exploring solutions from the perspective of corporate social responsibility, it is argued that the diversifying non-state actors certainly require more comprehensive legal arrangements on a broader basis.

In addition, there are several other regional institutions and initiatives that also have water-related issues on their agenda, such as the United Nations' Economic and Social Commission for Asia and the Pacific, the Global Water Partnership Southeast Asia,[227] the United Nations Development Programme's

222 International Rivers and BankTrack, *Western Banks Violate Rights, Law in Lao Dam Deal*, International Rivers (17 November 2009) <http://www.internationalrivers.org/resources/western-banks-violate-rights-law-in-lao-dam-deal-3779>.

223 Australia and New Zealand Banking Group Limited, *ANZ Outlines New Regional Growth Focus in Vietnam, Cambodia and Laos* (2 March 2010) <http://media.corporate-ir.net/media_files/irol/24/248677/mediareleases/2010/100302–ANZ-outlines-new-regional-growth-focus-in-Vietnam-+Cambodia-and-Laos.pdf>.

224 The Equator Principles are a voluntary set of standards for determining, assessing and managing social and environmental risk in project financing.

225 International Rivers and BankTrack, above n 222.

226 See Middleton, Garcia and Foran, above n 10.

227 See Hirsch et al., above n 66, 71.

(UNDP) Regional Environmental Governance Programme for Asia-Pacific and the International Union for Conservation of Nature (IUCN) and its partners.[228] Combined with the efforts to shape water governance and reform in the region by the MRC, the GMS, ASEAN, the ADB and the World Bank, a lack of cooperation and coordination among the multiple agendas and initiatives unavoidably lead to confusion and controversies. In addition to the multilateral cooperation, riparian states can seek to enter into bilateral relationships with each other or with foreign aid agencies regarding river development in the region which could add another dimension to the polycentric water governance landscape.[229] Meanwhile, development decisions can be strongly influenced by powerful local families, such as the case of the Don Sahong Project in Laos, where the politics still has a "highly personal nature" despite the country's embracement of some form of collective leadership.[230]

Despite the vulnerability of the local communities towards the possible impact of water-related projects (such as inundation, resettlement, the impact on agriculture and the wild fish catch) and the valuable role of NGOs as an effective watchdog (the Yali Falls Dam case is illustrative on this point),[231] civil society in this region still has very constrained political opportunities and resources to participate in the decision-making process, with the exception of a relatively advanced situation in Thailand. Along with the gradual political reform in this region, there is nevertheless an increasing tendency towards a more open political atmosphere for enhancement of public participation and transparency. Progress in this area is taken at a very unbalanced pace. Relevant difficulties and aspirations will be subject to further discussions later. Last, but not least, the engagement of civil society should be enhanced at the regional level to improve local communities' ownership of regional decision-making platforms.

---

228 Keskinen, above n 171, 86; Hirsch et al., above n 66, 71.

229 See Hirsch et al., above n 66, 58.

230 Osborne, above n 31, 31–2.

231 In the Yali Falls Dam (Vietnam) case, ex ante impact assessments in Cambodia were not conducted according to the MRC guidelines and the first reports calling attention to the plight of downstream communities on the Se San in Cambodia came not from a government or official body but from two international NGOs, the Oxfam America and the Bangkok-based TERRA (Towards Ecological Recovery and Regional Alliance). See generally Ratner, above n 99, 71.

## III Difficulties, Aspirations and Directions for Mekong Water Management Reform in a Polycentric Context

Based on the above analysis, it is obvious that the status quo of Mekong water resources management is highly polycentric, in terms of the multifaceted governance structures and various water-related initiatives and agendas at sectoral, local, national and regional levels, through which diverse players and stakeholders (state/non-state and internal/external) have participated in shaping the water governance landscapes. Sandwiched between the internationally accepted environmental law principles, best practice and the entrenched water governance regimes, the Mekong region is highly diversified in the "extent, nature, and direction of its environmental reforms".[232]

To date, the promotion of IWRM at the domestic level has been largely focused on restructuring institutional and power arrangements (such as the establishment of IWRM iconic river basin organisations) and the development of an overarching water legislation framework (including the endorsement of a comprehensive water law). These efforts, especially the former, have proved to be extremely complicated and contested in the context of Mekong. Even for countries such as Laos and Cambodia which managed to make dramatic changes in this area, the reform process has been externally driven for the most part and new structures and legislation have not necessarily been effective, often representing more rhetoric than reality and thus having limited impact on entrenched systems of governance.

Due to the competitive nature of different water uses, the limited environmental measures in this region often shift risks to different stakeholders, rather than actually reducing it. In addition, there are considerable discrepancies among riparian states in their water-related legislative frameworks and in the way their respective water administrative agencies are established and how they operate,[233] which further increase the difficulties of harmonisation and integration at the regional level. The attempts to configure hydrological boundaries into the existing political boundaries at this regional level are also facing enormous challenges, including the lack of legal teeth to address transboundary water issues, the existence of various uncoordinated and even competing water-related agendas initiated under different platforms, institutional dissonances between national and regional decision-making landscapes and the discrepancies among riparian states' domestic legal and political arrangements.

232 Hirsch, above n 8, 189.

233 Hirsch et al., above n 66, 42.

The difficulties and increased ineffectiveness of the ongoing water reforms raises the question of whether the ambitious principles of IWRM are indeed applicable in the context of Mekong.[234] To a large extent, what went wrong was not the concept of IWRM itself. Rather, more problems lie in how we interpret this concept and promote its application in the Mekong context.

Attention should be paid to the disconnection and tension between externally driven reform and the entrenched political, social and cultural circumstances. Past experiences have repeatedly demonstrated that simply urging more holistic institutional and legal arrangements without due regard for pre-existing patterns of resource use and decision-making can do little to bring IWRM into reality in the field. Instead, the starting point for IWRM should be "the history of uses and means of management among diverse actors and interest groups that have evolved over time".[235] One may argue, however, that it is extremely difficult to reconcile the donors' vision of sustainable water management and the entrenched water governance regime, especially at this critical moment of trying to hold back riparian states' strong intention toward hydropower expansion.

Nevertheless, it should be noticed that "as opposed to the assumption of a singular, objectively definable national interest, there is an array of diverse political and social interests within each country".[236] Avenues do exist for different actors (not so much for the civil society though) to influence the way that countries' interests are framed, and to influence the actions of governments, intergovernmental agencies and business sectors in Mekong basin development decisions.[237] In addition, each country has "different ways and mechanisms for understanding, negotiating, optimising and mediating these diverse interests".[238] While this diversified situation can pose many difficulties and uncertainties on the reform process, it also provides various opportunities and spaces for further engagement with the internal forces towards more sustainable water governance.

With regard to IWRM itself, the word "integration" in practice often entails

> a tension between the shift to more decentralized approaches associated with more participatory resource decision making and the institution

234 See Middleton and Lee, above n 74, 16; Molle and Hoanh, above n 51, 5.

235 Fiona Miller and Philip Hirsch, 'Civil Society and Internationalized River Basin Management' (Working Paper No. 7, Australian Mekong Resource Centre, 2003) 16.

236 Hirsch et al., above n 66, 45.

237 Ratner, above n 99, 76.

238 Hirsch et al., above n 66, 45.

> building that has occurred with attempts at more holistic planning, as reflected in the creation of river basin organisations.[239]

So far, more attention seems to be paid to the latter aspect of water reform. Given the increasing polycentric nature of water governance in the region, however, the institutional reform and restructure has often proved to be either too controversial to move forward or just "old wine in new bottles" in practice. Moreover, in light of the top-down decision-making traditions in the region, the one-sided emphasis on more centralised institutional structures often fails to incorporate the decentralised aspect of IWRM, which is characterised by more negotiated, cooperative, coordinated and bottom-up approaches. In fact, a holistic perspective of water governance does not necessarily require or at least rely on a centralised institutional structure. Instead, it more depends on effective exchange and disclosure of information, cross-sectoral and cross-boundary cooperation and coordination, and the involvement of various stakeholders, especially the local communities. This is especially true in the case of international rivers, for integration under such circumstances often relies on horizontal cooperation and coercion among riparian states rather than achieved in a hierarchical manner.

Institutional restructuring and capacity building is nevertheless necessary in the case of Mekong water governance, though it does not essentially requires a more centralised design, at least not in the beginning. Rather, it requires a more clear and rational demarcation of responsibilities to reduce the excessive bureaucracy due to the overlaps and vacancies of water-related powers, and developing platforms and mechanisms to foster and guide a more participatory and cooperative decision-making process. While the former is often "highly contested, bringing competing interests and value systems into collision",[240] the latter seems easier to promote under the current circumstance and can be used as an initial step of integration. But such cooperation in practice may be less effective due to the problematic institutional and power arrangements and the lack of a more enabling political and legal environment, and operational and enforceable legal tools.

While IWRM has been questioned for the "plausibility of actually integrating all aspects of water resources management both institutionally and physically",[241] it is argued that a fully integrated approach is not always needed for successful implementation. The more critical issue for water governance

---

239 Miller and Hirsch, above n 235, 8.

240 Hirsch, above n 8, 190.

241 Suhardiman, Giordano and Molle, above n 115, 1.

actually lies in the way in which decisions are taken.[242] Considering the difficulties and opportunities created by the polycentric feature of the current Mekong water governance regime, what is urgently needed and could be a more realistic and constructive approach of promoting IWRM in the Mekong region is to enhance decision-making processes in order to promote cross-boundary and cross-sectoral cooperation and coordination, suggest legal mechanisms to institutionalise sustainability concepts at both program and policy levels, as well as in relation to specific cases, through SEA and EIA respectively. By these means, transparency, accountability and public participation will also be encouraged.

The limitations of procedural mechanisms will also be discussed in the final chapter, both in theory and in practice, based on selected case studies which will give a more comprehensive picture on how to promote sustainable water governance in this region. Specific attention will be paid to the roles of hard law (i.e. legislative mechanisms) and soft law (non-enforceable guidelines) in managing transboundary water resources and the compliance of procedural requirements in the regional context.

242 International Rivers, 'Mekong under Threat: New Strategy Promotes Dams and Diversions' (Fact Sheet, International Rivers, 2006) 3.

CHAPTER 3

# Information Acquisition and Exchange on a Regular Basis

## I International Water Law and Selected Cases

### A *Rationale under the International Water Law*

Data collection and information exchange on a regular basis for shared freshwater resources among riparian states is an initial and fundamental step towards transboundary cooperation, contributing to a more informed discussion on transboundary water issues among riparian states. As viewed by McCaffrey, without relevant data and information sharing among co-riparian states, it will be very difficult, if not impossible, for states to ensure equitable and reasonable utilisation and prevent significant harm.[1] In addition to the inherent connection to the substantive principles and targets, this mechanism can be regarded as a part of the general obligation to cooperate.[2] Not only can it reduce misunderstanding and build trust among basin countries, the increasing communication and the cultivation of goodwill through this process will also lead to forms of closer cooperation among states.[3]

The value of regular exchange and collection of hydrological and hydrogeological data and information has been recognised by a variety of international documents and has been practiced in various basin contexts. Early in 1966, riparian states were recommended by the Helsinki Rules to "furnish relevant and reasonably available information" to the other co-riparians.[4] More detailed stipulations were achieved through the adoption of Article 9 of the United Nations' (UN) *Watercourses Convention* and the United Nations Economic Commission for Europe's (UNECE) *Water Convention*. In particular,

1 Stephen C. McCaffrey, *The Law of International Watercourses* (Oxford University Press, 2007) 478.

2 Patricia Birnie, Alan Boyle and Catherine Redgwell, *International Law and the Environment* (Oxford University Press, 3rd ed, 2009) 570.

3 McCaffrey, above n 1, 479.

4 See International Law Association, 'Helsinki Rules on the Uses of the Waters of International Rivers' (Report of the Committee on the Uses of the Waters of International Rivers, International Law Association, 1967) art XXIX.

 | DOI 10.1163/9789004266797_004

the latter represents an advanced example in this area. As a general requirement, two criteria of information exchange are highlighted under the *UNECE Water Convention*, namely the "widest" in terms of scope and "as early as possible" in terms of timing.[5]

In order to operationalise this provision, the Convention further clarifies the range of information as "reasonably available data", especially with respect to the environmental conditions of transboundary rivers, experience regarding best available technology and research results, emission and monitoring data, national regulations on emission limits, measures to tackle the transboundary impact and permits or regulations for waste-water discharges.[6] This is combined with another requirement to ensure several types of information are made available to the public. The Convention also covers the situation when the information requested is not available and urges endeavours to comply with the request which could be conditioned upon the payment of reasonable charges. Other than framing the obligations of states on this issue, river basin organisations are also required to facilitate this process by collecting, compiling and evaluating data, providing a forum for information sharing among states and promoting the exchange of information on the best available technology.

These requirements, however, do not affect the rights and the obligations of states in relation to industrial and commercial secrecy or national security. Although this is just a normal practice in international law, similar provisions in fact could be easily subject to different interpretations on what actually falls into this category, especially those relating to national security. With more detailed elaboration and legal arrangements on what information should be shared among countries and how, it is more likely to ensure that the confidentiality of information is just the exception rather than the rule. Since all riparian states of the Rhine River are bound by this Convention, the implementation of information exchange in the Rhine basin could be an enlighten case study.

In addition, numerous transboundary water treaties also entail requirements on information exchange to varying degrees, such as the *1944 United States-Mexico Boundary Waters Agreement*, the *1960 Indus Waters Treaty*, the *1961 Columbia River Basin Treaty*, the *1964 River Niger Treaty* and the *1994*

---

5 *Convention on the Protection and Use of Transboundary Watercourses and International Lakes*, opened for signature 17 March 1992, 1936 UNTS 269 (entered into force 6 October 1996) art 6.

6 Information in this paragraph is based on the content of the *UNECE Water Convention*. Ibid. arts 8, 9, 13, 16.

*Danube River Protection Convention*.[7] In particular, the *1944 United States-Mexico Boundary Waters Agreement*, together with the *1983 United States-Mexico Agreement for Transboundary Environmental Protection*, provides a fundamental legal basis for transboundary cooperation between the United States and Mexico regarding the utilisation and protection of their shared water resources, especially the Rio Grande River. Considering the fact that the United States is a strong upstream state in this case, it is to some extent comparable to the situation of China in the Mekong. Moreover, the transboundary dispute in the Rio Grande basin is also highly relevant to the emergence of the "Harmon Doctrine", namely the theory of absolute sovereignty.[8] It is interesting to see the transition of the United States from that initial position to transboundary cooperation with the relatively weak downstream state of Mexico through mechanisms such as information exchange. Although this case only involves bilateral cooperation, valuable experience can be drawn from it to enlighten the development of information exchange in the Mekong region, particularly with regard to the dialogue relationship between China and the lower Mekong countries.

## B *Selected Cases*

### 1 Information Exchange and Data Collection in the Governance of the Rhine

The Rhine, with a length of some 1320 km, is one of the longest and most important rivers in Europe.[9] From its source in Switzerland, the Rhine flows via France, Germany[10] and the Netherlands into the North Sea. Its catchment area also covers parts of Italy, Austria, Liechtenstein, Luxembourg and Belgium.[11] The Rhine is of crucial ecological, economic, political, social and cultural significance in the region and is certainly a much more intensively used watercourse compared to the Mekong. The development of vast industrial complexes along the river, such as the Ruhr, has led to serious chemical, salt and thermal pollution since the mid-twentieth century.[12] The canalisation

7 Birnie, Boyle and Redgwell, above n 2.

8 McCaffrey, above n 1, 77.

9 United Nations Environment Programme, *Freshwater in Europe: Facts, Figures and Maps* (2004) 66 <http://www.grid.unep.ch/products/3_Reports/freshwater_atlas.pdf>.

10 Before the German reunification in 1990, it was the Federal Republic of Germany (Western Germany) that participated in the cooperation in the Rhine region.

11 Ine D. Frijters and Jan Leentvaar, 'Rhine Case Study' (PCCP Series 17, UNESCO-IHP, 2003) 2.

12 See J. G. Lammers, *Pollution of International Watercourses* (Martinus Nijhoff, 1984) 171–5.

of the Rhine River and the construction of numerous dams also raise concerns on the ecological health of the river system.[13] Moreover, due to the impact of climate change, severe floods and droughts are expected to occur more often in the Rhine basin,[14] which has been identified as another high-profile issue in this area.[15]

In July 1950, the International Commission for the Protection of the Rhine against Pollution (renamed into the International Commission for the Protection of the Rhine in 1999, hereinafter referred to as ICPR) was established, but only after the occurrence of the severe 1986 Sandoz accident that countries began to take more effective cooperative actions on the protection of the Rhine.[16] Currently, the ICPR is operating under the *1999 Convention on the Protection of the Rhine* (*1999 Rhine Convention*) and its member states are also parties to a range of important UNECE agreements, including the *UNECE Water Convention*. In particular, data collection and information exchange in the Rhine basin can be examined at three levels: international commitments, the EU requirements and river basin arrangements. Notably, although Switzerland is the only Rhine state that is not an EU member, it maintains a very close relationship with the EU in various aspects. Having outlined the relevant obligations of the Rhine states under the *UNECE Water Convention*, more specific attention will be paid to the other two aspects to paint a more comprehensive picture of information exchange in the context of the Rhine basin.

At the EU level, several directives and decisions have dealt with this issue. Notably, the *Council Decision 77/795/EEC* in 1977 established a common procedure for the exchange of information on the quality of surface fresh water in the European Community.[17] It has been further amended by other EU decisions

13 See Koos Wieriks and Anne Schulte-Wulwer-Leidig, 'Integrated Water Management for the Rhine River Basin, from Pollution Prevention to Ecosystem Improvement' (1997) 21(2) *Natural Resources Form* 147, 147–8.

14 H. Middelkoop et al., 'Impact of Climate Change on Hydrological Regimes and Water Resources Management in the Rhine Basin' (2001) 49 *Climate Change* 105, 105.

15 Tom Raadgever, 'Transboundary River Basin Management Regimes: The Rhine Basin Case Study' (Background Report of the NeWater Project, Centre for River Basin Management, Delft University of Technology, August 2005) 1.

16 See generally Lammers, above n 12, 169–91; Marco Verweij, 'A Watershed on the Rhine: Changing Approaches to International Environmental Cooperation' (1999) 47 *GeoJournal* 453; Wieriks and Schulte-Wulwer-Leidig, above n 13, 151.

17 *Council Decision of 12 December 1977 Establishing a Common Procedure for the Exchange of Information on the Quality of Surface Fresh Water in the Community* [1977] OJ L 334/29.

and regulations.[18] This rather technical document standardises the process of regular information exchange and collection, and facilitates its implementation through the platform of the EU Commission. Requirements are made relating to the frequency of sampling, sampling stations, intercalibration, sample preservation and measuring methods to secure timely, transparent, reliable and abundant information sharing among the EU countries. Several sampling and measuring stations located along the Rhine River in Germany and Netherlands are involved in this exchanging mechanism at the EU level.[19] It is further complemented by the *Directive on Measurement Methods and Sampling Frequencies*.[20] Moreover, information exchange and common synergy is required under the *2007 Flood Directive*, including information on the first flood hazard maps, flood risk maps, the first flood risk management plans and their subsequent reviews.[21] In March 2007, the Commission launched the Water Information System for Europe as a comprehensive platform for information collection and sharing.[22]

At the basin level, however, the *1999 Rhine Convention* does not explicitly require information exchange among the Rhine states and relevant organisations, except for the obligation on member states to report regularly to the ICPR regarding their implementation of the Convention and the ICPR's decisions, upon which the ICPR could evaluate the effectiveness of the actions and take further decisions.[23] This in part can be attributed to the intensive requirements on this issue put in place by international conventions and the EU documents that are effective in the region. In addition, it is related to the fact that a large part of the work is handled by another professional organisation

18 It can be subjected to amendments of national legislation as well, but the Rhine states have not made such changes.

19 *Council Decision of 12 December 1977 Establishing a Common Procedure for the Exchange of Information on the Quality of Surface Fresh Water in the Community* [1977] OJ L 334/29, Annex 1.

20 *Council Directive 79/869/EEC of 9 October 1979 concerning the Methods of Measurement and Frequencies of Sampling and Analysis of Surface Water Intended for the Abstraction of Drinking Water in the Member States* [1979] OJ L 271/44.

21 *Directive 2007/60/EC of the European Parliament and of the Council of 23 October 2007 on the Assessment and Management of Flood Risks* [2007] OJ L 288/27, arts 6, 9.

22 See *The Water Information System for Europe* <http://water.europa.eu/>.

23 *Convention on the Protection of the Rhine* [2000] OJ L 289/31, arts 8, 11(3) (5). In fact, considering the principles and targets of the Convention and the quite successful cooperation in the field, an extensive and effective information exchange mechanism is unavoidable.

discussed below on hydrology in the region. Among others, the following arrangements have been made to facilitate the process:

To begin with, the member states take the main responsibility of data and information collection, which is assessed and compiled by the delegates of member states through the ICPR working group meetings.[24] After approved by the heads of delegations and the plenary meeting of the ICPR, information is published on the website of the ICPR and is free to be downloaded by anyone, including the public. It reflects a strong connection between information exchange and the public's right of access to information. In addition, there is a network of experts that meets frequently in the working groups to facilitate the exchange of information. In addition, the ICPR also serves as a platform to share various monitoring results and reports produced by the different programs of the Rhine.[25]

Other than the role of the ICPR in the exchange of information in the region, another organisation has contributed to this process significantly, namely the International Commission for the Hydrology of the Rhine Basin (CHR). Founded in 1970, it has served as a platform for the scientific institutes of the Rhine states to "formulate joint hydrological measures for sustainable development of the Rhine basin".[26] It aims to expend the knowledge of the hydrology in the Rhine basin through joint research; exchange of data, methods and information; development of standardised procedures; and publications. Moreover, it contributes to the resolution of transboundary issues through the formulation, management and provision of information systems and models. Further, cooperation between the ICPR, the EU Commission and the CHR has been promoted to synergise this process. For example, the secretary of the ICPR attends the CHR meetings and the CHR members also take part in ICPR working groups.[27] The ICPR also plays an important role in coordinating the implementation of the *EU Water Framework Directive* in the Rhine basin.[28]

---

24 Unless otherwise indicated, information in this paragraph is derived from: Ain Sokhna, 'International Conflict Management in the Basin of the Rhine' (Report, Egyptian-Dutch Advisory Panel on Water Management, 2010) 4.

25 Jonathan L. Chenoweth and Eran Feitelson, 'Analysis of Factors Influencing Data and Information Exchange in International River Basins' (2001) 26(4) *Water International* 499, 505.

26 Unless otherwise indicated, information in this paragraph is derived from the website of the International Commission for the Hydrology of the Rhine Basin: http://www.chr-khr.org/en/general.

27 Frijters and Leentvaar, above n 11, 7.

28 See European Commission, *Interesting Links concerning the Water Framework Directive* <http://ec.europa.eu/environment/water/water-framework/links/index_en.htm>.

The success of regular exchanges of information and collection of data in the Rhine basin is prominent. A comprehensive system has been established at different levels to govern and facilitate information sharing in various degrees and through diverse approaches, including the exchange of data independently collected, data standardisation and synergy, joint collection of data, the exchange of forecasts of water utilisation and the exchange of plans and the situation of national implementation. The process has benefited from the transparency of domestic water governance, the regional arrangements on the public's right of access to information, the long history of transboundary cooperation in the region, the general acceptance of international environmental rules, the EU integration process and the advanced economic and technology situation.

## 2 Information Exchange and Data Collection between the United States and Mexico

The United States and Mexico share several transboundary rivers. The beds of the Rio Grande and the Colorado River coincide with the United States-Mexican border for approximately half of its length.[29] The watersheds are located in a semi-arid region and limited water supplies have been challenged by increasing demands ever since American westward expansion. In the late 19th century, increasing diversions of Rio Grande waters by farmers in the United States sharply decreased the water supply to Mexican communities.[30] As a response to whether the diversions in the United States violated Mexico's rights under principles of international law, Judson Harmon (the United States Attorney General at the time) strongly argued that the United States enjoys absolute sovereignty over its water resources and is under no obligation to Mexico to restrain its use of the Rio Grande.[31]

It has become known as the "Harmon Doctrine" and was taken as the formal legal position of the United States in its dispute with Mexico.[32] However, the United States government did not actually act on Harmon's advice in

29 Marie J. Gunning, 'The Projected Impact of the North American Free Trade Agreement on Transboundary Water Management between Mexico and the USA' in J. Ganoulis et al. (eds), *Transboundary Water Resources Management: Institutional and Engineering Approaches* (Springer, 1996) 71, 71.

30 McCaffrey, above n 1, 76, 113.

31 United States Department of Justice, *Official Opinions of the Attorneys General of the United States: Advising the President and Heads of Departments in Relation to their Official Duties Volume 21* (Government Printing Office, 1985) 274, 283.

32 Stephen C. McCaffrey, 'The Harmon Doctrine One Hundred Years Later: Buried, not Praised' (1996) 36 *Natural Resources Journal* 549, 588.

dealing with this transboundary dispute.[33] It is also interesting to notice the positions taken by the United States during its negotiations with Canada in the 1950s regarding the Columbia River (the United States is a downstream state in this case). They were in fact quite similar to that of Mexico in the Rio Grande dispute.[34] The geographical fact that the United States could either be an upstream or downstream state in different occasions is probably an important practical reason of why the United States is more open to transboundary water cooperation.

A more fundamental reason, however, lies in the lack of rationale support for Harmon's conclusion.[35] While he attempted to rely on the idea of self-preservation (similar to the doctrine of "state of necessity"), scholars have pointed out that it was not a right, but an excuse that "prevents what would otherwise have been an internationally wrongful act from being regarded as wrongful".[36] Following the rationale underlining this doctrine, the United States will find it logically impossible to obtain a sound legal position in the Rio Grande case.[37]

Although the international watercourses law was still quite immature at the time, the reality of interdependence among states ultimately led to goodwill cooperation and reciprocity in dealing with transboundary issues. In this sense, the fact that the United States is also a downstream state in several instances does provide a strong case to illustrate the necessity for cooperation.

In 1889, the International Boundary Commission was established to jointly ascertain the facts and report on its findings.[38] In order to carry out these tasks, the exchange of information and data was unavoidable. In 1906, a bilateral agreement was signed to promote *equitable* distribution of the Rio Grande waters for irrigation purposes.[39]

The initial cooperation on equitable water allocation was then upgraded by the *1944 United States-Mexico Boundary Waters Agreement* which expanded

33 Herbert Smith concluded that "Mr. Harmon's attitude seems to have been merely the caution of the ordinary lawyer who is determined not to concede unnecessarily a single point to the other side." In fact, according to McCaffrey, it was probably just "a piece of advocacy that might be useful as a negotiating device but hardly provided a basis for resolving the concrete controversies". McCaffrey, above n. 1, 76, 93, 110 (citation omitted).

34 Ibid. 107.

35 See McCaffrey, above n 32, 560–9.

36 Ibid. 567.

37 See McCaffrey, above n 1, 91.

38 McCaffrey, above n 32, 569.

39 See McCaffrey, above n 1, 92–7 (emphasis added).

the jurisdiction and responsibilities of the Commission.[40] The Commission was then renamed to the International Boundary and Water Commission (IBWC). In particular, both sides agreed to keep a complete record regarding the waters delivered to Mexico and the flows of the river, which will be periodically compiled and exchanged between the two national sections of the IBWC in the United States and Mexico.[41]

Since the mid-1960s, the power of the IBWC has been gradually expanded to solve transboundary water pollution problems, such as salination, sewage treatment and industrial and pesticide contamination.[42] In 1983, an environmental protection agreement, the *La Paz Agreement*, was signed by both countries, which established a rather loose dialogue forum led by two national coordinators.[43] Some general arrangements were made regarding information exchange.[44] In 1992, both sides agreed that the IBWC will develop a monitoring program and an appropriate database for a systematic observation of the water quality in boundary waters.[45]

---

40 *Treaty regarding Utilization of Waters of Colorado and Tijuana Rivers and of the Rio Grande*, signed 3 February 1944, 3 UNTS 313 (entered into force 8 November 1945) art 2.

41 Ibid. arts 12(d), 24(f).

42 This is achieved through the issue of IBWC minute records, inter alia the Minute 261. As further agreements by the two parties to take cooperative actions, the IBWC minutes are used as an important approach to implement the *1944 Agreement*. International Boundary and Water Commission, *Minutes between the United States and Mexican Sections of the IBWC* <http://www.ibwc.state.gov/Treaties_Minutes/Minutes.html>; Chenoweth and Feitelson, above n 25, 506.

43 Coordinators can make recommendations to the governments and organise annual meetings between the governments and the meetings of the experts. John H. Knox, 'The North American Commission for Environmental Cooperation and Transboundary Pollution' (2004) 34 *Environmental Law Reporter: News and Analysis* 10142, 10143; *Agreement between the United States of America and the United Mexican States on Cooperation for the Protection and Improvement of the Environment in the Border Area*, signed 14 August 1983, 1352 UNTS 67 (entered into force 16 February 1984) art 8.

44 For example, the periodic exchange of information and data on likely sources of pollution which may produce environmental polluting incidents is listed as a possible cooperative measure. In addition, it is required that "all technical information obtained through the implementation of this Agreement *will* be available to both Parties". *Agreement between the United States of America and the United Mexican States on Cooperation for the Protection and Improvement of the Environment in the Border Area*, signed 14 August 1983, 1352 UNTS 67 (entered into force 16 February 1984) arts 6, 16 (emphasis added).

45 See generally United States Environmental Protection Agency and Mexico's Secretariat of Urban Development and Ecology, *Integrated Environmental Plan for the Mexican-U.S.*

A decade later, an environmental side agreement was signed by members of the North American Free Trade Agreement (NAFTA, members include Canada, the United States and Mexico) to develop common environmental policies. Under the Agreement, states are obliged to "periodically prepare and make public available reports on the state of the environment".[46] Meanwhile, the Council of the newly established Commission for Environmental Cooperation is responsible for "promoting the exchange of information on criteria and methodologies used in establishing domestic environmental standards".[47] It also has the power to consider and develop recommendations regarding the "comparability of techniques and methodologies for data gathering and analysis, data management and electronic data communications".[48] States, however, are protected from releasing information that could impede its environmental law enforcement or in cases that is against the domestic law regarding business or proprietary information, personal privacy or the confidentiality of governmental decision-making.[49]

Despite the above efforts to promote environmental cooperation between the United States and Mexico, it is argued that real progress has been slow.[50] But as an initial step for transboundary cooperation, two countries have managed to move away from absolute sovereignty to a more active exchange of information and data. The early practice on information sharing was limited to water allocation and maintaining the quantity of water flows. The collection and exchange of data lays down a foundation for further cooperation, such as

---

*Border Area* (*First Stage, 1992–1994*) (1992) <http://pdf.usaid.gov/pdf_docs/PNABM228.pdf>.

46 *North American Agreement on Environmental Cooperation*, signed 14 September 1993, 32 ILM 1480 (entered into force 1 January 1994) art 2(1).

47 Ibid. art 10 (3).

48 Ibid. art 10 (2).

49 Ibid. art 39.

50 This is partly due to the different legal and institutional frameworks between the two counties. And the power gaps and overlaps resulted in a complex and competitive political environment for the cooperation under the IBWC. In addition, the IBWC itself has limited legal strength to promote environmental cooperation on water issues and often only maintains a technical focus in practice. Moreover, the *La Paz Agreement* falls short of more specific mechanisms and arrangements to implement its goals. Further, the absence of a definite, articulated role for the IBWC under the *La Paz Agreement* also illustrates the disconnection between them. There has been funding challenges to meet the demand for environmental infrastructure as well. See Gunning, above n 29; Chenoweth and Feitelson, above n 25, 506; Good Neighbor Environmental Board, 'Water Resources Management on the United States-Mexico Border' (Eighth Report to the President and the Congress of the United States, Good Neighbor Environmental Board, 2005).

joint construction, operation and maintenance of storage dams and hydroelectric plants. Eventually, information exchange has been extended to the area of water quality. The IBWC has endeavoured to detail the arrangements on information collection and exchange regarding the quality of border waters. Some technical issues have been discussed, such as the location of sampling sites, parameters to be analysed and the capabilities of laboratories in each country.[51] Based on some agreements on these issues, several joint programs have been initiated to gain more understanding on water pollution in the region.[52]

Nonetheless, the mechanism of information exchange between the United States and Mexico is still facing several challenges. Despite the existence of relevant domestic legislation and bilateral arrangements, a certain degree of reluctance to share data between the two nations still exists in practice (ironically, it is the downstream state Mexico that is more likely to hold data).[53] Combined with the exceptional provision on information sharing under the environmental side agreement under NAFTA, more detailed clarification should be made on what kinds of information shall be shared among the two nations. Interestingly, however, it is also revealed that water managers and stakeholders have more chance to agree on information sharing and cooperative management at a more informal level, for example, through the development of personal relationships.[54]

In addition, the data collection systems of the two countries are quite different and complex. Compared to the United States system, the Mexican counterpart is generally more centralised.[55] Moreover, within each country, data management responsibilities are further divided among domestic water sectors and between federal and state agencies. This situation requires more coordination at both regional and domestic levels, the lack of which often leads to data gaps and inconsistencies on water quantity and quality.[56] Despite efforts of the IBWC, there remain considerable differences between the methods used by two countries to collect information and the current cooperation still

51 International Boundary and Water Commission, *Joint Report of the Principle Engineers relative to Determination of Presence of Toxic Substances in the Waters of the Rio Grande in its International Boundary Reach* (11 November 1992) <http://www.ibwc.gov/Files/Minutes/JR289.pdf>.

52 Ibid.

53 Good Neighbor Environmental Board, above n 50, 26.

54 Ibid.

55 Linda Fernandez, 'Transboundary Water Management along the U.S.-Mexico Border' in Renan-Ulrich Goetz and Dolors Berga (eds), *Frontiers in Water Resource Economics* (Springer, 2006) 153, 161.

56 Good Neighbor Environmental Board, above n 50, 24.

falls short of more systematic arrangements on the regular exchange of water-related data.[57]

Non-state actors can also contribute to the process of information exchange. In the US, the public's right of access to information has been better secured and tribes, academia and NGOs have participated in the process of water data collection.[58] But there is a lack of proper arrangements to combine them with the joint information collection and data exchange among states at the regional level. The involvement of non-state actors in information collection should to be further enhanced in Mexico.

Although the IBWC has the primary responsibilities on coordinating transboundary water governance in the region, the process of information exchange in the field is further burdened by the lack of coordination within the two sections of the IBWC[59] and insufficient cooperation between IBWC, the *La Paz Agreement* and the Commission for Environmental Cooperation under the NAFTA regime

### C *Lessons*

The exchange of information on a regular basis is inherent in the fundamental theories of international water law. As demonstrated by McCaffrey, the rationale of the Harmon Doctrine falls short of support from international law and has "seldom, if ever, been reflected in the resolutions of actual controversies".[60] Combined with the community of interest created by the natural and physical integrity of shared water resources, modern theories of transboundary water governance is shaped by the principle of equitable and reasonable utilisation, the obligation to prevent significant harm and the obligation to cooperate. The adoption of these principles can logically lead to the necessity of information exchange. In turn, the adoption of this mechanism can be viewed as an implicit positive sign of embracing the fundamental values of the contemporary international water law.

Despite the convincing legal rationale at the theoretical level regarding the exchange of information on a regular basis, the situation in practice varies in different socio-economic and political settings. Nowadays, countries often

57 Ibid. 27.

58 Ibid. 19.

59 Scholars have suggested the governments to reorganise the two national sections of the IBWC into a single office to improve bilateral coordination. See Mary Kelly and Alberto Székely, 'Modernizing the International Boundary and Water Commission' (Policy Paper 1, Center for Latin American Studies, 2004) 14.

60 See McCaffrey, above n 1, 90–92, 125.

do not explicitly claim for absolute sovereignty over shared water resources located in their own territories. Instead, the reluctance to follow the fundamental principles could be disguised by the creation of information barriers. Scientific uncertainties and controversies of water-related development decisions can in part be attributed to the absence of necessary information exchange, the manipulation of monitoring data or simply the lack of capacity to obtain reliable data. The knowledge gaps among riparian countries regarding the domestic arrangements for water governance also increases the difficulty on taking coordinated measures at the regional level.

The content and timing of information exchange is crucial. Rather than an ad hoc system, more regular, frequent and timely exchange of information is preferred. It is argued that any delay in the release of reports containing new data could be detrimental to its value.[61] Such delay and inefficiency can result from the reluctance to cooperate, excessive bureaucracies or a lack of capacity or resources to facilitate this process.[62] With regard to the content, key criteria are transparency, reliability and abundance. The *UNECE Water Convention* provides an illustration of the wide-ranging information that should be regularly exchanged among riparian states, including several types of monitoring data, experiences regarding best available technology and scientific research, and a range of domestic legal measures and arrangements of water managements.[63] Among others, the exchange of monitoring data is fundamental in providing a common basis for transboundary cooperation.

In order to better secure the accuracy and compatibility of the data, more detailed arrangements should be made regarding the process and technology used for data collecting and analysis. In light of different monitoring systems and capacities of riparian states and possible technical variations, however, the actual process of information exchange is often troubled by the difficulties to synergise the work of each riparian state and to compile outcomes gaining through varied monitoring techniques. Efforts can be identified in the above cases attempting at increasing consistency and compatibility of state behaviour in this area. Other than coordinating data collection carried out by each state separately, arrangements are made to promote joint investigation and monitoring. Specific organisations are designated to facilitate and lead the joint efforts. While it is important to promote more standardised practice for

61 Good Neighbor Environmental Board, above n 50, 26.

62 See ibid.

63 *Convention on the Protection and Use of Transboundary Watercourses and International Lakes*, opened for signature 17 March 1992, 1936 UNTS 269 (entered into force 6 October 1996) art 13.

monitoring, attention should also be paid to better understand and acknowledge the existing discrepancies of relevant state practices. This could help calibrate and interpret the data more accurately.

In addition, scientific data should be accompanied by information on national arrangements and implementation, which are essential to better evaluate and analyse the reasons behind the monitoring results. It is also a part of the non-compliance mechanism to assess the implementation of state commitments. Cooperation on relevant technology and scientific research can improve the capacity on providing more reliable data as well. Since there may be several regional cooperation institutions exist in one area, the requirements on information exchange under different cooperative regimes should be coordinated. Arrangements should be made to facilitate communication among regional institutions regarding the collection and sharing of information. Finally, although information exchange mainly requires cooperation among countries, the involvement of non-state actors in data collection and research can help improve the accuracy of data. But there could be a risk of information manipulation under the influence of powerful corporations. Nevertheless, combining the process of information exchange with the public's right of access to information can increase the transparency of information. The linkage between information exchange and the public's right to access to information is reflected in Article 5 of the *Aarhus Convention*. The openness of this process could certainly allow more room for debate on the validity of relevant information and the specific ways in which it is collected and analysed. Hence the reliability of information may be better secured through discussion. This issue will be further discussed in future chapters.

## II Status Quo and Prospects in the Mekong Region

In light of the polycentric feature of transboundary cooperation in the Mekong region, the status quo of water-related information collection and exchange in the region can be examined from several perspectives, including the relevant cooperation among four member countries of the Mekong River Commission (MRC) and between the MRC and China. Attention will also be paid to information exchange systems under the Greater Mekong Subregional (GMS) Program and the Association of Southeast Asian Nations (ASEAN) (including its dialogue relationship with China). Recommendations will be given on what needs to be further improved in this area and more importantly, how to cultivate and facilitate changes towards this direction.

### A *Information Acquisition and Exchange under the MRC*

The requirement on information exchange and collection on a regular basis is incorporated in the *1995 Mekong Agreement*. The Joint Committee of the MRC is obliged to "regularly obtain, update and exchange information and data necessary to implement this Agreement".[64] Under the supervision and direction of the Joint Committee, the Secretariat is responsible for maintaining the databases of information. The interconnection between information collection and exchange and the principle of equitable and reasonable utilisation is reflected in Article 26. Based on this principle, it requires the Joint Committee to prepare and propose rules for the location of hydrological stations, the flow level requirements at each station and the monitoring mechanisms for intra-basin use and inter-basin diversions from the mainstream. But these procedural documents are fairly general, mainly focusing on the objectives, principles and institutional arrangements of monitoring and information exchange. Instead of really making the mechanisms operational and functional in practice, the documents more closely resemble framework arrangements pending further consensus on many detailed issues. Moreover, the institutional arrangements mainly focus on the responsibilities of the MRC bodies, especially the Secretariat, and only address the roles of member states through some general requirements on the National Mekong Committees (NMC).

As illustrated in chapter two, MRC's reliance on the NMCs to engage with domestic water governance regimes has often proved to be less effective in practice. While the NMCs are responsible for linking the MRC's work on information collection and exchange with relevant domestic agencies and practices, their strengths in the field are limited by their varied domestic settings, the fragmentation of domestic water governance and the general tensions between the donor-driven Secretariat and the member states. While various responsibilities have been put on the MRC bodies to ensure the accuracy, transparency and efficiency of the system, the procedural documents often fail to elaborate on what approaches they can use to achieve that.

Pursuant to Article 25 of the Agreement, the Procedures for Data and Information Exchange and Sharing and the Procedures for Water Use Monitoring were approved through the MRC Council resolutions in 2001 and 2003 respectively. The Procedures for Water Quality also briefly requires the

64 Information in this paragraph is based on the content of the Agreement. *Agreement on the Cooperation for the Sustainable Development of the Mekong River Basin*, opened for signature 5 April 1995, 2069 UNTS I-35844 (entered into force 5 April 1995) arts 24(C), 24(E), 26, 30(E).

member states to strengthen the existing programs and establishing new joint programs (if necessary) for water quality monitoring. Further, the prior notification mechanism established under the MRC Procedures for Notification, Prior Consultation and Agreement is used as a general approach to collect and exchange information on all intra-basin uses and inter-basin diversions on both tributaries and mainstream of Mekong. Relatively detailed arrangements have been made regarding the content and procedures of such notification, which will be discussed in the next chapter.

The above MRC procedural documents are further supported by several guidelines. Among others, the Guidelines on Custodianship and Management of the MRC Information System, the Guidelines for Management of the MRC Hydrometeorological Network and the Guidelines on Implementation of the Procedures for Water Use Monitoring are highlighted. Notably, increasing attention has been paid to the roles of the NMCs and relevant domestic line agencies. Overall, these guidelines are more action oriented, focusing on providing and promoting more detailed technical arrangements regarding information gathering and exchange. In particular, the MRC Information System has been developed as a structured communication and management system for data and information.[65] Correspondingly, a support team with members from the MRC Secretariat and the NMCs is established to help the development of guidelines and standards for information collection and exchange.[66] The guidelines further elaborate on the roles of the MRC Secretariat, the NMCs and domestic line agencies in operating this mechanism. In addition, the scope of information exchange is enumerated by the procedural documents and guidelines. Cost sharing and the obligations and responsibilities of information users are addressed as well.[67] Although these documents mentioned the public's right of access to information, requirements in this area remain to be general and ambiguous.

Further, the Information and Knowledge Management Programme (IKMP) was initiated by the MRC in 2006 as one of the key data acquisition and analysis services in the lower Mekong basin.[68] This programme is funded by the governments of Australia, Finland and France and numerous preparation

---

65 Joint Committee of Mekong River Commission, 'Guidelines on Custodianship and Management of the MRC Information System' (Guidelines, Mekong River Commission, 2002) 2.

66 Ibid. 1.

67 See ibid.

68 Mekong River Commission, *Information and Knowledge Management Programme* <http://www.mrcmekong.org/about-the-mrc/programmes/information-and-knowledge-management-programme/>.

works have been done with foreign supports and in collaboration with other external organisations.[69] Again, it generates discussions on how member states see the role of the IKMP in promoting information sharing when "data collection is driven primarily by donors' development ideas rather than focused on countries' needs".[70]

The above documents and program depict the outline of information collection and exchange under the MRC. Along with the implementation of the IKMP, there has been a general tendency towards a more comprehensive information system. Increasing technical issues have been addressed to improve the quality and compatibility of data and to facilitate the sharing of information and knowledge. In particular, the following issues should be noted:

A large amount of attention has focused on developing a basin-wide (at least in the lower Mekong basin) river monitoring network. To date, monitoring services include, but are not limited to, water level information, water quality information, hydro-meteorology data and bio-monitoring data.[71] In addition, sediment and ground water monitoring has also been put in place.[72] National line agencies for hydrological and meteorological services have been identified[73] and a range of monitoring stations (on both mainstream and tributaries of the Mekong) and laboratories has been designated for varied monitoring and analysis purposes.[74] A list of indexes and parameters has been agreed by all member states regarding water use monitoring.[75] Moreover, some coordinated arrangements have been made on the sampling frequency as well.[76]

---

69 Mekong River Commission, 'The Information and Knowledge Management Programme 2011–2015' (Programme Document, Mekong River Commission, 2010) 4; World Meteorological Organization and Mekong River Commission, 'Establishment of a Hydrological Information System in the Mekong River Basin' (Project Document, World Meteorological Organization and Mekong River Commission, 2006) 5.

70 Diana Suhardiman, Mark Giordano and François Molle, 'Scalar Disconnect: The Logic of Transboundary Water Governance in the Mekong' (2011) 0 *Society and Natural Resources: An International Journal* 1, 10 <http://www.tandfonline.com/doi/abs/10.1080/08941920.2011.604398>.

71 See Mekong River Commission, *Information Services*, Mekong River Commission Data and Information Services <http://portal.mrcmekong.org/cms/information-services>.

72 See Mekong River Commission, above n 69, 7.

73 World Meteorological Organization and Mekong River Commission, above n 69, 28.

74 See Mekong River Commission, above n 71.

75 Mekong River Commission, above n 69, 43.

76 See Mekong River Commission, *Water Quality Index*, Mekong River Commission Data and Information Services <http://portal.mrcmekong.org/cms/lower-mekong-basin-water-quality-index>.

In order to improve the capacity of the NMCs and line agencies in providing and transmitting good quality data, capacity building plans have been made and implemented in areas such as technical assistance, financial support, human resources training, institutional development and legal, regulatory and procedural development.[77] Other than information obtained through monitoring, the IKMP also collects information on fisheries, hydropower development, irrigation projects and areas, and other geospatial information.[78] The above information has been compiled into various databases, through which information services are delivered on a real-time or near real-time basis, or subject to annual or as-available updates.[79] This is generally in line with the requirement on exchanging information in a timely manner as reflected in the case studies.

As demonstrated before, data collection should not be limited to scientific monitoring. A large amount of information regarding the relevant social, economic and environmental impact following changes in river system conditions should also be gathered through various modelling and assessment approaches. Through the MRC Information System, a set of assessment tools has been provided to support regional planning in the area.[80] Some environmental and social-economic data has been incorporated in various databases. The Decision Support Framework has been recently established as an important knowledge base for the MRC countries, containing historical and current information on the environmental and socio-economic conditions of the Mekong.[81] The MRC's efforts in this area, however, do not seem to be appreciated by member states in many cases. The tension between the donor-driven MRC Secretariat and strong national water sectors limits the actual outputs of knowledge production in this area and undermines its influences on water-related decision-making process.

The knowledge production on ecosystem impact scenarios and assessments illustrates the blurring of boundaries between politics and science: power structures, diverging interests among stakeholders and different policy motivations all have an impact on the modelling and assessment process.[82] As the

77 World Meteorological Organization and Mekong River Commission, above n 69, 37.

78 See Mekong River Commission, above n 71.

79 Ibid.

80 See Mekong River Commission, *Modelling Toolbox*, Mekong River Commission Data and Information Services <http://portal.mrcmekong.org/cms/models-and-scenarios>.

81 Mekong River Commission, above n 71.

82 See Mira Käkönen and Philip Hirsch, 'The Anti-Politics of Mekong Knowledge Production' in François Molle, Tira Foran and Mira Käkönen (eds), *Contested Waterscapes in the Mekong Region: Hydropower, Livelihoods and Governance* (Earthscan, 2009) 333, 350.

current core of the MRC information collection in this area, the hydrological models are still criticised for simplifying the complex ecosystem and related social-economic dynamics of the basin.[83] Despite the initial ambitious plans of creating comprehensive and integrated assessments, the MRC's knowledge production on ecosystem impact scenarios and assessments is in fact limited.

Even if the quality of information in this area can be improved, it is not self-evident that they would actually influence the decision and policy making.[84] Along with the developments in this area, however, if countries continue to ignore such information during the decision-making process without reasonable explanations, they will find themselves in a very unfavourable position to justify their behaviour under the requirement of due diligence. While problems continue to exist in how to give more strength to implement the *Mekong Agreement*, improving information collection and exchange in this area can certainly play a commendable role in supporting state behaviour changes. The influence of the information exchange mechanism has to be combined with other procedural requirements in order to better secure a real impact on decision-making.

Another important content of information exchange is information on domestic water management, particularly the relevant legislation, administrative arrangements and the domestic implementation of the *Mekong Agreement*. But cooperation in this area under the MRC is still very much incipient and mainly exists on an informal and ad hoc basis. This in part arises from the language barriers among the riparian states. More fundamentally, problems lie in the lack of requirement on the member states to regularly report to the MRC under the *Mekong Agreement*. In light of international experiences, self-reporting system is often used as the main approach in this area and is generally viewed as a part of the non-compliance mechanism as well. A lack of this system illustrates the disconnection between the MRC and its member states. It is also systematically detrimental to the implementation of the Agreement and results in notable knowledge gaps at the regional level. While some information in this area has been gathered by other institutions (such as the Global Water Partnership—Southeast Asia and the Asian Development Bank), academics and NGOs, information fragmentation and varied institutional agendas behind it often lead to further controversies and could weaken the roles of the MRC in regional water governance.

With regard to information exchange between the MRC and national water agencies, the current knowledge hub focuses on capacity building for trans-

83 Ibid. 341.

84 Ibid. 350.

boundary water resources management. It is more of a transfer process of international best practices and theories to the Mekong states. There seems to be limited active feedback from the member states and less attention has been paid to the experiences and challenges reflected in domestic water governance and reforms. More systematic information exchange in this area under the MRC could be an important step to move away from its strong technical feature to actually strengthen its impact on water governance in the region.

In general, the information collection and exchange system under the MRC has been established with a relatively comprehensive vision and has provided an improving common knowledge base for decision-making. For example, real-time monitoring data on precipitation and water level is an important reference for flood forecasting. Information regarding aquatic ecosystem and water quality is also valuable for relevant policy-making and further researches. But the knowledge production on ecosystem impact scenarios, related social-economic dynamics and domestic political and legal arrangements on water governance remains constricted to varying degrees. In particular, it is argued that the MRC should improve the information exchange on more localised water governance experiences and lessons.

Another problem is the varied capacities of different domestic agencies in fulfilling their duties on information collection and exchange and the existence of some geographical, culture and language obstacles. While it is necessary to build capacity for information collection from various aspects, efforts should be made to identify and reduce the variations of state practice in this area. Discrepancies in part arise from the lack of capacity to collect information to varying degrees. More importantly, they could result from different domestic regimes of water governance and numerous institutional problems faced by each country. Given the unique setting of the NMC in each riparian state and disconnection between the MRC and domestic water governance regimes, the NMC's ability to coordinate relevant works among domestic agencies and between the NMCs and line agencies is subject to challenges in the field.

While it is commendable that the current system facilitates information exchange between member states and among different MRC programmes, the cooperation between the MRC and other regional institutions on sharing information is still limited. As mentioned in chapter two, some preliminary cooperative arrangements have been made between the MRC, the GMS Program and ASEAN. The involvement of the MRC in the GMS program remains largely in the form of technical support and the cooperation so far mainly focuses on climate change adaptation (particularly in the area of flood and drought management). Thus the suggestion here is that the MRC and the GMS program should enhance cooperation through two-way information exchange rather than one-way technical support on the MRC side. Other than climate change adaptation, a more regular information exchange system should be established between the two institutions regarding hydropower development and relevant infrastructure development.

A project database is currently available at the ADB website which could provide a large amount of information regarding projects funded by the ADB through the GMS program. But since the GMS is becoming increasingly Asian and less "ADB-driven", it is argued that more systematic arrangements should be made between the GMS and the MRC. As a loosely structured forum, however, information exchange under the GMS mainly relies on meetings at different political levels, reflecting a strong feature of the "ASEAN Way". As shown in the case of the Rio Grande, informal and flexible approaches can be valuable to cultivate further cooperation in this area. But at least it is more prudent to reflect the consensus in a legally-binding form. Along with the development of the GMS, if it is to become a formal organisation in the future, the adoption of more formal and regular arrangements is essential, including information exchange mechanism. Considering the dynamic economic cooperation facilitated by the GMS and the gradually increasing environmental initiatives under the GMS program, more pressures should be put on the GMS to develop a more cooperative relationship with the MRC. From the MRC's perspective, the shift of focus from the rationale of technical rendering to increasing engagement and interaction with the polycentric landscape of water-related decision-making in the region could in fact further enhance the role of the MRC in water governance.

Moreover, the development of information exchange mechanism under the MRC can benefit from the ASEAN initiative on harmonising environmental policies, legislation, regulations, standards and databases among the ASEAN countries.[85] Efforts have been made at the national and the ASEAN level to support environmental monitoring, analysis, modelling, forecasting and reporting.[86] In particular, regional and national environmental reports prepared by ASEAN and its member countries could provide a valuable way of information exchange. On the first summit of MRC (2010), the ASEAN Secretariat announced that it will cooperate with the MRC Secretariat in the development and management of the Mekong water resources as well as in

85 Koh Kheng-Lian (ed), *ASEAN Environmental Law, Policy and Governance: Selected Documents (Volume I)* (World Scientific, 2009) 501.

86 Ibid.

addressing challenges common to the two organisations.[87] More regular and intensive information exchange between two organisations is necessary to facilitate further cooperation in this area.

Last, but not least, the public's right of access to information and participation should be better secured during the process of information collection and exchange. While some rudimentary requirements in this area can be identified in the above procedural documents and program, the general political opportunities in this respect are still very much restricted. Public participation in this mechanism can contribute to redressing the power imbalances that shape the production of knowledge.[88] More comprehensive studies regarding the involvement of non-state actors will be done in chapter five.

It should be admitted, though, that public involvement in information collection and exchange is still "rarely a sufficient remedy for the unequal power structures underlying the process".[89] It is further argued that through the process of information exchange, the MRC should be more focused on fostering a "political dialogue between and within riparian countries that is informed by a better understanding of the implications of particular decisions and policy approaches".[90] Combined with the need to collect and share more information on localised water governance experiences and lessons, it is clear that the MRC should take measures to encourage and facilitate more active participation of member states in information exchange, rather than mainly led by the MRC.

### B *Information Acquisition and Exchange under the MRC-China Dialogue Relationship*

Compared to the information system established among four member states of the MRC, relevant cooperation between the MRC and China is still at an initial stage. To date, the only formal outcome is the signing of an agreement in 2002 to provide hydrological information on the Lancang River.[91] However, this information sharing arrangement is limited to a particular time period and very restricted types of information. According to the Agreement, China has provided the MRC Secretariat with daily water level and rainfall data from two

---

87 MRC Summit 2010, *ASEAN, MRC to Boost Cooperation on Mekong Issues* (4 April 2010) <http://www.mrcsummit2010.org/ASEAN-MRC-to-Boost-Cooperation-4-apr-10.htm>.

88 Käkönen and Hirsch, above n 82.

89 Ibid. 351.

90 Ibid.

91 Mekong River Commission, *Upstream Partners* <http://www.mrcmekong.org/about-the-mrc/upstream-partners-2/>.

Lancang monitoring stations during the flood season.[92] For the last decade, the near real-time data provided by China has contributed to water-level monitoring, flood forecasting and mitigation in the lower Mekong region. In August 2013, China renewed this agreement with the MRC and agreed to extend the period of hydrological data sharing and increase the frequency of information exchange during the flood season.[93] Efforts have also been made to expand the data sharing agreement to include dry season levels.[94] During the severe drought in 2010, China agreed to provide water level data from the two dams until the end of the drought.[95] The above information, however, is far from enough to provide a comprehensive information foundation for resolving the hydropower disputes between China and the lower Mekong states.

The biggest legal obstacle for China to share flow information of the Mekong River actually comes from its domestic regulation, according to which the hydrologic data, water resources development and utilisation information, river basin plans and certain information about hydroelectric project are all confidential in the case of a transboundary river, unless certain international agreements exist.[96] While such information is not even accessible to its own public, it is even more difficult to get the Chinese government to share such information with other riparian states and their public. This reflects a rather broad interpretation of protecting information for state security reasons. Within China, however, tension is getting fierce between the current confidentiality of information regarding international rivers and the increasing need for more transparency on government decision-making and the public's right of access to information and participation. This is obvious during China's ongoing dam planning on another international river—Nu River (the upper Salween River)—in which case the Chinese public was denied access

92 The two stations are Yunjinghong and Man'an. Mekong River Commission, *Agreement on Provision of Hydrological Information Renewed by China and MRC* (29 August 2008) <http://www.mrcmekong.org/news-and-events/news/agreement-on-provision-of-hydrological-information-renewed-by-china-and-mrc/>.

93 Mekong River Commission, *Mekong River Commission and China Boost Water Data Exchange* (30 August 2013) <http://www.mrcmekong.org/news-and-events/news/mekong-river-commission-and-china-boost-water-data-exchange/>.

94 Mekong River Commission, above n 91.

95 Bangkok Post, *China to Provide Water Data on Dams* (2010) <http://bangkokpost.newspaperdirect.com/epaper/viewer.aspx>.

96 See《水利工作中国家秘密及其密级具体范围的规定》[Regulations on State Confidentiality in Water Resources Management and its Specific Scope and Security Classification] (People's Republic of China) 水利部及国家保密局 [Ministry of Water Resources and State Secrets Bureau], 29 December 2000, arts 3, 4.

to the strategic environmental assessment report despite a strong demand for the release of relevant information through environmental movements. The increasing domestic demand for transparency has put more pressures on the Chinese government and the current legislation. For the lower Mekong countries, the only possible way to overcome this legal barrier is to achieve further agreements with China on sharing information relating to the Mekong.

China's recent experiences on other transboundary rivers could provide more reference for future prospects of information exchange in the region. In particular, China has signed two bilateral agreements with Kazakhstan and Russia regarding the utilisation and protection of transboundary rivers in 2001 and 2008 respectively.[97] The agreements recognise the principle of equitable and reasonable utilisation and the need to prevent and alleviate significant transboundary harm in the preambles or through general provisions.[98] Joint committees have been established to coordinate and facilitate the implementation of the agreements. Chairmen and members of the committees are selected by each side from national departments, especially the agencies which take main responsibilities on water resources management and environmental protection. With regard to information collection and exchange on a regular basis, both sides agreed to prepare and propose rules on monitoring, share information on monitoring data, arrange joint water research, cooperate on water-related technologies and exchange experiences and measures of transboundary water management.[99]

---

97 China shares several international rivers with Kazakhstan. The key issue concerning the Irtysh River and the Ili River is water allocation. China and Russia share the Heilong River, the Argun River, the Ussuri River, the Suifen River and the Khanka Lake, etc. The major problem for the Heilong River is transboundary water pollution.

98 See《中华人民共和国政府和哈萨克斯坦共和国政府关于利用和保护跨界河流的合作协定》[Cooperation Agreement between China and Kazakhstan on the Utilisation and Protection of Transboundary Rivers], signed 12 September 2001 (entered into force 23 September 2002) preamble, arts 2, 3;《中华人民共和国政府和俄罗斯联邦政府关于合理利用和保护跨界水的协定》[Cooperation Agreement between China and Russia on the Reasonable Utilisation and Protection of Transboundary Waters] (2008) 外交部 [Ministry of Foreign Affairs of the People's Republic of China], preamble <http://www.fmprc.gov.cn/mfa_chn/ziliao_611306/tytj_611312/tyfg_611314/t708160.shtml>.

99 See《中华人民共和国政府和哈萨克斯坦共和国政府关于利用和保护跨界河流的合作协定》[Cooperation Agreement between China and Kazakhstan on the Utilisation and Protection of Transboundary Rivers], signed 12 September 2001 (entered into force 23 September 2002) arts 5, 6;《中华人民共和国政府和俄罗斯联邦政府关于合理利用和保护跨界水的协定》[Cooperation Agreement between China and Russia on the Reasonable Utilisation and Protection of Transboundary Waters] (2008)

Many provisions of the two agreements are quite ambiguous and hortatory. The agreement with Russia is relatively more specific and clearer in terms of the areas of cooperation. The general requirements on information collection and exchange remain to be clarified and more operational guidelines should be made through further cooperation. The information exchange systems under these agreements are also subject to obvious restrictions. For example, in case one side requested for information and data that does not fall into the category agreed by the two parties, the other side should provide such information if conditions allow, but could attach "additional conditions" for the exchange of such information. There is no further clarification on "additional conditions". Compared to the similar arrangements under the UNECE *Water Convention*, there is certainly more room for political bargaining.

In addition, countries are not required under these agreements to provide any information that is viewed as state secrets and the exchange of such information should be subject to other bilateral agreements that specifically address this issue. As mentioned earlier, the requirement for protection of information is not unusual and is included the UNECE *Water Convention* and the environment side agreement of NAFTA. But this restriction should be better combined with detailed requirements on what information should be shared and how. Otherwise, if there is a conflict or uncertainty between the ambiguous commitments on information exchange and the domestic restrictions on information disclosure, the former will have much less chance of being implemented and the actual scope of information exchange will be largely limited in practice. Moreover, unless other agreements exist, all information shared between two countries should be kept as confidential and cannot be provided to a third party. It basically rules out the possibility for the public to have access to such information.

Despite the above disadvantages, at least some progress can be identified in the field. China and Russia established a basic information exchange system through the Joint Committee and regular conferences. They also cooperate on joint monitoring. Initially, a memorandum on joint monitoring of boundary rivers was signed to guide the cooperation during 2002 and 2003.[100] In 2006, it was upgraded into a five-year program (2007–2012) that covers four

---

外交部 [Ministry of Foreign Affairs of the People's Republic of China], arts 2, 4, 5 <http://www.fmprc.gov.cn/mfa_chn/ziliao_611306/tytj_611312/tyfg_611314/t708160.shtml>.

100 新华社 [Xinhua News Agency],《中俄界河水环境联合监测 2005 年启动》[China and Russia Decided to Deepen Cooperation on Joint Monitoring in 2005] (25 September 2004) <http://news.xinhuanet.com/newscenter/2004–09/25/content_2019525.htm>.

transboundary rivers and one transboundary lake.[101] More detailed arrangements are made regarding monitoring locations, joint sampling, timing and frequency of data collection, and the parameters to be analysed. But notable variations do exist in the methods and criteria of evaluation. In March 2012, an outline was signed by two countries to guide the joint monitoring of water quality of the Heilong River from 2012 to 2017.[102] In addition, cooperation will be extended to bio-monitoring in the Songhua River.[103] With regard to the cooperation with Kazakhstan, information exchange on the meteorological data, hydrological data and water quality information is viewed as necessary to provide a scientific foundation for transboundary water allocation. Some minutes documented the common understandings in this area and initial practice can be identified.[104]

The above experiences represent China's gradual progress in information exchange on transboundary water management. Although the relevant agreements and implementations are still incipient and immature in many ways, they can open a door for further developments in information exchange between China and the MRC countries. But China's involvement in transboundary water governance is also dependent on different geopolitical considerations and interests. Due to the varied environmental concerns and development agendas in different river basins, information exchange in the above cases is likely to be less sensitive than the situation in the Mekong region. With regard to the hydropower controversies between China and lower Mekong countries, the domestic classification of state secrets and regional political landscapes remain the major barriers for further information exchange between China and the MRC.

---

101 新华社 [Xinhua News Agency],《中国俄罗斯开展跨界水体水质联合检测》[China and Russia Agreed to Jointly Monitor the Water Quality of Their Transboundary Waters] (29 June 2007) <http://news.xinhuanet.com/society/2007-06/29/content_6306824.htm>.

102 东北网 [Northeast.com],《中俄联合跨界监测界江水质，黑龙江水质趋于好转》[China and Russia Jointly Monitor the Water Quality of Their Transboundary Waters: Water Quality of the Heilong River has Improved] (16 March 2012) <http://heilongjiang.dbw.cn/system/2012/03/16/053748868.shtml>.

103 Ibid.

104 See 水利部综合事业局 [Bureau of Comprehensive Development of the Ministry of Water Resources],《中哈利用和保护跨界河流联合委员会第四次会议在阿拉木图召开》[Fourth Conference of the Joint Committee between China and Kazakhstan on Utilisation and Protection of Transboundary Rivers Held in Alma-Ata] (7 November 2006) <http://www.zhsyj.org.cn/zwgk/ywdt/19893.html>.

Nonetheless, as illustrated in the Rio Grande case, absolute sovereignty has proved to be an outdated and questionable theory, both logically and realistically. Although China recognised the fundamental principles of modern international watercourse law on some level through its transboundary cooperation with Russia and Kazakhstan, the provisions in the agreements and their implementation in the field in fact send out mixed signals. From China's perspective, the above two cases could be counted as the relatively advanced practices so far in terms of transboundary water management. But compared to the best practices in the world, it is obvious that China has a long way to go. The current arrangements reflected in these cases are obviously too soft and insufficient to actually secure a sustainable outcome, especially when there is a strong conflict of interest due to the burgeoning economic development. Even so, as an overall tendency, internal and external pressures will eventually, if not already in some cases, reach a breaking point that China has to cooperate with neighbouring countries more actively on transboundary water issues and increase government transparency for its own citizens rather than denying their rights to know and participate for the convenient excuse of so-called "national security". This is in line with China's domestic trend of political reform and its regional policy to promote closer and more amiable partner relationships with its neighbours. While the Chinese government has promised that China will not pose any threat to the region, it is important for the government to actually present a peaceful, responsible and cooperative image to the world.

With respect to the Mekong issues, China has denied the possibility of a significant negative impact of its Mekong hydrological expansion on the downstream states and its own local communities. But such a promise sounds much less convincing without proper transparency. In light of the status quo, it is argued that China should further enhance cooperation with the lower Mekong countries on monitoring. Providing upstream water level information during the drought season of Mekong could be the next goal.

It should be noted, however, that the current cooperation on information exchange only involves the water resources department in China and the environmental protection agencies have not been involved. The latter also has a monitoring system and is a more credible source for environmental data. The existence of two monitoring systems is generally viewed as a deficiency of China's water governance regime, which often leads to inconsistency of the data and is a huge waste of government resources. Having recognised this situation, it is important to get the environment protection agencies involved in the Mekong cooperation. Precedents could be found in China's cooperation with Russia. Otherwise, there is no way to exchange environmental information such as the data gained from bio-monitoring. The participation of environmental protection sectors may bring some balance of power in transboundary water cooperation between China and the MRC.

To date, the Ministry of Environment Protection in China is already involved in environmental cooperation with ASEAN and both sides are seeking further cooperation on transboundary water issues. In the 2010 Joint Statement on Sustainable Development, China and ASEAN agreed to explore ways of further enhancing exchange of information and experiences. The MRC should develop a more close cooperative connection with ASEAN and the ASEAN-China dialogue relationship. Meanwhile, as a prominent economic cooperation regime in the region, the GMS program could be a good source of information regarding China's development agendas, which is also related to the hydropower development in the lower Mekong countries.

In addition to monitoring data, it is argued that China should deepen its dialogue relationship with the MRC by exchanging more information regarding domestic legislation, measures and policies on water governance, especially those related to the Mekong. The development of trans-sectoral/provincial/municipal cooperation on water issues within China's territory could provide valuable experiences and lessons on how to deal with transboundary water governance at the regional level. Relevant experience should be shared among riparian states and research should be encouraged in this area. This could be a good starting point for information exchange on political and legal arrangements for water governance and the participation of environmental protection agencies is necessary. Meanwhile, cooperation on technology could be another way of information exchange.

Despite the need to break the domestic legal barriers on information exchange through international negotiations, attention will be paid in chapter five on how to improve government transparency at the national level, particularly through enhancing the public's right of access to information and participation. The growing transparency and public involvement will generate more momentum for information exchange at the regional level. Moreover, the mechanisms of information exchange has to be combined with the enhancement of the environmental assessment procedures, which can provide more direct information on hydropower development in the region. This issue will be addressed in chapter six.

CHAPTER 4

# Notification and Consultation in Good Faith

The procedure of notification and consultation in good faith is another important element of procedural mechanisms of transboundary water management. Before any detailed analysis, it is prudent to clarify its application in different circumstances. With regard to notification, other than the obligation to notify the potentially affected states on *planned activities* that may have a significant negative transboundary environmental effect, early notification/warning is viewed as an important initial response to *natural disasters and other emergencies* that might cause transboundary harm. While the former can be implemented during the process of hydropower planning in the region, the latter is applicable in cases like flooding and water pollution accidents.

Consultation is a natural extension of notification. It provides an opportunity for the potentially affected states to review and discuss with the originating states any issues to prevent damage to their territory due to the planned activities, to cooperatively mitigate the impact of emergencies and to seek compensation for human factors in accidents. In the broader sense, consultation on a regular basis is considered as a basic approach to facilitate negotiations on transboundary cooperation and often leads to or assisted by the development of joint bodies and relevant operation rules.[1] In addition, consultation is also useful as a form of public participation. Although the different roles played by consultation are all important and interconnected, this chapter will mainly focus on prior consultation regarding planned activities, since the issue of regular consultation seems too general to be discussed as a unique procedural mechanism and public consultation will be dealt with in chapter five. In addition, consultation can be used as a part of the non-compliance mechanism, which will be addressed in the final chapter.

This chapter is separated into two sections: one is about prior notification and consultation on planned activities and another is with regard to emergency notification and cooperation in its response. Discussions will begin by exploring the rationale of each mechanism, followed by analysis on important international documents. Specific attention will then be paid to the Mekong region, focusing on the existing notification and consultation arrangements

1 See Stephen C. McCaffrey, *The Law of International Watercourses* (Oxford University Press, 2007) 476–7.

 | DOI 10.1163/9789004266797_005

among the lower Mekong countries and the prospects of relevant development between China and other Mekong countries.

## I Prior Notification and Consultation on Planned Activities

### A *Rationale and Key Issues under the International Environmental Law*

Based on the principle of good faith[2] and in the spirit of good neighbourliness,[3] prior notification and consultation on planned activities is considered as an important means of the general obligation to cooperate, the due diligence requirement under the obligation to prevent harm, the obligation of equitable and reasonable utilisation, and more specifically, for avoiding and resolving disputes among riparian states over the benefits and burdens of river development.[4] Other than transboundary water management, it has been applied to deal with other risks posed by activities like nuclear installations near border, continental-shelf operations, dumping and land-based developments that can result in marine pollution, and transboundary air pollution.[5] This is reflected in a variety of treaties, cases, declarations and other hard and soft law documents.[6]

---

2 In the *Lake Lanoux Arbitration*, the Tribunal (Permanent Court of Arbitration) provides an elaboration on the rules of good faith:
"according to the rules of good faith, the upstream State is under the obligation to take into consideration the various interests involved, to seek to give them every satisfaction compatible with the pursuit of its own interests, and to show that in this regard it is genuinely concerned to reconcile the interests of the other riparian State with its own".
*Lake Lanoux Arbitration* (*France v. Spain*) (*Decision*) (1957) 24 ILR 101, 139.

3 Notably, the *Iron Rhine Arbitration* addresses the dispute on whether Netherlands should consult with Belgium before the designation of a nature reserve where Belgium soon proposed a major reactivation programme according to its right of transit under international law. Good neighbourliness is referred to in the award. See generally *Iron Rhine Arbitration* (*Belgium v. Netherlands*) (*Award*) (2005), 27 RIAA 35, 78.

4 McCaffrey, above n 1, 472–3; Patricia Birnie, Alan Boyle and Catherine Redgwell, *International Law and the Environment* (Oxford University Press, 3rd ed, 2009) 177, 565.

5 Birnie, Boyle and Redgwell, above n 4, 178.

6 Such as the *1997 UN Watercourses Convention*, the *1979 Convention on Long-range Transboundary Air Pollution*, the *1972 Convention on the Prevention of Marine Pollution by Dumping of Wastes and other Matter*, the *1991 Espoo Convention*, the *1960 Convention on the Protection of Lake Constance against Pollution*, the *1994 Danube River Protection Convention*, the *1960 Indus Waters Treaty*, the *1995 Mekong Agreement*, the *Pulp Mills Case*, the *North Sea Continental Shelf Cases*, the *Iron Rhine Arbitration*, the *Lake Lanoux Arbitration* and the 1992 Rio Declaration.

In the area of international watercourse law, key issues regarding this mechanism can be concluded as follows:

The first question is in what circumstances notification should be made. The general practice is to require notification for activities that may have a significant adverse environmental impact on other states. This is coherent with the threshold set for the obligation to prevent harm.[7] Although it is widely accepted that the obligation to prevent harm arises if there is a risk of significant harm to the environment, risk identification can be very controversial in practice. In 2001, the International Law Commission adopted the Draft Articles on Prevention of Transboundary Damage from Hazardous Activities, which defines "risk of causing significant transboundary harm" to encompass both "a high probability of causing significant transboundary harm and a low probability of causing disastrous transboundary harm".[8]

In such context, the application of precautionary approach or principle is of immense practical importance. In the area of international watercourse law, it is incorporated in the text of several treaties, including the *UNECE Water Convention* (article 2(5)), 1994 *Danube Convention* (article 2(4)) and the 1999 *Rhine Convention* (article 4). Notably, however, it is not included in the *1997 UN Watercourses Convention*. In fact, the legal status of precautionary principle or approach at the international level remains controversial.[9] As observed by Birnie, Boyle and Redgwell:

> in determining whether and how to apply 'precautionary measures', states have evidently taken account of their own capacities, their economic and social priorities, the cost-effectiveness of proposed measures, and the nature and degree of the environmental risk when deciding what preventive measures to adopt.[10]

Currently, states are generally more willing to be more precautionary about ozone depletion, dumping at sea or whaling than about other international environmental issues.[11] It is still too early to claim that precautionary approach or principle widely applies in assessing due diligence requirement under the obligation to prevent harm.

7 See generally McCaffrey, above n 1, 437–45.

8 *Prevention of Transboundary Harm from Hazardous Activities*, UN GAOR 56th sess, Supp No 10, UN Doc A/56/10 (2001) art 2.

9 Birnie, Boyle and Redgwell, above n 4, 159–64.

10 Ibid. 163.

11 Ibid.

Value judgments about how to respond to environmental risk are also reflected in the development of detailed criteria or in the design of decision-making process. In order to further clarify the word "significant", during the negotiation of an agreement, countries tend to develop some screening standards or list certain kinds of activities as subject to the rules. While notification is often initiated by the proposing state, in case it did not act, some international documents also explicitly entitle the affected state to initiate the process.[12] Through the above consultation process and procedural design, international law provides opportunities for countries to communicate and negotiate in relation to issues on how to respond to environmental risk. With regard to timing, several terms are often referred to in framing the requirement on notification and consultation, namely, "prior", "timely", "at an early stage" or "as early as possible".[13] But most agreements do not provide further explanations of the above wordings. In order to better ensure the meaningfulness of this process, it is argued that this process should be initiated as early as possible before implementation. In addition, time-frame for response and the duration of the consultation period are used to avoid unnecessary postponement. As represented by the *1997 UN Watercourses Convention*, six months are often considered to be a reasonable maximum period for the notified states to reply.[14] According to the International Law Commission Commentaries, this period is left for the notified state to study and evaluate the possible effects of the planned activities.[15] The Convention does allow the notified state to request for an extension of another six months on the ground of "the evaluation of the planned measures poses special difficulty".[16] This provision could be trig-

12 Such as Article 18 of the *1997 UN Watercourses Convention*. It should also be noted that in the *Lake Lanoux Arbitration*, the tribunal observed that "a state wishing to do that which will affect an international watercourse cannot decide whether another state's interests will be affected; the other state is *sole* judge of that and has the right to information on the proposals." See *Lake Lanoux Arbitration* (*France v. Spain*) (*Decision*) (1957) 24 ILR 101, 119.

13 For example, the Principle 19 of the Rio Declaration frames it in the following terms: "States shall provide *prior* and *timely* notification and relevant information to potentially affected States on activities that may have a significant adverse transboundary environmental effect and shall consult with those States *at an early stage* and in good faith". *Report of the United Nations Conference on Environment and Development*, UN Doc A/CONF.151/26 (vol. I) (28 September 1992) (emphasis added).

14 Birnie, Boyle and Redgwell, above n 4, 568.

15 International Law Commission, 'Draft articles on the Law of the Non-navigational Uses of International Watercourses and Commentaries thereto and Resolution on Transboundary Confined Groundwater' (1994) 2(2) *Yearbook of the International Law Commission* 89, 113.

16 *Convention on the Law of the Non-navigational Uses of International Watercourses*, UN GAOR 51/229, 51st sess, Supp No 49, UN Doc A/51/869 (21 May 1997) art 13(b).

gered in case additional time is needed to collect necessary information. But if the states concerned agreed otherwise, the six-month time-frame will not be applied.[17] From the perspective of the notifying state, however, it is less likely that it could agree to a period longer than what stipulated in the Convention.

Failure to respond to notification can be viewed as tacit consent to the proposed activity.[18] In such circumstances, the notifying country is still subject to the obligation of equitable and reasonable utilisation and the obligation to prevent harm.[19] But any claim for compensation by the notified state may be offset by the costs incurred by the notifying state for action which would not have been undertaken if the notified state had objected within the designated period.[20] In addition, a six-month limit is set for the notified country to resolve the matter with the proposed state through consultation, which can be extended if both sides agreed to do so.[21] According to the Commentaries, if countries cannot reach an agreement, the notifying state can only proceed with the implementation of its plans after this period has expired.[22] Therefore, this time-frame is meant to set a minimum standard for consultation period. In fact, as observed by Birnie, Boyle and Redgwell, state practice undoubtedly suggests that the consultation process is often much more protracted than the initial agreement envisages.[23]

Notification should be accompanied by adequate information on proposed activity, which provides the foundation for a meaningful prior consultation. The *UN Watercourses Convention* requires the provision of available technical data and information, including the results of any EIA, to enable the notified states to evaluate the possible effects of the planned activities.[24] But there is no explicit requirement under the Convention for conducting an EIA.[25] Even if the proposed country has conducted an EIA according to its domestic legislation, such a process often does not take into account of any transboundary

---

17 International Law Commission, above n 15.

18 See *Convention on the Law of the Non-navigational Uses of International Watercourses*, UN GAOR 51/229, 51st sess, Supp No 49, UN Doc A/51/869 (21 May 1997) art 16; Charles B. Bourne, 'Procedure in the Development of International Drainage Basins' (1972) 22 *University of Toronto Law Journal* 172, 181.

19 *Convention on the Law of the Non-navigational Uses of International Watercourses*, UN GAOR 51/229, 51st sess, Supp No 49, UN Doc A/51/869 (21 May 1997) art 16(1).

20 Ibid. art 16(2).

21 Ibid. art 17.

22 International Law Commission, above n 15, 116.

23 Birnie, Boyle and Redgwell, above n 4, 570.

24 *Convention on the Law of the Non-navigational Uses of International Watercourses*, UN GAOR 51/229, 51st sess, Supp No 49, UN Doc A/51/869 (21 May 1997) art 12.

25 McCaffrey, above n 1, 475.

impact. The best way to evaluate adverse effect on the notified state, as argued by McCaffrey, is through a transboundary EIA or SEA, with participation of the affected public and other stakeholders.[26] It is clear that there is a close connection among the processes of notification and consultation, transboundary EIA/SEA and public participation. In addition, it can also benefit from a regular exchange of information among riparian states. Information gained through these mechanisms could provide a relatively sound foundation for consultation.

In particular, the implementation of the general obligation to notify and consult on proposed activities should be coordinated with the notification and consultation during the transboundary EIA or SEA process, especially when the latter falls short of detailed regulation. For example, according to the *Espoo Convention*, the state of origin should notify the affected state "as early as possible and no later than when informing its own public about that proposed activity".[27] This stipulation relies on the non-discrimination principle or the principle of equal access[28] and combines the timing issue with the domestic requirements on public's right to know and participate. As a part of the transboundary EIA process, consultation under the *Espoo Convention* is based on the completed transboundary EIA document and is not directly aimed at reaching agreement on proposed activities.

In order to maximise the strengths of these procedural mechanisms, the notification process should be combined with the transboundary EIA or SEA process, which often provides an earlier opportunity for the affected states to participate in decision-making. Consultation under the transboundary EIA or SEA process is more refrained to the factual issues of the potential transboundary environmental effects and measures to reduce or eliminate such an impact.[29] It reflects the attempt to de-politicise disputes by causing parties to focus on the technical issues arising from the proposed activity. But for the general obligation to consult on proposed activities, it should include a broader agenda to reach agreement between the two sides on this particular

26 Ibid. 474–5.

27 *Convention on Environmental Impact Assessment in a Transboundary Context*, opened for signature 25 February 1991, 1989 UNTS 309 (entered into force 10 September 1997) art 3(1).

28 The principle of non-discrimination entails giving equivalent treatment to the domestic and transboundary effects of environmentally harmful activities.

29 *Convention on Environmental Impact Assessment in a Transboundary Context*, opened for signature 25 February 1991, 1989 UNTS 309 (entered into force 10 September 1997) art 5. This issue will be further discussed in chapter six.

matter. In addition, since the *Espoo Convention* does not explicitly require consultation prior the completion of the EIA report, it is argued that the consultation process should be encouraged and welcomed before that. The Convention also allows the notified state to request for additional information, but only when it is "available" and "necessary" for an "accurate evaluation".[30] If the necessary information is not yet available, according to the provision on regular exchange of data, the requested state should comply with the request in its best efforts but may condition its compliance on payment for the extra costs.[31] Again, there could be potential conflicts with the six-month time-frame set for consultation. Further, similar to the mechanism of information exchange, the provision of information through the notification process can be subject to limitations on protection of information under domestic legislation. Although the Convention requires the notifying states to actively provide additional information, the time-frame and the convenient excuse of national security can in fact serve as disincentives for them to do so.

During the notification and consultation period, the state proposing the activity should refrain from implementing or permitting the implementation of the planned activities.[32] The aim of consultation process is to achieve a solution regarding the proposed activity.[33] But as argued by Birnie, Boyle and Redgwell, an obvious shortcoming in this approach is that finding a solution to the dispute may depend on the ability to negotiate one.[34] In 1997, the International Court of Justice (ICJ) ordered in the *Gabčíkovo-Nagymaros Case* that both sides should "find an agreed solution within the cooperative context of the Treaty".[35] However, no such agreement had been concluded at the time of writing.[36] When negotiations are unsuccessful, although the proposed country is still required to take due account for the interests of affected state, the latter does not have the veto power against the decision.[37] As reflected

30 *Convention on the Law of the Non-navigational Uses of International Watercourses*, UN GAOR 51/229, 51st sess, Supp No 49, UN Doc A/51/869 (21 May 1997) art 14.

31 Ibid. art 9.

32 Ibid. arts 14(b), 17(3).

33 This is reflected in Article 17 of the *UN Watercourses Convention* and Article 11 of the *Danube River Protection Convention*. See also Owen McIntyre, *Environmental Protection of International Watercourses under Interna tional Law* (Ashgate Publishing Group, 2007) 337; Birnie, Boyle and Redgwell, above n 4, 569.

34 Birnie, Boyle and Redgwell, above n 4, 179.

35 *Gabčíkovo-Nagymaros Project (Hungary/Slovakia) (Judgment)* [1997] ICJ Rep 7, 78.

36 Birnie, Boyle and Redgwell, above n 4, 179.

37 See *Lake Lanoux Arbitration (France v. Spain) (Decision)* (1957) 24 ILR 101, 128–141; Frederic L. Kirgis, Jr., *Prior Consultation in International Law* (University Press of Virginia, 1983) 361.

in the *Lake Lanoux Arbitration*, the international law supports neither the theory of absolute territorial sovereignty nor the principle of absolute territorial integrity.[38] While some form of prior consent is required in several areas of international environmental law, such as the transportation and disposal of hazardous wastes, it only applies when one country actually seeks to act through or within the territory of another.[39]

In regards to international watercourse law, when countries fail to reach a consensus through consultation, the proposed state can proceed with the project, but remains bound by the obligation to prevent harm and the principle of equitable and reasonable utilisation.[40] If significant transboundary harm eventually happened due to the activity under dispute, the proposed country may find it in a more unfavourable place to justify its behaviour according to the due diligence requirement. But since many negative environmental effects are unlikely to be irreversible, the sole reliance on consultation and consensus-building as an approach to seek resolution to the proposed activity often falls short of enough strength to deliver sustainable outcome in practice. In the cases when countries do reach an agreement to allow the implementation of the proposed activity, it is suggested that the decision should be accompanied by measures to prevent, monitor and mitigate environmental impact.

The following study will incorporate the above discussion into a detailed analysis on the status quo of prior notification and consultation in the Mekong region, focusing on the content and implementation of the relevant procedural document and guideline of the Mekong River Commission (MRC). In addition, the prospect of developing such mechanism between China and the lower Mekong countries will be considered.

## B *Prior Notification and Consultation Process in the Mekong Region*

### 1 The MRC Prior Notification and Consultation Process: A Theoretical Analysis

Prior notification and consultation is expressly required under Article 5 of the *1995 Mekong Agreement*[41] and is elaborated by a specific yet non-binding

38 Absolute territorial integrity means that the upstream state cannot affect the natural flow of the water into the downstream state unless the latter give the consent to do so. See generally McCaffrey, above n 1, 126–33.

39 See David Hunter, James Salzman and Durwood Zaelke, *International Environmental Law and Policy* (Foundation Press, 3rd ed, 2007) 528–9.

40 International Law Commission, above n 15, 116.

41 *Agreement on the Cooperation for the Sustainable Development of the Mekong River Basin*, opened for signature 5 April 1995, 2069 UNTS I-35844 (entered into force 5 April 1995) art 5.

procedural document (Procedures for Notification, Prior Consultation and Agreement) and an implementation guideline prepared by the MRC Council and Joint Committee respectively. Among the guiding principles stated in the procedural document, there is no explicit reference to the obligation to prevent harm. To a large extent, it is implied through the principle of equitable and reasonable utilisation and the respect for rights and legitimate interests.[42] In addition, the principle of good faith and transparency is highlighted to guide the process.[43] Notably, prior notification in the context of the Mekong region is not just a prerequisite for consultation. Rather, it also serves as a general approach to collect and exchange information on intra-basin uses and inter-basin diversions on both tributaries and mainstream of the Mekong River. The following research will focus on notification and consultation on proposed projects that may have a significant negative impact to other riparian states. Notification in emergency situations, as required by Article 10 of the Agreement, will be addressed separately.

With regard to threshold setting, instead of imposing a general requirement on projects with a potential significant transboundary impact, the MRC documents enumerates several kinds of projects that are ought to go through this process before implementation.[44] If any proposed country failed to initiate this process, the MRC Joint Committee can request its National Mekong Committee (NMC) to fulfil the duty.[45] This, however, only includes developments on the Mekong mainstream river, while tributary river developments are completely left out of the mechanism. Although it is obvious that mainstream development certainly have a higher potential for a more serious transboundary impact, such stipulation does significantly reduce the scope of application of this mechanism and more generally limits the impact of the MRC on tributary Mekong river development, which also triggers more and more transboundary disputes among riparian states and may have an accumulation effect on the mainstream river.

---

42 Mekong River Commission, *Procedures for Notification, Prior Consultation and Agreement* (30 November 2003), art 3 <http://www.mrcmekong.org/assets/Publications/policies/Procedures-Notification-Prior-Consultation-Agreement.pdf>.

43 Ibid.

44 See ibid. art 5(1). According to Article 5(1) of the Procedures, three types of development are subject to consultation, namely the inter-basin diversion from mainstream during wet season; the intra-basin use on the mainstream during the dry season; and the inter-basin diversion of the surplus quantity of water during the dry season.

45 Ibid. art 5(6).

For example, the proposed Sesan 2 Dam located in north-eastern Cambodia is alleged to have a significant negative impact (especially on fish species), not only to Cambodia, but also to the Mekong Delta in Vietnam and the middle Mekong River in Laos and Thailand.[46] Not requiring such tributary dams to go through a prior consultation process in fact left out a major part of hydropower expansion in the region. While Vietnam and Cambodia have expressly urged more comprehensive transboundary EIA of the Xayaburi Dam in Laos, they themselves are reluctant to apply the same standards to the tributaries dams located in their territories that may also have a significant transboundary impact. The selective policy implementation raises doubt over the political willingness for genuine embracement of environmental discourses in the region, particularly considering the existing geo-political concerns. Given the early stage of river basin cooperation in the region, however, one may argue that the limited implementation of the mechanism at this stage is realistic compromise considering the priority issues in the region. During the negotiation of the *Mekong Agreement*, Article 5 was fiercely debated and its three-scenario standard for threshold setting has been criticised for a number of conceptual inconsistencies.[47] The current threshold requirement for prior consultation set according to Article 5 is at least better than nothing, even though it is not in the form of legally-binding rules. Along with its implementation, there may be more pressure on the tributary dams to adopt more stringent environmental standards and more environmental awareness can be raised among the public regarding these projects.

The MRC procedural document further elaborates on the content of notification by requiring the provision of a feasibility study report, implementation plan, schedule and *all other available* technical data and information on the proposed activity for the notified states to evaluate its impact.[48] Only in the guideline is the *summary* of impact assessment documents expressly required.[49] The impact assessment here is not limited to transboundary environmental effects (the available summary information on any transboundary

46 Ian G. Baird, 'Best Practices in Compensation and Resettlement for Large Dams: The Case of the Planned Lower Sesan 2 Hydropower Project in Northeastern Cambodia' (Report, River Coalition in Cambodia, 2009) 14.

47 See Greg Browder, 'An Analysis of the Negotiations for the 1995 Mekong Agreement' (2000) 5 *International Negotiations* 237, 253–5.

48 Mekong River Commission, above n 42, arts 4(2), 5(2) (emphasis added).

49 Mekong River Commission, *Guidelines on Implementation of the Procedures for Notification, Prior Consultation and Agreement* (31 August 2005), 5 <http://www.mrcmekong.org/assets/Publications/policies/Guidelines-on-implementation-of-the-PNPCA.pdf> (emphasis added).

social impact should be provided as well). The notified states also have the right to request for additional information and even a field visit to the project site in order to better evaluate the possible impact of the proposed use.[50] Correspondingly, however, the notifying state is only required to provide *available* data based on such request.[51] Confusingly, the guideline interprets the requirement of providing "all available data" as an effort to provide "sufficient relevant data, meaning the data *necessary* for the notified parties to be informed of and to understand the proposed project and use of water to determine impacts upon them".[52] While it seems to indicate that the notifying state should make efforts to collect and provide the information that is not yet available, this process could easily go beyond the six-month time-frame and the notifying state may refuse to extend it. In addition, political and scientific controversies remain as to whether certain information is necessary or not and the relevant information could be subject to the protection of information under domestic legislation. Since there is no general obligation or detailed guidelines for the Mekong countries to conduct a transboundary EIA or SEA, it is doubtful whether the available information on Mekong mainstream projects is sufficient and adequate enough to evaluate the transboundary effects.

Although transparency is viewed as a guiding principle for this process, the existing procedural requirements on notification and consultation fails to incorporate requirements to ensure the public's right of access to relevant information and participate in the evaluation process. Given the limited domestic political opportunity for public participation in the region, the opinions of affected local communities on the proposed project are often difficult to be heard. This represents another kind of necessary information that may not be available by the time of notification. Although there is an increasing recognition of public participation in the region and it is reflected in many of the MRC programs and initiatives,[53] domestic and regional legal protection in this respect remains highly restrained, with an exception of Thailand. This problem will be further discussed in the Xayaburi case study.

In light of the above uncertainty on the content of information, the time-frame set by the procedural document may in fact pose further problems in practice. The notification is required to be initiated in "a timely manner

---

50 Mekong River Commission, above n 42, art 5(4).

51 Ibid. (emphasis added).

52 Mekong River Commission, above n 49, n 8 (emphasis added).

53 For example, this is reflected in the MRC Strategy (2007–2011), the Basin Development Plan Programme and the SEA of mainstream dams.

prior to implementation".[54] Combined with the six-month time-frame set for consultation,[55] the notification should be made at least six months before implementation. In fact, the guideline further suggests the notification process to be initiated at a much earlier time in practice due to the considerable analysis required to evaluate the impact of mainstream projects.[56] While the *Espoo Convention* resorts to the non-discrimination principle to solve this issue, the linkage between notifying the affected states and its own public may not necessarily be a realistic choice for the Mekong region at this stage, for most Mekong countries still fall short of adequate transparency and public involvement during the domestic decision-making process. This issue will be further considered in chapter six. Based on the guideline, it is suggested that a more suitable interpretation is that notification process here (namely, not as a process during the transboundary EIA) should be initiated "as early as possible" before implementation.

The time-frame for consultation is set for six months, but an extended period can be granted by a unanimous decision of the MRC Joint Committee. Different from the setting under the *UN Watercourses Convention*, there is no six-month period (maximum one year) granted for the notified state to reply and the consultation process is triggered almost immediately after the notification documents are received and processed.[57] While it is clear that all projects subject to the mechanism have to go through the consultation process after the notification, the requirement here indeed shortens the whole process to a mere period of half year, which is very likely to be insufficient without any extension.

During this process, the notifying state should not implement the proposed activity.[58] According to the Commentaries on the UN Watercourses Convention, this covers "not only measures planned by the state, but also those planned by private entities".[59] However, there is a fine line between preparation works and actual implementation of the main project. The current arrangements are not clear on this issue. In addition, as illustrated in chapter two, the relevant infrastructure development, such as the construction of an electricity transmission

---

54 Mekong River Commission, above n 42, art 4(5).

55 Ibid. art 5(5).

56 Mekong River Commission, above n 49.

57 Mekong River Commission, above n 42, art 5(5). According to the guideline, the internal processing alone under the MRC Secretariat could take up to one month. Mekong River Commission, above n 49, n 15.

58 Mekong River Commission, above n 42, art 5(4).

59 International Law Commission, above n 15, 111.

line and the improvement of transportation to the proposed project site, are often initiated separately from the proposed project and the economic interests involved will urge the permission for the proposed project, not to mention the fact that the MRC has little influence on their decision-making process. The project-based notification and consultation process under the MRC platform does not have enough leverage to influence such uncoordinated and scattered development.

The initial purpose for setting a time-frame is to avoid unnecessary delay, since states are not really forbidden from creating sources of risk to others.[60] It provides an opportunity for the notifying state to end the consultation process without reaching agreement on the proposed project. The procedural document does expressly stipulate that consultation is "neither a right to veto the use nor unilateral right to use water by any riparian without taking into account other riparian's rights".[61] But other than encouraging states to reach a resolution on the proposed project, the MRC procedural document does not expressly clarify the issue of whether a consultation process will automatically come to an end if no agreement can be reached and the notifying country refuses to extend it. The Commentaries on the UN Watercourses Convention implies that while consensus is required for countries to extend the consultation process, the decision to end the process after the minimum six-month consultation period does not require consensus.[62] According to the *UN Watercourses Convention*, after a six-month consultation, the notifying state can proceed with the project but is still obliged to comply with the general obligations under international watercourses law. But in light of the considerable analysis required during the process, the shorter period of the whole process under the MRC procedural document compared to the requirements under the *UN Watercourses Convention* and the common phenomenon of extension in other state practices, such behaviour can raise reasonable doubt on whether the notifying state indeed followed the principle of cooperation in good faith and complied with the due diligence requirement, or just merely treated the process as a necessary formality to go through.

Nonetheless, even if countries cannot reach a resolution within six months and the notifying state refused to extend the consultation, there is another provision under the *Mekong Agreement* requiring states to settle disputes through

60 Birnie, Boyle and Redgwell, above n 4, 179.

61 Mekong River Commission, above n 42, art 1.

62 International Law Commission, above n 15, 116.

negotiation.[63] However, it is not clear whether countries have to suspend the implementation of the project during the dispute settlement process. It should be noted that while in some other cases, the notified state may also resort to other forms of dispute settlement, such as arbitration and judicial settlement, the Mekong regional cooperation regime is solely reliant on diplomatic means to settle dispute.[64] The reluctance for countries to relinquish some sovereignty to any international tribunal is not unusual and it is even less likely for the Mekong countries to seek judicial resolution in the face of settling the issue in the traditional "ASEAN Way". In addition, the immature domestic judicial systems in many Mekong Countries fail to provide a domestic platform for environmental protection which plays an important role in resolving environmental issues that may have a significant transboundary impact, for example, the case of the Rhine basin.[65] At the domestic level, there is limited opportunity in both political and legal contexts within most Mekong countries for launching administrative or civil cases against administrative agencies or enterprises involved in hydropower decision-making. Although Thailand has made more progress on this issue, it is difficult to prove a Thai court has the jurisdiction to hear such case, for most hydropower projects are located outside its territory. At the time of writing, some NGOs and public interest lawyers are trying to bring the Xayaburi Dam issue to court, targeting at the approval given by the Thai Cabinet permitting the Electricity Generating Authority of Thailand (EGAT) to sign the power purchase agreement with the Xayaburi project developer necessary to move the project forward. This case will be further discussed in chapter five.

## 2 The Implementation of Prior Notification and Consultation Process in the Xayaburi Case

According to the *Mekong Agreement*, all lower Mekong mainstream dam proposals must go through the prior notification and consultation process. Despite some preliminary information on these projects, this process had not

63 *Agreement on the Cooperation for the Sustainable Development of the Mekong River Basin*, opened for signature 5 April 1995, 2069 UNTS I-35844 (entered into force 5 April 1995) arts 34, 35.

64 See ibid. art 35.

65 Both the national courts and the European Court of Justice have the jurisdiction and powers to hear civil actions regarding the damage occurring in downstream states. For example, chlorides pollution in the Rhine basin has been the subject of several civil actions in national courts and before the European Court of Justice. See Birnie, Boyle and Redgwell, above n 4, 575; McCaffrey, above n 1, 301–2.

been triggered until an official submission was made to the MRC Secretariat by the Lao government regarding the Xayaburi Dam on 20 September 2010. The consultation process officially started on 22 October 2010 and a MRC Joint Committee Working Group was established to guide the MRC Secretariat and report to the Joint Committee.[66]

The Ch. Karnchang (one of Thailand's largest construction companies), in conjunction with the Lao government, has been working on the development of the Xayaburi Dam, the furthest advanced mainstream project in the lower Mekong region since 2007. At least four Thai banks have expressed their interest in funding the project. Opponents, however, have argued that this dam will have devastating effects on important fish habitats and block natural sediment flows in the Mekong River to the detriment of downstream agriculture.[67]

Along with the notification, the Lao NMC provided reports conducted by the project developer, including a feasibility study, an EIA report and a social impact assessment report.[68] These reports were then heavily criticised over very limited geographical coverage within Laos (not to mention the lack of consideration of transboundary effects) and failure to consider many necessary indicators and factors.[69] In addition to the information provided by the Lao NMC, the MRC Secretariat established a task group as a cooperative mechanism among the MRC programs to undertake a technical review on the transboundary impact of the Xayaburi project and external experts also contributed to the final review report. The report further incorporates two important reports developed or commissioned by the MRC, namely the Basin Development Strategy and the SEA of hydropower on the lower Mekong mainstream. In particular, the SEA process had gone through a 16-month period of evaluation and was completed right before the start of the consultation process. Notable information gaps and uncertainties were expressly stressed in these findings and the SEA report specifically recommends a 10-year deferral

66 Mekong River Commission, *Proposed Xayaburi Hydropower Project Prior Consultation Process* <http://www.mrcmekong.org/news-and-events/consultations/proposed-xayaburi-hydropower-project-prior-consultation-process/>.

67 International Rivers, *Xayaburi Dam* <http://www.internationalrivers.org/campaigns/xayaburi-dam>.

68 The Lao government also provided two plans on environmental management and resettlement.

69 See Eric Baran et al., 'Review of the Fish and Fisheries Aspects in the Feasibility Study and the Environmental Impact Assessment of the Proposed Xayaburi Dam' (Report, World Wildlife Fund, 2011).

for mainstream hydropower development.[70] Due to the above reviews and findings, Cambodia, Thailand and Vietnam called for further study and consultation beyond the six-month limit. Similar concerns were also raised at the public consultation meetings held in these countries.

While it is clear that Cambodia and Vietnam, as the downstream states, certainly hold a negative position on the Xayaburi Dam, it is interesting to notice the standpoint of Thailand on this issue. The Department of Water Resources in the Ministry of Natural Resources and Environment in Thailand raised concerns in public forums that the sustainability of the project is still questionable and that the stipulated time-frame for the prior consultation process should be extended.[71] The Thai representative of the MRC Joint Committee is also from this ministry and officially supports an extension of the prior consultation study and the conducting of further studies. This reflects the political wrestling within Thailand between the Ministry of Natural Resources and Environment and the EGAT, which is in favour of the project.

Due to the wide divergences on relevant issues, by the end of the six-month period, the Lao government and three other member states could not agree on whether the Xayaburi Dam can be properly constructed with a necessary safeguard to the environment, nor could they reach an agreement to extend the consultation period. Finally, they decided to table the issue for consideration at the ministerial level through the MRC Council.[72] At the MRC Council meeting in December 2011, the countries agreed to postpone the decision on the Xayaburi until a joint study on the transboundary impact of the Mekong mainstream dams was carried out.[73] Although this appeared to be a positive signal at the time, this result did not explicitly address the issue of whether the prior consultation process is extended pending further study.

---

70 See generally International Centre for Environmental Management, 'Strategic Environmental Assessment of Hydropower on the Mekong Mainstream: Final Report' (SEA Report, ICEM, 2010).

71 Factual information in this paragraph is based on news release available on the Mekong River Commission website. Mekong River Commission, *Lower Mekong Countries Take Prior Consultation on Xayaburi Project to Ministerial Level* (19 April 2011) <http://www.mrcmekong.org/news-and-events/news/lower-mekong-countries-take-prior-consultation-on-xayaburi-project-to-ministerial-level/>.

72 Ibid.

73 World Wildlife Fund Cambodia, *Xayaburi Dam Delay Pending Further Studies is a Positive Step* (8 December 2012) <http://m.cambodia.panda.org/news_cambodia/?202755/Xayaburi-dam-delay-pending-further-studies-is-a-positive-step>.

Technically speaking, the Lao government does have a point in arguing the process was ended based on the current arrangements. As mentioned earlier, an extended period of consultation should be permitted by the decision of the MRC Joint Committee. Therefore, failure to reach a unanimous decision on this matter in April 2011 can be viewed as the end of the consultation process. Also, the current requirements do not impose a clear obligation on the notifying state to provide information that is not yet available. Further, according to the *Mekong Agreement*, what was triggered by the Joint Committee's decision to refer the issue to the Council is indeed a separate dispute settlement process.[74]

Following this logic, while the Mekong countries are no longer subject to specific obligations and restrictions under the prior consultation process, the Lao government is still bound by the obligation to prevent harm and the principle of equitable and reasonable utilisation. While countries can argue that ignoring the obvious information gaps and uncertainties should be viewed as a breach of the due diligence requirement, there are limited legal measures at the regional level to secure the implementation of these general obligations. Moreover, the construction of the Xayaburi Dam will very likely trigger a domino effect on the construction of other mainstream dams. Once the existence of these dams became a *fait accompli*, even if they did have a significant adverse impact on the downstream states, it is unlikely the damage will be reversed and consequently the whole regime fails according the standard established by the precautionary and preventive principles.

With regard to suspension of the project, advocates have criticised that the initial stages of construction at the site have already forced some of the local population to relocate and the preparation work has already been in progress for more than a year.[75] This observation was later confirmed by an official statement from the Lao government issued on 19 November 2012, which states that "the first stage of construction has begun in late 2010 and is currently on going which includes preparatory infrastructure works, right bank coffer dams, navigation locks, spillway, sediment flushing outlets, and an intermediate block".[76]

---

74 See *Agreement on the Cooperation for the Sustainable Development of the Mekong River Basin*, opened for signature 5 April 1995, 2069 UNTS I-35844 (entered into force 5 April 1995) art 18(c).

75 Voice of America, *Thai Company Says Work on Disputed Dam Has Started* (19 April 2012) <http://blogs.voanews.com/breaking-news/2012/04/19/thai-company-says-work-on-disputed-dam-has-started/>.

76 Department of Energy Business, *19th November 2012—Statement of the Government of Lao PDR on Xayaburi Hydropower Project* (2012) <http://www.poweringprogress.org/index

It is obvious that the so-called "suspension" of the project during the consultation process in fact did not have much real impact.

The attempt to end the Xayaburi consultation process triggered strong protests from downstream states and civil society groups, citing the beforementioned Council decision or alleging that the Lao government cannot unilaterally end the consultation process. Since there is no satisfactory procedural arrangement left available to address the Xayaburi issue at the regional level, there is a desperate need to hang on to the consultation process as an important political strategy to gain more leverage and win more time for downstream states and dam opponents to take the next step.

These heated disagreements were finally dealt with by the Lao government. While reaffirming that the prior consultation process had ended in April 2011, it also reassured the opponents that the construction of the project will not proceed "before gaining *approval* from the international community and in particular the downstream countries".[77] It then stated that the ongoing work on the site was only for preparation, mostly in the primary and exploration stage.[78] At first glance, the above statement appears to suggest that the downstream countries have some sort of veto power against the decision to proceed with the Xayaburi Project. As mentioned earlier, however, the requirement for prior consent under international environmental law is in fact limited to the situation when one country actually sought to carry out activities within the territory of another.[79] The Lao government's statement here does not reflect general international practice. Considering the fact that the *Mekong Agreement* specifically clarifies that prior consultation is not a veto right for the affected states, it would be unnecessary for the Lao government to end the consultation process while committing to a more stringent restriction. A realistic interpretation, as held by many civil society groups in the field, is that this is just another typical Southeast Asian way of face saving, instead of a serious legal commitment. This is in line with the tradition of avoiding open and public disagreement among the ASEAN countries.

---

.php?option=com_content&view=article&id=947:19th-november-2012-statement-of-the-government-of-lao-pdr-on-xayaburi-hydropower-project&catid=85:press-releases&Itemid=50>.

77 Supalak Ganjanakhundee, *Laos: No Work on Xayaburi Dam until Green Concerns Solved* (4 May 2012) The Nation <http://www.nationmultimedia.com/politics/Laos-no-work-on-Xayaburi-dam-until-green-concerns--30181251.html> (emphasis added).

78 Ibid.

79 See Hunter, Salzman and Zaelke, above n 39.

Since the current regional arrangements cannot suspend the preparation work, both on the site and with respect to commercial arrangements, the increasing economic interests involved will continue to move the project forward. Although the Lao government's statement still maintains a strong feature of the "ASEAN Way", there are increasing open disagreements on this issue by the other member states. The controversial nature of the mainstream Mekong development continues to challenge the comfort level of consultation and test the limits of the "ASEAN Way" in resolving disputes. As discussed in chapter two, the "ASEAN Way" has proved to be less effective when dealing with issues involving opposing interests. As the situation gets more intense, the entrenched "ASEAN Way" and the emerging rules-based and people-oriented way of regional cooperation will continue to influence the dam debate.

Although theoretical analysis suggests that the Lao government should agree to extend the consultation period due to the due diligence consideration, there is no legal approach available to impose it in practice. It is clear that, in the Xayaburi case, the Lao government managed to circumvent the restrictions under the current MRC arrangements. Combined with the fact that the MRC decisions and procedural documents are not legally-binding in nature, there are few legal avenues available to promote sustainable development of hydropower in the region.

In addition to the aforementioned deficiencies of this mechanism in the context of the Mekong region, what is also exemplified in this case is the lack of proper support from other procedural mechanisms, including information exchange, the public's right of access to information and participation and transboundary EIA and SEA. As identified during the Xayaburi Dam prior consultation process, the current information collection and exchange system in the lower Mekong region cannot provide necessary information on the transportation of sediment due to the failure to include all size fractions and nutrients.[80] Uncertainties are particularly significant with regard to sediment yields, sediment properties and the potential geomorphic responses to altered sediment loads.[81] Moreover, due to the difficulties of conducting relevant research and a lack of investment, a shortage of sufficient empirical information on how important the area is to fish migration in terms of biomass and

80 Colin Thorne et al., 'Review of Sediment Transport, Morphology, and Nutrient Balance' (Sediment Experts Group Report, Mekong River Commission, 2011) 19.

81 Mekong River Commission Secretariat, 'Proposed Xayaburi Dam Project: MRCS Prior Consultation Project Review Report' (Report, Mekong River Commission, 2011) 54.

species diversity also results in huge information uncertainty regarding the evaluation on the impact on aqua species.[82]

Although not required by the notification and consultation documents, public participation was included as part of the process.[83] But the implementation varies a lot across the region. In Thailand, where there is a relatively more open political culture and more legal protection for public participation, the participants are mainly constituted by NGOs and community groups. In Cambodia and Vietnam, however, the process is in fact dominated by officials and experts. Many local communities still fall short of proper awareness of the mainstream dam issue. It reflects the limited influence of civil society on their domestic decision-making processes. In the case of Laos, the stakeholder participation during the preparation of the project was more focused on resettlement instead of the environmental impact.

In addition to public consultation facilitated by member states, the MRC launched a webpage to allow public comments on the development of hydropower projects in the lower Mekong region and a series of conferences were held outside the framework of MRC with the participation of academic and research instructions, NGOs and representatives of community groups.[84] These conferences could help raise the public's awareness of the hydropower development issue and facilitate a valuable network among academics, NGOs and local communities. While relevant work in this area can certainly lay a better foundation for public participation, without more political freedom and opportunities, it is still difficult to really empower the civil society in the decision-making process. Despite the general political and legal restrictions, more specific problems can also be identified during the Xayaburi public consultation process. This includes, but not limited to, a lack of timely release of information before consultation; language barriers and the lack of availability of some documents in local languages; the involvement of public is not early enough in the prior consultation process; and the lack of effective communication between the project developer and the affected public during the participation.[85]

Another important issue is the relationship between prior notification and consultation and transboundary EIA and SEA. As demonstrated before,

82 Ibid. 39.

83 See Mekong River Commission Secretariat, 'Prior Consultation Project Review Report Volume 2: Stakeholder Consultations related to the Proposed Xayaburi Dam Project' (Report, Mekong River Commission, 2011).

84 Ibid. 16–7.

85 See ibid. 17–8.

transboundary EIA or SEA is the best way to evaluate the transboundary environmental impact. The ICJ even considers transboundary EIA as a necessary element of the due diligence requirement under the obligation to prevent harm.[86] For countries that already embraced the *Espoo Convention* and the *SEA Protocol*, such development disputes can be dealt with based on rather detailed regulations on the EIA and SEA processes, which also incorporate a notification and consultation process. Notably, the judgment of the *Pulp Mills Case* considers transboundary EIA as a requirement under general international law for proposed industrial activities that may have a significant transboundary adverse impact.[87] But the Court also argues that the scope and content of an EIA are not specified by general international law.[88] For countries that are not bound by relevant international agreements, these issues are left for each state to decide in its domestic legislation or on a case by case basis.[89] In the context of the Mekong region, although a SEA report has been done, the process falls short of necessary regional requirements and relevant domestic legal support is also insufficient. Moreover, the SEA report only considers the lower Mekong mainstream hydropower development as a whole and does not specifically address the transboundary impact of the Xayaburi Dam. In April 2012, Japan agreed to fund the study on the transboundary impact (not limited to environmental effects) of the Xayaburi Dam which was agreed by the lower Mekong countries in the form of the MRC Council decision in 2011.[90] But there are no regional requirements on when a transboundary EIA should be conducted and how. A transboundary EIA or SEA is not just about scientific research, it also aims at getting the affected states and their public involved in the decision-making process. Simply conducting transboundary EIA research can do little to resolve the dispute. In addition, since the Lao government did not adopt the conclusions of the SEA report, it is unlikely that this transboundary EIA research at the last minute will make any real change. In fact, on 5 November 2012, the Lao government officially approved the Xayaburi project and formal groundbreaking ceremony was held two days later.[91] It is unclear

86 *Pulp Mills on the River Uruguay* (*Argentina v Uruguay*) (*Judgment*) [2010] ICJ Rep 14, para 204.

87 Ibid.

88 Ibid. para 205.

89 Ibid.

90 Phnom Penh Post, *Xayaburi Study Locks in Funding* (23 April 2012) Eco-Business <http://www.eco-business.com/news/xayaburi-study-locks-in-funding/>.

91 Reuters, *Laos Holds Groundbreaking Ceremony for Contentious Mekong Dam* (7 November 2012) <http://www.reuters.com/article/2012/11/07/us-laos-dam-idUSBRE8A618I20121107>.

if that transboundary EIA study was in fact done, not to mention be discussed by the member states. Following this decision, the Lao government notified the MRC on 3 October 2013 with regard to the decision to proceed with the Don Sahong Dam from November 2013. Although it is generally viewed as a Mekong mainstream project, the Lao government only notified it to the MRC as a tributary dam project,[92] which does not require prior consultation with the other MRC countries under the MRC Procedures for Notification, Prior Consultation and Agreement. This of course, triggered another round of fierce debates in the region. It should be pointed out that the divergence of opinions on this issue is more focused on scientific aspects instead of on the prior consultation process itself.

In fact, the Xayaburi issue itself seems a bit too big for the MRC to deal with effectively. The infrastructure development that is directly linked to the Xayaburi Dam, such as the electricity transmission line and road, is completely out of the MRC's control. These projects are decided separately either through the GMS program or solely by the Lao government, with limited environmental requirements imposed on them. The unbalanced and fractured development of environmental protection at both domestic and regional level has proved to be difficult to integrate environmental concerns with economic development.

Based on the Xayaburi case, one can conclude that without more support from other procedural and substantive mechanisms within or outside the MRC regime, the prior notification and consultation process under the MRC alone is not enough to resolve the hydropower disputes in the region. This is further complicated by the non-binding nature of the process itself and the existing deficiencies and uncertainties of the procedural documents on this issue. In order to improve the implementation of this process for other lower Mekong mainstream projects, it is suggested that more procedural arrangements should be developed in the region, particularly with regard to public participation and transboundary EIA. Relevant domestic legislation should be improved as well. In addition, it is necessary to review the MRC documents regarding prior notification and consultation to formally clarify the existing uncertainties and negotiate on possible changes of the process, especially with regard to the time-frame set in the procedural document and interpretations

---

92 Mekong River Commission, *Lao PDR Submits Notification on Don Sahong Hydropower Project* (3 October 2013) <http://www.mrcmekong.org/news-and-events/news/lao-pdr-submits-notification-on-don-sahong-hydropower-project/>. The map included in this news report illustrates the site of the proposed Don Sahong dam. It is generally viewed that this dam is located on a branch of the Mekong mainstream, instead of on a Mekong tributary river.

on what conducts should be suspended during the process. Since there is no immediate danger that the member states will completely ignore this procedure or obviously violate the current procedural document, the non-binding nature of the current detailed arrangements does not seem to be much of a problem for now and may make it easier for countries to agree on further amendments. But over the longer term, upgrading these arrangements to a formal agreement and expanding its scope of application should be considered.

### 3 Prospects of Introducing Prior Notification and Consultation Process between China and the Lower Mekong Countries

Compared to the situation in the lower Mekong region, China's record on prior notification and consultation for proposed projects on transboundary rivers is almost zero. In particular, China's eight-dam cascade plan on middlestream and downstream of Lancang River has never been formally notified to other riparian states. It was not until the mid-1990s that there was any general awareness of its scope,[93] by then the first dam (Manwan) was almost completed and the construction of the second one (Dachaoshan) was about to begin. In the 1980s and 1990s, environmental protection in China was still quite rudimentary, with a brief requirement for EIA in *1989 Environmental Protection Law* and some administrative rules and guidelines in place for conducting an EIA. No form of SEA was required at the time. As mentioned in chapter three, information regarding a water utilisation plan on transboundary rivers is labelled as confidential. In addition, due to the remoteness of Yunnan Province and the high-profile economic development in the coastal areas, China's hydropower development on the upper reaches of the Mekong River did not attract much attention at the time, either domestically or regionally. The first decade of the 21st century then witnessed the construction of another four upper Mekong hydropower projects. The implementation of all the Mekong hydropower projects had not been in consultation with other riparian states, even though the downstream countries and civil society groups strongly requested so after they became aware of the issue through informal channels. China's hydropower development on the Lancang River is still expanding. As mentioned in chapter two, China has planned another eight-dam cascade on the upstream of Lancang within the Yunnan Province and a six-dam cascade on the Dza Chu River (the name of the Mekong mainstream known in Tibet and Qinghai

93 This was achieved by the presentation of a paper by EC Chapman and He Daming in a conference held in Melbourne in October 1996. Milton Osborne, 'River at Risk: The Mekong and the Water Politics of China and Southeast Asia' (Working Paper No 2, Lowy Institute, 2004) 11.

Province). So far, China has no intention of consulting them with the downstream states.

China, however, already signed the Stockholm Declaration in 1972, which expressly recognises a state's sovereignty over its natural resources and the obligation to prevent environmental harm to other countries. While the former is very much welcomed by all developing countries, the latter often falls short of more specific mechanisms to implement. The progress of transboundary water governance between China and neighbouring countries is slow and unbalanced, with some bilateral or multilateral agreements signed with Russia, Kazakhstan, Mongolia and North Korea. Although China also shares several important international rivers with South and Southeast Asian Countries, no agreement has been signed with them regarding transboundary water governance, except a hydrological data sharing agreement with the MRC.

As mentioned in chapter three, China's cooperation with the neighbouring countries on transboundary water governance is set in very different geopolitical landscapes and is facing various environmental concerns. The major issues regarding international rivers running through northeast, north and northwest parts of China are water allocation and pollution prevention. With regard to prior notification and consultation, only the agreement signed with Russia briefly mentions notification on planned activities. Although Kazakhstan complained that China's construction of water towers on the upstream of Irtysh River may increase water usage on China's side to the detrimental of Kazakhstan economic interests and environment, there was no prior notification and consultation process available to deal with such disputes in advance.[94]

According to the agreement with Russia, both sides will notify each other through a pre-agreed process on planned and *existing* hydraulic projects that may have a significant transboundary impact and take necessary measures to prevent, control and mitigate such an impact.[95] The mechanism

---

94 韩啸 [Han Xiao],《水资源挑战迫近中国》[Challenge of Water Resources Approaching China] (26 April 2011) 人民论坛 [People's Tribune] <http://paper.people.com.cn/rmlt/html/2011-04/11/content_804553.htm?div=-1>. China shares several international rivers with Kazakhstan. Currently a joint water division project is under construction on Huoerguos River to allow both sides to each claim 50% of its water. See 关俏俏，刁甜甜 [Guan Qiaoqiao and Diao Tiantian],《中哈两国共同建霍尔果斯河友谊联合引水枢纽工程》[China and Kazakhstan Jointly Construct Huoerguos Water Division Project] (16 April 2011) 新华网 [Xinhua News Agency] <http://www.xj.xinhuanet.com/2011-04/16/content_22539842.htm>.

95 《中华人民共和国政府和俄罗斯联邦政府关于合理利用和保护跨界水的协定》[Cooperation Agreement between China and Russia on the Reasonable Utilisation and Protection of Transboundary Waters] (2008) 外交部 [Ministry of Foreign Affairs of the

here only applies to hydraulic projects, namely development projects along transboundary rivers that may result in significant water pollution are not included. Considering the fact that point source water pollution is an important environmental concern in this area, the lack of notification for these activities can weaken the legal strength to implement the general commitments to prevent pollution. But even for the hydraulic projects that are subject to this requirement, there is no clear requirement on what measures are considered to be necessary under such circumstances. Based on the wording of the agreement, such efforts are more focused on seeking technology solutions rather than resolving the issue through bilateral consultation or other mechanisms (i.e. transboundary EIA), leaving spaces for taking unilateral measures. While both sides do agree to settle disputes through consultation, it is still different from a prior consultation mechanism which requires a suspension of the planned activity.

In addition, the implementation of this provision is based on the existence of an agreed process to facilitate notification. Unfortunately, there is no further information on whether such a process has been clarified or not. If the answer is "yes", it is more likely that such notification will be organised through the Joint Committee established between the two sides. Moreover, it is unclear what kind of information should accompany the notification and when the notification should be made. Further, it is interesting to notice that notification is not only required for planned projects, but also applies to existing projects. A possible explanation is that hydraulic projects may be already completed before the agreement was signed in 2006. Although China is unlikely to withdraw these projects, efforts should at least be made to reduce and prevent their environmental impact.

This in fact resembles a rudimentary form of post-project analysis which is stipulated under the *Espoo Convention*. Although these projects may be subject to domestic EIA under Chinese legislation before they were implemented, the transboundary impact is not included in the domestic EIA process. Without a requirement for conducting transboundary EIA under the agreement, it is difficult to actually predict and prevent transboundary effects. But other mechanisms established under the agreement regarding information collection and exchange on a regular basis and notification in emergency situations may benefit the process of identifying and eliminating the environmental impact. The former has been discussed in chapter three and the latter will be analysed in the next section.

---

People's Republic of China], art 2(8) <http://www.fmprc.gov.cn/mfa_chn/ziliao_611306/tytj_611312/tyfg_611314/t708160.shtml> (emphasis added).

Considering the rapid development of the first eight-dam cascade on the upper Mekong, it is already too late to apply prior notification and consultation on these dams. At the time of writing, the Ganlanba project was still in the process of conducting a domestic EIA. While it remains technically feasible for China and other downstream countries to enter into consultation regarding this particular project, it is more likely that the project will continue without engaging in regional dialogues. Since notification and consultation is yet to be recognised as a customary international law and there is no pre-existing agreement between China and other Mekong countries regarding this mechanism, it is also unlikely for China to engage in prior notification and consultation for the rest of dam plans on the upper Mekong in China. It is probably hard to argue that China violates international law by not engaging in notification and consultation with downstream states. But it is reasonable to criticise that China's behaviour does not comply with international best practice in this area and risks violating the general obligation to prevent harm and the principle of equitable utilisation. Another notable situation is that downstream states are currently preoccupied with mainstream dam proposals on the lower Mekong and China's dam construction is no longer a high priority issue on their schedule.

At the domestic level, there is still a strong belief in science and a heavy reliance on improving technology as the solution to water-related environmental problems. Institutional and legal reform is very much stagnated due to the lack of enough political will and the existence of vested interests. Reflected at the regional level, China is still reluctant to really embrace western discourses on transboundary water cooperation, including prior notification and consultation. Indeed, it is the ongoing non-transparent development of the upper Mekong projects and the lack of cooperation that result in most of the current criticisms. This cannot be offset even if these projects did not cause any significant transboundary impact. As a first step to shift towards modern water management, the Chinese government should learn how to better communicate with neighbouring countries and it own public.

From a pragmatic point of view, a more important concern about China's hydropower development on the upper Mekong should be the operation of existing dams. Therefore, it is suggested that a regular exchange of information and monitoring is a relatively realistic option for further cooperation between China and the MRC countries to prevent and reduce the negative transboundary impact of these projects.

Nonetheless, prior notification and consultation still has value for future environmental cooperation in the region. Along with the economic development in the Mekong area, water pollution is likely to become an increasingly important environmental issue. Therefore, other than hydraulic projects, other activities along the Mekong River that may result in significant transboundary water pollution should be subject to prior notification and consultation as well. This could be another perspective of developing prior notification and consultation between China and the lower Mekong countries. In addition, in order to increase reciprocity and promote more general acceptation of the notion of prior notification and consultation, the discussion on this mechanism can be extended to other environmental protection areas, such as biodiversity and marine environment protection. Increasing the practice of notification and consultation between China and other Mekong countries on less controversial environmental issues may in fact contribute to the adoption of this mechanism in transboundary water cooperation. To facilitate more general application of this mechanism, the GMS program and the ASEAN-China dialogue relationship may provide a more suitable platform than the MRC.

## II Emergency Notification and Cooperation in Its Response

### A *International Experiences*

The duty to notify in emergency situations is supported by various non-binding documents, treaties, cases and state practice and is based on the obligation to cooperate, the obligation to prevent harm and the consideration of humanity.[96] Applied in cooperation on shared water resources, the *UN Watercourses Convention* represents a comprehensive international document in this area. The Convention frames the term "emergency" with two fundamental criteria, namely the seriousness of the harm involved and the suddenness of the emergency's occurrence. Under such circumstances, not only should the affected riparian states be notified, "other states" are also mentioned in the Convention, implying that coastal states may be affected due to the interconnection between the freshwater environment and marine environment. Emergencies

96 For example, Principle 18 of the Rio Declaration, Article 5(6) of the *1999 Rhine Convention*, Article 28(3) of the 1997 *UN Watercourses Convention*, Article 16 of the *Danube River Protection Convention*, Article 14 of the *UNECE Water Convention*, Article 194(3) of the *Convention on the Law of the Sea*, Article 5 of the *Aarhus Convention*, the *Corfu Channel Case*, the *Convention on the Transboundary Effects of Industrial Accidents*, the *Convention on Oil Pollution Preparedness, Response and Co-operation*, the *Convention on Early Notification of Nuclear Accidents*. In the 1986 Sandoz Chemical Accident, Switzerland was criticised by other Rhine states for its failure to offer timely warning under the *1976 Chemical Pollution Convention*. For more information, see Birnie, Boyle and Redgwell, above n 4, 182–4.

include both natural disasters and disasters induced by human conduct. The enumeration on natural disasters reflects a relatively broad consideration of water-related environments.[97] Moreover, it is clear that the implementation of this obligation is irrelevant to the issue of liability.[98]

The Convention then goes on to require the originating state to notify the affected states and competent international organisations "immediately upon learning of the emergency" and "by the most rapid means of communication that is accessible".[99] In addition to the mere obligation to notify, Article 28 of the Convention takes one step further by requiring the relevant countries to "immediately take all practicable measures necessitated by the circumstances to prevent, mitigate and eliminate harmful effects of the emergency". The word "practicable" means measures that are feasible, workable and reasonable. Paragraph four of the Article 28 then calls for anticipatory rather than responsive action, namely, the joint development of contingency plans for responding to emergencies.

To a large extent, the key elements of the above provisions can be identified in state practice. Instead of fully embracing the high degree of integration indicated in the Convention, this mechanism is often tailored based on unique regional circumstances, reflecting priority choices made to promote integrated water resources management (IWRM) in different river basins. For example, the *1999 Rhine Convention* obliges the originating state to immediately notify the International Commission for the Protection of the Rhine (ICPR) and affected member states "in the event of incidents or accidents that might threaten the quality of the water of the Rhine or in the event of imminent flooding" according to the warning and alert plans.[100] Here, this mechanism only applies to emergencies regarding water quality and flooding, which are two of the most serious water issues in the Rhine basin. In fact, they are the two cooperation areas where early warning enjoys the most support from state practice compared to other transboundary water issues. The *1999 Rhine*

97 According to the Convention, natural disasters include, but are not limited to, floods, the breaking up of ice, landslides and earthquakes.

98 Even if there is no liability on the originating state for the harmful effects caused by the emergency, the obligation to notify in emergency situations should still be applied under such circumstances. International Law Commission, above n 15, 130.

99 The discussion on the obligation to notify in emergency situations under the *1997 UN Watercourses Convention* is based on the provisions of the Convention and relevant commentaries made by the International Law Commission. See ibid.; *Convention on the Law of the Non-navigational Uses of International Watercourses*, UN GAOR 51/229, 51st sess, Supp No 49, UN Doc A/51/869 (21 May 1997) art 28.

100 *Convention on the Protection of the Rhine* [2000] OJ L 289/31, art 5(6).

*Convention* does not expressly require emergency notification to other non-riparian states that may be affected. But since the European Community is a member of this Convention, the notification to it can trigger further notification to other affected EU countries. In addition, the provision implies an obligation for member states to develop warning and alert plans for the Rhine. The ICPR is expressly required to coordinate these plans under Article 8. The emergency notification mechanism established under the *1999 Rhine Convention* is further supported by other conventions and EU directives.

As a highly industrialised region, pollution resulting from industrial accidents has been one of the most high-profile issues in the Rhine basin. Following the 1986 Sandoz accident,[101] the ICPR began to inventory warehouses and production sites of hazardous substances in the Rhine basin. It drafted specific recommendations to address many technical issues regarding the prevention of accidents, and the security of industrial plants and transportation of hazardous substances.[102] The inventories certainly provide a basic knowledge foundation for the early warning system. The Warning and Alarm Plan is developed to provide emergency notification and seven International Main Alert Centres along the river are responsible for issuing timely warning to all affected water users in case serious water pollution accidents happened.[103] Moreover, the Warning and Alarm Plan is used as an instrument for the Rhine states to exchange reliable information on water pollution, especially regarding excessive pollutants. This is further linked to the drinking water works as a precautionary measure. Each alert centre can also issue search report in order to find polluter of the Rhine in cases it is not located within the area of its responsibility.[104] Each year's warning and other forms of reports are then compiled and analysed in the annual report, providing a continuous source of analytical data for future decision-making concerning pollution prevention.

In addition to the warning system established under the ICPR to address water pollution accidents, this issue has been dealt more comprehensively across different environmental sectors via the United Nations Economic Commission for Europe's (UNECE) *Convention on the Transboundary Effects of*

101 In 1986, a catastrophic fire at a chemicals factory near Basel, Switzerland resulted in serious chemical pollution of the Rhine and caused the death of almost all of the aquatic life downstream as far as Koblenz.

102 International Commission for the Protection of the Rhine, *Prevention of Accidents and Security of Industrial Plants* <http://www.iksr.org/index.php?id=87&L=3>.

103 See International Commission for the Protection of the Rhine, 'Warning and Alarm Plan Rhine Reported Incidents 2010' (Report No. 191, ICPR, 2010).

104 Ibid. 1.

*Industrial Accidents* and the *Major Accidents (Seveso II) Directive.*[105] Major accident reporting systems have been established at the member state, the UNECE and EU levels. The compatibility and efficiency of these systems are highlighted. The obligations of the operator and the member states are specified. Timely notification of accidents is just one of a series of mechanisms established to tackle with emergencies. This is further complemented by numerous requirements on the collection and exchange of information regarding the holding of large quantities of a dangerous substances and measures taken to prevent accidents and to limit their impact. Information to and participation of the public during the process is also highlighted.

Flood prevention and protection is another major priority concern in the Rhine basin. As a consequence of the great floods of the Rhine in 1993 and 1995, the ICPR adopted the Action Plan on Floods, which has been proved to be another effective soft law initiative in the region.[106] Efforts have been made to reduce damage risks and extreme flood stages, conduct flood risk assessments, draft and publish maps of flood danger and flood risk, and develop early, prompt and long term flood announcements.[107] In 2007, the EU adopted the new *Floods Directive* which specifically requires the EU countries to develop flood risk management plans, including flood forecasts and early warning systems.[108] In particular, flood warning and forecasting centres have been established in the Rhine states. All flood forecasting and monitoring data exchanged among countries and the forecasting of downstream centres is based on monitoring values and forecasts of those upstream.[109] This requires a high degree of trust among countries and the compatibility of monitoring

---

105 Discussions in this paragraph are based on the two documents. See *Convention on the Transboundary Effects of Industrial Accidents*, opened for signature 17 March 1992, 2105 UNTS 457 (entered into force 19 April 2000); *Council Directive 96/82/EC of 9 December 1996 on the Control of Major-Accident Hazards Involving Dangerous Substances* [1996] OJ L 10/13. On 21 December 2010, the EU Commission adopted a proposal for a new directive that would repeal and replace the current *Seveso II Directive* by 1 June 2015.

106 International Commission for the Protection of the Rhine, *Action Plan on Floods* <http://www.iksr.org/index.php?id=123&L=3>. The application of the Rhine Action Programme, a soft law document, is another successful example.

107 Conference of Rhine Ministers, *Living and Linking Rhine—Common Challenge of a Watershed* (18 October 2007) International Commission for the Protection of the Rhine <http://www.iksr.org/fileadmin/user_upload/Dokumente_en/MIN07-02e.pdf>.

108 *Directive 2007/60/EC of the European Parliament and of the Council of 23 October 2007 on the Assessment and Management of Flood Risks* [2007] OJ L 288/27, art 7.

109 International Commission for the Protection of the Rhine, *Flood Warning and Forecasting Centres* <http://www.iksr.org/index.php?id=140&L=3>.

and modelling systems. In addition, it is necessary to ensure that the affected public can get access to such information in a timely and easy fashion. It relies on the increase of public awareness on flood risk through the releasing of more reliable and detailed flood hazard and risk maps, and more effective linkage between flood warning centres and local agencies and communities.

The early warning systems established in the Rhine basin regarding water pollution accidents and flooding represent the most favourable examples so far. The effectiveness of these systems benefits from the existing regular information collection and exchange mechanisms in the region. And the compiled information on these warnings, in turn, provides another regular data source for further research and policy-making. Moreover, the warning systems within the Rhine basin are complemented by other emergency notification networks and requirements established at the UNECE and EU levels. Not only do relevant conventions and EU directives provide another layer of legal coercion outside the Rhine cooperation regime, they also contribute to a higher degree of integration in terms of linking other EU or UNECE countries with the Rhine states on water-related issues. Further, the early warning systems in the Rhine basin reflects a close relationship between emergency notification and the need to make sure that such notification can get to the affected public in a timely and convenient manner. This is expressed required by Article 5 of the *Aarhus Convention*. Last, but not least, as a part of the whole arrangements to tackle water pollution and flooding, emergency notification should be combined with necessary preventive and responsive measures. While it is encouraged that countries should have relevant plans in place before emergency situation actually took place, in cases that they do not have such arrangements ready in advance, the originating state should immediately enter into consultation with the affected states to take cooperative measures to mitigate any negative impact.

### B *Evaluation of the Current Arrangements under the MRC Regime*

According to the *1995 Mekong Agreement*, any water quantity or quality problem that constitutes an emergency should be notified to and in consultation held with affected states and the MRC Joint Committee without delay in order to take appropriate remedial action.[110] Compared with the provisions under the *1997 UN Watercourses Convention* and the *1999 Rhine Convention*, the requirement under the *1995 Mekong Agreement* is more moderate and

110 *Agreement on the Cooperation for the Sustainable Development of the Mekong River Basin*, opened for signature 5 April 1995, 2069 UNTS I-35844 (entered into force 5 April 1995) art 10.

ambiguous. For example, the term "emergency" is described as a situation that "requires an immediate response". But there is no further clarification on the seriousness of the harm involved. In addition, the idea of taking "appropriate remedial action" is too obscure to provide necessary guidance or legal certainty in practice, especially when the Agreement does not specifically require the preparation of early warning and response plans.

The application of this mechanism in the lower Mekong region targets emergencies regarding water quantity and quality. As identified in a MRC report, transboundary pollution is not yet a big problem in the Mekong region.[111] But along with the development of mining,[112] the exploration for oil and gas, and other industries, there will be increasing substantial pressure on water quality and higher risk of accidents result from such activities. While the lower Mekong countries have developed a water quality monitoring system, there is not much information and research available regarding water quality issues arising from the above economic developments.[113] Since water pollution is not yet an imminent threat to the region, limited focus on this aspect is understandable due to the priority concerns. However, it is argued that close attention should be paid to the future changes in this area and more preparation work should be done in order to better prevent the occurrence of such accidents. Based on the experiences in the Rhine basin, initial steps can be taken to collect more information on the potential point sources of water pollution along the river and to conduct more research on the influences of development in different economic sectors to water quality in the Mekong region. Compared to the situation in the lower Mekong region, there is stronger evidence indicating transboundary transmission of pollutants from upper Mekong in China into the lower Mekong basin.[114] Therefore, it is prudent to consider the development of an emergency notification system between China and other Mekong countries regarding water quality.

Flooding, on the other hand, has been one of the major concerns in the region for a long time. The Mekong River is characterised by a unique floodpulse hydrology which plays a vital role in agriculture and drives ecosystem

---

111 Mekong River Commission, 'An Assessment of Water Quality in the Lower Mekong Basin' (Technical Paper No. 19, Mekong River Commission, 2008) 59.

112 Ibid. 7. In the lower Mekong region, the main potential problems with mining are likely to be associated with catastrophic failure of retention dams (tailings dams), poorly constructed or managed retention dams and spill of chemicals such as cyanide during transport on the Mekong River.

113 See ibid. 5–7.

114 Ibid. 59.

productivity in the Mekong floodplain and Tonle Sap area.[115] While the annual flooding cycle requires adaptive measures, extreme flooding can cause significant loss of lives and economic, environment and social damages. This is further complicated with the potential impact of climate change in the region. Notably, approximately two-thirds of the region's total annual flood damage occurs in Cambodia and Vietnam.[116] Against the above background, the lower Mekong countries have cooperated closely on flood management and mitigation, including the development of a basin-wide flood forecast and warning system. It reflects a mixed feature of both regular information exchange and notification in emergency situations, which further demonstrates a close relationship between the two mechanisms.

The history of transboundary flood forecasting and warning in the Mekong region can be traced back to the 1970s.[117] Currently, based on the data gained from 138 hydrometeorological stations (including two on the upper Mekong in China), the Regional Flood Management and Mitigation Centre (a permanent physical centre of the MRC Secretariat) issues daily flood forecasts and warnings during the June–November flood season. Daily bulletins are exchanged via fax, email and MRC websites to NMCs, NGOs, the media, and most importantly, the flood-prone communities. In order to reach a wide audience throughout the basin, especially in the remote areas, other tools like flood markers, community billboards and radio communication are used. In addition, guidebooks, workshops and regional forums are also used to raise public awareness on the warning.[118]

Even so, problems and difficulties still exist in several aspects, inter alia, the lack of enough funding and training, insufficient compatibility of monitoring

115 During the southwest monsoon, from May to September, the swollen Mekong causes the Tonle Sap River in Cambodia to reverse flow, which in turn, causes a six-fold increase in the area and a 38-fold increase in the volume of the Tonle Sap Lake. Matti Kummu et al., 'Sediment: Curse or Blessing for Tonle Sap Lake?' (2008) 37 *Ambio* 158, 158.

116 Mekong River Commission, *Flood & Drought* <http://www.mrcmekong.org/topics/flood-and-drought/>.

117 See generally Erich J. Plate and Thanongdeth Insisiengmay, *Early Warning System for the Mekong River* (2002) 9 <http://www.cws.net.cn/cwsnet/meeting-fanghong/v10101.pdf>.

118 Information in this paragraph is derived from the MRC website. Mekong River Commission, *Flood Management & Mitigation Programme* <http://www.mrcmekong.org/about-the-mrc/programmes/flood-management-and-mitigation-programme/>. For more information, see Chusit Apirumanekul, 'Flood Forecasting and Early Warning System in Mekong River Commission' (Speech delivered at the 4th Annual Flood Forum, Siem Reap, 18–19 May 2006) <http://ns1.mrcmekong.org/download/free_download/AFF-4/session4/4-Flood_Forecasting_and_Warning_in_MRC.pdf>.

and modelling systems and varying risk and impact assessment technologies.[119] All these factors could have a negative impact on the effectiveness and accuracy of transboundary emergency warnings. For example, the accuracy of five-day forecast is not yet quite satisfactory.[120] Considering the difficulties for remote communities to get access to flood warnings, one-day forecasts may not leave enough time for them to get prepared. In addition to the above tools used to facilitate remote communities' access to flood warnings, more coordinated measures should be taken among the Regional Flood Management and Mitigation Centre, MRC, NMCs, line agencies, local governments and local communities to promote a more responsive and accountable system for flood warnings. Besides, flood-related education and support should be improved for local communities to actively respond to flood warnings.

As illustrated in the case of Rhine basin, a flood-related emergency warning system is often combined with domestic flood management action plans and regional coordination of these plans. While the drafting of the national flood action plan still faces some technical and financial difficulties to varying degrees in the field, it should also be noted that current regional coordination of these plans remains substantially insufficient. As observed by the MRC, flood risks can be minimised through various forms of land-use, development and building controls, regional flood emergency planning and improved preparedness.[121] Therefore, the coordination of national flood mitigation plans would require the MRC to assume a stronger role in governance. This is in contrast with the current technical focus of the MRC on providing basin-wide flood forecast and warning. Again, the limited role of the MRC in promoting regional water governance beyond the technical level has proved to be a bottleneck for further development of basin-wide flood mitigation.

Recent years have also witnessed a gradual increase of regional attention on sub-basins flood forecasting. The Flood Management and Mitigation Programme under the MRC is in the process of developing a flash flood (due to intense rainfall) guidance system for tributaries to indicate the likelihood of flooding of small streams over wide areas.[122] Meanwhile, boundaries data is also supplied by the MRC for more detailed food predictions for sub-basins that

---

119 See Plate and Insisiengmay, above n 117; Guillaume Lacombe, *Effectiveness of Early Warning Systems and Monitoring Tools in the Mekong Basin* (2009) 2 <http://www.adbi.org/files/2009.06.09.cpp.day2.sess3.2.lacombe.paper.early.warning.systems.mekong.pdf>.

120 Plate and Insisiengmay, above n 117.

121 Mekong River Commission, above n 116.

122 Mekong River Commission, above n 118.

are undertaken by national agencies.[123] Since the tributaries of the Mekong River can create significant transboundary flood issues as well, it is argued that more subregion-specific cooperation on flood forecasting and warning should be promoted. As an initial step, more information is needed to identify the major tributary areas that are prone to severe transboundary flood damages and pilot projects should be encouraged and supported to provide opportunities for learning by doing.

The flood warning system should also be considered under the background of burgeoning tributary dam construction in the region. Over one hundred dam projects are currently planned or operating on the Mekong tributaries. They can have cumulative effects on the mainstream river's natural flood pulse. But only until recently has the Flood Management and Mitigation Programme began to interact with hydropower expertise by requesting a list of completed hydropower projects in the lower Mekong region for the consideration of effects on the system of flood forecasting and warning.[124] Such information is still insufficient to accurately predict the impact of these dams on natural flood cycles. It is the information regarding the management of these projects that actually provides more valuable reference for flood prediction. In fact, as identified in the SEA report, flood protection benefits from storage reservoirs on the Mekong tributaries and on the upper Mekong mainstream still remain to be seen and are currently highly debated.[125] In several instances, large amounts of dam release have resulted in unexpected flash floods in the downstream areas, such as the case of the Yali Fall Dam in Vietnam, which caused damages to communities in northeastern Cambodia.[126] This often occurs without proper early warning to the downstream governments or communities. Even if early warnings were issued, which in fact is the case after Cambodia and Vietnam reached agreement on this matter in 2000, these warnings often got through on an erratic basis, due to the lack of accuracy, excessive bureaucracy,

123 Mekong River Commission, 'The Flood Management and Mitigation Programme 2011–2015' (Programme Document, Mekong River Commission, 2011) 11.

124 Ibid. 18.

125 See International Centre for Environmental Management, above n 70, 68.

126 The Vietnamese government ordered the dam builder to provide such information. This notification was transmitted through the Vietnam NMC and the Cambodian NMC and was then passed to the local Water Resource Ministry in Ratanakiri, to the districts, communes, villages and individual villagers. See NGO Forum on Cambodia, *Down River: The Consequences of Vietnam's Se San River Dams on Life in Cambodia and Their Meaning in International Law* (NGO Forum on Cambodia, 2005) 53–5; Oxfam Australia, *Yali Fall Dam* <https://www.oxfam.org.au/explore/infrastructure-people-and-environment/save-the-mekong/3s-critical-environmental-zone/yali-falls-dam/>.

remoteness of the affected communities and the shortage of electronic communications infrastructure in some areas.[127] While the debates on lower Mekong mainstream dam proposals continue to hit the headlines, cooperation regarding the management of the existing tributary dams remains largely stalled. As a part of the solution, flood warning systems and consultation on responsive or remedial measures should be introduced and improved as an important approach to manage and mitigate the transboundary impact of the tributaries dams operation.

The accessibility of information to the public and public participation regarding the emergency notification should be highlighted as well. This is partly reflected in the current Flood Management and Mitigation Programme. In addition to the problematic domestic legal arrangements and implementation concerning the public's right to know and to participate,[128] the restricted resources and capacity on informing the public should be noted in the context of emergency notification. Even under the current circumstances, the civil society's ability to participate in the emergency notification system should not be neglected. For example, NGOs, such as the Red Cross, have cooperated with the MRC in expanding the flood early warning system to remote and flood-prone villages.[129] In addition, the local communities can help gather information in high risk areas.

### C *China's Experiences on Emergency Notification in Transboundary Water Management and the Potentials for Relevant Discussion in the Mekong Region*

Among China's unbalanced experiences on transboundary water management, an emergency notification system has been established between China and Russia. This was directly triggered by a severe water pollution accident that occurred on the Songhua River in mid-November 2005 due to an explosion in a petrochemical plant (belonging to PetroChina) in Jilin Province, China.[130] In this case, the blast resulted in the release of 100 tons of benzene

127 See Probe International, *Heavy Water Release from Vietnam's Yali Falls Dam Floods Communities in Northeastern Cambodia* (29 July 2008) <http://eprf.probeinternational.org/node/4179>.

128 See chapter five.

129 Mekong River Commission, *Public Participation in the Lower Mekong Basin* (2005) 11 <http://www.mrcmekong.org/assets/Publications/governance/Public-Participation.pdf>.

130 Factual information regarding this accident is based on the following resources: United Nations Environment Programme, 'The Songhua River Spill' (Field Mission Report, United Nations Environment Programme, 2005); Yuqiong Liu, 'Monitoring Chinese-Russian Transboundary Waters' (2006) 5 (3) *Southwest Hydrology* 38.

and other chemicals into the Songhua River, the largest tributary to the Heilongjiang River (referred to as the Amur River in Russia). PetroChina and the local government were criticised for concealing information regarding the discharge of chemicals into the river for around one week from the central government, the downstream governments, the affected public and Russia. During that period, the Jilin petrochemical plant continued to deny any pollution to the Songhua River, but the Jilin Provincial government and environmental protection bureau notified the Heilongjiang government five days later about the possible water pollution that resulted from this accident. It then took another several days before the affected public had a general awareness of the issue. When the Harbin municipal government (Harbin is the capital city of the downstream Heilongjiang Province) finally notified its citizens about the decision to cut off water supply for four days, the initial reason given by the government was very obscure, only referring to the need to ensure water usage safety. It was the second notice issued in the same day that openly confirmed severe water pollution due to the blast. The lack of transparency and information credibility caused panic throughout the entire city.

Russia was formally notified of the accident the next day after the notification to Harbin citizens and both the Chinese President and the Prime Minister extended their apologies to the Russian government. Fortunately, this notification was still in time for Russia to respond appropriately, since the water froze and took approximately one month for most pollutants to reach Russia's territory. While China had already taken measures to reduce the impact of the accident before it went public, a joint monitoring team was then established with the participation of Russian experts and officials and China, who agreed to donate equipment and materials to assist Russia to mitigate the impact. By the end of December, water quality in the Heilongjiang River reached China's safe drinking standard before it crossed Russia boarder. Monitoring data showed that the groundwater resources were not polluted and no poisoning of humans or livestock was reported. But the ecosystem along the corridor of Songhua River may take a long time to recover.

Although the mitigation measures seemed to be effective to a large extent, PetroChina (a large state-owned oil company) and local government's initial attempt to cover up the water pollution accident was strongly criticised both within and outside China. Lessons from this incident called for transparency regarding environmental emergencies and more stringent and accountable requirements for polluter and local government to report to relevant authorities. It also added more momentum for the promulgation of the National Master Plan for Rapid Response to Public Emergencies and the National Plan for Rapid Response to Environmental Accidents in January 2006. Both plans highlight the requirement for a timely and accurate release of information regarding emergencies and institutionalise the domestic arrangements for emergence response. They are further supported by China's enactment of *Emergency Response Law* and *Regulations on Government Information Disclosure* in 2007. In addition, as a typical case of trans-provincial boundary water pollution within China, the Songhua River Spill exemplified the necessity for long-term cross-boundary and cross-sector cooperation to respond to water-related environmental emergencies. The development of emergency notification and response systems for transboundary water management within China is currently in progress, represented by the establishment of warning systems among eight provinces along the Yellow River.[131] This could lay a better foundation to expand such cooperation at the regional level.

In March 2006, China and Russia signed a quite pragmatic agreement to cooperate on prevention and elimination of emergency situations, which includes, but is not limited to, environmental incidents and accidents.[132] Monitoring and emergency notification is required under the Agreement, but most of the Agreement focuses on detailed arrangements on how to provide mutual aid in case of emergencies. Early warning is further required by the bilateral agreement between China and Russia regarding the utilisation and protection of transboundary rivers in 2008, which specifically refers to the *2006 Agreement* to deal with transboundary water-related emergencies. The *2008 Agreement* expressly requires both sides to immediately notify each other regarding emergency situation and take necessary and reasonable measures to eliminate and mitigate the negative impact.[133] The language used in this provision is to a large extent comparable to other international practices, although

131 See 李晓莹 [Li Xiaoying],《黄委携手流域8省（区）建立突发水污染事件信息沟通与协作机制》 [The Yellow River Conservancy Commission, together with Eight Riparian Provinces, Developed Information Exchange and Collaboration Mechanisms for Water Pollution Accidents] (14 July 2011) 中国水利 [China Water Resources News] <http://www.chinawater.com.cn/newscenter/ly/huangh/201107/t20110714_154665.html>.

132 See《中华人民共和国政府和俄罗斯联邦政府关于预防和消除紧急情况合作协定》[Agreement between China and Russia regarding Cooperation on Prevention and Elimination of Emergency Situations] (21 March 2006) <http://www.fsou.com/redirect/index.asp?url=http://vip.chinalawinfo.com/newlaw2002/slc/slc.asp?db=eag&gid=100669464>.

133 《中华人民共和国政府和俄罗斯联邦政府关于合理利用和保护跨界水的协定》[Cooperation Agreement between China and Russia on the Reasonable Utilisation and Protection of Transboundary Waters] (2008) 外交部 [Ministry of Foreign Affairs of the People's Republic of China], art 6 <http://www.fmprc.gov.cn/mfa_chn/ziliao_611306/tytj_611312/tyfg_611314/t708160.shtml>.

there is no further explanation on threshold requirements for emergencies. The *2008 Agreement* also reflects a close relationship between regular collection and exchange of information and emergency notification.

In addition, a memorandum was signed in 2008 between the Ministry of Environmental Protection of China and the Ministry of Natural Resources and Environment of the Russian Federation regarding the establishment of notification and information exchange mechanisms for transboundary environmental emergencies. It provides a standardised format for such notification and information exchange. The above arrangements serve as the foundation for China and Russia to deepen their cooperation on water-related emergencies. Interestingly, since the Heilong River is a contiguous river (which forms an international boundary), transboundary water management regarding this river is more reciprocal than the case of a successive river (which traverses the territories of two or more states). In 2008, Russia notified China on a water pollution accident which was later confirmed to have originated from Russia.[134]

Other than the more advanced example of emergency notification between China and Russia, such mechanism has not yet been formally established in transboundary water management between China and other countries. In the agreement signed between China and Kazakhstan in 2001, both sides agreed to take appropriate measures to prevent or mitigate significant transboundary damage due to floods and accidents caused by human factors.[135] This provision should imply the need for timely notification in emergency situations. Otherwise, it would be difficult to implement this requirement in practice.

Support for this mechanism can be also identified in China's domestic legislation. According to the *2007 Emergency Response Law*, the Chinese government shall cooperate and communicate with foreign governments and relevant international organisations regarding emergency incidents and accidents on relevant prevention, monitoring, warning, response and aid, ex post recovery and reconstruction.[136] This domestic requirement can open a

---

134 See 陈义龙 [Chen Yilong],《纪实：中俄跨界河流污染事件处置》[Report: China and Russia Respond to Transboundary Water Pollution Accidents] (20 June 2009) 中国价值 [China Value] <http://www.chinavalue.net/Finance/Article/2009-6-20/181849.html>.

135 《中华人民共和国政府和哈萨克斯坦共和国政府关于利用和保护跨界河流的合作协定》[Cooperation Agreement between China and Kazakhstan on the Utilisation and Protection of Transboundary Rivers], signed 12 September 2001 (entered into force 23 September 2002) art 3.

136 《中华人民共和国突发事件应对法》[Emergency Response Law of the People's Republic of China] National People's Congress Standing Committee, Order No 69, 30 August 2007, art 15.

door for the development of emergency notification system between China and other Mekong countries. To date, the cooperation between China and the lower Mekong countries on flood forecasting and warning remains limited to the provision of hydrological data from two monitoring stations in Yunnan. Since several upper Mekong mainstream dams are already completed, whether these dams can provide benefits to downstream states in terms of flood control remains to be seen. Therefore, it is prudent to combine the negotiation on post-project analysis and monitoring of these dams with the need for a more accurate basin-wide flood warning and mitigation system. But as pointed out in chapter three, such information is often marked as confidential under China's domestic legislation.

Moreover, although water pollution is not yet a major issue in the Mekong region, along with the economic growth in Yunnan Province, it is more likely that there will be increasing possibilities for transboundary water pollution accidents on the upper Mekong River. China's experience with Russia on handling water pollution accidents can provide a valuable reference in context of the Mekong region. However, it should be noted that the case of Heilong River reflects more reciprocity features than is the case of the Mekong region. In addition, as demonstrated in the Songhua River Spill case, transboundary emergency notification is highly related to the soundness of domestic emergency response system, the improvement of the public's right of access to information and the regular collection and exchange of necessary information.

CHAPTER 5

# Access to Information and Public Participation

## I Introduction

In addition to states and inter-governmental organisations, recent decades have witnessed a proliferation of non-state actors in international affairs. Correspondingly, international environmental law has developed some rights and obligations which attach to individuals, corporations and non-governmental organisations (NGO). Inter alia, the emergence of environmental human rights represents the most significant development in this area. Instead of environmental quality, however, the strongest argument for specific environmental rights actually lies in procedural rights,[1] with this chapter focusing primarily on access to information and public participation.[2]

The increasing significance of these procedural rights is also derived from the growing popularity of deliberative democracy since the late 20th Century, which considers democratic decision-making to be the process of reasoned, public discussion amongst equal citizens.[3] Based on the theories of environmental democracy, it is argued that governments which operate with openness, transparency, accountability and public participation are more likely to promote environmental justice and sustainable development.[4] Moreover, as demonstrated in the case of the Rhine, a greater inclusion of civil society has been instrumental in promoting transboundary water management through a decentralised approach. It was pointed out in chapter two that the ongoing water reforms in the Mekong countries is too dependent on centralised institutional structures and often fails to incorporate the decentralised aspect of

1 See Malgosia Fitzmaurice, 'Some Reflections on Public Participation in Environmental Matters as a Human Right in International Law' (2002) 2 *Non-state Actors and International Law* 1, 10–22; Patricia Birnie, Alan Boyle and Catherine Redgwell, *International Law and the Environment* (Oxford University Press, 3rd ed, 2009) 288.

2 Although access to justice is also an important part of the procedural rights, detailed discussion on this issue could easily go beyond the length of this book. In addition, access to justice regarding environmental issues remains largely constrained in the Mekong region. Therefore, this chapter will only focus on access to information and public participation, but will address this issue briefly in the final chapter.

3 Joshua Cohen, 'Deliberation and Democratic Legitimacy' in James Bohman and William Rehg (eds) *Deliberative Democracy: Essays on Reason and Politics* (MIT Press, 1997) 72.

4 Birnie, Boyle and Redgwell, above n 1, 289.

 | DOI 10.1163/9789004266797_006

integrated water resources management (IWRM). Therefore, it is necessary to highlight the discussion of transparency and public participation in the context of the Mekong region.

This chapter will begin by analysing the development of access to information and public participation under international environmental law and more specifically watercourses law. Notably, the *Aarhus Convention*, officially known as *Convention on Access to Information, Public Participation in Decision-making and Access to Justice in Environmental Matters*, represents the most advanced international development of individual procedural rights so far. The evolution and the contents of these important international documents can shed light on the rationale and best practices of promoting procedural rights at the international level. Attention will then be paid to the Mekong region to identify and evaluate the existing and potential regional efforts on promoting transparency and public participation through the Association of Southeast Asian Nations (ASEAN), the Mekong River Commission (MRC), the Greater Mekong Subregion Program (GMS), the ASEAN-China Free Trade Area (ACFTA) and major multilateral development banks like the Asian Development Bank (ADB).

Having considered these procedural rights from an international perspective, the focus of discussion will be shifted to relevant domestic political and legal arrangements, which are more fundamental in securing the implementation of these procedural rights. Detailed research will be done on the diverse domestic legislation and political initiatives regarding access to information, public participation and the corresponding civil society development in different Mekong countries. Some case studies will be referred to in order to gain lessons in the field and provide a more vivid picture of the current landscape. Combined with regional efforts on promoting further improvement of transparency and participation, recommendations will be given on how to better utilise the constrained political and legal rights in the context of reform opportunities that are opening across the Mekong region. Incorporated into the discussion in this chapter will be the interaction between these procedural rights and other procedural mechanisms.

## II Access to Information and Public Participation under International Environmental Law

In 1966, the *International Covenant on Civil and Political Rights* only briefly confirmed that every citizen has the right and the opportunity to take part in the conduct of public affairs.[5] The World Charter for Nature in 1982 then put forward a more environment-focused interpretation of public participation.[6] In both documents, however, no clear requirement was made regarding the public's right of access to information, which is often viewed as a prerequisite for effective participation. At the regional level, it is notable that the EC countries adopted the *Directive 90/313/EEC* in 1990 to specifically address the freedom of access to information on the environment.[7]

A more comprehensive and probably most oft-quoted provision on both information access and public participation is Principle 10, which mainly focuses on information access and participation at the national level. In the United Nations Economic Commission for Europe's (UNECE) *Convention on Transboundary Effects of Industrial Accidents*, the participation right is granted to the affected public without regard to national borders based on the non-discrimination principle. Similar arrangements are also made in the 1991 *Espoo Convention*, providing the public of the affected countries equivalent participation opportunities to that given to the public of the state of origin during the transboundary environmental impact assessment (EIA) process.[8] It should be noted, however, in the *Pulp Mills Case*, the International Court of Justice (ICJ) held the view that "no legal obligation to consult the affected populations arises for the Parties from the instruments invoked by Argentina".[9] Neither party of the Case is bounded by the *Espoo Convention* invoked by Argentina. And the other documents cited by Argentina are not legally-binding in nature. Following the logic of this ICJ judgment, since general international law does not impose specific obligations on states in this regard, international obligations on consulting the affected public during transboundary EIA can only rise from bilateral or multilateral commitments. Many scholars, however, criticise

5 *International Covenant on Civil and Political Rights*, opened for signature 16 December 1966, 999 UNTS 1057 (entered into force 23 March 1976) art 25.

6 *World Charter for Nature*, GA Res 37/7, UN GAOR, 48th plen mtg, UN Doc A/RES/37/7 (28 October 1982) para 23.

7 This Directive was later replaced by the Directive 2003/4/EC to implement the *Aarhus Convention*.

8 *Convention on Environmental Impact Assessment in a Transboundary Context*, opened for signature 25 February 1991, 1989 UNTS 309 (entered into force 10 September 1997) art 2(6).

9 *Pulp Mills on the River Uruguay (Argentina v Uruguay) (Judgment)* [2010] ICJ Rep 14, para 216.

this part of the judgment and argue that public participation is a necessary element of the EIA process.[10]

With respect to transboundary water management, the *1997 UN Watercourses Convention* makes no mention of non-state actors and relevant procedural rights.[11] But regional practices and international soft-law documents indicate an increasing momentum towards international recognition of non-state actors and their procedural rights in water management. In the 1992 Dublin Statement on Water and Sustainable Development, experts ambitiously declared that water development and management should be based on a participatory approach incorporating a strong feature of the decentralised nature of IWRM.[12]

Meanwhile, the *UNECE Water Convention* specifically requires the riparian states to ensure the public can have access to information regarding transboundary waters, including the conditions of river system; measures taken or planned to be taken to prevent, control and reduce the transboundary impact; and the effectiveness of those measures.[13] Such information should be available to the public at all reasonable times and facilities should be provided by the governments as well.[14] More detailed requirements on access to information are included in the *1994 Danube River Protection Convention*, focusing on information disclosure regarding the quality of riverine environment in the Danube basin. The Convention elaborates on the forms of information and sets out the exemptions regarding this obligation and the procedures for

10 See Alan Boyle, 'Developments in the International Law of Environmental Impact Assessments and their Relation to the Espoo Convention' (2011) 20(3) *Review of European Community & International Environmental Law* 227, 227.

11 With regard to Article 7 on obligation not to cause significant harm, the Commentaries refers to Article 2 of the *Espoo Convention* to deduce the obligation of due diligence. Public participation is included in Article 2. See International Law Commission, 'Draft articles on the Law of the Non-navigational Uses of International Watercourses and Commentaries thereto and Resolution on Transboundary Confined Groundwater' (1994) 2(2) *Yearbook of the International Law Commission* 89, 103.

12 The decisions should be made at the lowest appropriate level, with full public consultation and involvement of users in the planning and implementation of water projects. *The Dublin Statement on Water and Sustainable Development* (1992) Global Development Research Center, principle 2 <http://www.gdrc.org/uem/water/dublin-statement.html>.

13 *Convention on the Protection and Use of Transboundary Watercourses and International Lakes*, opened for signature 17 March 1992, 1936 UNTS 269 (entered into force 6 October 1996) arts 11(3), 16.

14 Ibid. art 16.

responding to information request.[15] Compared to other water conventions, this Convention adopts the most advanced position on the public's right of access to information.

The above documents laid the foundation for the development of a comprehensive agreement on the public's procedural rights culminating in the *Aarhus Convention*. Opened for signature in 1998, this Convention remains the most comprehensive international convention for giving legally-binding normative significance to Rio Principle 10. Notably, the "public authority" defined in the Convention not only includes different levels of government, but also refers to natural or legal persons that perform public administrative functions, have public responsibilities or provide public services in relation to the environment.[16] The word "public" is also interpreted in a broad sense to include both natural and legal persons, and their associations, organisations or groups.[17] It provides a clear legal basis for the involvement of various NGOs. Although the Convention focuses on the application of these procedural rights at the domestic level, it also refers to the non-discrimination principle to apply such requirements in a transboundary context.[18]

### A *Access to Information under the* Aarhus Convention

Under the *Aarhus Convention*, access to information is addressed both as a separate procedural right and as a part of the public participation process to ensure the public can make an informed decision. The latter will be incorporated into the discussion on public participation processes. Article 4 sets out a comprehensive framework to ensure the public can have access to a very broad range of environmental information held by public authorities.[19] The freedom of access to such information is "not dependent on being personally affected or having some right or interest in the matter".[20] The Convention first addresses access to environmental information upon request, requiring such information to be made available "as soon as possible" and a maximum time

15 *Convention on Cooperation for the Protection and Sustainable Use of the Danube River*, signed 29 June 1994, ROD 21997A1212(03) (31997D0825) (entered into force in 22 October 1998) art 12.

16 *Convention on Access to Information, Public Participation in Decision-making and Access to Justice in Environmental Matters*, opened for signature 25 June 1998, 2161 UNTS 447 (entered into force 10 October 2001) art 2(2).

17 Ibid. art 2(4).

18 Ibid. art 3(9).

19 Ibid. art 2(3).

20 This is based on the fact that the phrase used in Article 4 is "the public" instead of "the public concerned". Ibid. art 4(1); Birnie, Boyle and Redgwell, above n 1, 292.

limit is set to respond to the information request in order to prevent unreasonable delay.[21]

The Convention then goes to great lengths to list the *only* circumstances under which exceptions to the above general rules may apply.[22] This includes, but is not limited to, the confidentiality of the proceedings of public authorities, international relations, national defence or public security and the confidentiality of commercial and industrial information.[23] With regard to the first exception, the confidentiality must be provided for under national law. Theoretically speaking, this leaves the possibility for the public to express their opinions on whether a particular proceeding should be marked as confidential through their participation in the preparation of executive regulations, which is encouraged in Article 8. Although countries may deny the request for information based on the ground of international relations and national security, it is suggested that such terms should be interpreted restrictively and in consistent with international law.[24] Moreover, information concerning pollutant emissions relevant for environmental protection may not be claimed as confidential commercial information.[25] Therefore, it is clear that even though a range of exceptions is recognised in the Convention, strict interpretation of these provisions should apply and a more democratic process should be introduced at the national level to put in place such restrictions.

Another exception is that if information exempted from disclosure can be separated out without prejudice to the confidentiality of the information exempted, public authorities should make the remainder of the environmental information available to the public.[26] This illustrates the high standard imposed by the Convention to ensure the refusal to release environmental information is exceptional rather than usual. In practice, countries like Netherlands go even further to require the public authorities to indicate

---

21 *Convention on Access to Information, Public Participation in Decision-making and Access to Justice in Environmental Matters*, opened for signature 25 June 1998, 2161 UNTS 447 (entered into force 10 October 2001) art 4(2).

22 *The Aarhus Convention: An Implementation Guide*, UN Doc ECE/CEP/72 (2000) 53 (emphasis added).

23 *Convention on Access to Information, Public Participation in Decision-making and Access to Justice in Environmental Matters*, opened for signature 25 June 1998, 2161 UNTS 447 (entered into force 10 October 2001) art 4(4).

24 *The Aarhus Convention: An Implementation Guide*, UN Doc ECE/CEP/72 (2000) 59.

25 Ibid. 60.

26 *Convention on Access to Information, Public Participation in Decision-making and Access to Justice in Environmental Matters*, opened for signature 25 June 1998, 2161 UNTS 447 (entered into force 10 October 2001) art 4(6).

"where information has been removed and, in a general way, the substance of the information withheld".[27] However, for countries that do not have a history of transparent governance, this provision will be very difficult to implement.

The Convention also establishes procedures for refusing to provide information.[28] In addition to the time limit mentioned above, a refusal of information request should be made in a written form and reasons for such decision should be given. The applicant should also be informed of any review procedure to exercise the right of access to justice. Moreover, if a requested public authority does not hold the environmental information requested, it should, "as promptly as possible, inform the applicant of the public authority to which it believes it is possible to apply for the information requested or transfer the request to that authority and inform the applicant accordingly". The above requirements are generally in line with the due process provisions that are often imposed under national administrative law, but may not be effectively implemented in practice. More discussion regarding these issues will be provided in the context of China where similar regulations exist under its domestic law.

From the perspective of member states, the Convention imposes the obligation to collect and disclose environmental information.[29] With respect to information disclosure, a series of measures are listed to ensure an adequate flow of environmental information to public authorities and such information is "effectively accessible" to the public. This requires the information to be processed into an organised and user-friendly form. And technological and other practical arrangements should also be made to facilitate the process.

### B *Public Participation under the* Aarhus Convention

As an important element of environment decision-making, public participation is addressed in the Convention at three levels: specific activities; plans and policies; and executive regulations or generally applicable normative instruments. The most detailed and stringent requirements on public participation are with regard to specific activities that may have a significant impact on the environment.

---

27 *The Aarhus Convention: An Implementation Guide*, UN Doc ECE/CEP/72 (2000) 63.

28 Information regarding the *Aarhus Convention* in this paragraph is drawn from paragraphs 5 and 7 of Article 4.

29 See *Convention on Access to Information, Public Participation in Decision-making and Access to Justice in Environmental Matters*, opened for signature 25 June 1998, 2161 UNTS 447 (entered into force 10 October 2001) art 5.

Different from the general freedom of access to information, the right to participate in decisions on specific activities are granted only for the "public concerned".[30] This, however, broadly includes the "public affected or likely to be affected by, or having an interest in, the environmental decision-making". To a large extent, the latter secures the participatory rights of the environmental NGOs. Minimum standards are then set out in Annex I to clarify the term "significant", but countries can enact stricter requirements on this threshold issue.[31] National defence purposes can be used to exempt governments from the requirements, but only "on a case-by-case basis if so provided under national law".[32]

The Convention requires the public concerned to be involved *early* in an environmental decision-making procedure, namely when "all options are open".[33] Ideally, this could provide more scope for effective participation. But in reality, quite often, strong economic and political interests involved are likely to move the project forward despite the participation process, especially if the proposed project is a part of a more comprehensive development plan, program or policy that has already been approved. This raises questions both on the effectiveness of public participation at the project level and its relationship with other levels of participation, other environment management mechanisms and their enabling environment, which will be further analysed in this chapter in the context of the Mekong region.

The participation process begins by providing the public concerned certain information about the proposed activity and the envisaged procedure of participation. This is required to be done in "an adequate, timely and effective manner".[34] Some tools are recommended in the guidelines to resolve practical problems of notification.[35] Notably, the fact that the activity is subject to a national or transboundary EIA procedure should be notified as well.[36] This may be then followed by participation during the preparation of the EIA report under the national law or according to transboundary arrangements. Although the EIA itself is just a tool for decision-making rather than a permission or

---

30 Ibid. art 6.

31 See ibid. art 6(1)(b), annex I.

32 Ibid. art 6(1)(c).

33 Ibid. art 6(4).

34 Ibid. art 6(2).

35 *The Aarhus Convention: An Implementation Guide*, UN Doc ECE/CEP/72 (2000) 96–7.

36 *Convention on Access to Information, Public Participation in Decision-making and Access to Justice in Environmental Matters*, opened for signature 25 June 1998, 2161 UNTS 447 (entered into force 10 October 2001) art 6(2).

authorisation process,[37] it is argued that active involvement of the public during different stages of EIA is vital for the effectiveness of the process. As will be illustrated in detail later, domestic legislation on public participation during the EIA process usually represents the most advanced form of participation in Mekong countries, but even participation in this respect is insufficient and falls short of necessary legal foundation. Moreover, in a transboundary context, informing the public should be further combined with the notification and consultation process among states.

The Convention then requires states to set reasonable time-frames for different participation phases to allow sufficient time for informing the public and for the public to prepare and participate effectively.[38] Despite the preliminary information provided to the public, countries should also ensure that the public concerned can have access for examination of all information relevant to the decision-making that is available at that time, subject to the exceptions of information disclosure under the Convention.[39] A non-exhaustive list of information that is relevant to the decision is then made to set minimum standards to ensure the public's right of access to information at this stage, the contents of which are in line with the information provided by an EIA report under the *Espoo Convention*.[40] Namely, in order to implement the *Aarhus Convention*, some form of EIA process will be required.[41] And the Convention largely complements and enhances public participation requirements under the *Espoo Convention*.[42] Detailed forms of participation are left to a state's discretion. By the end of the participation process, public opinion gained from the process should be given due consideration in the final decision. Once the decision has been made, the public should be promptly informed.[43] But it is unclear in the Convention on whether reasons for rejecting the public opinion should be provided as well.

---

37 *The Aarhus Convention: An Implementation Guide*, UN Doc ECE/CEP/72 (2000) 90.

38 Ibid. art 6(3).

39 Ibid. art 6(6).

40 See ibid. art 6(6); *Convention on Environmental Impact Assessment in a Transboundary Context*, opened of signature 25 February 1991, 1989 UNTS 309 (entered into force 10 September 1997) annex II.

41 *The Aarhus Convention: An Implementation Guide*, UN Doc ECE/CEP/72 (2000) 91.

42 *Convention on Environmental Impact Assessment in a Transboundary Context*, opened of signature 25 February 1991, 1989 UNTS 309 (entered into force 10 September 1997) arts 2, 3.

43 *Convention on Access to Information, Public Participation in Decision-making and Access to Justice in Environmental Matters*, opened for signature 25 June 1998, 2161 UNTS 447 (entered into force 10 October 2001) art 6(8)(9).

Article 7 of the Convention then briefly addresses participation at other levels of decision-making. General requirements like necessary information to the public, early participation, reasonable time-frames and due account of participation outcomes should also be applied to the preparation of plans and programs. With respect to policies relating to the environment, the language used in the Convention is much more hortatory, using terms like "to the extent appropriate" and "shall endeavour".[44] Based on the guidelines, it is suggested that strategic environmental assessment (SEA) is one method of implementing this Article.[45] Further, general rules are set by the Convention to guide public participation in the development of laws and other normative acts.[46] Public participation at this level not only involves law-making on the substantive aspects of environmental protection, but also provides further procedural security for the freedom of access to information and the detailed arrangements for public participation at lower levels. Although the Convention recognises the "desirability of transparency in all branches of government", the Convention does not impose requirements for parliaments since countries consider this a prerogative of the legislative branch.[47]

### C *Comments*

The above requirements under the *Aarhus Convention*, combined with the support provided by the right of access to justice, establish a relatively systematic international regime to promote environment deliberative and more responsive decision-making. It focuses on the obligations of public authorities and does not elaborate on the relevant obligations of private actors. Other than the decision-making period, there is no specific requirement on information disclosure or public participation during the implementation period. These issues are left to the discretion of member states. But with regard to the implementation of the Convention, the member states later established a unique compliance monitoring mechanism, which allows even the public to bring issues of non-compliance before the Compliance Committee.[48]

44 See ibid. art 7.

45 *The Aarhus Convention: An Implementation Guide*, UN Doc ECE/CEP/72 (2000) 114.

46 See *Convention on Access to Information, Public Participation in Decision-making and Access to Justice in Environmental Matters*, opened for signature 25 June 1998, 2161 UNTS 447 (entered into force 10 October 2001) art 8.

47 *The Aarhus Convention: An Implementation Guide*, UN Doc ECE/CEP/72 (2000) 119.

48 Svitlana Kravchenko, 'Strengthening Implementation of MEAs: The Innovative Aarhus Compliance Mechanism' in Durwood Zaelke, Donald Kaniaru and Eva Kružíková (eds), *Making Law Work: Environmental Compliance and Sustainable Development* (Cameron May Ltd, International Law Publishers, 2005) vol 1, 245, 248–9. By 2005, 11 cases had been

The Compliance Committee meetings are open to the public, except for its deliberations.[49] The independent experts that constitute the committee can be nominated not only by parties, but also by certain NGOs.[50] The extent of public involvement and information transparency achieved under the Aarhus regime is commendable and represents significant progress.

The implementation of the Convention largely relies on domestic legislation and practice. Although the elements of procedural rights set out in the Convention are designed to operate together, they are often developed in an imbalanced way under different domestic circumstances. In addition, how to integrate these participation requirements with other mechanisms and their respective agreements can also pose serious challenges in the field. The effectiveness of access to information and participatory rights also depends on the overall improvement of environmental democracy and the judicial system to provide more comprehensive political and legal support. In practice, member states implement the Convention in a patchy and uneven way. However, by joining the Convention, at least these countries do share similar values on improving environment democracy by increasing transparency and further involving the public. Although countries are facing different domestic and regional circumstances, they are bound by the Convention to comply with the minimum standards agreed internationally and further enhance these procedural rights in different contexts.

Since many operating water treaties were signed before the *Aarhus Convention* was adopted, the limited reference to the public's procedural rights under the existing international watercourses law is to some extent understandable. After the adoption of the *Aarhus Convention*, the member states, particularly the EU countries, have taken various measures to incorporate these requirements into their domestic and regional legal systems and to apply them in their domestic and transboundary water cooperation practice. But a real challenge is how to introduce the provisions of the Convention to other non-member countries, many of which are still struggling with their

---

initiated by communications from NGOs. Moreover, the independent experts that constitute the committee can be nominated not only by parties, but also by certain NGOs. In addition, the Compliance Committee meetings are open for the public, except for the deliberations and decision-making.

49 United Nations Economic Commission for Europe, *Report of the First Meeting of the Parties (Addendum): Decision I/7 Review of Compliance (Adopted at the First Meeting of the Parties Held in Lucca, Italy, on 21–23 October 2002)*, UN Doc ECE/MP.PP/2/Add.8 (2 April 2004) annex IX(32).

50 Ibid. annex I(4).

immature domestic political and legal systems. Questions remain on how to design and promote these two procedural rights under the general political and legal background in the region and how to better interact with other existing mechanisms.

International experience in this area has adopted different approaches, which include, inter alia, a project-by-project approach, action programs,[51] developing a coordination organisation among the regional water-related advocacy groups,[52] enhancing the role of river basin organisations in information disclosure and public participation, and improving domestic legislation. In addition to riparian states, major international development banks have become involved in this process.[53] Due to the varied political, legal and economic situations in different basins, however, notable gaps often exist between rhetoric and reality and the performance in the field can be unstable. The following study will shift attention to the Mekong region in particular to evaluate the relevant developments and make further recommendations.

## III The Development of Access to Information and Public Participation in the Context of the Mekong Region

### A *Mekong Regional Arrangements: Between Rhetoric and Reality*

#### 1 Association of Southeast Asian Nations (ASEAN)

Recent development of regional cooperation in Southeast Asia has witnessed an emerging trend towards increasing involvement of non-state actors in regional affairs and more regional efforts toward promoting democracy and the rule of law. A cornerstone document is the *ASEAN Charter*, a legally-binding agreement entered into force in 2008. Article 1 of the Charter concludes

51 See generally Olli Varis, Virpi Stucki and Sylvie Fraboulet-Jussila, *The Senegal River Case* (2006) United Nations Development Programme <http://hdr.undp.org/en/content/senegal-river-case>.

52 See generally John Jackson, 'Citizens Working Across National Borders: The Experience in the North American Great Lakes' in Carl Bruch et al. (eds), *Public Participation in the Governance of International Freshwater Resources* (United Nations University, 2005) 118, 131–7.

53 See generally Aboubacar Fall and Angela Cassar, 'Improving Governance and Public Participation in International Watercourse Management: Experience of the African Development Bank in the Senegal River Basin' in Carl Bruch et al. (eds), *Public Participation in the Governance of International Freshwater Resources* (United Nations University, 2005) 216.

that one purpose of ASEAN is to "strengthen democracy, enhance good governance and the rule of law, and to promote and protect human rights and fundamental freedoms, with due regard to the rights and responsibilities of the Member States of ASEAN".[54] In order to promote and protect human rights and fundamental freedoms, a consultative inter-governmental body, the ASEAN Intergovernmental Commission on Human Rights was inaugurated in 2009 under Article 14 of the Charter. But no regional human rights convention or concrete standards have been developed accordingly. Comprised of representatives from all ASEAN countries, the Commission is required to disclose information regarding its work and activities to the public and engage in dialogue and consultation with civil society organisations.[55]

Other than the aspirational feelings and an opportunity provided for potential human rights development in the ASEAN region, these new developments were mainly labelled as "a tongue but no teeth".[56] This can be attributed to the huge divergence among member states over their vision for ASEAN's future. With an exception of Thailand, other lower Mekong countries all prefer to maintain ASEAN as a mediator among government instead of a more cohesive and effective regional organisation and are generally reluctant to make real commitments on human rights and democratic values.[57] In light of the current soft arrangements on promoting human rights through ASEAN and the lack of political will from most of the lower Mekong countries, whether the ASEAN Human Rights Commission can result in actual improvement in these countries is doubtful. Nevertheless, along with the continuing engagement of representatives from all ASEAN countries and civil society groups, the Commission can serve as a rudimentary regional platform to better utilise the limited political opportunities that are gradually opening to varying degrees in the region to promote human rights.

54 *The Charter of the Association of South East Asian Nations*, opened for signature 20 November 2007 (entered into force 15 December 2008) art 1.

55 See *Terms of Reference of the ASEAN Intergovernmental Commission on Human Rights*, ASEAN <http://www.asean.org/communities/asean-political-security-community/category/asean-intergovernmental-commission-on-human-rights-aichr>.

56 See Andrea Durbach, Catherine Renshaw and Andrew Byrnes, " 'A Tongue but No Teeth?': The Emergence of a Regional Human Rights Mechanism in the Asia Pacific Region" (2009) 31 *Sydney Law Review* 211.

57 The ASEAN human rights agenda is mainly promoted by Indonesia, Philippines and Thailand. See Lee Leviter, 'The ASEAN Charter: ASEAN Failure or Member Failure?' (2010) 43 *International Law and Politics* 159, 194.

## 2 The Mekong River Commission (MRC)

If the human rights and democracy discourses are mainly driven by Thailand and a few other ASEAN countries located outside of the Mekong region, the prospects of introducing them in the context of Mekong water management are even more challenging. Not surprisingly, the *Mekong Agreement* makes no reference to non-state actors or their procedural rights. But the MRC has allegedly viewed transparency and public participation as important components of good governance almost from the outset.[58] This phenomenon in part reflects the gaps between the member states and the donor-driven MRC, and illustrates the disconnection between the MRC and domestic Mekong management. So far, some measures have been undertaken by the MRC to promote transparency and public participation. The design and implementation of relevant arrangements will be examined.

### (a) *Information Disclosure*

Freedom of access to water-related information is partly reflected through the MRC's agenda to improve information collection and exchange across the region. One objective of the Procedures for Data and Information Exchange and Sharing is to "make available, upon request, basic data and information for public access as determined by the National Mekong Committees (NMC) concerned".[59] But this document has no legally-binding force and it does not provide any further elaboration or detailed guidance on how to ensure its implementation. Moreover, the word "basic" used in the provision is confusing and indicates a limited range of information available for the public. Detailed arrangements are completely left to the discretion of the NMCs, with no standard or clarification applicable at the regional level. In addition to access to information upon request, there is no obligation on the government to actively disclose information on a broader basis, which, in contrast, is emphasised in the *Aarhus Convention*.

The public's right of access to information is not expressly recognised in the procedures for notification and consultation on proposed projects. With regard

58 This is reflected in various MRC program documents and reports, i.e., the 1999 MRC Public Participation Policy: "Public Participation in the Context of the MRC", the Environmental Programme, the Basin Development Programme and the MRC Communication Strategy and Disclosure Policy. A hortatory and general provision on raising public awareness and promoting public participation is also included in the MRC Procedures for Water Quality.

59 Mekong River Commission, *Procedures for Data and Information Exchange and Sharing* (1 November 2001), 2 <http://www.mrcmekong.org/assets/Publications/policies/Procedures-Data-Info-Exchange-n-Sharing.pdf>.

to notification in emergency situations, the *Mekong Agreement* only addresses notification to the affected states and the MRC Joint Committee, while the public's right to know is treated more like a subordinate matter. In practice, effective access to information remains difficult for many local communities, due to technological and geographic difficulties, a lack of subregional arrangements for early warning, and the insufficient arrangements and requirements for governments to disseminate information actively and effectively.

The most notable progress of information disclosure through the MRC is the adoption of the MRC Communications Strategy and Disclosure Policy in 2009. In addition to information disclosure and communication regarding the public, this document aims to improve the responsiveness of the MRC to its member states, partners and other stakeholders.[60] It incorporates a specific MRC Disclosure Policy in the appendices to regulate access to information held by the MRC Secretariat and the materials more generally available. Namely, it only addresses the transparency of the MRC, instead of reflecting common commitments of the member states on information disclosure at the domestic level (even the NMCs are not directly targeted in the Policy).

The Policy highlights the advantages of enhancing transparency of the MRC and gives definition for "data", "information" and "knowledge". Different from the *Aarhus Convention*, these definitions are based more on their literal interpretation and form, rather than the contents. As argued in chapter three, the current information collection and exchange system mainly focuses on technical and scientific information regarding the river. Information on water-related legislation, domestic administrative arrangements and the implementation of the *Mekong Agreement* in each country is much more limited. Under such circumstances, information available for the MRC to share is largely restrained and there is no regional commitment from the member states to require the disclosure of such information in a user-friendly manner.

Three categories are then required by the Policy to address different levels of information accessibility: unrestricted information is available to the general public, while restricted information "may be provided to a specific audience following the appropriate approvals". Confidential information is not for release beyond the author and addressees. More concrete standards are applied to confidential information, including national defence and security, copyright, internal processing, communications behind the scenes between the MRC and

60 Information in the next few paragraphs regarding the Policy is derived from: Mekong River Commission, *Communication Strategy and Disclosure Policy* (2009) <http://www.mrcmekong.org/assets/Publications/policies/Communication-Strategy-n-Disclosure-Policy.pdf>.

its member states, commercial secrets, personal data or information provided to the MRC on a confidential basis. Notably, the prevailing "ASEAN Way" means that a lot of communications between the MRC and member states can be marked as confidential. The Policy then sets out the categorisation process for documents in terms of definitions, the approval of classification and declassification. It also briefly addresses access to information upon request. No time-frame is set for response, but an authority is identified to handle such requests and is required to give reasons if the requested information cannot be provided.

In addition, the Policy favours the use of electronic data and information. Recent years have witnessed a rapid development of electronic databases and an increasing utilisation of the MRC and the MekongInfo websites to disseminate information. The development of the electronic information system is required under the *Aarhus Convention* as well. But the latter is targeted at member states.[61]

Although the electronic information system can arguably make information more easily accessible to the public, it is less likely to be the case for local communities who do not understand English or cannot afford the necessary equipment to access it. The only approach that is adopted in the Policy to improve local accessibility is through more translation,[62] while in fact more fundamental reforms need to be made with cooperation of NMCs, other water sectors in the member states, the media, NGOs and other stakeholders. Some examples are already available in this area, such as publication and distribution of easy to read material in riparian languages; the use of radios, community billboards, local forums and other media; the identification of points of contact; the cooperation with locally-based NGOs, etc. But the practice is uneven across the region and the kind of information that is available through these measures can be very selective. A more fundamental issue in need of redress lies in the problematic domestic water regime and the lack of legal protection and political will in most Mekong countries to secure the public's right of access to information. At the regional level, the MRC remains largely disconnected from this aspect of the problem and most member states are not really interested in making common commitments on information disclosure.

Therefore, it can be concluded that the current MRC Policy on Information Disclosure has a real impact only on the organisation itself rather than the

---

61 *Convention on Access to Information, Public Participation in Decision-making and Access to Justice in Environmental Matters*, opened for signature 25 June 1998, 2161 UNTS 447 (entered into force 10 October 2001) art 5(2).

62 See Mekong River Commission, above n 60, 14–5.

member states. Its current major approach of information disclosure remains distant from local communities. This situation, however, can be largely attributed to the member states rather than the MRC, since the latter is not a supernational organisation. The lack of political will, legal environment and necessary resources at the domestic level remain the biggest obstacles for bringing information disclosure down to the ground. The increasing transparency of the MRC itself does have some positive influence on the current restrained political environment and the information available from the MRC is quite beneficial for the work of local media, academics and advocates, who can subsequently serve as bridges to link the MRC and local communities.

(b) *Public Participation*

The MRC often states that since 1995 it has "adopted a participatory approach in the work of all its core programs and sector programs and is envisaging ways to expand the opportunities for collaboration with both internal and external stakeholders".[63] This, however, has proved to be a very uneven and problematic performance across different subregions and programs. Before any detailed discussion, it is necessary to clarify some often used concepts that may cause confusion, bearing in mind that the following concepts are often developed as the result of discussions on participation from different disciplines.

There is the difference between "public" participation and "stakeholder" participation. The latter can be referred to in both a narrow sense and a broad sense. In a narrow sense, the "stakeholder" can be interpreted as the "public concerned", namely any person, group or institution that is affected or likely to be affected by, or having an interest in the decision-making.[64] Under the *Aarhus Convention*, this concept is used in public participation on proposed activities while participation at other decision-making levels should be open for the general public. But in the MRC documents, participation at these levels is often open to "stakeholders". If interpreted strictly, this may narrow the scope of those members of the public that can be involved in the decision-making process.

In a broad sense, however, the "stakeholder" at the Mekong regional level can include the MRC internal agencies, riparian governments, government agencies, business sector and civil society. Stakeholder participation in this sense also includes inter-governmental cooperation or internal cooperation with other MRC institutions. Civil society is often referred to as the "third sector" of

63 Mekong River Commission, *Public Participation in the Lower Mekong Basin* (2005) <http://www.mrcmekong.org/assets/Publications/governance/Public-Participation.pdf>.

64 Ibid.; *The Aarhus Convention: An Implementation Guide*, UN Doc ECE/CEP/72 (2000) 40.

society which is distinct from government and business.[65] It can either mean the "aggregate of non-governmental organisations and institutions that manifest interests and the will of citizens" or "individuals and organisations in a society which are independent of the government".[66] "Civil society" and "public" are overlapping terms and the development of civil society, especially the NGOs and other civil society organisations, is an important aspect of participatory democracy. In addition, in various discussions on public participation, it is the local communities and NGOs that are often highlighted. The former is usually the most vulnerable group among all stakeholders. The latter can serve as an important watch dog on government's decision-making and help raise the voice of the disadvantaged groups.

The word "participation" is often linked with "involvement", "consultation" and "communication". However, these terms can be understood as involving lower levels of participation (tokenism) according to the Arnstein's ladder. At the risk of oversimplification, the ladder indicates different degrees of public participation from the perspective of power relationships between the public and those holding or exercising the power.[67] Higher levels of participation involve power redistribution between citizens and power holders, while the degrees of tokenism are characterised by one-way information flow or the public taking an advisory role but having no guarantee that their voice will be heard. At the bottom of the ladder there are forms of nonparticipation when "people are placed on rubberstamp advisory committees or advisory boards for the express purpose of educating them or engineering their support".[68] The Global Water Partnership also argues that public participation should be more than consultation.[69]

The development of real participation in practice is challenged by the lack of political will and pressure to redistribute power.[70] This is typically featured

65 Many people hold the view that a free and vigorous press is an essential element in civil society. But most newspapers and TV stations are run as for-profit businesses. Therefore, whether the media should be a part of the civil society is under dispute. Civil Society International, *What is Civil Society* <http://www.civilsocietyinternational.org/whatisCS.htm>.

66 Dictionary.com's 21st Century Lexicon, *Civil Society* <http://dictionary.reference.com/browse/civil+society>.

67 The following description of the ladder is based on the paper published by Sherry R. Arnstein in 1969. Sherry R. Arnstein, 'A Ladder of Citizen Participation' (1969) 35(4) *AIP Journal* 216.

68 Ibid. 218.

69 Global Water Partnership Technical Advisory Committee, 'Integrated Water Resources Management' (Background Paper No 4, Global Water Partnership, 2000) 16.

70 Arnstein, above n 67, 217.

by the reluctance to reform the political process, to strengthen the legislation and to improve its implementation to protect procedural rights. From the public's perspective, it is argued that "simply creating participatory opportunities will do nothing for currently disadvantaged groups unless their capacity to participate is enhanced".[71] This includes inadequacies in their political, socio-economic infrastructure and knowledge base. It requires not only "awareness raising, confidence building and education, but also the provision of the economic resources needed to facilitate participation and the establishment of good and transparent sources of information".[72] During this process, the role of NGOs should not be neglected.

Against the above background, the following section will focus on the development of public participation facilitated by the MRC. In late 1996, a study on public participation in the context of the MRC was initiated. It directly led to the adoption of the MRC Secretariat Report on public participation in 1999 by the Joint Committee. The report addresses the basic concepts, terminologies and principle guidelines for public participation regarding the work of the MRC. In the report, the term "public" also includes the government and business sector.[73] Therefore, the so-called public participation agenda under the MRC indeed refers to broad stakeholder participation. The interchangeable use of public participation and stakeholder participation can also be identified in other MRC plans and programs.[74]

Whilst it is of crucial significance is to improve the involvement of governments and business sectors in the MRC cooperation regime, the confusing use of some basic concepts like "public", "stakeholder", "civil society" and "NGOs" reflects the MRC's poorly developed recognition of public participation. Simply adding public participation to the larger pool of general stakeholder participation is not a prudent approach to study and promote public participation in the context of the Mekong region. Without more specific, systematic attention and policy-making on the inherent characteristics of public participation, issues concerning the use of this mechanism can be easily neglected. The involvement of governments, business sectors or even experts may be used

---

71 Global Water Partnership Technical Advisory Committee, above n 69, 17.

72 Ibid.; Arnstein, above n 67, 217.

73 Mekong River Commission Secretariat, 'Public Participation in the Context of the MRC' (Report, Mekong River Commission, 1999) 1.

74 For example, the more recent MRC Communication Strategy and Disclosure Policy aims to improve the MRC communication with various stakeholders and enhance stakeholder participation through "close communication and collaboration with civil society, NGOs and emerging River Basin Organizations". In addition, the Basin Development Plan Programme, the Environment Programme and the Flood Programme also use the term "public participation" when they actually mean stakeholder participation.

to avoid actual participation on the part of local communities. Evaluations based primarily on stakeholder participation in a broad sense can easily conceal the degree of actual public participation in the field. Therefore, it is strongly recommended that the MRC should clarify the existing confusion and ambiguity of public participation and develop more specific policies accordingly, or at least develop a more precise process for public participation in the context of the current general stakeholder policy.

Public participation is viewed as "a normal and essential process in MRC and NMC activities" and should occur "throughout the lifecycle of a project or programme".[75] Transparency is highlighted in the report and information should be available in an "understandable" way. The report also elaborates on information gathering and dissemination, including suggested tools. In particular, printed materials, information centres in accessible locations, public hearings, and community meetings can make the information more accessible to the local communities. The report obviously pays more attention to addressing these technical issues than elaborating on what kinds of information should be available to the public. Since the MRC does not differentiate specific activities with the more general plans, programs and policies, it is in fact difficult to develop a specific list of what should be included. For example, in the context of the MRC, the term "project" can either mean a specific development activity initiated by member states and developers, or projects run by the MRC Secretariat as components of the various programs and plans. In addition, it should be noted that public participation on specific activities is open to the "public concerned", while participation on plans, programs and policies is often open to the general public, with or without an interest in the decision. This issue needs to be further clarified, especially since the MRC is currently considering developing a MRC procedural document on transboundary environmental impact assessment (EIA). How to link the transboundary EIA process with public participation should be a major component during the preparation of this document. But it should be borne in mind that public participation policy adopted for the operation of an international organisation is different from the one that directly targets the obligations of member states.

Another principle is that public participation should start "as early as possible in project or program cycles—preferably in the formation stage and be evident throughout the entire cycle".[76] This is reflected in the processes of "consultation" and "participation". Although the report differentiates between the

75 Mekong River Commission Secretariat, above n 73, 3, 6.

76 Ibid. 6.

two terms, it is not based on different levels of participation. Rather, "consultation" is the participation process during the formation and design of the project or program, while "participation" refers to public involvement during the implementation of the projects and policies. Technically, this is a way forward considering the *Aarhus Convention* only requires public participation during the decision-making process. The participation process during the implementation period does bear some features of higher levels of participation in the sense that theoretically not only can the public influence the decision on the formulation of the plans and programs, they can also take part in the decision-making process during the implementation period, especially regarding the allocation of resources, costs and benefits.

Nevertheless, since decision-making at this stage is mainly through negotiation and bargaining, it is very doubtful whether the public do have such power to bargain with other powerful stakeholders. In addition, considering the level of participation, the public involved at this stage should have enough capacity to utilise this opportunity. The report does call for the MRC and NMCs to build capacity for public participation, but no attention is paid to capacity building for the public which is a more crucial issue in the region. The local communities often have insufficient ability to participate, even at the lower participation levels. It is obvious that participation at this level will require a vibrant and strong civil society which generally is not the case at present in the Mekong region.

Combined with the fact that the report addresses stakeholder participation in a broad sense, it is very likely that participation at the implementation level refers more to the governments, donors and business sectors rather than the public. Although the report focuses on so-called public participation, an inordinate amount of attention is in fact paid to the participation of stakeholders other than the public. It mainly addresses participation on plans, programs and policy, but largely ignores public participation on specific development activities, thus providing very limited guidance on the decision-making with respect to the mainstream hydropower projects. It does not call for improvement of public participation at the domestic level and this participation agenda is very much disconnected to what is happening in the field. Given the fact that tributary hydropower development is completely left for the discretion of member states, the lack of regional arrangements on promoting public participation at the domestic level cannot contribute to a more sustainable decision-making process for these projects.

Currently, some elements of public participation are reflected in the MRC programs and plans. Due to the different issues addressed in each program and the corresponding political will and resources available for promoting public participation, these programs reflect varying degrees of participation.[77] The Basin Development Plan Programme (BDP) adopted a specific stakeholder participation strategy in 2004 to promote multi-stakeholder participatory planning forums at sub-area, country and basin levels through different BDP working groups. Again, participation here includes governments, private sector, donor agencies, civil society organisations, individuals with relevant knowledge and the media.[78] No representative of local communities is expressly listed as a stakeholder and the individuals have to possess relevant knowledge in order to be qualified to participate.

The directly affected people, as one of the stakeholders, are better recognised in the 2009 BDP Phase 2 Stakeholder Participation and Communication Plan.[79] It includes workers, farmers and fisherfolk who depend on river resources for their livelihoods. And minorities, poor people and women are identified as the least powerful among the most vulnerable groups. NGOs are given more prominence in the new plan. This improved stakeholder identification comes along with the recognition that:

> The representation of stakeholder representatives should include processes that promote social equity, ensure gender balance and enable the interests and needs of affected peoples to be taken into consideration. Interests and needs of the poor will be taken into consideration as a priority, and opportunities will be provided for them to engage effectively.[80]

Different from the 2004 stakeholder participation strategy, improved access to information is expressly set as a target of the Plan. Notably, timely distribution, non-technical and easily understandable terms, and accurate translation into the riparian languages are highlighted to improve the accessibility of information. In addition to openness and transparency, the Plan also requires stakeholder participation to be initiated as early as possible in the formula-

77 The so-called public participation is partly reflected in almost all MRC programs, such as the Environment Programme and the Flood Programme. The Basin Development Plan Programme is chosen as a typical example here.

78 Mekong River Commission, 'The MRC Basin Development Plan: Stakeholder Participation' (Programme Document, Mekong River Commission, 2005) 5–6.

79 Information on the Plan in the next few paragraphs is mainly based on: Mekong River Commission, 'Stakeholder Participation and Communication Plan for Basin Development Planning in the Lower Mekong Basin' (Programme Document, Mekong River Commission, 2009).

80 Ibid. 12.

tion of MRC programs, projects, other activities and the decision-making in the MRC Council and Joint Committee. It is further emphasised that stakeholders should be able to participate during all stages of the MRC activities. Again, since this refers to the participation of all stakeholders, to what extent the local communities and NGOs can participate is less clear. The Plan does mention the need to "empower local decision-makers and communities to take the lead in data provision, analysis, working with national research institutions and experts, and implementing local forums in their sub-areas".[81] Here, the reference to local communities in addition to local decision-makers contains more rhetoric than reality, with no specific measure or arrangement dedicated to raise their voice and power during the communication and consultation.

Communities, along with other local stakeholders, mainly participate through sub-area forums. The Plan only emphasises that they should be consulted and provided with opportunities to participate in these sub-area forums, but no attention is paid to improve their capacity to participate. The aim of such forums is to build common understanding, increase communication, and build consensus on sub-area development scenario and IWRM strategy. The benefit of participation at this level (namely information exchange and providing a platform for them to express their opinions) is very limited, not to mention that the impact of the BDP strategies and scenarios on domestic development decision-making remain relatively low.

Despite the adoption of some encouraging principles and limited improvement on participation at the local level, the whole Plan pays scant attention to the directly affected people. It is highly doubtful to what extent their participation can be weighed during the implementation of the new Plan. In fact, the Plan also speaks to the responsibilities of the main stakeholders during its implementation. While government stakeholders and the MRC internal stakeholders are given more detailed roles during the implementation of the Plan, the responsibilities assigned to the local communities and NGOs are in more flexible terms, such as to be engaged and involved in the BDP Phase 2 processes "where appropriate". In addition to participation in stakeholder forums and providing comments on the BDP Program documents, their major roles are restricted to training activities and data contribution. In comparison, line agencies and local governments can participate at higher decision-making levels and are required to "take the lead" in sector reviews and sub-area activities.

Overall, the development of public participation under the MRC regime does have some potential to increase transparency of the MRC, raise public awareness on Mekong issues and provide a forum or platform for the public

81 Ibid. 18.

to express their opinions. But participation at these levels are relatively low according to the Arnstein's ladder, not to mention that the MRC's arrangements on these lower levels of participation are still very immature. The degree of participation by the public remains the most unsatisfactory among all stakeholders. The MRC relies on the NMCs and domestic line agencies to provide necessary channels for information dissemination and facilitate national and local public consultations. Such structural settings call for more support from the domestic political and legal environment. Otherwise, it is unlikely that the MRC arrangements on public participation alone can make much difference in the field. As illustrated in chapter two, the lack of real influence on water development decision-making by the MRC creates a more fundamental challenge on the effectiveness of public participation under the MRC regime. Even if the arrangements under the MRC regarding public participation can be significantly improved, the impact of public participation through the MRC regime may remain limited due to the polycentric feature of water governance in the region and the lack of more stringent requirements on public participation under other regional cooperation regimes or at the domestic level.

Moreover, under the current circumstances, it is doubtful whether the comments made through such dialogues and communications really represent the true public voice. Combined with the fact that public participation is incorporated with the participation of other stakeholders, the lack of power and capacity of many local communities can easily lead to manipulation of their opinions by the powerful stakeholders. This can be resulted from political pressure, selective information disclosure, control over the selection of the representatives of the local communities and NGOs, bribery and a small number of economic interests or promises to the public which are often not realised in practice. This would require more effective domestic legislation and regional commitments on securing the public's right to know and participate. It also calls for detailed and strategic measures to improve the participation capacities of local communities. The capacity requirement often relates to the more general issues like poverty alleviation and improving public education.

The enhancement of public participation relies on the development of a vibrant civil society. Among different civil society actors, the participation of experts is often more common than the participation of the local communities in the Mekong countries. Although experts and scholars have professional knowledge and are likely to have a strong sense of social responsibility, their opinions should not replace those of the local communities. The latter's capacity to participate is often limited in the Mekong region and their participation is more politically sensitive. The opinions of the local communities have less chance, compared to experts, to be heard or considered seriously during the decision-making process. Further, due to the different restrictions on the development of NGOs across the region, it is very difficult to establish local NGOs in countries like Laos. To what extent the international NGOs operating in such areas can really represent the interests of local communities is difficult to quantify.[82] In addition, some NGOs in the region have a very close relationship with the government and their independence is therefore in doubt.

Therefore, while it is necessary to improve public participation arrangements under the MRC, it is clear that this participatory agenda led by the MRC will continue to be problematic unless more fundamental changes can be made at the domestic level, under other regional cooperative organisations or through international banking policies. In particular, more detailed requirements under domestic legislation or banking policies regarding public participation during the decision-making process of specific projects and their effective implementation are crucial in promoting sustainable hydropower development. Along with the increasing emphasis on public participation at the regional level, there is growing momentum and pressure for the transformation and improvement of domestic decision-making processes. The development of participatory democracy is a progressive process and different platforms for participation and various participation levels all have their unique roles in promoting meaningful change.

## 3 Multilateral Development Banks

As identified in chapter two, the Asian Development Bank (ADB) and the World Bank mainly influence the Mekong river water governance by funding specific projects and promoting the development of IWRM and relevant legislation or strategies at the domestic level. Access to information and public participation is addressed through a series of environmental and social safeguard policies and procedures, policies on information disclosure or public communication, guidelines on public participation and the establishment of an accountability mechanism or inspection panel. While both the World Bank and the ADB have decided not to provide funding for any of the lower Mekong

82 For example, in the case of the Theun-Hinboun Dam, the most affected people had no knowledge of the actions being undertaken on their behalf at certain points in the campaign project, which raised question of accountability of the advocacy work. See Lindsay Soutar, 'Asian Development Bank: NGO Encounters and the Theun-Hinboun Dam, Laos' in Barbara Rugendyke (ed), *NGOs as Advocates for Development in a Globalising World* (Routledge, 2007) 200, 217–8.

mainstream dams,[83] it is the relevant infrastructure developments and tributary hydropower developments that are more directly affected by their information disclosure and participation policies. These arrangements target the development and implementation of policies and strategies of the World Bank and the ADB, as well as their decision-making processes regarding specific loans (investment and policy-based), grants and technical assistance. The following discussion will use the relevant experiences of the ADB to illustrate the roles and limitations of multilateral development banks in promoting more transparent and participatory water-related development.

With regard to information disclosure, the ADB has recently adopted the Public Communications Policy (2011) as a review of the 2005 Policy which includes contributions from civil society. Compared to the previous version, the new Policy expressly recognises the right to access to information and the ADB make a general commitment to provide information in a "timely, clear and relevant manner".[84] The accessibility of information, although later mentioned several times in the Policy, is not highlighted as much as other information standards or principles. Instead, it is mainly addressed as one of the detailed issues during information disclosure and the primary responsibility for providing information indeed lies with the borrower and/or client, namely the government and the private sector.[85] The reliance on them to ensure the accessibility of information is to a large extent unavoidable, but given the restricted domestic environment for transparency, its effectiveness cannot be secured.

The real contribution of the ADB on improving the accessibility of information is by undertaking translations in accordance with its translation framework adopted in 2007. But overcoming the language barriers is only an initial step towards more accessible information and the extra time required for translation may undermine the standard of timely disclosure. Similar to the MRC, the ADB relies on its website as the primary vehicle for proactive disclosure, which is also criticised for the lack of accessibility for poor communities. Civil society groups even claim that this "manifests the pro-business bias of the Bank's disclosure policy".[86] To some extent, this can be compensated by

83 The World Bank and the ADB's decisions on not to provide funding for the lower Mekong mainstream projects are also used as another demonstration on the potential negative impact of these projects.

84 Asian Development Bank, 'Public Communications Policy 2011: Disclosure and Exchange of Information' (Policy Document, 2011) 3.

85 Ibid. 16.

86 NGO Forum on ADB, *Forum's Campaign on the Public Communications Policy* <http://www.forum-adb.org/inner.php?sec=13&ref=extras&id=8>.

more active information disclosure through specific public participation processes, utilising the media and engaging the civil society groups as another channel to disseminate information. But in reality, the Mekong governments can often influence the process by passive information disclosure, controlling the media or restricting the operation of civil society groups. The ADB falls short of more stringent requirements and arrangements to evaluate the compliance of its borrower and/or client on this issue. The 2011 document does delineate exceptions to the Policy and provides an independent appeals panel for denied requests of access to information.[87] This, however, only addresses the decisions of the ADB on information requests and does not consider the information disclosure requirement on the borrower and/or client. Therefore, even though the ADB did manage to improve its transparency through its website, various limitations still exist for the local communities to effectively access such information. In addition, the dual accountability setting between the ADB and its borrower and/or client opens the door for the ADB to shift the blame onto the latter for ineffective information disclosure. The ADB itself falls short of detailed measures and the political will to urge or compel the latter to actively comply with the Policy in practice. Due to the variations of domestic circumstances, the transparency situation also differs from country to country. But there is no country-specific plan on how to implement the Policy.

Ideally, the ADB facilitates public participation at three levels: at the policy level, at the country strategy level and on a project specific basis.[88] The ADB itself claims that civil society has been "actively consulted" in the development and review of institution-wide ADB policies, strategies and the country partnership strategy in each developing member country. An oft-cited example in this area is the process of reviewing the 2005 Public Communication Policy and the development of the new one in 2011. This was mainly achieved by allowing public comment on the 2005 Policy and two drafts of the new policy, and organising consultations with NGOs and the affected people in the ADB project sites.[89]

---

87 Asian Development Bank, above n 84, 2, 4.

88 Asian Development Bank, *Civil Society Participation* <http://www.adb.org/site/ngos/civil-society-participation>.

89 See Asian Development Bank, 'Strengthening Participation for Development Results: An Asian Development Bank Guide to Participation' (Guidelines, Asian Development Bank, 2012) 13; Asian Development Bank, *External Comments and ADB Response* <http://www.adb.org/site/disclosure/policy-background-history/comments-external-stakeholders>; Asian Development Bank, *Consultation Workshops* <http://www.adb.org/site/disclosure/policy-background-history/consultation-workshops>.

The public comment process was web-based consultations with the involvement of some civil society organisations (none of which, however, is based in countries in the Mekong region). The ADB collected comments from these groups and responded to this feedback in a detailed manner.[90] This form of participation is less dependent on the support of the borrower and/or client. Whilst this represents a two-way flow of information and to a large extent indicates that the ADB considered these comments seriously, the web-based approach remains distant from most local communities. The ADB Guidelines for Participation encourages more approaches to facilitate participation at this level for those who do not understand English or have access to the internet.[91] In this case, the ADB did organise face-to-face consultations with NGOs and the affected people in the ADB project sites, but such consultation only needs to be held in a representative sample of the ADB member countries (the donor countries and the developing member states).[92] This process can be highly selective as well, leaving ample opportunity for the ADB to control the consultation result by choosing countries which the ADB has better relationships with, or by choosing ADB projects that are less controversial, or selecting the representatives of the public mainly from the village leader or men instead of women. Moreover, the government often has significant influence over this consultation process.

For example, the consultation workshops held by the ADB for the 2011 Policy included only two Mekong countries: China and Cambodia,[93] while Laos and Vietnam, two countries that are keen on Mekong hydropower development and have many relevant ADB projects, were not consulted. The participants from China did not include the local communities of any ADB project. Only NGOs and academics participated as representatives of civil society along with the participation of government agencies and international donor

90 See Asian Development Bank, *Key Recommendations from External Stakeholders on the Second Consultation Draft (November 2010) of the Public Communications Policy (PCP) and ADB's Response* (16 February 2011) <http://www.adb.org/sites/default/files/external-comments-2nd-draft_0.pdf>; Asian Development Bank, *Key Recommendations from External Stakeholders on the First Consultation Draft (June 2010) of the Public Communications Policy (PCP) and ADB's Response* (26 November 2010) <http://www.adb.org/sites/default/files/external-comments-1st-draft.pdf>.

91 Asian Development Bank, 'Strengthening Participation for Development Results: An Asian Development Bank Guide to Participation', above n 89, 12.

92 Ibid.

93 Asian Development Bank, *Consultation Workshops*, above n 89.

organisations.[94] The Cambodia consultation process incorporated more local communities and NGOs, but the representatives of some local communities claimed that they had never been informed or consulted about the ADB projects, which provides a perspective on the implementation of the 2005 Policy in the field.[95] It is clear that the current consultation practice for the ADB policies remains far from being really effective, with varying degrees of implementation in different countries.

Opportunities for the public to participate in the preparation of the ADB country strategy are even less secure. As the primary planning instrument guiding the ADB operations in each member country, the ADB guidelines require that the development of such strategy should fully involve non-government stakeholders.[96] But the ADB only works directly with borrowers and/or clients (mostly governments) to provide support for the activities of NGOs and other members of the public or civil society during the preparation of the country partnership strategy. Namely, the implementation of public participation at this level is largely dependent on domestic legislation and political will. Although the ADB itself also interacts with civil society through Civil Society Programmes at the ADB Annual Meetings, the NGO and Civil Society Centre and the Accountability Mechanism, these processes are indeed separate from the preparation of the country partnership strategy.

Consultations with civil society in developing the Cambodia Country Partnership Strategy are cited as an example in the Guidelines, but there is less evidence indicating to what extent public opinion can have an impact on the final decision reached under the strategy. Another driving force for a relatively more consultative process during the development of the country strategy in Cambodia is probably that the ADB has been actively promoting integrated water resources management (IWRM) reform in Cambodia. As illustrated in chapter two, water reform in Cambodia is largely driven by external actors like the ADB, allowing more foreign influence on its water management and development. But the reform measures and the consultative features introduced

94 See Asian Development Bank, *ADB Public Communications Policy Review 2010: PCP Consultation Workshop Summary (PRC Resident Mission, ADB)* (6 July 2010) <http://www.adb.org/sites/default/files/prc-consultation-pcp.pdf>.

95 Asian Development Bank, *Consultations on ADB's Public Communications Policy: PCP Consultation Workshop Summary (Nongovernment Organizations) (Cambodia Resident Mission)* (5 July 2010) <http://www.adb.org/sites/default/files/cam-consultation-cso-pcp.pdf>.

96 Asian Development Bank, 'Strengthening Participation for Development Results: An Asian Development Bank Guide to Participation', above n 89, 14.

by the ADB do represent the reality in the field. The 2012 Guidelines also states that the developing member country recipients/clients should negotiate with the ADB and agree on objectives and plans for participation in the country partnership strategy. But this is certainly not the case for most strategies that have just been updated. They either make no reference to public participation at all or just briefly mention civil society consultation but provide no plans or measures on how to promote it in practice.[97]

With regard to participation at the level of projects (namely specific loans, both investment and policy-based; grants; and technical assistance), the ADB Guidelines often refer to the broad stakeholder participation rather than public or civil society participation. Most parts of Guidelines are dedicated to facilitate cooperation with government and the private sector. But different from the MRC documents, these Guidelines at least clearly differentiate civil society participation with that of government and the private sector. The ADB develops some specific tools and measures that directly target and promote participation from these stakeholders.[98] In particular, the role of civil society organisations, among other civil society actors, is highlighted in the Guidelines.[99] Stakeholder participation at this level should be incorporated throughout the project cycle, such as individual project planning, implementation, monitoring and post-evaluation. During the project planning period, participation is mainly incorporated into various impact assessments processes, such as social and environment impact assessments.

The ADB Safeguard Policy requires:

> borrowers/clients to engage with communities, groups, or people affected by proposed projects, and with civil society through information disclosure, consultation, and informed participation in a manner commensurate with the risks to and impacts on affected communities.[100]

---

97 For example, civil society consultation or communication is briefly mentioned in the country partnership strategy in Cambodia and China, but the Lao Strategy does not include any provision or sentence on this matter. In the Thailand Strategy (2007–2011), cooperation with civil society organisations is mentioned several times as a part of the lessons and experiences gained from past practices.

98 Information on the Guidelines in the next three paragraphs is derived from the guideline document. See Asian Development Bank, 'Strengthening Participation for Development Results: An Asian Development Bank Guide to Participation', above n 89, 27, 15–6, 17, 19–20, 42–6, 51–60.

99 A specific tool is developed regarding working with civil society organisations.

100 Asian Development Bank, 'Safeguard Policy Statement' (Policy Paper, Asian Development Bank, 2009) 20.

But due to the variety of projects, specific measures are not delineated for participation. Instead, it requires the participation plan designed for each project to "define the engagement of specific stakeholders and the approach, depth and methods for use at each stage of the project cycle, taking into account time and resource constraints".[101] Some tools and methods are provided to develop such a plan, but no minimum standards are set for the key issues identified in the checklist. Therefore, the degree and approaches used to encourage participation in one specific project could be quite varied from the others due to the nature of the project and different domestic environment.

While participation at the project planning stage under the Guidelines does not specifically highlight civil society during the implementation, monitoring and the post-evaluation periods, the role of civil society organisations has become more apparent, allowing them to provide services or monitoring independently. In practice, it is often at this later stage of the project cycle that civil society manages to have a bigger voice with respect to the project and attracts wider attention. Correspondingly, the Guidelines develop specific tools on how to work with civil society organisations and how to involve civil society during the monitoring and evaluation processes.

Many of such tools are strongly ADB-oriented, paying more attention on how to identify such organisations and assess their capacities to collaborate or partner with the ADB or a developing member country. Instead of ensuring the right for civil society organisations to participate, the tools provide advices outlining ways for the ADB and the government to maintain a good relationship. Although such suggestions include elements like early involvement and transparency, the aims of taking such measures should go beyond merely maintaining a good relationship. Two methods for individuals and local communities to participate in the monitoring and evaluating processes include citizen report cards and community-based monitoring, but it is unclear to what extent these methods can be applied in practice. Whilst such measures may be more likely to be introduced in projects regarding public services, such as health, it is certainly less likely to be implemented in projects regarding economic development.

It is obvious that most ADB policies on public participation rely on the government and private sector clients to commit to a participatory approach. Despite some direct interactions between the ADB and civil society organisations mentioned earlier, most public participation arrangements are indirect and the ADB documents fall short of more concrete standards to evaluate the

101 Asian Development Bank, 'Strengthening Participation for Development Results: An Asian Development Bank Guide to Participation', above n 89, 20.

participation measures adopted by the clients during the approval process. Working with civil society is increasingly "subordinate to working with governments", who are the major clients of the ADB.[102]

Past experience has shown that between the formal channels arranged by the government or the private sector and those that allow more direct interaction with the ADB, it is the latter that is more favoured by the NGO advocates. This is especially true in cases where the domestic political freedom to challenge development projects and agendas are not available or highly-constrained (i.e. Laos).[103] But even if civil society organisations were able to participate more actively, their influence on decisions would remain very limited, such as in the cases of the Song Bung 4 Dam in Vietnam and the Theun-Hinboun Dam in Laos. In the Guidelines, the former is cited as a positive example of NGO involvement in monitoring social safeguards, including implementation of resettlement plans. But NGOs were critical that relevant information was not disseminated in a timely manner and their recommendations had little influence on the results.[104] In the case of Theun-Hinboun dam, locally-based communities and NGOs were not able to speak out against the project. Even when the ADB admitted the validity of the NGO critiques about the project's impact, such acknowledgements resulted in little concrete action.[105]

The direct participation approaches offered by the ADB are not in practice functioning well. Although the ADB does provide another platform for civil society to express their views and to influence the decision-making, there are concerns that the capacity of the ADB's NGO and Civil Society Centre has been "undermined by its small size, lack of resources and limited influence within the Bank".[106] The duel accountability system itself creates problems for the effectiveness of public participation. Despite the possibility for civil society to bring issues to the ADB Accountability Mechanism, this mechanism often cannot solve problems of project-affected people due to the fact that under the current arrangements most of the relevant responsibility lies primarily with the domestic government and the ADB lacks the necessary incentives to urge its major clients to comply with its policies or to effectively implement appropriate mitigation and compensation measures.

---

102 Soutar, above n 82, 209.

103 Ibid. 203.

104 See Bank Information Centre, *Song Bung 4 Hydropower Project* <http://www.bicusa.org/en/Project.Concerns.10516.aspx>.

105 Soutar, above n 82, 213–4, 217.

106 Ibid. 210.

Despite the above deficiencies, it remains valuable to continue promoting public participation through multilateral development banks like the ADB. But along with the need for more stringent requirements under the ADB and the World Bank, there is an increasing concern that the hydropower developers and the government may seek alternative funding from domestic or foreign investors that adopt lower standards. The diversification of funding sources calls for more fundamental public participation commitments and arrangements by the governments through regional economic cooperation organisations and at the domestic level.

## 4 Regional Economic Cooperation

Currently, it is the GMS program and the newly established ACFTA that function as the major regional economic cooperation platforms in the Mekong region. The former focuses on infrastructure development and the latter aims at promoting free trade and facilitating investment among ASEAN countries and China. Both cooperative mechanisms are now mainly driven by countries within this region, instead of being strongly influenced by donors and other foreign actors. The two mechanisms are state-centred but fall short of policies on information disclosure and necessary opportunities for civil society to participate in regional economic cooperation and relevant environment protection initiatives.

For the GMS projects that are funded or supported by the ADB, the ADB policies on public participation at the project level should apply, but the GMS itself does not include any express requirement for access to information and public participation. As mentioned before, the operation of GMS follows a flexible, results-oriented and activity-based approach.[107] Along with its development, more systematic arrangements should be made to crystallise the experiences of the GMS. As a loosely structured forum, it is probably too early to expect the GMS to adopt any policy on transparency and public participation. But such notions should begin to be introduced into the discussions during the ministerial and prime ministerial meetings. Since the GMS has taken some preliminary measures on environmental protection and has adopted methods like environmental performance assessment and strategic environmental assessment (SEA), further development of environmental cooperation under the GMS should incorporate more advanced transparency and participation requirements.

107 Asian Development Bank, 'Midterm Review of the Greater Mekong Subregion Strategic Framework (2002–2012)' (Report, Asian Development Bank, 2007) 2.

Regional and international economic integration regimes such as the World Trade Organisation (WTO), North American Free Trade Agreement (NAFTA) and EU are increasingly concerned about the environment and the democratic feature of their decision-making processes. For example, the NAFTA environmental side agreement emphasises the importance of public participation and highlights transparency and public participation as one of the objectives of the Agreement.[108]The compliance mechanism established under the Agreement also allows submissions from NGOs and individuals.[109] Recent years have witnessed an increasing discussion on transparency and public participation under the WTO regime, urging more strategic measures to promote public participation in the WTO policy-making and dispute resolution processes.[110] To date, two WTO documents are especially important in this area, namely the Decision of the General Council on the Procedures for the Circulation and De-restriction of WTO Documents and the Guidelines for Arrangements on Relations with NGOs. While the implementation of the above arrangements is not shielded from criticism, at least an initial step has been made under these economic cooperation regimes toward more transparent and participatory decision-making. As a general tendency in economic cooperation, it is argued that the future development of ACFTA should promote the regional recognition of these procedural values and gradually develop suitable mechanisms to increase transparency and allow more opportunities for civil society to participate.

### B *The Status Quo of Procedural Rights in the Mekong Countries*

International and regional efforts on promoting procedural rights can have a positive impact on domestic implementation. Meanwhile, the development of relevant international and regional arrangements and their effective implementation are to a large extent dependent on domestic legal, political and economic circumstances. After all, it is countries that should take the primary responsibility to promote and protect human rights and fundamental freedoms regarding the environment. In particular, the improvement of rule of law and specific legislation on procedural rights, the increasing political will

108 *North American Agreement on Environmental Cooperation*, signed 14 September 1993, 32 ILM 1480 (entered into force 1 January 1994) preamble, art 1.

109 Ibid. art 14.

110 See generally Yves Bonzon, 'Institutionalizing Public Participation in WTO Decision Making: Some Conceptual Hurdles and Avenues' (2008) 11(4) *Journal of International Economic Law* 751; Jeffrey L. Dunoff, 'Public Participation in the Trade Regime: of Litigation, Frustration, Agitation and Legitimation' (2004) 56 *Rutgers Law Review* 961.

and democratic reforms, the development of civil society and the availability of resources are some of the key factors regarding the transformation towards environmental democracy in the context of the Mekong region. Due to historical differences with respect to politics, legal systems, cultures and economic development, it is not unreasonable to expect a lack of homogeneity across the region. Considering the developing nature of the Mekong countries, the challenge of poverty certainly adds another level of complexity.

## 1 China

Standing at the crossroads of political and administrative reforms, deliberative democracy is attracting increasing interest in China as a possible direction for progressive political reform. Though it should be admitted that without proper representative democracy, there is a high risk that the deliberative measures will end up as a mere formality or be manipulated by the more powerful stakeholders, increasing legislation and arrangements for transparency and participation will certainly open more political opportunities for the public to get involved in public affairs and try to have their voices heard. As argued by Cai Dingjian, public participation and increasing transparency will add more momentum and provide more opportunities for shifting Chinese politics towards real representative democracy.[111] Meanwhile, the evolution of relevant legislation also interacts with China's development of civil society. The increasingly open and high-profile discussions on transparency and public participation can contribute to the awareness-raising of the Chinese public. Growing pressures from civil society inside China will trigger attempts to not only further conceal information, suppress and manipulate the public, but will also urge the government to take real steps to promote the transition towards more transparent, participatory and accountable decision-making.

While more radical advocacy campaigns for human rights and democracy discourses remain sensitive, there is more toleration for discussions and efforts in the context of more modest and progressive initiatives in these areas. The Chinese government has just released its second National Human Rights Action Plan which recognises and aims to promote the right to know, the right to participate and the environmental right.[112] Although questions remain on

111 蔡定剑主编 [Cai Dingjian (ed)],《公众参与：风险社会的制度建设》[Public Participation: Constructing a Framework for the "Risk Society"] (法律出版社 [Law Press · China], 2009) 20.

112 See 《国家人权行动计划 (2012–2015)》 [National Human Rights Action Plan] (11 June 2012) 新华社 [Xinhua News Agency] <http://news.xinhuanet.com/politics/2012-06/11/c_112186014.htm>.

whether this will be more lip service, it is increasingly acknowledged that the only meaningful way forward will be through encouraging political reforms and to improve the protection of basic human rights. As the Chinese government highlights the goal of building a harmonious and stable society, more transparency and public participation is considered an important and more effective approach to that end.[113] With regard to environmental protection, the Amendment on Environmental Protection Law (draft for second reading) expressly recognises the public's rights to know and to participate.[114] This provision, if finally adopted, will be a breakthrough in terms of formally recognizing such procedural rights. This human right perspective is rather implicit under the current legislation in this respect.

(a) *Access to Information*

Other than the *2007 Emergency Response Law* which requires a timely and accurate release of information regarding emergencies, the public's right to know in China is only specifically addressed by one general regulation and several more detailed administrative rules and ordinances. These regulations only enjoy lower levels of legal recognition compared to the *State Secrets Protection Act* and the *Archives Act*. But even this level of protection is not particularly enlightening. The adoption of the Regulations on Government Information Disclosure in January 2007 was considered a legal breakthrough in this area. Notably, it did not enter into force until 1 May 2008. This unusually long preparation time set in the Regulation indicates the degrees of complexity and difficulty involved in comprehending and implementing the new Regulation in the context of the existing administrative legal system and traditions.

According to the new Regulation, governments are obligated to disclose information actively and to provide certain information upon request.[115]

---

113 蔡定剑主编 [Cai Dingjian (ed)], above n 111.

114 《中华人民共和国环境保护法修正案（草案二次审议稿）》[Amendment of Environmental Protection Law (Draft for Second Reading)] (17 July 2013) 中国人大网 [National People's Congress of the PRC], art 43 <http://www.npc.gov.cn/npc/xinwen/lfgz/flca/2013-07/17/content_1801189.htm>.

115 The Regulation also applies to other organisations that are authorised by law or regulation to perform public administrative functions. But it only has reference value to information disclosure of enterprises and public institutions. The nature of these public authorities could be quite confusing in practice and can be used as legal loopholes to be exempted from the Regulation. See《中华人民共和国政府信息公开条例》[Regulations on Government Information Disclosure of the People's Republic of China] (People's Republic of China) State Council, 17 January 2007, arts 36, 37.

Active disclosure of information is guided by four general principles, including information that is relevant to the vital interests of citizens, legal persons and other organisations; that needs to be known by the general public or requires their participation; that reflects the administrative setting, functions and procedures; and that should be actively disclosed according to other statues and regulations.[116] But as will be explained later, the application of these principles can be easily constrained by two controversial exemption provisions. The Regulation further requires the government to disclose information in ways that are easily accessible for the public.[117] In practice, however, the implementation of this provision is rather selective. The media's role in information disclosure is largely controlled by the government as well. Compared to the more ambiguous requirements on the obligation to disclose information actively, the procedures on providing information upon request is much more systematic and to a large extent in line with the *Aarhus Convention* and the general practice of the national administrative law.[118] The Regulation also provides some remedies ranging from administrative measures to judicial remedies.[119] In 2011, the Supreme Court of China issued a detailed judicial interpretation with regard to providing judicial remedies for the right of access to information.[120]

The government cannot disclose any information regarding state secrets, commercial secrets and individual privacy. While there is no exception for state secrets, in the other two cases certain information can be revealed if the obligee agrees to do so[121] or the government believes that the failure to reveal such information may have a significant impact on public interest. This is further bound by another exemption clause. Pursuant to Article 8 of the Regulation, information disclosure shall not endanger national security, public security, economic security and social stability.[122] In particular, "social stability" is the

116 Ibid. art 9.

117 Ibid. art 15.

118 See ibid. arts 21–22.

119 Ibid. arts 29–35.

120 最高人民法院 [Supreme People's Court],《最高人民法院关于审理政府信息公开行政案件若干问题的规定》[Provisions of the Supreme People's Court about Several Issues Concerning the Trail of Administrative Cases on Government Information Disclosure] (15 August 2011) 新华网 [Xinhua News Agency] <http://news.xinhuanet.com/legal/2011-08/15/c_121860879.htm>.

121 The government is required to make written inquiry to the third party when such information is requested.

122 《中华人民共和国政府信息公开条例》[Regulations on Government Information Disclosure] (People's Republic of China) State Council, 17 January 2007, art 8.

most notorious term which has proved to be a very convenient excuse for the government not to disclose information. How to decide on what information may cause social instability falls short of universal standards and is completely left to the discretion of the government. This can be very confusing in practice. Even for those officials who want to be more active in promoting government transparency, they are often afraid of causing social instability and risking their own positions. The Regulation itself does not interpret these limitations in a restrictive manner and information that falls into the categories under the Article 8 can be easily labelled as state secrets. Although social stability is not expressly cited as a ground for state secret determination under the *2010 State Secret Protection Law*, the word "political interest"[123] can be interpreted to include state stability concerns, which is a very broad interpretation of a state secret.

Therefore, although most provisions of the Regulation seem to aim at protecting the public's right of access to information, the broad exemption provisions are in fact very powerful and leave ample opportunities for the government to decline information requests. Although it is recognised that disclosure should be the rule rather than the exception, it is often not the case for information regarding highly controversial development activities and human rights violations. Considering the massive amount of information held by various governmental sectors and different levels of governments, the implementation of this Regulation also require more specific sub-decrees and ordinances. To date, however, the implementation of the Regulation varies significantly across different regions, at different levels of governments and among various government sectors.[124]

Immediately following the release of the Regulation, the State Environmental Protection Administration at the time (upgraded to the Ministry of Environmental Protection in 2008) adopted a Trial Regulation on Environmental Information Disclosure. Compared to other government sectors, this gesture already represented a quick response to the Regulation. The Trial Regulation addresses the release of environmental information held by the environmental protection agencies and also includes some requirements for the release of

123 《中华人民共和国保守国家秘密法》[State Secret Protection Law of the People's Republic of China] (People's Republic of China) Standing Committee of the National Congress, 5 September 1988, revised at 29 April 2010, art 9.

124 See 公众参与研究与支持中心 [Centre for Public Participation Studies and Supports], 《中国行政透明度报告·2009（摘要）》[The 2009 Report on Chinese Administration Transparency (Abstract)] (29 September2010) <http://www.cppss.cn/news_body.asp?id=808>.

environmental information held by business sectors.[125] The Trial Regulation does elaborate in great detail regarding what kinds of information should be disclosed actively by the environmental protection agencies, but it is also subject to exemptions set out in the Regulation.

With respect to environmental information disclosure by business sectors, the general principle is that the government "encourages" them to reveal certain kinds of environmental information. Only some big polluters are obligated to disclose certain information and commercial secrets cannot be used as an excuse.[126] The environmental protection authorities have the power to examine the environmental information that should be made public, but only a small fine (maximum 100,000 RMB) is applicable if business does not comply with the obligation. Government can also provide incentives for a business to voluntarily disclose information and comply with environmental protection legislation, but given the costs of doing the exact opposite are often significantly lower, the effectiveness of these modest incentives are less likely to work in practice.

The implementation of the above regulations and arrangements remains far from satisfactory. Despite the variations in different regions, departments and levels of governments, five problematic areas remain very common in the context of government information disclosure:

One area of concern relates to the availability of information. Although the environmental protection authorities are required under the *1989 Environmental Protection Law* to develop national standards for environmental quality and the corresponding monitoring system, some important parameters or indicators may not be considered under the existing system. A typical example in this area is the controversy surrounding PM2.5 monitoring that generates considerable public interest and debate.[127] This case also raises another con-

125 Factual information regarding the Trial Regulation in these two paragraphs is based on its text. See《环境信息公开办法（试行）》[Trial Regulation on Environmental Information Disclosure] (People's Republic of China) State Environmental Protection Administration, 8 February 2007.

126 See 水利部 [Ministry of Water Resources of the People's Republic of China],《政府信息公开目录》[Catalogue for Government Information Disclosure] <http://zwgk.mwr.gov.cn/index2.htm?classInfoId=18>.

127 The old air pollution monitoring system in China only covers PM10, namely coarse dust particles between 2.5 and 10 micrometers in diameter. Comparably, the same amount of PM2.5 has a more severe impact on human health than that of PM10. Along with the deterioration of air quality in many Chinese cities, there is an increasing demand for PM2.5 monitoring and it is added to the new air quality standards (draft for comment) in the end of 2011. Dramatically, the release of PM2.5 monitoring data from the US Embassy

cern about the accuracy of the monitoring and forecast information.[128] How to draw a line between science and politics is a highly divisive issue in China regarding monitoring and information disclosure.

Another aspect of the problem is that information should be disclosed under the current legislation, but the government is either reluctant to release it or too cautious to do so due to the difficulties of interpreting and understanding the exemption provisions. Government officials are often willing to take the chance of breaching information disclosure regulations rather than to risk violating the legislation on the state secret provision.[129] There remains a large gray area between the scope of information disclosure and that surrounding the exemptions. The existing legal ambiguity in this area can be resolved through interpretation. In light of the general trend toward government transparency and the development of a more vibrant civil society, it is likely that the use of exemptions will be more limited. On the positive side, this is still the part of

---

in Beijing attracted attention from the public and became an important environmental event in China in 2012. Before the new standards become effective in 2016, domestic pressures already pushed the environmental authorities to speed up the piloting works for PM2.5 monitoring.

128 Although Beijing has begun to monitor PM2.5 in 2012, quite often, the official monitoring data differs from the one released by the US Embassy in Beijing or the pollution level forecasted based on similar data is different. This involves a lot of technical issues and also raises the question on whether China should adopt the environmental standards in developed countries or develop its own pollution standards based on the economic and social circumstances in China. The former may be too difficult to be achieved, given the severe environmental situations in China. But the latter approach can be over-politicised, especially regarding concerns on economic growth and social stability.

129 For example, several environmental volunteers have submitted their requests for the release of lists on major emission sources of dioxin (a highly toxic known carcinogen) to the Ministry of Environmental Protection and 31 provincial environmental protection bureaus since the end of 2011. Before the submissions, only four provinces have already disclosed relevant information. The responses for their requests are not optimistic at all. Only one province responded by providing the information requested. Another six provinces declined the requests on the ground that they do not have the capacity to collect such information. Seven provinces rejected the request by claiming that such information cannot be disclosed, but no reasons were provided to support the decision. The Beijing Environmental Protection Bureau expressly stated that such information is state secret, while the authority in Xinjiang held the view that revealing such information can pose a negative impact on social stability. The rest of the provincial authorities have not responded to the request by mid-April, 2012. See 王静怡 [Wang Jingyi], 《垃圾焚烧厂急上马，二恶英信息难公开》 [Rush for the Waste Incineration Plant: Difficulties to Gain Access to Information on Dioxin] (22 April 2012) 南方周末 [Southern Weekly] <http://www.infzm.com/content/74373>.

the problem that has a better chance of success through the judicial system in China and the political will for challenging such administrative decisions is more encouraging.

A more challenging issue is the information that is clearly labelled as a state secret. As discussed in chapter three, a large amount of information is marked as confidential by the Chinese government in the context of international rivers. This was highlighted by several influential domestic environmental events in 2005 and early 2008 which requested the disclosure of the SEA report on the Nu River hydropower plans. There are two potential directions to improving information disclosure in such circumstances. The long-term aim is to revise the existing legislation on state secret protection to reflect the principle of restrictive interpretation on state secrets. Another relatively feasible solution is to better utilise Article 22 of the Regulation, which states: where a part of the requested information is exempted from disclosure but can be separated out, government should make available the remainder of the information that has been requested.[130] In the context of China, the application of this clause is very difficult. Technically, however, this could serve as a ground for filing administrative cases, thus providing another opportunity to deal with the relevant controversies.

An equally important issue is that even if the information is available to the public, it may not in a form that is easily accessible or understandable. This is another prevailing phenomenon in China. Information disclosed via official gazette or government website is less likely to attract much public attention. Combined with the loosening but still strong control over the media, the government can often find a way to disclose information without most of the public knowing of it. In many occasions, the content of information is either too technical or too brief, causing difficulties for the general public to interpret or comprehend the real message behind the released information. Even though the existing legislation on government transparency still suffers from numerous deficiencies, it opens additional political opportunities for civil society to promote further developments in this direction. But government transparency cannot be achieved automatically; it also requires civil society organisations, the media and most importantly, individual citizens to cherish the right to know and exercise their restrained rights more actively in order to keep pushing the existing boundaries to enlarge the scope of information disclosure and improve the quality and accessibility of the information disclosed.

130 See《中华人民共和国政府信息公开条例》[Regulations on Government Information Disclosure] (People's Republic of China) State Council, 17 January 2007, art 22.

### (b) *Public Participation*

As illustrated in the *Aarhus Convention*, public participation can be incorporated at different levels of decision-making concerning laws and executive regulations; plans, programs and policies; and specific activities. In addition, under national law, best practice indicates that the public can participate not only during the preparation period, but also during the implementation and evaluation periods. The following discussion will try to identify and review the piecemeal development of public participation in China. The concept of public participation was first introduced into China around the 1990s, but it was not legally recognised as a formal procedure until a decade later. There is currently no legislation that has expressly recognised public participation as a right. Instead, the existing legislation treats public participation merely as a mechanism or procedure. This situation may be changed by the future revision of the *Environmental Protection Law* (1989). The Amendment on Environmental Protection Law (draft for second reading) not only embraces public participation as one of the environmental protection principles in China, but also clearly recognises the public's right to participate.[131] The current draft of the amendment, however, fails to provide sufficient framework requirements on how to secure the right to participate. Instead, it authorises and requires government to improve the process of public participation.[132] This requirement apparently gives too much discretion to government and it is difficult to expect the government itself to develop proper participation procedures that will act as a restriction to its own power.

Under China's Constitution, some relevant rights are already recognised, such as the right to speak, the right to demonstrate, the right to criticise and advise and freedom of association.[133] But it is no secret that these rights are constrained in China. It should be noted that except for public participation at the legislative level, all participation requirements can be exempted if the content of plans, programs, policies or special activities need to be kept confidential. This is a fundamental restriction on public participation. Although many countries may have similar requirements, the state secret protection requirements in China are exceedingly powerful and devoid of reasonable constraints. In addition, the status and role of civil society organisations in the public participation process is not clear in the existing legislation. Although the term "organisation" or "institution" is used several times in relevant provisions, as

131 Above n 114, arts 6, 43.

132 Ibid. art 43.

133 《中华人民共和国宪法》[Constitution of the People's Republic of China] (People's Republic of China) National People's Congress, 4 December 1982, arts 35, 41.

will be further illustrated later, it is in fact a mixed term reflecting remaining features of unfinished political, social and economic reforms.

The first legislative enactment addressing public participation is the *2000 Legislation Law*. According to Article 35, important legal bills that are added to the agenda of the National Standing Committee Conferences "can" be disclosed to seek opinions and comments from government authorities, organisations and citizens.[134] Obviously, this is not a compulsory procedure. The drafting of administrative regulations, however, is required to take into account the views of government authorities, organisations and concerned citizens via hearings or other forms of consultation.[135] Recent years have witnessed a gradually increasing public consultation during the preparation of legislation. But in many cases the public are not aware of the release of draft for comments, for they are usually only disclosed via governmental websites which only a few members of the public would browse. In addition, a large percentage of the public still have no awareness of their right to participate in such decision-making processes. Since public consultation is only a part of the general stakeholder consultation and there are no specific regulations on how to undertake this process, the practice often varies across different geographic areas and in different fields. Besides, while it is a general practice that legal professionals are consulted or commissioned to draft the legislation, their participation should not replace the participation of the general public. Over the past few years, some detailed local or provincial regulations on public participation at this level have been promulgated, such as in Guangzhou and Chongqing, but this phenomenon remains rather rare across the whole country.

At the level of plans, programs and policies, there is no general requirement for public participation, except some brief provisions on public participation during the SEA process (required only for plans). Participation during the formulation of programs and policies is almost vacant. Several local authorities have developed some rules on public participation during city planning, such as Huangshan, Anyang and Qingdao. But this procedure is still far from becoming a regular practice during the preparation of plans. Public participation during the SEA process is required under the *2002 EIA Law* for specific/sector-based plans prepared at or above the municipal (municipalities with district setting) level and is set out in the 2006 Interim Measures of Public Participation in EIA and further crystallised in the 2009 Regulations on Environmental Impact

134 《中华人民共和国立法法》 [Legislation Law of the People's Republic of China] (People's Republic of China) National People's Congress, 15 March 2000, art 35.

135 Ibid. art 58.

Assessment of Planning (the SEA Regulation).[136] Public participation is not required in the preparation of comprehensive plans. Comprehensive plans refer to those concerning the utilisation of land; the exploitation, development and construction at the regional level, and river basin and marine area levels. Notably, river basin planning is not subject to public participation. Therefore, public only have the opportunity to participate in fragmented sectoral plans, which further restricts the opportunities for public participation.

Sectoral plans that may cause a negative environmental impact and directly relate to the environmental interests of the public should be subject to consultation with institutions, experts and the public. The time set for public participation during the preparation of plans is before submitting the plan for approval, which is in line with the timing requirement for the SEA of sectoral plans. However, experience has shown that the SEA integrated into the plan-making process has more impact on decision-making than those carried out after the plan is mostly completed.[137] This will be discussed in more detail in chapter six. At present, it is obvious that public participation during China's SEA process cannot compensate for the fact that there is no requirement for the public to be involved during the drafting of the plans themselves, not to mention that environmental considerations are not the only issues that warrant public consultation during the plan-making process.

In the event of a significant divergence between public opinion and the conclusions of the draft plan, the drafting authority is required to hold further consultations. Public opinion should be considered seriously and the responses to public opinion should be included in the SEA report, namely whether their opinions are adopted or not and why. In instances where the SEA report failed to provide such information or did not have reasonable grounds for accepting public comments, the approval authority should order the SEA report to be revised and resubmitted. The decision not to accept public opinions should be made in writing and archived. Instead of disclosing it actively, such

136 Information regarding public participation during the SEA of plans is based on the normative documents in Chinese. See 《中华人民共和国环境影响评价法》 [Environmental Impact Assessment Law of the People's Republic of China] (People's Republic of China) Standing Committee of the National People's Congress, 28 October 2002, arts 5, 8, 11; 《环评公众参与暂行办法》 [Interim Measures of Public Participation in EIA] (People's Republic of China) State Environmental Protection Administration, 22 February 2006, arts 33–37; 《规划环境影响评价条例》 [Regulations on Environmental Impact Assessment of Planning] (People's Republic of China) State Council, 12 August 2009, arts 13, 19, 20, 22, 25, 26.

137 See Strategic Environmental Assessment Course Module, *Timing of the SEA* (3 September 2006) <http://sea.unu.edu/course/index.html%3Fpage_id=110.html>.

information is only accessible upon request. Public opinion on the environmental impact of the plan should also be considered during post-evaluation, which is required subsequent to the implementation of plans that have a significant negative environmental impact.[138]

Despite the general criticisms on the effectiveness of SEA in China,[139] public participation itself during the SEA process suffers from the limited scope of public participation in SEA, late introduction of public participation, no requirement for active disclosure of responses concerning public opinion, no detailed arrangements on participation procedures and the broad interpretation of state secrets.

The most detailed legislation and arrangements for public participation in China are with regard to its application during the EIA process. This is addressed by the *2002 EIA Law*, the 2006 Interim Measures of Public Participation in EIA and 2011 Technical Guideline for Public Participation in EIA (Draft for Comments).[140] Under the *EIA Law*, projects that may cause a significant environmental impact should go through the public participation process before submitting the EIA report for approval and reasons should be given in the report on whether to accept the public's views or not. Notably, public participation is introduced in the EIA process when the EIA report is almost finished, instead of commencing at an earlier stage, such as scoping.[141]

---

138 Notably, only when plans may have a significant negative environmental impact *and* the authority cannot provide feasible and achievable measures or strategies to prevent or mitigate such an impact, should the SEA report not be approved. The other ground for disapproval is that no scientific judgment can be made regarding the degree or scope of the negative environmental impact of the plan based on the existing knowledge and technology.

139 See chapter six.

140 Information regarding public participation during the EIA process is based on the normative documents in Chinese. See《中华人民共和国环境影响评价法》[Environmental Impact Assessment Law of the People's Republic of China] (People's Republic of China) Standing Committee of the National People's Congress, 28 October 2002, arts 5, 21;《环评公众参与暂行办法》[Interim Measures of Public Participation in EIA] (People's Republic of China) State Environmental Protection Administration, 22 February 2006, arts 1–32; 环境保护部 [Ministry of Environmental Protection of the People's Republic of China],《环境影响评价技术导则：公众参与（征求意见稿）》[Technical Guideline for Public Participation in Environmental Impact Assessment (Draft for Comments)] (30 January 2011) <http://www.es.org.cn/download/2011/1-6/2135-1.pdf>.

141 Scoping determines the "content and extent of the matters to be covered in the environmental information to be submitted to a competent authority". European Commission, 'Report from the Commission on the application and effectiveness of the EIA Directive (Directive 85/337/EEC, as Amended by Directives 97/11/EC and 2003/35/EC)' (Report,

In principle, public participation can occur at every stage in the EIA process and usually the earlier it starts the more chances it has to be effective.

The Interim Measures then details information disclosure requirements for the project developer. For projects located within an environmental sensitive area, the developer should provide the public with some preliminary information regarding the project, the EIA process and major issues relating to public participation within seven days after the decision for conducting an EIA is determined. This reflects a relatively higher standard of publicity set for such projects. But the relevant arrangements under the Draft Guideline seem to indicate that information disclosure at this stage is a general practice applicable for all projects that are subject to EIA. Together with the information disclosure after the preparation of the EIA report, there are two separate procedures for access to information. It is uncertain at this moment which interpretation will be finally adopted. Either way, however, as observed by an official from the Ministry of Environmental Protection, this early information disclosure requirement often fails to be implemented in practice and the information is usually not provided in an easily understandable fashion.[142] The public can be easily misled by partial or even false information given by the developers.

After finishing the EIA report and before submitting it for approval or revaluation (at least ten days prior to submission according to the Draft Guideline), the developer or the institution responsible for conducting the EIA should disclose brief information concerning the project, the key points of the EIA report and the envisaged procedures for public participation. In particular, this includes approaches and time-frame set for the public to have access to the summary of the EIA report and for requesting additional information; the scope of consultation and key issues concerned; and the approaches and time-frame set for the public to express their opinions. The above issues are

European Commission, 2009) 3. The importance of public participation at the scoping and other stages in EIA has been increasingly recognised by competent authorities and other participants in the EIA process within the EU countries. See generally, Environmental Resources Management, 'Guidance on EIA Scoping' (Guiding Document, European Commission, 2001).

142 任景明 [Ren Jingming],《公众参与何时成为润滑剂》[When can Public Participation actually Become the Lubricant during Decision-making Process] (19 September 2012) 湖北省环境保护厅 [Hubei Environmental Protection Bureau] <http://www.hbepb.gov.cn/hbdt/hjzl/201209/t20120919_55903.html>.

addressed in a more detailed way, but not as specific as the *Aarhus Convention*.[143] In particular, only the summary of the EIA report is required to be revealed instead of the whole draft report. According to the Draft Guideline, summary of the EIA report attempts to make information more understandable for the general public. But this is not an excuse for failing to release the full draft report, since the devil is often in the detail[144] and there are people and NGOs with professional knowledge that will need the full information in order to be in a position to provide more informed comment.

The time-frame set for public consultation is at least ten days, which is quite short compared to many other countries where the period is at least thirty days or more.[145] This is another major deficiency surrounding public participation during EIA process in China. In fact, considering the historically poor communications between the developer, government and the public, it is recommended that the consultation period in China should be more than thirty days. The Interim Measures suggests possible approaches for public participation, including questionnaires, expert consultation, discussion meetings and hearings. It also sets out specific requirements regarding public hearing as well as administrative procedures concerning different forms of participation. Requirements are much simpler for regular discussion meetings, which are often preferred over the public hearing as a formal administrative procedure.[146] The factors to be considered for public representation at the meetings or hearing are also listed, requiring the representatives of the affected public to be included. But the process of deciding who is to be consulted still leaves room for manipulation, especially when there is no free media and the local government often has ultimate power to decide. In reality, the public is often

143 For instance, the *Aarhus Convention* also requires an indication of: (1) the public authority from which relevant information can be obtained and to which comments or questions can be submitted; and (2) what environmental information relevant to the proposed project is available.

144 The summary of the EIA report can only provide partial information on its quality.

145 For example, the United States, Australia, Russia, Sweden, Italy, Finland, the United Kingdom, France, Belgium, Denmark, Germany and the Netherlands. See *Guidance on Public Participation in Environmental Impact Assessment in a Transboundary Context*, UN ECE/MP.EIA/7 (2006) 18.

146 The application of public hearing under the Chinese administrative law is not a compulsory procedure in most circumstances, except for the decisions on some kinds of administrative penalties and permissions. But in many cases of the administrative permissions, the public are unfamiliar with the legislation and have no idea of their rights to request for public hearing or to participate via this approach.

involved only via questionnaires, which are mainly designed based on similar templates and the public often finds it difficult to participate actively through this approach.[147]

After the environmental protection authorities receive the EIA report, they are required to notify the public via governmental websites or in other easily accessible ways. In practice, what is disclosed at this stage often includes only the basic information of the project, developer, contacts and the date of receiving the report. The full EIA report is not required to be disclosed, nor is the added section documenting public participation. Therefore, the public do not have access to the responses to their comments.

The environmental protection authorities can seek public opinion a second time for controversial projects. Similar to the requirements for public participation during the SEA process, the public's comments and the responses from the developer are supposed to be reviewed and taken into account seriously by the government, but since there is no requirement to release the full EIA report, the public cannot know whether their comments are indeed considered or even accurately documented by the developer and the government. In fact, as revealed by an official from the Ministry of Environmental Protection, many EIA reports are very brief or ambiguous concerning opponents' objections to a project and the reasons on whether their views should be accepted or rejected are often not provided.[148]

The issue of full EIA report disclosure causes some confusion in practice. In a response letter from the former State Environmental Protection Administration to the Shanghai Environmental Protection Bureau, it replied that the EIA report is not the kind of information that should be disclosed actively by the government and the environmental protection authority can only provide contact information for the public to request the EIA report from the developer or institutions that prepared the EIA report.[149] The response also cited the provisions from the Regulations on Governmental Information Disclosure regarding commercial secrets. But this response is based on flawed logic. It did not deny the fact that an EIA report is itself a form of governmental information and by admitting that implicitly, the environmental protec-

147 任景明 [Ren Jingming], above n 142.

148 Ibid.

149 国家环境保护总局 [State Environmental Protection Administration of the People's Republic of China],《关于公众申请公开建设项目环评文件有关问题的复函》[Response Concerning the Issues of Public's Request for the Disclosure of the EIA Document] (30 January 2008) <http://www.zhb.gov.cn/info/gw/huanhan/200802/t20080202_117941.htm>.

tion authority should not simply divert the request to the developer or the institution that conducted the EIA. Even if it is relevant to an issue relating to commercial secrets, it is still the government's responsibility to consult with the third party in writing to ascertain whether such information should be revealed and then make a formal decision.[150] Diverting the responsibility for releasing an EIA report to a non-governmental third party is a blatant attempt of trying to avoid the risk of litigation. This situation could be improved along with the future revision of Environmental Protection Law. The most recent draft amendment requires the environmental authorities to make public of the EIA report after receiving it, with an exception of matters in relevant to state or commercial secrets.[151]

Based on the above analysis, it is safe to say that current public participation in EIA in China remains largely controlled by the developer and the government and the degree of participation by the public is generally low. As indicated in the language used in the legislation, the words "seeking public opinions" is often used instead of consultation or participation, indicating a strong feature of one-way information flow and a superior attitude on the part of the developer and government. The extent to which the so-called public opinion can have any credibility or impact on decision-making is highly questionable, considering the lack of proper transparency of the project and of the EIA process itself, as well as the problematic settings for public participation. The formality surrounding the process also significantly impedes the ability of the public to actively participate. The lack of trust by the public in resolving disputes through normal channels of communication often lead to more confrontational and violent outcomes,[152] rather than peaceful outcomes. A major lesson from such violent protests is that similar issues must be dealt with in an open and transparent manner and law-based conclusions should be drawn.[153] Unfortunately, another common phenomenon in China is that the opportunity and effectiveness of public participation is more influenced by decision-makers than secured by the system. This contrasts the differences and tensions in China between the rule of law and the rule by powerful institutions or individuals. The EIA process is the only mechanism in China that has

---

150 See《中华人民共和国政府信息公开条例》[Regulations on Government Information Disclosure] (People's Republic of China) State Council, 17 January 2007, arts 21, 23.

151 Above n 114, art 46.

152 Such as the Shifang protests. See BBC News, *China Morning Round-Up: Shifang Protest* (4 July 2012) <http://www.bbc.co.uk/news/world-asia-china-18700819>.

153 Global Times, *Shifang Protest Needs Law-Based Conclusion* (5 July 2012) <http://www.globaltimes.cn/content/719095.shtml>.

developed a relatively detailed legal framework to regulate public participation. The improvement of public participation in China also relies on a more vibrant civil society and an increasing awareness among the public concerning their rights and social responsibilities. As the third sector of society, the development of civil society is now an important feature underlying changes in Chinese society as a whole. NGOs and the ordinary citizenry have played a vital role in recent environmental protection movements. But in many cases their voice are not expressed or heard through institutionalised channels for public participation, as they were in the Shifang and Xiamen protests against the construction of mineral and chemical plants.[154] In some other cases, individual citizen's or expert's comments were reported by the traditional media forcing the developer to enter into public consultation or correct its behaviour, i.e. the Yuanmingyuan Lakebed Seepage Project.[155] The emergence and popularity of new technologies and new media (like mobile phones, the internet and especially social networking websites) provides prominent tools or platforms for fostering public debate and raising public awareness on environmental concerns.

Nevertheless, the development of civil society, especially civil society organisations, remains constrained by many political, legal and financial problems.[156] The development of civil society organisations in China is largely a top-down process with increasing bottom-up features. Many civil society organisations are closely connected or in fact controlled by the government and often represent a mixture of different social sectors, such as research and professional associations, workers' union and women's unions. The registration of these organisations is relatively easier. They have more political opportunities to operate and usually have a good relationship with the government. They are often in a better financial situation and can attract more trained personnel. Many of them are bureaucratic to varying degrees and usually lack enough

154 For detailed information on the 2007 Xiamen Protest, see BBC News, *'Text Protest' Blocks China Plant* (30 May 2007) <http://news.bbc.co.uk/2/hi/asia-pacific/6704359.stm>.

155 See People's Daily Online, *Yuanmingyuan Lakebed Project Questioned* (30 March 2005) <http://english.peopledaily.com.cn/200503/30/eng20050330_178760.html>.

156 Factual information in the following discussions is based on 高丙中，袁瑞军主编 [Gao Bingzhong and Yuan Ruijun (eds)], 《中国公民社会发展蓝皮书》 [Blue Book on Civil Society Development in China] (北京大学出版社 [Peking University Press], 2008); 《社会团体登记管理条例》 [Regulations on Social Groups Registration Management] (People's Republic of China) State Council, 25 October 1998; 《民办非企业单位登记管理暂行条例》 [Provisional Regulation on the Registration of People-run Non-enterprise Unit] (People's Republic of China) State Council, 25 October 1998; 《基金会管理条例》 (Regulation on the Administration of Foundations of the People's Republic of China) (People's Republic of China) State Council, 11 February 2004.

incentives to take real action in the field to represent the needs of vulnerable groups. But they generally have more credibility than unregistered grassroots organisations in their daily operations in China where social identity and government connections are important. In order to influence the government's decision-making, interaction with many of the so-called "official" civil society groups (contradictory as it is) is indeed necessary in practice. This is also true for international NGOs in China. Many of them choose to operate like an "official" civil society group or seek registration as profitable associations, risking either of the two most important features of NGOs: independence from government and a not-for-profit status. For these "official" civil society groups, their legitimacy to represent the voice of the public is doubtful, especially since many of their operations are disconnected to the local communities.

Comparatively, the increasing bottom-up civil society development is still constrained in many aspects. The biggest and most fundamental obstacle is the complicated and problematic registry system. Not only should a civil society organisation be registered at the Civil Affairs Department, it also has to find another authority to supervise its operation in order to be qualified for registration. In reality, the latter is often very difficult to find. Government authorities usually lack incentives to take on such responsibility and do not trust grassroots organisations. Even if a civil society organisation manages to find a supervisory authority, this relationship can be easily ended unilaterally by the latter. This situation means that a large number of grassroots civil society organisations are unable to get registered, facing not just legal and political risks, but also the accompanying difficulties on establishing credibility, fund raising and recruiting better trained personnel. Although many of them are welcomed by disadvantaged groups, they themselves are usually in a constant struggle to survive and have very limited resources to actually enhance the public's voice or influence decision-making. In light of the above difficulties, some organisations alternatively choose to be registered as a company or other forms of profitable associations.

Other problems exist for registered civil society organisations. For one thing, whether they are allowed to operate nationally, trans-jurisdictionally or mere locally depends on the level of the government under which they registered. Except for national organisations, they have to specify where they are going to operate and cannot expand their operation outside the designated area. This out-dated requirement further restricts the development of civil society organisations, especially considering current population mobility and the nature of many environmental issues. In order to be qualified for registration, another requirement is that there cannot be another organisation that has a similar scope of activities. This restriction can significantly reduce the number of civil society groups and the lack of competition among similar organisations is very detrimental for both capacity building and effective operation. The definition of civil society organisations under the administrative law is also confusing from a civil law perspective. The legal person or partnership status is less clear under the administrative law regarding civil society groups, creating problems for their daily operation. The troubles between administrative requirements and the civil law system are most severe in terms of the establishment and operation of foundations. Civil society developments involving environmental protection issues currently enjoy some government support and attention. But instead of focusing on environmental victims or environmental law violations by the government and business sectors, a large number of registered civil society groups in this area are research or professional associations and mainly promote environmental technology and public awareness.

As exemplified in the Nu River case in chapter three, in the case of international rivers, there is still no legal basis for formal channels of public participation. Under such circumstances, the campaigning by civil society organisations and reputable individuals remains the most feasible way of introducing an environmental issue into public debate and forcing the government to respond to the voices of public. In addition to the more confrontational relationship with the government, it is important to maintain some level of cooperative interaction and make full use of restricted participation opportunities. Finding a balance in practice is challenging, since opinions on issues like hydropower development are often polarised among different stakeholders. Meanwhile, it is crucial to highlight the development of grassroots civil society groups and promote a more relaxed environment for their establishment, capacity building and operation. More attention should also be paid to the rapid development of new media and the protection of journalists' rights. For individuals, awareness raising for environmental protection, individual rights and social responsibilities should be some of the priority areas. At the legislative level, it is necessary to incorporate requirements for transparency and public participation in water-related legislation. Not only should access to information and public participation be expressly recognised as rights and be provided higher levels of protection, efforts should also be made to provide more detailed guidance and regulations in this respect.

## 2 Thailand

The improvement of access to information and public participation in Thailand has been closely linked with the contemporary history of its transition to democracy. Despite the instability and challenges during this process, such as temporary military rule and the 2008 political crisis, it is generally recognised that Thailand has gained a more progressive reputation in terms of its developing representative democracy and the basic recognition and protection of human rights compared to other Mekong countries.[157] Other than issues regarding the Royal family, the political will for transparency and public participation are much better than the rest of the Mekong countries. Meanwhile, the burgeoning environmental movement since the 1980s (with varying degrees of success in terms of influencing decision-making), represented by the cancellation of the Nam Choan Dam and the high-profile dispute over the Puk Mun Dam,[158] also made it much more difficult to build dams within Thailand's own territory. NGOs, such as the Project for Ecological Recovery and Toward Ecological Recovery and Regional Alliances, have played an important role during this movement and the ongoing strong civil society movement in turn triggered the more vibrant development of environmental NGOs since the late 1980s.

(a) *Access to Information*

The public's right of access to information is expressly recognised in the *Thai Constitution* (both the 1997 and 2007 versions) and information disclosure is dealt with by the *1997 Official Information Act*. The Act was promulgated right before the enactment of the *1997 Constitution*. The right of access to information was soon embraced by the *1997 Constitution* which is often hailed as a landmark in Thailand democratic political reform. Different from China, where there is no judicial review available for violation of constitution, the Constitutional Court of Thailand has been established under both Constitutions with jurisdiction over the constitutionality of legislation. This arrangement certainly makes the Thai Constitution more enforceable than that of China.

Both the 1997 and 2007 Constitutions explicitly stipulate that:

> A person shall have the right to get access to public information in possession of a State agency, State enterprise or local government organisation, unless the disclosure of such information shall affect the security of

157 Thailand is a party to the *International Covenant on Civil and Political Rights* and several other core UN human rights treaties. At the ASEAN level, Thailand is also the only lower Mekong country that is more active towards the ASEAN's human right agendas.

158 See generally Jonathan Rigg, 'Thailand's Nam Choan Dam Project: A Case Study in the "Greening" of South-East Asia' (1991) 1(2) *Global Ecology and Biogeography Letters* 42; Tira Foran and Kanokwan Manorom, 'Pak Mun Dam: Perpetually Contested?' in François Molle, Tira Foran and Mira Käkönen (eds), *Contested Waterscapes in the Mekong Region: Hydropower, Livelihoods and Governance* (Earthscan, 2009) 55.

> the State, public safety or interests of other persons which shall be protected as provided by law.[159]

Notably, the public's right of access to information not only applies to information held by administrative authorities, but also covers information held by state enterprises. This is important considering state-owned Thai banks and developers are active participants in regional hydropower development. But to what extent can this be achieved in practice is doubtful, since commercial secrets could be used to get around the legislation. The *Information Act* also sets out several types of information that falls into the category of confidential information, among which include information that may jeopardise the Royal Institution, national security, international relations, or national economic or financial security.[160] But according to the Rule on Maintenance of Official Secrets (2001), state security is linked to domestic or international politics, state defence, the economy, society, science, technology, energy and the environment.[161] Therefore, the range of information that is actually available for the public is more restricted than it appears under the Constitution. It is difficult to claim that the above exemptions have violated the Constitution, since there is no constitutional standard for national security and interpretation of the exemptions is left for the legislative body and administrative authorities with the power to issue executive regulations. But different from the Chinese system, representative democracy in Thailand can provide some protection at the legislative level and public participation requirements in Thailand provides another approach to protect the public's right to know.

The *Information Act* established the Official Information Commission to supervise and make recommendations on its implementation by state agencies.[162] Based on the Act, currently five quasi-judicial Information Disclosure Tribunals have been appointed by the Council of Ministers

159 *Constitution of the Kingdom of Thailand 1997* (Kingdom of Thailand) s 58; *Constitution of the Kingdom of Thailand 2007* (Kingdom of Thailand) s 56. The *1997 Constitution* was approved by the National Assembly, while the *2007 Constitution* was approved via a public referendum.

160 See *Official Information Act* (Kingdom of Thailand) National Assembly, 2 September 1997, ss 14–5.

161 *Rule on Maintenance of Official Secrets* (Kingdom of Thailand) Council of Ministers, 5 February 2001, s 5.

162 *Official Information Act* (Kingdom of Thailand) National Assembly, 2 September 1997, ss 27–34.

upon the recommendation of the Commission.[163] Correspondingly, the members of the public have the right to lodge a complaint to the Commission or appeal through the Commission to the Tribunals regarding the decision prohibiting the disclosure of information.[164] These institutional settings aim at improving the implementation of the Act and providing dispute resolution opportunities in addition to traditional judicial process.[165] This is followed by the Cabinet's resolution asserting that state agencies shall comply with the Commission's recommendations and the Tribunal's order.[166]

Compared to China where there is no specific administrative authority dedicated to oversee the implementation of the 2007 Regulation in different government sectors or at different levels of government, the above provisions under the *Information Act* certainly show more determination on improving government transparency. Ever since the Act entered into force, an increasing number of complaints and appeals have been submitted to the Commission. Local administrations have been the subject of most number of complaints over the years.[167] The Commission further develops guidelines and manuals in order to assist the implementation of the Act and standardise procedures. A report system between the Commission and state agencies has been established as well.[168] Both the Commission and the Tribunals are supposed to be independent, but such independency is doubted by some scholars.[169] Further, the implementation of tribunal decisions has been difficult due to overlapping legislation.[170] In the Thai bureaucratic context, making government

163 Ibid. ss 35–9. Information on members of the Board and the settings of the five tribunals is available on the official website. See Office of the Official Information Commission, *Committee* <http://www.oic.go.th/content_eng/committee.htm>.

164 *Official Information Act* (Kingdom of Thailand) National Assembly, 2 September 1997, s 18.

165 The Tribunal decisions are deemed final except for appeals to the administrative court by citizens who believe that the decision of the tribunal was unjust. Ibid. s 36; David Banisar, 'Freedom of Information around the World 2006' (Report, Privacy International, 2006) 147; *Act on Establishment of Administrative Courts and Administrative Court Procedure* (Kingdom of Thailand) National Assembly, 10 October 1999, s 3.

166 Chungtong Opassiriwit, *Thailand: A Case Study in the Interrelationship between Freedom of Information (FOI) and Privacy*, Official Information Commission <http://www.oic.go.th/content_eng/privacy.html>.

167 Official statistics for complaints and appeals are available at: Office of the Official Information Commission, *Diagram of Appeal and Complaint by Ministry* <http://www.oic.go.th/iwebstat/istatministry.asp?language=En>.

168 See Nakorn Serirak, *Challenges of Thailand's Freedom of Information* <http://www.worldlii.org/int/journals/PLBIN/2000/29.html>.

169 See Banisar, above n 165, 148.

170 Ibid.

information easily accessible for the public remains a continuing battle, but with the current legislation, there are at least several legal tools available for the public to employ to protect their rights. Civil society groups and the media can play an active role during this process.

### (b) *Public Participation*

Public participation in Thailand is addressed by the 1997 and 2007 *Constitution*, the *1992 Enhancement and Conservation of National Environmental Quality Act* (NEQA) and the 1996 Public Hearing Regulation (which has been updated by the 2005 Regulation of the Office of the Prime Minister regarding Listening to Public Opinion).[171]

The *NEQA Act*, as a replacement of the 1975 version, introduces public participation into the area of environmental protection. This is achieved by setting out the individual's rights relating to public participation and specifying the rights of registered NGOs. The former includes the right of access to information, the right to seek remedies or compensation for environmental damages caused by the government, the right to petition or lodge complaints for violations of environmental law and the right to cooperate and assist the government with efforts to protect the environment.[172] But the language used in the legislation states that the above rights "may be" accorded to individual persons as provided by this Act and other related legislation, suggesting that more might be required to firmly confirm the existence of the above rights and facilitate their implementation. The *NEQA Act*, however, does not make any specific provisions for public participation, except with respect to the status and rights of NGOs. Although the *NEQA Act* also serves as the key framework document for EIA in Thailand, relevant provisions make no reference to how to incorporate public participation into the EIA procedures.[173] It is worth noting that the SEA process is not referred to under the *NEQA Act*. The lack of more specific requirements is certainly a major deficiency of the current legislation, but this does not necessarily mean that the public cannot be involved in the EIA process.

The major contribution of the *NEQA Act* with respect to public participation is its formal recognition of the registered NGOs in promoting environmental

171 See Chutarat Chompunth, *An Evaluation of the Public Participation Practice in Environmental Development Projects in Thailand: A Case Study of the Hin Krut Power Plant Project* (PhD Thesis, University of East Anglia, 2011) 6.

172 *Enhancement and Conservation of National Environmental Quality Act* (Kingdom of Thailand) National Assembly, 29 March 1992, s 6.

173 Chompunth, above n 171, 8.

protection and its provisions on the registration and operation of environmental NGOs. This is in contrast with the Chinese environmental legislation which makes no specific mention of NGOs. In contrast to the dual supervision system in China for NGO registration, the Act only requires a NGO to satisfy the following requirements in order to be qualified for environmental NGO registration: (1) to obtain a juristic person status under domestic or foreign legislation; (2) be directly engaged in environmental protection activities; (3) be classified as non-governmental; and (4) be classified as non-profitable.[174] But in the event that the activities of any registered NGO causes disturbances or is contrary to public order or deemed unsuitable, the Minister of Science, Technology and Environment shall have the power to revoke the registration of the NGO involved in such activities.[175] It is uncertain what the terms "disturbance" and "unsuitable" mean legally and there is the potential for the government to tighten controls over NGOs. How threatening this provision might be in practice depends on the overall development of democracy in Thailand.

The Act then goes on to allow the registered environmental NGOs to request government assistance or support for their operations. But correspondingly, whether the government will provide such support or assistance upon request is totally up to the government itself. Moreover, other than providing legal aid to affected people and acting as representatives of environmental victims to bring lawsuit to seek legal remedies (which is a different issue regarding the role of NGOs with regard to access to justice), the remaining activities listed in the provision rank as lower degrees of participation according to the Arnstein's ladder. These include: assisting the work of government officials, disseminating information, raising public awareness, public relations campaigns, initiating environmental projects or activities, conducting research, etc. The structure of this provision is more focused on the interactions between NGOs and individuals rather than between NGOs and government. Apart from the non-enforceable promise of governmental support, there is no express obligation on the government to provide formal opportunities for the NGOs to participate in its decision-making. And it is necessary to note the language used in this provision: instead of "participation", environmental NGOs can "assist" the performance of government, which indicates a strong sense of government-led and controlled participation.

The right to participate is more strongly protected by the 1997 and 2007 *Constitution*. Both versions stipulate that:

---

174 *Enhancement and Conservation of National Environmental Quality Act* (Kingdom of Thailand) National Assembly, 29 March 1992, s 7.

175 Ibid. s 8.

> A person shall have the right to receive information, explanation and reason from a State agency, State enterprise or local government organisation before permission is given for the operation of any project or activity which may affect the quality of the environment, health and sanitary conditions, the quality of life or any other material interest concerning him or her or a local community and shall have the right to express his or her opinion on such matters to agencies concerned for consideration of that matters.[176]

A very broad approach is taken in terms of the levels of participation ("any activity") and the threshold setting (the impact does not need to be significant). In addition, the 1997 Constitution also expressly recognises the participation right of traditional communities in the management, maintenance, preservation and exploitation of natural resources and the environment.[177]

As part of compensation for the lack of a public participation requirement for the EIA process under the *NEQA Act*, the Constitution expressly confirms that the public has the right to participate in the decision-making process of projects or activities that may have a significant impact on the environment.[178] These activities shall not be permitted unless the environmental and health impact is studied and evaluated by an independent commission which must be comprised of representatives from environmental NGOs and academics from higher education institutions.[179] It does provide a specific approach for some parts of civil society to participate, but this process does not explicitly require the participation of affected communities. Also, it is unclear how this independent review process will be combined with the EIA process in practice. It is more likely that this process will be inserted after the EIA report is prepared, thus providing no opportunity for civil society to be involved during the preparation of the EIA report. There is no requirement for the government to take due account of the public opinion. Although the public does have the right to receive explanations and reasons from the government before the permission is granted, such explanations and reasons can be made in the context of the permission itself.

---

176 *Constitution of the Kingdom of Thailand 1997* (Kingdom of Thailand) s 59; *Constitution of the Kingdom of Thailand 2007* (Kingdom of Thailand) s 57.

177 *Constitution of the Kingdom of Thailand 1997* (Kingdom of Thailand) s 46. This is stipulated in s 66 of the *2007 Constitution*.

178 Ibid. s 56. This is stipulated in s 67 of the *2007 Constitution*.

179 Ibid. This is stipulated in s 67 of the *2007 Constitution*.

Compared to the *1997 Constitution*, the *2007 Constitution* expanded and improved the requirements for public participation. In particular, an additional paragraph was inserted after the paragraph referred to in the 1997 Constitution quoted above regarding public hearings:

> In undertaking any social, economic, political, and cultural development planning, appropriation of immovable property, city planning, land use zoning, and issuance of regulations which may affect the interests of the people, the State shall thoroughly hold public hearings procedure prior to implementation.[180]

Hence, public hearings became a compulsory procedure for planning and the preparation of regulations in Thailand since 2007. The screening standard here does not require these activities to have a potentially "significant" impact on people. This is a notable development considering the fact that a public hearing is still an optional procedure in China at these levels and even the public participation requirement is not yet widely adopted as a compulsory procedure for planning. But this procedure in Thailand is only required to be carried out "prior to implementation", indicating that the decision could have already been made before the public could participate in this process. As observed by Chompunth, many public hearings in Thailand are held, not because the government actively choose to do so, but because of strong requests and pressure from the public. Considering the fact that public hearings in Thailand often happen after the decisions are already made, this process is usually criticised for occurring too late to solve conflicts.[181]

Detailed provisions for public hearings in Thailand were first made by the 1996 Public Hearing Regulation and then updated by the 2005 Regulation of the Office of the Prime Minister regarding Listening to Public Opinion. But problems remain in the existing public hearing legislation and it has been outdated since the new Constitution was promulgated.[182] The Convention requires public hearings for plans and regulations, whilst the majority of hearings in Thailand are in the area of specific projects. Under the above Regulations, public hearing committees are required to be set up to monitor and organise the whole process and to prepare reports on the hearings. It is constituted by academics, members of parliament, representatives from the Council of Lawyers

180 *Constitution of the Kingdom of Thailand 2007* (Kingdom of Thailand) s 57.

181 Chompunth, above n 171, 10.

182 Ibid. 9, 14, 16.

and some technical experts.[183] Therefore, civil society members with professional knowledge have the chance to be involved and provide guidance to the process. But it should also be noted that the participation of experts cannot and should not replace the involvement of affected people.

From the perspective of the government, several directive principles are required to be complied with during the implementation of policies regarding natural resources and environment, among which setting the participation standards and providing opportunities for public participation are highlighted. The *2007 Constitution* then lists directive principles of the Public Participation Policy which requires the government to encourage, promote and support public participation at different decision-making levels and in various decision-making areas.[184] Equality between men and woman during participation is noted as well.

The most obvious feature of public participation arrangements in Thailand is probably the notable gaps appeared between the rather strong *Constitution* on public participation and the lack of more specific legislation or administrative rules in this area. It raises the question of whether the Constitutional requirements can be implemented in practice. For example, some Thai public interest lawyers, representing several Thai villagers in the Northeast of Thailand who allegedly would be effected by the Xayaburi Dam in Laos, recently brought a lawsuit to the Thai Administrative Court arguing that the Cabinet approval that allows the Electricity Generating Authority of Thailand (EGAT) to sign a power purchase agreement with the Lao government regarding the Xayaburi Dam was taken without public participation and violated their constitutional rights. Although the dam itself is located outside Thailand, the power purchase decision was indeed made by a Thai state enterprise under the Ministry of Energy and approved by the Cabinet. The lawyer for the plaintiff cites Section 57 of the 2007 *Constitution* and argues that the government should provide information and an explanation to the public and allow them to express their opinions for any *activity* that may *affect* the quality of the environment. Reasonable as it sounds, rulings on administrative cases are not given based on the *Constitution*

183 Thawilwadee Bureekul, 'Access to Environmental Justice and Public Participation in Thailand' in Andrew Harding (ed), *Access to Environmental Justice: A Comparative Study* (Martinus Nijhoff Publishers, 2007) 271, 277.

184 *Constitution of the Kingdom of Thailand 2007* (Kingdom of Thailand) s 87.

directly and this specific Cabinet decision is not eligible for judicial review by the Constitutional Court either.[185]

The public participation process in Thailand is yet to be specified and institutionalised. Practice in the field is largely uncoordinated and unstable. Issues like early involvement, transparency, appropriate time-frames, capacity-building, selection of participants and proper ways of responding to public opinion are still waiting to be better defined and clarified via legislation or guidelines.

From the perspective of outcomes, the general impression on the effectiveness of the participation process on influencing the final decision is probably more negative than positive. In a more confrontational situation, whether public opinion can actually change the final decision usually provides a direct answer to the question of effectiveness. However, it can be argued that even if the government does not adopt the views of the public, as long as it has actively engaged the public in the discussion leading up to a decision and provides reasonable explanation for not complying with their comments, this process can also lead to a peaceful resolution of conflicts and contribute to trust-building between government and the public. Regrettably, quite often it is the third situation that is more common in Thailand. The late involvement of the public and problematic participation arrangements often lead to unsuccessful dispute resolution, increased social unrest and the loss of public faith in the formal participation process. In this sense, the participation practices in China and Thailand face similar challenges and criticisms, though to varying degrees in different circumstances.

Among the Mekong countries, Thailand probably has more potential of enhancing public participation in the future than the other countries. It enjoys the openest political environment for public participation and the development of civil society is the most vibrant in the region.[186] This can be attributed to its democratic system of government, the fundamental recognition of the right to participate under the Constitution, the more relaxed control over civil society organisations, a free media and the legal right of the NGOs to directly participate in environmental litigation.

185 For detailed powers of the Constitutional Court, see Constitutional Court of the Kingdom of Thailand, *Powers and Duties of the Constitutional Court* <http://www.constitutionalcourt.or.th/dmdocuments/Powers%20and%20Duties%20of%20the%20Constitutional%20Court.pdf>.

186 See Asian Development Bank, 'Civil Society Briefs: Thailand' (Briefs, Asian Development Bank, 2011).

In fact, one of the reasons why the environmental legislation in Thailand is not as specific and abundant as some other Mekong countries is that the public does have opportunities to participate in preparation of normative documents and the process is more time consuming than in other Mekong countries.[187] Although public participation via formal channels provided by the government may not be that systematic or effective, there are other approaches available for the public to have their voice heard and to protect their procedural and substantial rights. Thailand's environmental movement is largely driven by various forms of protests, petitions and campaigns, and the media plays an important role in this process. The less reliance on formal public participation processes to resolve environmental disputes illustrates the initial stage of deliberative democracy development in Thailand. But the availability of other alternative approaches, though perhaps not ideal, can help shape an enabling environment for deliberative democracy and persuade the government to take more genuine measures to enhance the effectiveness of public participation channels.

## 3 Vietnam

Vietnam, as a one-party socialist country, is another emerging economy in the region and is undergoing economic reforms following a similar pattern of China's Reform and Open Policy. Political reform in this country has lagged behind changes in the economic sector. Slowly, however, new political opportunities are arising in Vietnam, including those for public participation and the development of civil society. Similar to the *Chinese Constitution*, the *1992 Vietnam Constitution* upholds basic civil rights which are nevertheless difficult to be delivered in practice.[188] Vietnam even goes one step further than China by ratifying the *International Covenant on Civil and Political Rights* in 1982.

In terms of government transparency, there is currently no general policy or specific legislation available in Vietnam. But under the *2005 Law on Environmental Protection*, certain environmental information is required to be made public as long as it is not classified as state secrets. This includes: EIA reports, decisions on the approval of the EIA reports and plans for the implementation of such decision. Information disclosure should be easily accessible and accurate.[189] But the timing of information disclosure is not

187 See Philip Hirsh, 'Water Governance Reform and Catchment Management in the Mekong Region' (2006) 15(2) *Journal of Environment and Development* 184, 190.

188 The right to receive information is stipulated in Article 69.

189 *Law on Environmental Protection* (Socialist Republic of Vietnam) National Assembly, 29 November 2005, art 104.

addressed. There is no further guidance on how to ensure the implementation of the existing requirements and civil society has no opportunity to question the government's behaviour on these issues. Press freedom in Vietnam is severely constrained by the government.[190] In 2008, Vietnamese authorities decided to draft the *Law on Access to Information*.[191] This process was assisted by several international organisations and bilateral partners. For example, in June 2009, the NGO "Article 19" published detailed and critical commentaries on the draft law.[192] But the process of actually passing this draft law is now suspended since the bill was not dealt with at the 11th Party Congress in January 2011.[193] Even if it is finally promulgated someday, based on the experience in China it is less likely that it would be effectively implemented in the near future.

This situation is associated with strict control over the development of civil society organisations and rudimentary provisions with regard to public participation. In response to local uprisings and protests in the mid-1990s due to the ineptitude and corruption among local officials, Vietnam passed the 1998 Regulations on Democracy in Communes and was later updated by the 2003 Grassroots Democracy Decree.[194] The 2003 Decree reflects the Communist Party's policy on citizen participation, namely allowing people to be informed and to participate during the formulation, implementation and monitoring of local government plans and spending.[195]

Compared to other decision-making levels, it should be acknowledged that the culture of challenge and assertion of alternative ideas is most vibrant at the local level and the issuance of such Decrees do have some positive

---

190 See generally Robert W. Vaagan, 'Media Systems, Access to Information and Human Rights in China and Vietnam' (2011) 29(4) *Nordic Journal of Human Rights* 302.

191 Ibid. 309.

192 See Article 19, *Vietnam: Article 19 Assists with Drafting Freedom of Information Law* (11 May 2009) <http://www.article19.org/data/files/pdfs/press/vietnam-article-19–assists-with-drafting-freedom-of-information-law.pdf>.

193 Vaagan, above n 190, 311.

194 Charles Hostovsky, Virginia Maclaren and Geoffrey McGrath, 'The Role of Public Involvement in Environmental Impact Assessment in Vietnam: Towards a More Culturally Sensitive Approach' (2010) 53(3) *Journal of Environmental Planning and Management* 405, 410.

195 Bach Tan Sinh, 'Civil Society and NGOs in Vietnam: Some Initial Thoughts on Developments and Obstacles' (Paper presented at the Meeting with the Delegation of the Swedish Parliamentary Commission on Swedish Policy for Global Development to Vietnam, 2 March 2001) 5.

impact on government performance at the communal level.[196] But in order to reconcile the Party's desire for associations that promote economic and social development with concerns that NGOs may oppose party and state policies, the above two Decrees, combined with the *1957 Law on Association* and the 2003 Decree on Operation of Association, give the state ample power to strictly control the formation and operation of associations.[197] The new draft Law on Association, which attempts to ease restrictions over the formation of associations, is currently blocked in the National Assembly.[198]

At present, the term "civil society" is still a relatively new concept in Vietnam. It is neither widely recognised by authorities nor completely independent from the party-state discourse.[199] Any relevant development in Vietnam is strongly led by the government and the dominant forms of civil society organisations are "official" mass organisations like those in China. Among the Vietnamese NGOs that are registered, most of them focus on charity, health and educational areas and are less of a threat to the government.[200] Some environmental NGOs that are able to be registered are the Vietnam Union of Science and Technology Associations, the Vietnam Association for Conservation of the Nature and Environment and the Centre for Water Resource Conservation and Development. But the operation of these NGOs usually does not directly target the behaviour of the government or state enterprises and is more focused on seeking scientific and technologic solutions rather than political or legal ones. The operation of International NGOs is relatively less restricted than local NGOs but the development of grassroots NGOs is very much restricted under the current system, comparable to China, if not worse. Unfinished political and economic reforms leave numerous ideological, political, institutional and legal obstacles to overcome in order to really embrace the theory of civil society and facilitate the development of deliberative democracy.

---

196 Mira Käkönen and Philip Hirsch, 'The Anti-Politics of Mekong Knowledge Production' in François Molle, Tira Foran and Mira Käkönen (eds), *Contested Waterscapes in the Mekong Region: Hydropower, Livelihoods and Governance* (Earthscan, 2009) 333, 347.

197 See John Gillespie, 'Localizing Global Rules: Public Participation in Lawmaking in Vietnam' (2008) 33(3) *Law and Social Inquiry* 673, 682; Scott Robertson and Tran Thi Hai, 'NGO/Civil Society Development in Vietnam' (Working Reference, Vietnam Assistance for the Handicapped, 2004).

198 Gillespie, above n 197, 682–3.

199 Irene Nørlund, *Civil Society in Vietnam: Social Organisations and Approaches to New Concepts* (2007), 68 <http://www.asienkunde.de/content/zeitschrift_asien/archiv/pdf/a105_ref_art_norlund.pdf>; Asian Development Bank, 'Civil Society Briefs: Vietnam' (Briefs, Asian Development Bank, 2011) 1.

200 See Nørlund, above n 199, 77.

Some elements of public participation are reflected in the environmental protection legislation in Vietnam, particularly regarding SEA and EIA processes. Under the *Law on Environmental Protection*, no public participation is required during the preparation of the SEA report. The reports do, however, need to be reviewed by an appraisal council that is comprised of government officials, experts and representatives of other organisations and individuals.[201] It should be noted that organisations here do not necessarily mean NGOs and there is no express requirement for the participation of individuals that are directly affected by the plan or strategy. Since the council members are handpicked by government agencies, it is very easy to manipulate the views of the public reflected in this process.[202]

Another way to participate is to send petitions and recommendations to government agencies and the latter are required to take them into account during decision-making.[203] This, however, is dependent on whether the public can receive information regarding the proposed plan or strategy. There is no way to know whether the government agency does consider the public opinion during decision-making and no explanation or reasons are required to be given to the public in response. The lack of basic flow of information and the strong government-led feature of the process will provide ample opportunity for the government to control the outcome. Therefore, although the above provisions apply to all strategies and plans that are subject to SEA (in contrast to China where public participation only applies to the SEA of sectoral plans), the participation requirements under the *Law on Environmental Protection* are still quite limited.

Similar requirements are made for public participation during the EIA process.[204] In addition to the rather ambiguous references to public participation, the provision on the content of the EIA report actually reflects more stringent requirements in this respect. It states that the EIA report should include opinions of representatives of local communities and must present opinions that are against the project location or against environmental

201 *Law on Environmental Protection* (Socialist Republic of Vietnam) National Assembly, 29 November 2005, art 17. The results of such appraisal should serve as a basis for approval of the plan or strategy. More than 50 percent of the members must have the expertise in environment and other areas related to the contents of the project, while persons who are directly involved in the preparation of the SEA report cannot participate in the appraisal process.

202 See ibid. The members of the council are decided by the agency competent to set up the appraisal council.

203 Ibid.

204 Ibid. art 21.

protection solutions.[205] But without more enforceable arrangements on the participation process itself and an enabling environment for participation, it is difficult to ensure that public opinion can be effectively reflected in the EIA report. As mentioned earlier, the government is required to disclose the EIA report to the public. But this requirement is not incorporated into the EIA procedures, thus there is no further guidance on how and when the report should be made public.

The decision on approving the EIA report should be notified to local People's Committees by the competent authority.[206] This process resembles more of an internal administrative procedure and the public is not directly the recipient of such notification. It is not clear whether this provision also applies to circumstance when the EIA report is not approved. The project owners are responsible for reporting the above information to the local People's Committees as well. In addition, as part of the post-EIA analysis process, the owners are required to publicly post information on the categories of wastes, relevant environmental standards, environmental protection solutions and technologies employed at project sites for local communities in order to respect their right to know and facilitate their supervision and inspection.[207] Considering the local government's eagerness for development projects and the potential economic interests regarding government revenue, including corruption attributed to local officials, it is unlikely that the local communities will have their voices heard by the government or by the public through the media.

The Law, however, does provide guidances on how to exercise grassroots democracy in environmental protection as a way of implementing the Grassroots Democracy Decree. The public should be informed on environmental matters and measures to prevent and alleviate any negative environmental impact. Dialogues should be held with the public on environmental issues as well. Such dialogues much be held at the request of dialogue-seeking parties or in response to complaints, petitions and lawsuits filed by concerned organisations or individuals.[208] There is no detailed information on the procedural requirements of such dialogues and it is less clear on how to incorperate these general requirements into the SEA or EIA process.

Currently, Vietnam is in the process of reviewing and revising the *Law on Environmental Protection*. In addition to the need to further improve the

205 Ibid. art 20.
206 Ibid. art 23.
207 Ibid.
208 Ibid. art 105.

existing legislation, attention should be paid to the question of implementation in practice. With regard to hydropower development in the Mekong region, since the Vietnamese government is officially against the construction of mainstream dams, it is relatively less controvercial for the NGOs and individuals to involve themselves on this particular issue in Vietnam. The degree of political tolerance, however, cannot be guaranteed, due to the fluid relationship between Vietnam and Laos. Considering Vietnam's intendtion to win support from Laos regarding its territorial dispute with China in the South China Sea, there seems to be a tendency to supress the heated critisism of Vietnam NGOs on Laos' mainstream hydropower plans.[209]

As a country where the development of public participation and civil society is still largely controlled and led by the government, there is certainly a reasonable concern that public participation can be merely employed as a political strategy to collect information to serve the needs of foreign affairs. By allowing some relaxation of restrictions on public participation and civil society, there is nevertheless a real possibility of momentum for further improvement of these reforms and a wider application in practice. In light of the growing investment in this country by the World Bank and the ADB, their policies on public participation and EIA can, to varying degrees, help to raise standards for specific projects in this country.

## 4 Laos

Laos is one of the poorest countries in Southeast Asia and the political environment for transparency and public participation is the most constrained among four lower Mekong countries. Compared to China and Vietnam, Laos lags behind in terms of economic, political and legal reform. So far, there is no national policy or legislation on government transparency. Under the *1999 Environmental Protection Law*, governmental authorities are granted the power and responsibility to collect and disseminate environmental information.[210] But there are no specific provisions in this area and the public's right to know is not expressly recognised by the *Constitution* or the *Environmental Protection Law*. Similar to the situation in China and Vietnam, some forms of civil rights, like lodging complaints, petition and making suggestions are set out in the

209 Yumiko Yasuda, 'Institutional Influence on NGO Advocacy: Comparative Case Studies of Xayaburi Dam Advocacy' (Speech delivered at the Southeast Asia Seminar Series, University of Sydney, 7 September 2012).

210 *Environmental Protection Law* (Lao People's Democratic Republic) National Assembly, 3 April 1999, arts 4, 37–9.

revised *Constitution* in 2003.[211] But in reality such rights can be easily restricted and often have limited impact on decision-making. Without independent judicial system or rule of law in the country, petitions or complaints often serve as an alternative way of seeking remedies for injustice and usually occurs after the decision are made. The terms used in the Constitution may share some elements of western concepts of public participation, but fundamentally they are based on divergent political systems and thus have different implications in the context of most Mekong countries.

Over the past decade, some notable progress with respect to public participation in Laos has occurred in the area of EIA. Under the *1999 Environmental Protection Law*, environmental assessment[212] shall include the participation of mass organisations and people that are likely to be affected by the development projects or operations.[213] This is further elaborated by the 2010 Decree on EIA.[214] The Decree specifies the relevant rights and duties from both the perspectives of the public and the government and outlines more detailed requirements on the participation process. The public has the right to receive information on (1) the development project and its potential positive and negative impact; (2) the EIA report, the environmental management and monitoring plan and the social management and monitoring plan; as well as (3) the report on the progress in implantation of preventive measures.[215]

In addition, the public have the right to participate in (1) the consultation meetings at all levels to deliberate the EIA report and relevant plans; (2) the discussions on compensation, resettlement and restoration measures; and (3) the discussions on implementation of environmental and social measures and plans.[216] Correspondingly, the government and project developers *must* notify the local communities via village dissemination meetings and collect opinions from the affected public. This is followed by the obligation to organise consultation meetings at village, district and provincial levels during the preparation and examination of the EIA report. Further, local communities

---

211 *Constitution of the Lao People's Democratic Republic* (Lao People's Democratic Republic) National Assembly, 6 May 2003, art 41.

212 A more general term of "environmental assessment" is used in Lao rather than "environmental impact assessment".

213 *Environmental Protection Law* (Lao People's Democratic Republic) National Assembly, 3 April 1999, art 8.

214 See Asia Development Bank, 'Lao People's Democratic Republic: Environment and Social Program' (Progress Report, Asian Development Bank, 2006) 6.

215 *Decree on Environmental Impact Assessment* (Lao People's Democratic Republic) Prime Minister's Office, 18 February 2010, art 7.

216 Ibid.

should also be informed by the project developer during the construction and operation periods regarding any activities which may affect the environment and society.[217]

The above provisions use rather strong language for public participation. Not only do they expressly recognise the public's rights to access to information and to participate during the EIA process, but also highlight the relevant obligations of the government and developer. Such clear requirements on public participation during the EIA process are even more advanced than what current exists in Thailand and Vietnam. Compared to the relevant legislation in China, the Lao requirements for public participation cover three different stages of the EIA process: the preparation and review of the EIA report and the implementation of the environmental measures and plans. In particular, participation during the EIA preparation period represents an early involvement of public. The evolution of the public participation requirements for the EIA procedure in Laos is supported and promoted by the ADB's Environment and Social Program loan, which is intended to support the policy reform agenda of the Lao government to improve environmental management and social safeguards in the energy and transport sectors.[218] This indicates the potential positive impact of foreign and international investors and donors on the legal reforms in Laos. Having expressly recognised the relevant rights and obligated the different levels of participation, the existing legislation still needs to be further developed with respect to more detailed guidance concerning the principles of information disclosure and the process for public participation.

These improvements with respect to public participation, however, are undermined by the lack of political will and a challenging legal and economic environment to ensure adherence to the above provisions in practice. The general public are often not aware of their participation rights and the current Lao political and judicial systems fall short of effective channels for the public to challenge government violations. This is further restricted by the highly controlled media environment. Difficulties also arise from the fact that only slightly more than half of the population can speak the official and dominant language in Laos (the reminder speaks a variety of ethnic minority languages), not to mention the relatively low literacy and education rates in the country. Laos is sparsely populated and many people live in extremely remote areas. The lack of necessary resources and infrastructure due to poverty further exacerbates these difficulties.

---

217 Ibid. art 8.

218 See Asia Development Bank, above n 214.

Under the Article 44 of the *Lao Constitution*, Lao citizens have the freedom of association. But this right is in fact highly restricted due to political concerns, excessive bureaucracy and a lack of standards and procedures for the establishment of associations and organisations. In addition, there is no clear designation of government agency that is responsible for relevant management.[219]

The development of civil society organisations remains largely led by the government and in many ways still relies on personal relationships or recommendations. Before 2009, only a few independent local organisations were active. As observed by ADB, "these groups generally existed under ad hoc arrangements, including being registered as companies or training institutes, or through arrangements with specific ministries".[220] While international NGOs have more political leeway to operate in Laos, local NGOs can be more "attuned to the local culture, as well as needs at the community level" and the international NGOs cannot reach many of the remote areas.[221]

Recent years have witnessed the Lao government taking some steps to reduce the ambiguities and obstacles and slowly improve the opportunities for the development of civil society.[222] This is illustrated by the approval of the Decree on Associations in April 2009.[223] Notably, the Lao registration system does not adopt China's dual supervision system, which has proved to be a major obstacle for the establishment of civil society organisations in China. Nor is there is an express competition restriction under the Decree. The Decree does, however, adopt a regulation system based on the operation of associations at the national, provincial or local levels.[224] The associations are not allowed to engage in activities that can threaten national stability and social order.[225] Based on the experiences in China, the so-called national stability and social order provision is a very convenient excuse for restricting or prohibiting the operation of organisations. Although registrations opened in November

219 Gretchen A. Kunze, *New Decree Opens Way for Civil Society in Laos* (2 June 2010) In Asia: the Asia Foundation Blog <http://asiafoundation.org/in-asia/2010/06/02/new-decree-opens-way-for-civil-society-in-laos/>.

220 Asian Development Bank, 'Civil Society Briefs: Lao People's Democratic Republic' (Briefs, Asian Development Bank, 2011) 1.

221 Integrated Regional Information Networks, *Laos: Government Boost for Local NGOs* (12 May 2009) <http://www.irinnews.org/Report/84347/LAOS-Government-boost-for-local-NGOs>.

222 Kunze, above n 219.

223 See Integrated Regional Information Networks, above n 221.

224 *Decree on Associations* (Lao People's Democratic Republic) Prime Minister's Office, 29 April 2009, art 8.

225 Ibid. art 20.

2009, no organisation had completed the process or achieved permanent registration by early 2011, reflecting the complexity of the registration process and the potential political concerns and distrust from both the government and the existing grassroots organisations.[226]

Despite the existing deficiencies, the issuance of this Decree is groundbreaking[227] and has the potential to open new political opportunities for the establishment and operation of local NGOs. For example, local NGOs are increasingly involved in promoting government information transparency and improving the accessibility of government information. This is represented by the work of the Coalition for Lao Information, Communication and Knowledge.[228] Along with the fledging civil society movement, it is likely that the Lao government will have to introduce more initiatives designed to enhance the disclosure of government information and improve relevant legislation. With regard to hydropower development, since the power sector in Laos serves two vital national priorities,[229] it is much more sensitive for the local NGOs to challenge the dam projects. That said, the Mekong mainstream dam projects in Laos attract a lot of attention from international NGOs and are under pressure from neighbouring governments and their citizens. Nevertheless, further development of local NGOs in Laos is still crucial to help protect the interests of local communities that are affected by the dam projects.

## 5 Cambodia

After years of isolation and civil war, a large percentage of the population in Cambodia are still struggling below the poverty line despite the rapid economic growth over the last decade. As an emerging democracy, Cambodia suffers from many problems associated with a post-conflict society relating to a lack of bureaucratic capacity and widespread corruption.[230] Although Cambodia is undergoing rapid legal reforms in water management under the

226 Asian Development Bank, above n 220, 3.

227 Kunze, above n 219.

228 More information regarding the Coalition for Lao Information, Communication & Knowledge can be found on its website: http://helvetas-laos.org/la/index.php?option=com_content&view=article&id=16&Itemid=31&lang=en.

229 It promotes economic and social advancement by providing a reliable and affordable domestic power supply and earns foreign exchange from electricity exports. Xaypaseuth Phomsoupha, 'Hydropower Development Plans and Progress in Lao PDR' (2009) 4 *Hydro Nepal* 15, 15.

230 Philip Hirsch et al., 'National Interests and Transboundary Water Governance in the Mekong' (Report, University of Sydney, 2006) 15.

influence of various foreign and international donors and investors, its legislation on information disclosure and public participation remains insufficient.

In terms of government transparency, the public's right to know is not expressly recognised under the *1993 Constitution*. It was not until December 2010 when a draft law on access to information was finally brought to the National Assembly.[231] The bill was rejected one year later without review or debate and another version of the bill was submitted by the same opposition party in March 2012. The latest bill recognises the right to access to information and elaborates on the information that should be actively disclosed. Similar to the Thailand *Official Information Act*, the draft law attempts to establish Information Disclosure Tribunals which have the power to make decisions on the appeals against decisions of the Information Commissioner. Such decisions can then be challenged in the Supreme Court. But the language used in the draft law is still ambiguous in many aspects and may be abused or misinterpreted by the government.

Currently, some information disclosure provisions are incorporated into the *1995 Press Law* and the *2005 Archive Law*. The former briefly recognises the right of the press to gain access to information in government held records and further provides some general requirements on the exemptions and information disclosure upon request.[232] The latter recognises the right of the public to access achieves for research purposes.[233] But documents that affect public order may be subject to longer periods of secrecy.[234] The existing legislation is obviously not enough to fully recognise and protect the public's right to know and the requirements on confidential information should be re-examined as well.

231 The first bill was introduced by the opposition Sam Rainsy Party representatives and then welcomed and reviewed by the Article 19 (a London-based NGO) in September 2011. Information regarding this draft law and relevant events is derived from a factsheet prepared by the International Freedom of Expression Exchange. International Freedom of Expression Exchange, 'Law Classification Series: Law on Freedom of Information' (Factsheet, International Freedom of Expression Exchange, 2012) 1. For efforts on promoting government transparency between 2004 to 2010, see Cambodian Centre for Human Rights, 'Freedom of Information in Cambodia: A Right to Know or a Culture of Secrecy?' (Report, Cambodian Centre for Human Rights, 2012) 11–2.

232 See *Law on the Regime of the Press* (Kingdom of Cambodia) National Assembly, 18 July 1995, art 5 (emphasis added).

233 *Law on Archives* (Kingdom of Cambodia) National Assembly, October 2005, art 13 (emphasis added).

234 Ibid. art 14.

While it is necessary to urge the promulgation of the Law on Access to Information, there are still many difficulties for the government to actively disclose information and to improve the accessibility of the information. Affecting factors include, but are not limited to: corruption, excessive bureaucracy, lack of human resources, a problematic judicial system, low literacy rates, the remoteness of many villages, the public's low awareness of their rights, low internet penetration and the lack of other infrastructure due to poverty. Therefore, even if the Law on Access to Information can be enacted in the near future, it will only serve a starting point for real improvement of government transparency.

Without proper information transparency, meaningful public participation cannot be guaranteed, even though it is a constitutional right in Cambodia to participate actively in the political, economic, social and cultural life of the nation.[235] For example, as observed by the Cambodian Centre for Human Rights:

> There appears to be a culture of secrecy within the legislative process in Cambodia, whereby access to information before bills become laws is severely limited and, in some cases, restricted to only a few days before the bill in question is due to be debated. This is particularly so when the draft law in question is considered to be politically sensitive ... consultation in relation to more politically sensitive laws, such as the Anti-Corruption Law, and the NGO law, has been more restricted and less forthcoming, with many in civil society regarding the consultation that followed the release of drafts of the laws as meaningless.[236]

With regard to plans and strategies, Cambodia has not yet adopted the SEA process, let alone the relevant requirements on information disclosure and public participation. The *1996 Law on Environmental Protection and Natural Resource Management* requires the Ministry of Environment to provide information on its activities "following proposals of the public" and shall "*encourage* participation of the public in the environmental protection and natural resource management".[237] Not only is there no obligation to actively disclose information, the Ministry is only required to encourage public participation,

---

235 *Constitution of the Kingdom of Cambodia* (Kingdom of Cambodia) Constitutional Assembly, 21 September 1993, art 35.

236 Cambodian Centre for Human Rights, above n 231, 28.

237 *Law on Environmental Protection and Natural Resource Management* (Kingdom of Cambodia) National Assembly, 24 December 1996, art 16.

which is basically a meaningless statement. According to the Law, detailed arrangements for public participation and access to information should be further determined by a sub-decree following a proposal by the Ministry, but no such document has come into force to date. The EIA procedure was the subject of a sub-decree in 1999. Although one of the objectives of the sub-decree is to "encourage public participation in the implementation of EIA process and take into account their conceptual input and suggestions for re-consideration prior to the implementation of any project",[238] there is in fact no further reference about these procedures in it. Along with the ongoing rapid legal reforms, it is obvious that the overarching environment protection law needs to be renewed and the EIA sub-decree should be reviewed and upgraded. As mentioned in chapter two, Cambodia's *2007 Law on Water Resources Management* includes provisions on information disclosure and supports the collaboration with and participation of civil society organisations in the sustainable development of water resources.[239] These provisions cannot be fully implemented without more specific and stringent requirements and a proper legal framework for the public to seek remedies for government violations. Meanwhile, the Cambodian government has attempted to increase public participation in the development process through political reforms towards decentralisation (illustrated by the establishment of local councils) and there appears to be some strong examples of cooperation between government and civil society organisations at the local level.[240]

Another issue regarding public participation is the development of civil society organisations in Cambodia. In a country that still largely relies on foreign and international donations and investments, the importance of civil society organisations being engaged in providing or supporting basic social services in Cambodia has been recognised by donors and multilateral investment banks.[241] Traditionally, the dominant form of social organisation was Pagoda-based association, but currently other kinds of grassroots organisations or community-based organisations are rapidly growing and usually linked to development projects.[242] The statistics in 2009 show that there are

238 *Sub-Decree on Environmental Impact Process* (Kingdom of Cambodia) Council of Ministers, 11 August 1999, art 1.

239 *Law on Water Resources Management* (Kingdom of Cambodia) National Assembly, 29 June 2007, arts 7, 8, 19.

240 Asian Development Bank, 'Civil Society Briefs: Cambodia' (Briefs, Asian Development Bank, 2011) 4.

241 See ibid. 2.

242 Ibid. 1.

about 450 registered local NGOs and 316 international NGOs that are believed to be active.[243] Civil society organisations are allowed to operate for the most part without government hindrance, despite the fact that the latter's attitude towards them is one of scepticism.[244] But this situation is not always consistent and varies in different circumstances.[245]

The establishment and operation of civil society organisations in Cambodia also falls short of clear and strong legal supports. In December 2010, the first draft of the Law on Associations and NGOs was released, which was then fiercely condemned by the international community and civil society organisations.[246] Major problems include: registration remains compulsory while unregistered associations are prohibited from operating; excessive registration and reporting procedures; and a lack of legal safeguards, meaningful judicial review mechanisms, or right to appeal.[247]

While there is an increasing need for more systematic legislation in this area, it is also important to make sure that such legislation can actually be more beneficial to civil society development rather than having an adverse impact on the status quo. As mentioned earlier, consultation on this draft law is more restricted than other less sensitive ones. Although the political opportunities are relatively open, Cambodia still falls short of reliable political and legal procedures to allow the public to have a real impact on the decision-making process.

Media freedom in Cambodia is not unrestricted. Some of the major obstacles confronting the Cambodian media are dangers related to the safety of journalists, limited media infrastructure, widespread financial and geographical problems in maintaining regular publication schedules and having paid staff.[248]

---

243 Cooperation Committee for Cambodia, 'NGO Contributions to Cambodia's Development 2004–2009' (Report, Cooperation Committee for Cambodia, 2010) 6–7.

244 Sida Advisory Team, 'Civil Society and Democracy in Cambodia: Changing Roles and Trends' (Report, Sida Advisory Team, 2003) 13.

245 See Asian Development Bank, above n 240, 3.

246 Siena Anstis, *Cambodia's Troubling NGO & Associations Law* (11 May 2011) <http://siena-anstis.com/wp-content/uploads/2011/05/11/cambodias-troubling-ngo-associations-law/>.

247 See Human Rights Watch, *Cambodia: Withdraw Flawed Draft NGO and Association Law* (7 April 2011) <http://www.hrw.org/en/news/2011/04/07/cambodia-withdraw-flawed-draft-ngo-and-association-law>; Cambodian League for the Promotion and Defense of Human Rights, 'Draft Law on Association & NGOs Cambodian Civil Society under Threat' (Briefing Paper, Cambodian League for the Promotion and Defense of Human Rights, 2010).

248 See Kay Kimeong, *Cambodian Media Struggles through Hard Time*, ASEAN Mass Communication Studies and Research Centre <http://utcc2.utcc.ac.th/localuser/amsar/about/document18.htm>.

A major legal restriction on media freedom in this country is the Article 12 of the Press Law, which prohibits the press from publishing or reproducing any information that may cause harm to political stability.[249] Nevertheless, based on the Press Freedom Index 2011/2012, the Cambodian media ranked 117th out of 179 countries in 2011, giving it the top ranking among all ASEAN countries.[250] The ranking may not necessarily be that accurate, but it does reflect a relatively open media environment in Cambodia.

Cambodia and Vietnam are the most affected countries of the lower Mekong mainstream hydropower projects, most of which are located in Laos. This particular issue enjoys more political freedom in the two countries for civil society to express their opinions, despite the fact that a certain degree of unofficial pressure still can be felt by many NGOs working in the field.[251]

## 6 Myanmar

As a country that was under military rule for almost half a century and is still strongly influenced by the military after a general election in 2010, it is obvious that government transparency and public participation has been very poor or impossible in Myanmar's recent history. But since the elections, a series of reforms have been carried out by the government which have been welcomed by the world, such as the release of pro-democracy leader Aung San Suu Kyi and allowing the party led by her to join the by-elections held in April 2012, the establishment of the National Human Rights Commission and the relaxation of press censorship.[252] Although there is no formal channel available for the public to participate in decision-making, growing pressure from the public can sometimes lead to a change in government decisions.[253]

Whilst the overall tendency of ongoing reforms seems to be positive, caution should continue to be exercised by the international community and

---

249 *Law on the Regime of the Press* (Kingdom of Cambodia) National Assembly, 18 July 1995, art 12.

250 Reporters Without Borders, *Press Freedom Index 2011–2012* <http://en.rsf.org/press-freedom-index-2011-2012,1043.html>.

251 Yasuda, above n 209.

252 BBC News, *Burma's Aung San Suu Kyi Wins By-election: NLD Party* (1 April 2012) <http://www.bbc.co.uk/news/world-asia-17577620>; BBC News, *Burma Sets up Human Rights Commission* (6 September 2011) <http://www.bbc.co.uk/news/world-asia-pacific-14807362>; BBC News, *Burma Abolishes Media Censorship* (20 August 2012) <http://www.bbc.co.uk/news/world-asia-19315806>.

253 See Aung Hia Tun, *Myanmar Shelves $3.6 Billion Mega Dam, Officials Say* (30 September 2011) <http://www.reuters.com/article/2011/09/30/us-myanmar-dam-idUSTRE78T10H20110930>.

those who are working closely in promoting further progress in this country. Along with the acceleration of the reform process, there is a strong need for the drafting of new laws and regulations. During this process, it is necessary to promote the recognition of the basic rights to know and to participate and develop relevant mechanisms and arrangements which can be reflected and incorporated into different levels and areas of decision-making. The current reform process is still controlled by the government and military forces behind the scenes, but the emerging civil society, growing opportunities for the establishment and operation of NGOs, new political forces, and the relaxed control over media will increasingly allow other actors to influence the reform process.

## IV Towards Deliberative Decision-making Processes in the Mekong Region: Regional and Domestic Strategies

The above discussion identified and evaluated the development of information transparency and public participation from international, regional and domestic perspectives. Significant gaps exist between the status quo in the Mekong region and international best practice. The polycentric nature of water governance in the region corresponds with the piecemeal development of procedural rights at the regional level. Mekong countries are at different stages of political, social and economic reform with respect to the transition to representative democracy and market-based economies. Deliberative democracy, as a relatively new concept, remains unfamiliar to many of the Mekong countries and their citizens in the region.

Ideally, the concepts of access to information and public participation should be comprehended and promoted in the Mekong countries from the perspectives of human right and deliberative democracy. Simply introducing them as mechanisms or tools without proper recognition and understanding of their roots in western political and legal theories can open the door for them to be hijacked for different political purposes. But the situation in the field is not just black and white. The interaction and contradictions between the western and eastern cultures set the background for the introduction of these western discourses in the context of the Mekong region. In addition, the terms “rights” and “democracy” can be quite sensitive in many Mekong countries and advocacy groups often have to avoid direct reference to these words in order not to appear threatening to political regimes that are in the throes of transition.

Although the prevalent political ideologies and systems in many Mekong countries are different from those in the West, the will of the people is recognised as a major source of government legitimacy. Therefore, the introduction of government transparency and public participation is not in direct conflict with their political ideology. This provides an opportunity for the reformists from within the regime to promote progressive changes towards democracy and better protection of human rights. From a realistic point of view, although there is a high risk of formality (at least in the early stages) by interpreting these procedural rights from the perspective of the dominant political theories in many of the countries in the Mekong region, this could serve as a realistic foundation for political reforms during the transition period.

Whether representative democracy is a prerequisite for deliberative democracy in the Mekong region is controversial. Different answers can lead to diverging choices on revolution or reform. As discussed before, although a functional representative democracy system can provide a better environment for the development of deliberative democracy, it does not necessarily lead to the conclusion that improvements cannot be achieved without it. On the contrary, the effectiveness of representative democracy system is also reliant on or complemented by deliberative democracy.

Overall, China is currently leading reforms in this direction compared to Vietnam and Laos in terms of political opportunity and legislation. But some provisions under the legislation in Vietnam and Laos are considered to be more advanced than similar legislation in China, such as the introduction of public participation for the preparation of the EIA report or the implementation of environmental measures and plans. This can be partly attributed to the influences of foreign donors and investors.

With the exception of Thailand, other countries in the Mekong region fall short of formal recognition of access to information and public participation as rights under their existing legislation. The general environment and political tolerance for the development of deliberative democracy is much better in Thailand than the rest of the Mekong countries. A major problem for public participation in Thailand is the lack of more detailed regulations, which should be the focus of future efforts. The fact that Thailand has adopted an *Official Information Act* (instead of a mere regulation) and established quasi-jurisdictional boards and tribunals is considered to be a good example for future developments in China and the other countries in the Mekong region. For all the Mekong countries, public participation has not yet been introduced to all levels of decision-making, ranging from law-making to specific projects and from the preparation period to the implementation stage.

At the domestic level, the Mekong countries may take different paths of political reforms, but the overall tendency towards democracy and rule of law is undeniable despite the possibility of twists and turns along the way. Given these countries also suffer from widespread poverty, economic development and reforms are usually the most high-profile issues and priorities among the states' agendas. But it is argued that relevant political and social reforms must not be overlooked. While China's economic reform and success in the past few decades has set an intriguing example for other Mekong countries to follow, the prosperous appearance is increasingly challenged by the slow pace of political and social reform. More and more people are beginning to rethink the utilitarian and outcome-based philosophy rooted in the current reforms. Theories of justice and due process are increasingly being accepted as a good starting point to move forward.

As a country that has gone further down the reform road, relevant domestic changes in China will continue to have impact on domestic reforms in Vietnam and Laos. China is currently undergoing rapid changes amidst intense discussions on social value systems and there is a wide divergence of opinion on the issues mentioned in this chapter. Under current circumstances, it is necessary to continue raising awareness with respect to social justice, due process and the right of the public to know and to participate. For the Mekong countries, the reforms toward deliberative democracy occur against the backdrop of more profound and general social and political changes. A functional deliberative democracy appears to be a remote dream at this stage. Nevertheless, there are increasing internal and external pressures and incentives for the Mekong governments to take more measures to promote changes in this direction.

It is likely that the whole process will continue to be mainly led by respective governments. But along with the loosening of government control, the development of civil society and increasing awareness of the public, pressure is on the governments to make further changes. Nowadays, civil society development is suppressed to different degrees in the region and the public also lacks the means and social consciousness to actively engage in public affairs. Therefore, while a top-down process remains vital in the context of future reform, bottom-up approaches should attract more attention as well. Efforts should be made not only to raise awareness, but also to reduce political and legal restrictions on the establishment and operation of civil society organisations and to facilitate economic and social resources to build the capacity of the third sector. The conflicts between civil society and other social sectors should be seen as "contributing to a 'creative tension' in an evolving relationship".[254] Among the grassroots population, the affected public, particularly women, indigenous and minority ethnic communities should receive specific attention.

254 Soutar, above n 82, 221.

Guided by the above perspectives, domestic efforts and international support should be made or offered to improve deficiencies of legislation and implementation identified in Section II. In particular, the following issues should be highlighted: exemptions for access to information and the accessibility of information, the procedures to facilitate public participation in EIA processes, the regulation of associations and media, and the provision of corresponding judicial and quasi-judicial remedies.

To date, access to information and public participation has not yet been recognised as customary law under international law. The Mekong countries have to commit to relevant obligations based on consensus. The development of regional arrangements on access to information and public participation is a process underpinned through domestic responses to strengthen deliberative decision-making. In this sense, it is unlikely for the Mekong countries to agree on a formal recognition of access to information and public participation as procedural rights or to achieve consensus on how to improve government transparency and public participation domestically. The general application of the non-discrimination principle is also difficult to achieve in view of the notable gaps in domestic legislation and political opportunity, not to mention a strong sense of state sovereignty in these Mekong countries. Without some basic level of protection in each Mekong country or some minimum standards at the regional level, reliance on the non-discrimination principle may trigger disputes based on reciprocity. While it is still too early to expect all member states to agree on a particular MRC procedural document in this regard, the ASEAN Intergovernmental Commission on Human Rights and national human rights commissions in ASEAN countries are valuable tools and platforms to raise awareness of these procedural human rights. Despite the fact that the recommendations of these commissions do not have legally binding status in practice, their establishment is at least one step forward.

Although it is difficult to develop regional obligations or strategies for domestic development in this respect, it is relatively easier to promote regional arrangements on public procedural rights with respect to the operation of the MRC and the multilateral banks themselves. At this stage, the discourses on transparency and public participation have been generally accepted by the MRC Secretariat, the ADB and the World Bank. But they are not specifically mentioned under the platforms of the GMS and ACFTA. As an initial step, it is necessary to introduce and encourage a discussion of these issues within the GMS and ACFTA. For example, transparency and public participation could be incorporated into the GMS environmental protection agenda. In the context of the MRC, it has been argued that the existing policies on transparency and public participation are not well prepared, with numerous ambiguities and confusions on what these mechanisms are and how they might deal with more specific issues. It is important for the MRC to separate public participation with other kinds of stakeholder participation and to incorporate transparency and participation requirements with other MRC mechanisms.

With regard to the ADB, although the main responsibility of transparency and public participation lies in the government and business sectors, the ADB should adopt more stringent measures to promote the implementation of its relevant policies by member states. The accountability of the ADB in ensuring its projects follow and adhere to international standards of transparency and public participation should not be shifted to the member states or developers. Although the ADB policies are better than the arrangements under the MRC, there is no country-specific plan for communication of its policies to the public and more public participation agendas should be incorporated into the country partnership strategy. Meanwhile, it is recommended that the ADB should increase its lobbying and support for domestic legal reforms in this area and initiate programs to specifically focus on raising awareness, capacity building, and facilitating the implementation of information disclosure and public participation.

Despite the polycentric feature of the regional regimes, it is argued that at the very least they should strive to improve their relationship with NGOs and other civil society organisations and provide practical avenues for them to be heard and to bring issues to regional discussions. At the same time, due to the strong foreign influences on the MRC and ADB, it is necessary to be aware of the sensitivities of the Mekong countries, fearful of a new form of colonialism towards their operations.[255] As part of the solution, the MRC and ADB should better engage with the local NGOs and communities and to combine external pressures with the internal needs for reforms. Changes have to come from inside in order to really make any difference in the longer term.

---

255 Pål Arne Davidsen, 'Between Rhetoric and Reality—A Critical Account of Stakeholder Participation in Decision Making in the Mekong River Basin' in Anton Earle and Daniel Malzbender (eds), *Stakeholder Participation in Transboundary Water Management—Selected Case Studies* (InWEnt—Capacity Building International, 2006) 131, 135.

CHAPTER 6

# Transboundary Environmental Impact Assessment and Strategic Environmental Assessment

## I Introduction

Ever since environmental impact assessment (EIA) was first established in the United States via the *1969 National Environmental Policy Act*, it has been emulated by many other countries.[1] According to the definition given by the *1991 Espoo Convention*, it is "a national procedure for evaluating the likely impact of a proposed activity on the environment".[2] After decades of implementation, this mechanism is now functioning as a fundamental tool for domestic environmental protection. Further, the EIA procedure has been increasingly applied in a transboundary context to cope with environmental effects that spill across borders and has, in recent years, been a requirement directed at funding agencies that finance projects in developing countries. As will be discussed in detail later, the *Espoo Convention* and the European Union's (EU) *EIA Directive* represent the most stringent international requirements in this aspect.

More recently, strategic environmental assessment (SEA) has emerged as a response to the criticism that EIA often comes late in the planning process when economic benefits are already well defined and by which time it is difficult to analyse the potential environmental impact rigorously. It is argued that environmental evaluation should be employed and integrated into a more comprehensive decision-making process. This often refers to plans, programs and, to a lesser extent, policies in addition to the more common project-based assessments. The valuable role of SEA is also recognised as a promising approach to tackling global environmental concerns like climate change.[3]

---

1 *National Environmental Policy Act*, 42 USC § 4321–4347 (1969); Roger W. Findley and Daniel A. Farber, *Environmental Law in a Nutshell* (West Publishing, 2000) 52.

2 *Convention on Environmental Impact Assessment in a Transboundary Context*, opened of signature 25 February 1991, 1989 UNTS 309 (entered into force 10 September 1997) art 1.

3 See Wolfgang Wende et al., 'Climate Change Mitigation and Adaptation in Strategic Environmental Assessment' (2012) 32(1) *Environmental Impact Assessment Review* 88. Another linkage between EIA and climate change is reflected in the *EU Directive 2009/31/EC* which applies EIA to the capture and transport of $CO_2$ streams for the purposes of geo-

 DOI 10.1163/9789004266797_007

Compared to well-developed EIA processes, however, SEA is still a relatively new concept and the experience on the application of domestic SEA beyond the state remains very limited. The most important international documents in this area are the EU's *SEA Directive* and the United Nations Economic Commission for Europe's (UNECE) *SEA Protocol to the Espoo Convention* (*SEA Protocol*). At this stage, international obligations under the *SEA Protocol* only cover SEA of plans and programs, while SEA of policies and legislation is only mentioned on a voluntary basis.[4] Given the important value of SEA and its relatively immature status compared to EIA, the following discussion will certainly include considerations on SEA, but more specific attention will be paid to the development of transboundary EIA in the context of the Mekong region.

Both EIA and SEA processes provide legal mechanisms to consider sustainability on a case by case basis. In terms of water management, taking transboundary impact into consideration is also in line with the concept of integrated water resources management (IWRM). At the international level, transboundary EIA is considered as a valuable approach for countries to comply with the customary law obligations to prevent harm,[5] to cooperate and more specifically to utilise water resources equitably and reasonably. The non-discrimination principle also provides a theoretical foundation for transboundary EIA and SEA, which requires states to "assess transboundary impacts in the same manner as impacts on the state's own environment".[6] In particular, it addresses the issue of who should receive notification and be provided opportunities to participate, but it will not impose any minimum standards

---

logical storage. *Directive 2009/31/EC of the European Parliament and of the Council of 23 April 2009 on the Geological Storage of Carbon Dioxide and Amending Council Directive 85/337/EEC, European Parliament and Council Directives 2000/60/EC, 2001/80/EC, 2004/35/EC, 2006/12/EC, 2008/1/EC and Regulation (EC) No 1013/2006 (Text with EEA Relevance)* [2009] OJ L 140/114.

4 *Protocol on Strategic Environmental Assessment to the Convention on Environmental Impact Assessment in a Transboundary Context*, UN Doc *ECE/MP.EIA*/2003/2 (21 May 2003) art 13.

5 Notably, in the *Pulp Mills Case*, the International Court of Justice endorsed the view that EIA is a necessary element of the due diligence obligation.
"due diligence, and the duty of vigilance and prevention which it implies, would not be considered to have been exercised, if a party planning works liable to affect the régime of the river or the quality of its waters did not undertake an environmental impact assessment on the potential effects of such works".
*Pulp Mills on the River Uruguay (Argentina v Uruguay) (Judgment)* [2010] ICJ Rep 14, para 204.

6 Neil Craik, *The International Law of Environmental Impact Assessment* (Cambridge University Press, 2008) 57.

on the state of origin.[7] The question on reciprocity then arises, since states with strict domestic environmental measures will then have to provide more extraterritorial protection than states whose domestic protection is weak.[8] This issue will be further discussed with regard to public participation during the transboundary EIA and SEA processes. At this stage, it is safe to conclude that transboundary EIA and SEA mechanisms are neither derived from only one single principle under international law, nor can the influences be denied of domestic EIA and SEA legislation on their application in a transboundary context. This further implies potential pathways for the development of transboundary EIA and SEA: either through greater cooperation and institutionalisation of transboundary EIA and SEA in the region or through the development of internal capacity within domestic EIA and SEA legal system to include consideration of transboundary impact. The former is represented by the centralized EU model and the latter is exemplified by the more decentralized model used in countries like Canada.

The following analysis will begin by identifying and evaluating the development of both mechanisms under international law, including important treaties, soft-law documents and case law. The primary questions in this section are: What is the status quo of international arrangements on both mechanisms? Is transboundary EIA a customary rule and thus binding under international law? What are the key issues regarding the two processes or mechanisms? Which pathway is better for the development of transboundary EIA and SEA in the Mekong region?

Although the emergence of SEA is based on the theory and practice of EIA, the following discussion regarding these two mechanisms in the context of the Mekong region will begin with transboundary SEA. This is because SEA of plans is a higher level of environmental assessment and, in practice, transboundary SEA has already been done before any form of transboundary EIA has occurred on specific lower Mekong mainstream dam projects. The discussion on transboundary SEA in the context of the Mekong region will be based on the experiences and lessons from this case study. It will be complemented by a general analysis on the development of SEA at the national level and recommendations will be provided on how to improve domestic SEA across the region and explore whether there are other possible pilot opportunities to enhance its transboundary application.

---

7 Ibid.

8 John H. Knox, 'The Myth and Reality of Transboundary Environmental Impact Assessment' (2002) 96 *American Journal of International Law* 291, 313–4.

Research on transboundary EIA will start by identifying the current state of domestic EIA practice across the Mekong region. Although there is no prior experience on transboundary EIA in the region regarding hydropower development, China's experience of the joint EIA undertaken for the Mekong navigation channel improvement project and the transboundary EIA arrangements regarding the Greater Tumen Region (involving China, North Korea, Mongolia, South Korea and Russia) is enlightening. Through the above two case studies, this chapter will attempt to identify the progress and deficiencies and evaluate the general environment in the Mekong region for the future introduction and strengthening of transboundary EIA. It will then move on to focus on specific issues related to the design and promotion of transboundary EIA in the Mekong region, bearing in mind the limitations of domestic legislation and existing international arrangements in the region. Finally, conclusions will be drawn to offer some possible ways forward to encourage the development of transboundary EIA in the region.

## II Environmental Impact Assessment (EIA) and Strategic Environmental Assessment (SEA) Procedures under the International Law

International support for EIA can be identified in a range of conventions, soft-law documents and relevant case law.[9] In particular, evidence of *opinion juris* for domestic or transboundary EIA in non-legally binding documents are contained in the 1978 United Nations Environment Programme (UNEP) Principles on Shared Natural Resources,[10] the 1987 UNEP Goals and Principles

9 Timo Koivurova, Patricia Birnie, Alan Boyle and Catherine Redgwell provided a relatively systematic illustration on these documents and cases. See generally Timo Koivurova, 'Transboundary Environmental Impact Assessment in International Law' in Simon Marsden and Timo Koivurova (eds), *Transboundary Environmental Impact Assessment in the European Union* (Earthscan, 2011) 15, 15–25; Patricia Birnie, Alan Boyle and Catherine Redgwell, *International Law and the Environment* (Oxford University Press, 3rd ed, 2009) 167–72.

10 According to Principle 4 of the document: "States should make environmental assessment before engaging in any activity with respect to a shared natural resource which may create a risk of significantly affecting the environment of another State or States sharing that resource." *Environmental Law Guidelines and Principles on Shared Natural Resources*, UN Doc A/33/25 (May 19, 1978) principle 4.

of EIA,[11] the Rio Principle 17,[12] the 1997 Draft North American Transboundary EIA Agreement,[13] and the 2001 International Law Commission's Draft Articles on Prevention of Transboundary Damage from Hazardous Activities.[14] In addition, domestic EIA is now a common requirement for international institutions, especially multilateral development banks.[15] Both the World Bank's Operational Directive on Environmental Assessment and the Asian Development Bank (ADB) Environmental Assessment Guidelines are examples of these requirements.[16] Failure to conduct a transboundary EIA is also a key issue debated by states in the *Gabčíkovo-Nagymaros Case*,[17] the *MOX Plant*

11 *Goals and Principles of Environmental Impact Assessment*, UN Doc UNEP/WG.152/4 Annex (1987).

12 This principle requires EIA at the national level. *Report of the United Nations Conference on Environment and Development*, UN Doc A/CONF.151/26 (vol. I) (28 September 1992) principle 17.

13 Commission for Environmental Cooperation, *Full-Text of Proposed North American Transboundary Environmental Impact Assessment Agreement Now On-Line* (1997) <http://www.cec.org/Page.asp?PageID=122&ContentID=1906&SiteNodeID=366>.

14 International Law Commission, *Prevention of Transboundary Harm from Hazardous Activities*, UN GAOR, 56th sess, UN Doc A/56/10, art 7.

15 David Hunter, James Salzman and Durwood Zaelke, *International Environmental Law and Policy* (Foundation Press, 3rd ed, 2007) 532.

16 World Bank, *Policy* (26 April 2010) <http://go.worldbank.org/3LBMXIFF20>; Asian Development Bank, *Environmental Assessment Guidelines* (2003) <http://www.adb.org/sites/default/files/pub/2003/Environmental_Assessment_Guidelines.pdf>.

17 The Gabčíkovo-Nagymaros dams is a large barrage project on the Danube River that was initiated by former Czechosolovak and Hungary in 1977 via a formal agreement. In 1989, when most of the project on the Slovak side had been constructed (under the name of Gabčíkovo), the Hungarian government decided to suspend its share of the project and later unilaterally terminated the *1977 Treaty* in 1992 due to environmental concerns of the project. This is done "without having previously had recourse to the machinery of dispute settlement" indicated in the *1977 Treaty*. Both sides then agreed to take the dispute to the ICJ. In particular, whether the potential environmental impact of the projects has been properly considered and whether environmental concerns could justify or excuse the material breach of the *1977 Treaty* by the Hungarian government were fiercely debated between the two parties. Notably, Hungary proposed to carry out a joint environmental impact assessment in the region. And the Court stresses that "awareness of the vulnerability of the environment and the recognition that environmental risks have to be assessed on a continuous basis have become much stronger in the years since the Treaty's conclusion". As observed by Birnie, Boyle and Redgwell, this view of the relationship between EIA and post-project analysis reflects the practice of EIA in many national systems and in the provisions of the *Espoo Convention*. See *Gabčíkovo-Nagymaros Project*

*Case*[18] and the more recent *Pulp Mills Case.*[19] To date, the strongest support for EIA and SEA can be found in the context of the *1991 Espoo Convention*, its *2003 SEA Protocol* and the EU's *EIA and SEA Directives.*

At the outset it is necessary to differentiate between international obligations to implement EIA or SEA at a national level and those that specifically address transboundary applications. Domestic EIA and SEA arrangements provide a template for establishing international standards to promote the implementation of these mechanisms within one country. Specific requirements for transboundary EIA and SEA are derived from domestic experience and international support for these mechanisms can be traced back to obligations and principles under the international law. Other international requirements such as information exchange, notification, consultation and non-compliance mechanisms are also found within transboundary EIA and SEA processes.

## A *Transboundary EIA*

Some commentators argue that the obligation to conduct a transboundary EIA is probably now a requirement of customary law.[20] This is strongly supported by the recent International Court of Justice (ICJ) judgment on the *Pulp Mills*

---

(*Hungary/Slovakia*) (*Judgment*) [1997] ICJ Rep 7, 32, 44, 48, 59, 62, 68, 73, 77–8; Birnie, Boyle and Redgwell, above n 9, 170.

18 In 2001, the British Nuclear Fuels Limited (a government-owned UK Company) was granted the permit to operate the MOX (mixed oxide fuel) plant without any consultation with Ireland concerning the discharges. In October 2001, Ireland began proceedings under the *UN Conference on the Law of the Sea* (UNCLOS), claiming "there had been an inadequate EIA a failure to cooperate with Ireland over the protection of the Irish Sea and a failure to take measures to protect and preserve the Irish Sea". Due to the jurisdiction concerns, this claim was withdrawn by Ireland in 2007 and is currently dealt with by the European Court of Justice. But it is interesting to notice Ireland's reference to more than twenty different non-UNCLOS agreements which allegedly placed specific obligations upon the Untied Kingdoms, including the EU *EIA Directive* (as amended) and the *Espoo Convention*. See International Tribunal for the Law of the Sea, *The MOX Plant Case* (*Ireland v. United Kingdom*), *Provisional Measures* <http://www.itlos.org/index.php?id=102>; M. Bruce Volbeda, 'The MOX Plant Case: The Question of "Supplemental Jurisdiction" for International Environmental Claims under UNCLOS' (2006) 42 *Texas International Law Journal* 211, 219; Simon Marsden, 'MOX Plant and the Espoo Convention: Can Member State Disputes concerning Mixed Environmental Agreements be Resolved outside EC Law?' (2009) 18(3) *Review of European Community and International Environmental Law* 312, 314–5.

19 Details of the case will be discussed later. *Pulp Mills on the River Uruguay* (*Argentina v Uruguay*) (*Judgment*) [2010] ICJ Rep 14.

20 Hunter, Salzman and Zaelke, above n 15.

*Case* in 2010. The case concerns a dispute between Argentina and Uruguay (neither is a member state of the *Espoo Convention*) on the construction of pulp mills on the Uruguay River. By recognising the obligation to prevent harm as a customary rule, the Court argued that "a State is thus obliged to use *all the means* at its disposal in order to avoid activities which take place in its territory, or in any area under its jurisdiction, causing significant damage to the environment of another State".[21]

The Court's conclusion is carefully worded:

> In this sense, the obligation to protect and preserve, under Article 41 (a) of the Statute, has to be interpreted in accordance with a practice, which in recent years has gained so much acceptance among States that it may now be considered a requirement under general international law to undertake an environmental impact assessment where there is a risk that the proposed industrial activity may have a significant adverse impact in a transboundary context, in particular, on a shared resource.... due diligence,... would not be considered to have been exercised, if a party planning works liable to affect the regime of the river or the quality of its waters did not undertake an environmental impact assessment on the potential effects of such works.[22]

As observed by Boyle, this judgment considers EIA as a "distinct and freestanding transboundary obligation in international law".[23] Alternatively, it also indicates a strong connection between EIA and the due diligence requirement under the obligation to prevent harm. But as argued by Craik, it is important to remember that EIA is not the only way by which the obligation to prevent harm can be implemented.[24] Notably, although the ICJ's judgment in this case provides strong support for the customary law status of transboundary EIA, its decision "has no binding force except between the parties and in respect of that particular case".[25]

---

21 *Pulp Mills on the River Uruguay (Argentina v Uruguay) (Judgment)* [2010] ICJ Rep 14, para 101.

22 Ibid para 204 (emphasis added).

23 Alan Boyle, 'Developments in the International Law of Environmental Impact Assessments and their Relation to the Espoo Convention' (2011) 20(3) *Review of European Community & International Environmental Law* 227, 227.

24 Craik, above n 6, 122.

25 *Statute of the International Court of Justice*, opened for signature 26 June 1945, 3 Bevans 1179 (entered into force 24 October 1945) art 59.

Both parties to this case "agree on the necessity of conducting an environmental impact assessment", but differ on the scope and content of EIA that should be carried out.[26] As observed by Koivurova, the Court was careful in navigating between the arguments that "there already exists a fairly specific scope and content" for transboundary EIA and that it is enough that some sort of transboundary EIA is done.[27] Based on the UNEP Goals and Principles of EIA referred to by Argentina, the Court concludes that:

> it is for each State to determine in its domestic legislation or in the authorization process for the project, the specific content of the environmental impact assessment required in each case, having regard to the nature and magnitude of the proposed development and its likely adverse impact on the environment as well as to the need to exercise due diligence in conducting such an assessment. The Court also considers that an environmental impact assessment must be conducted prior to the implementation of a project. Moreover, once operations have started and, where necessary, throughout the life of the project, continuous monitoring of its effects on the environment shall be undertaken.[28]

In addition to the timing requirement and the optional obligation on post-project analysis which will be further discussed later, the Court is careful in arguing that the general international law does not specify any clear scope

26 According to the Judgment:

> "Argentina maintains in the first place that Uruguay failed to ensure that 'full environmental assessments [had been] produced, prior to its decision to authorize the construction . . .'; and in the second place that 'Uruguay's decisions [were] . . . based on unsatisfactory environmental assessments' , in particular because Uruguay failed to take account of all potential impacts from the mill, even though international law and practice require it, . . . Uruguay accepts that, in accordance with international practice, an environmental impact assessment of the Orion (Botnia) mill was necessary, but argues that international law does not impose any conditions upon the content of such an assessment, the preparation of which being a national, not international, procedure, at least where the project in question is not one common to several States. According to Uruguay, the only requirements international law imposes on it are that there must be assessments of the project's potential harmful transboundary effects on people, property and the environment of other States".

*Pulp Mills on the River Uruguay* (*Argentina v Uruguay*) (*Judgment*) [2010] ICJ Rep 14, para 203.

27 Ibid; Koivurova, above n 9, 24.

28 *Pulp Mills on the River Uruguay* (*Argentina v Uruguay*) (*Judgment*) [2010] ICJ Rep 14, para 205.

and content for EIA.[29] This illustrates the limitations of the discussion on the customary law status of any transboundary EIA obligation. On the positive side, increasing acceptance of transboundary EIA as a customary rule can certainly provide a powerful argument to urge countries that are not yet bound by any bilateral or multilateral commitments on this issue to engage in transboundary EIA in practice, and can serve as a starting point for countries to enter into more specific negotiations on detailed arrangements in this area. But in the absence of detailed commitments on the process of EIA, the customary law status of transboundary EIA alone would not substantially advance the implementation of the obligation to prevent harm,[30] not to mention the fact that without proper non-compliance mechanisms or other approaches to seek remedies for violation, it is doubtful that transboundary EIA will be effective in preventing or reducing transboundary harm. Even if countries can agree to conduct a transboundary EIA, disputes often centre on specific arrangements which are unable to be resolved by resorting to general international law. This is illustrated in the *Pulp Mills Case* and will be further discussed in case studies regarding the Mekong countries.

The above discussions are further linked with an understanding of transboundary EIA from two levels. On the one hand, transboundary EIA as a legal framework can be referred to as a "basic version", which has the general function of cultivating goodwill, increasing transparency and enhancing the involvement of a more vibrant civil society, especially with respect to developing stronger non-governmental organisations (NGO). Transboundary EIA at this level is mainly a framework and is easier to be accepted by riparian states. On the other hand, transboundary EIA as an institutional process can be referred to as a "classic version", which is represented by the EU's *EIA Directive* and the *Espoo Convention* together with other relevant agreements, including the *Aarhus Convention* and the *UNECE Water Convention*.[31] An institutionalised transboundary EIA certainly has a better chance to be effective, but consensus on such detailed regulation is much more difficult to achieve. Since this issue is addressed with difficulty by developed countries, it is unlikely to be any easier to deal with them in the context of Mekong region. The discussion on customary status of transboundary EIA is more valuable in promoting this mechanism at the basic level while more detailed arrangements tend to be more regionally based and often exist in more developed regions.

29 Koivurova, above n 9, 24.

30 Craik, above n 6, 122.

31 *Convention on the Protection and Use of Transboundary Watercourses and International Lakes*, opened for signature 17 March 1992, 1936 UNTS 269 (entered into force 6 October 1996) arts 3(1), 9(2).

Although it is probably more prudent to conclude that transboundary EIA has not yet developed into a fully formed customary obligation,[32] it should be recognised that this mechanism has been increasingly accepted and supported by state practices and will continue to spread both in terms of geographical coverage (especially in less developed regions and areas beyond national jurisdiction)[33] and its application areas (such as industrial activities and shared natural resources management). Meanwhile, along with increasing practices in the field, there is also a tendency to improve its implementation by developing or adopting more specific arrangements.

As a decentralized approach, some countries have already covered the transboundary impact under their domestic EIA legislation, such as the *1990 Act Concerning EIA* (amended 2006) in Germany, the *Federal Act Concerning Environmental Impact Assessment and Public Participation* in Austria and the *1992 Environmental Assessment Act* in Canada.[34] But domestic legislation does not create new procedural requirements for projects with potential transboundary effects.[35] In addition, as observed by Knox, the logic behind the outgrowth of transboundary EIA from domestic legal systems is more about the principle of non-discrimination instead of a logical extension of the obligation to prevent harm.[36] This unilateral approach can certainly provide an enabling foundation to promote transboundary cooperation on this issue, but any sole reliance on it to address transboundary issues can be very problematic, raising concerns on jurisdiction, reciprocity and difficulties for state agencies within one country to conduct a proper transboundary EIA.[37] Extraterritorial application of domestic EIA law is thus criticised to be elusive, the effectiveness of which is totally relied on the effectiveness of domestic EIA regimes.[38] Therefore, in order to address transboundary effects more efficiently, simply giving consideration to it under domestic legislation is not enough. It has to be combined with necessary international arrangements to facilitate and regulate its implementation at the international level. The capacity of conducting proper domestic EIA, nevertheless, does have a significant impact on the implementation of transboundary EIA, which will be further discussed later.

---

32 Craik, above n 6, 122.

33 Transboundary EIA in areas beyond national jurisdiction is discussed by Koivurova. See Koivurova, above n 9, 26–9.

34 Birnie, Boyle and Redgwell, above n 9, 169 n 362.

35 Knox, above n 8, 300.

36 Ibid.

37 See Craik, above n 6, 45–51.

38 Knox, above n 8, 316.

In addition to multilateral or supernational regulatory regimes represented by the *Espoo Convention* and the *EIA Directive*, the member states of these regimes also resort to bilateral agreements to provide more detailed or stringent requirements to regulate the transboundary EIA practice with their neighbours.[39] This is represented by the *Flanders (Belgium)-Netherlands Agreement on Transboundary EIA*, bilateral treaties on important public projects between France and Italy, Spain, Switzerland and Germany and Finland bilateral agreement with Estonia. Germany is also undergoing preparations on specific transboundary EIA agreements with Poland, the Netherlands, the Czech Republic, etc.[40] This bilateral approach is also encouraged by the *Espoo Convention* itself.[41]

Outside the Espoo and EU regimes, efforts have been made to promote other multilateral cooperation that may vary from one region to another, such as the 1997 Draft North American Transboundary EIA Agreement.[42] The draft agreement is only a partly finished document with several provisions still pending further negotiation.[43] But it does provide detailed requirements on issues like notification and information exchange, screening, scoping and public participation. Unfortunately, the effort towards formally adopting this agreement has stagnated ever since. A major divergence is that while the United States and Canada argue that it should only be applicable to the federal governments of the signatories, Mexico insists that any final treaty should cover the actions of state governments as well.[44] This case reflects the degree of difficulty for

39 Charles M. Kersten, 'Rethinking Transboundary Environmental Impact Assessment' (2009) 34 *Yale Journal of International Law* 173, 179.

40 See European Commission, 'Report from the Commission to the European Parliament and the Council on the Application and Effectiveness of the EIA Directive (Directive 85/337/EEC as Amended by Directive 97/11/EC): How Successful are the Member States in Implementing the EIA Directive' (Report, European Commission, 2003) 80.

41 *Convention on Environmental Impact Assessment in a Transboundary Context*, opened for signature 25 February 1991, 1989 UNTS 309 (entered into force 10 September 1997) art 8, app IV.

42 Commission for Environmental Cooperation, above n 13.

43 Issues pending further discussions include, but are not limited to: mitigation measures, post-project monitoring, exemption, relation to existing bilateral mechanisms/obligations, on-going consultations and dispute resolution.

44 Ignacia S. Moreno et al., 'Free Trade and the Environment: The NAFTA, the NAAEC and Implications for the Future' (1999) 12 *Tulane Environmental Law Journal* 405, 430 n 142. The most recent available information on this agreement is that on August 31, 2005, the Council of the Commission for Environmental Cooperation (CEC) "rejected a proposal for the CEC Secretariat to prepare Case Studies on Transboundary Environmental Impact Assessment on the basis that the parties were seeking to negotiate a TEIA

countries to achieve consensus on transboundary EIA in a regional-specific context outside the EU and Espoo regimes, with additional constitutional hurdles to surmount in federalist systems of government. Another potential EIA regime is the *2003 Framework Convention for the Protection of the Marine Environment of the Caspian Sea*, which includes hortatory requirements on member states to "take all appropriate measures" to introduce and apply EIA that may have a significant negative impact on the marine environment of the Caspian Sea and to cooperate in the development of protocols on transboundary EIA.[45] Discussions among member states regarding this specific protocol are underway and the current draft is in line with the *Espoo Convention* and the 2003 UNEP Guidelines on Transboundary EIA in the Caspian Sea Region.[46] Difficulties remain due to issues such as the highly varied national EIA procedures and former Soviet Union countries' unfinished reforms.[47]

The *Espoo Convention* and the *EIA Directive* remain the most influential regimes regarding transboundary EIA. Together with the *Aarhus Convention*, they shed light on the key issues of this mechanism: timing; screening (determines whether an EIA is required);[48] scoping (determines the content and extent of the matters to be covered in the EIA report);[49] notification; public participation; consultation; final decision, post-project analysis; and compliance. Details regarding the above issues will be discussed later, combined with relevant domestic legislation and the existing regional arrangements in the Mekong region.

---

agreement through the Security and Prosperity Partnership of North America." Neil Craik, 'Transboundary Environmental Impact Assessment in North America: Obstacles and Opportunities' in Kees Bastmeijer and Timo Koivurova (eds), *Theory and Practice of Transboundary Environmental Impact Assessment* (Martinus Nijhoff Publishers, 2008) 93, 113–4; Kersten, above n 39, 178 n 36.

45 This Convention is signed by Azerbaijan, Iran, Kazakhstan, the Russian Federation and Turkmenistan. *Framework Convention for the Protection of the Marine Environment of the Caspian Sea*, signed 4 November 2003, [2005] 44 ILM 1 (entered into force 12 August 2006) art 17; Kersten, above n 39.

46 Rie Tsutsumi and Kristy Robinson, 'Environmental Impact Assessment and the Framework Convention for the Protection of the Marine Environment of the Caspian Sea' in Kees Bastmeijer and Timo Koivurova (eds), *Theory and Practice of Transboundary Environmental Impact Assessment* (Martinus Nijhoff Publishers, 2008) 53, 56–7.

47 Ibid. 61–4.

48 European Commission, 'Report from the Commission on the application and effectiveness of the EIA Directive (Directive 85/337/EEC, as Amended by Directives 97/11/EC and 2003/35/EC)' (Report, European Commission, 2009) 3.

49 Ibid.

In particular, the *EIA Directive* was first adopted in 1985 via the *Directive 85/337/EEC*. It has been amended three times, in 1997, 2003 and 2009 and then codified by *Directive 2011/92/EU* in December 2011.[50] All future references to the *EIA Directive* in this chapter, unless otherwise specified, will be based on the contents of the *Directive 2011/92/EU*. The *Espoo Convention*, officially known as the *Convention on Environmental Impact Assessment in a Transboundary Context*, was signed by member states of the UNECE in 1991 and entered into force in 1997.[51] At the time of writing, it has been ratified by 45 countries from Europe and Central Asia, as well as Canada and the European Community, while Russia and the United States have signed the agreement but not yet ratified it.[52] In particular, its requirements on access to information and public participation during the EIA process is updated after the *Aarhus Convention* (signed by the member states of UNECE in 1998) entered into force in 2001. Therefore, the following discussion of this aspect will be mainly based on the *Aarhus Convention*. Considering the fact that a detailed analysis on the

50 It was first amended by the *Directive 97/11/EC* in order to widen the scope, strengthen the procedural stages and integrate the changes provided by the *Espoo Convention* and then revised by the *Directive 2003/35/EC* to align the provisions on public participation with the *Aarhus Convention*. The *Directive 2009/31/EC* further applies EIA to the capture and transport of $CO_2$ streams for the purposes of geological storage. European Commission, *Environmental Impact Assessment—EIA* (2012) <http://ec.europa.eu/environment/eia/eia-legalcontext.htm>; *Council Directive 85/337/EEC of 27 June 1985 on the Assessment of the Effects of Certain Public and Private Projects on the Environment* [1985] OJ L 175/40; *Council Directive 97/11/EC of 3 March 1997 Amending Directive 85/337/EEC on the Assessment of the Effects of Certain Public and Private Projects on the Environment* [1997] OJ L 73/5; *Directive 2003/35/EC of the European Parliament and of the Council of 26 May 2003 Providing for Public Participation in Respect of the Drawing up of Certain Plans and Programmes relating to the Environment and Amending with Regard to Public Participation and Access to Justice Council Directives 85/337/EEC and 96/61/EC* [2003] OJ L 156/17; *Directive 2009/31/EC of the European Parliament and of the Council of 23 April 2009 on the Geological Storage of Carbon Dioxide and Amending Council Directive 85/337/EEC, European Parliament and Council Directives 2000/60/EC, 2001/80/EC, 2004/35/EC, 2006/12/EC, 2008/1/EC and Regulation (EC) No 1013/2006 (Text with EEA Relevance)* [2009] OJ L 140/114; *Directive 2011/92/EU of the European Parliament and of the Council of 13 December 2011 on the Assessment of the Effects of Certain Public and Private Projects on the Environment* (*Codification*) (*Text with EEA Relevance*) [2011] OJ L 26/1.

51 *Convention on Environmental Impact Assessment in a Transboundary Context*, opened for signature 25 February 1991, 1989 UNTS 309 (entered into force 10 September 1997).

52 See United Nations Treaty Collection, *Convention on Environmental Impact Assessment in a Transboundary Context* <http://treaties.un.org/Pages/ViewDetails.aspx?src=TREATY&mtdsg_no=XXVII-4&chapter=27&lang=en>.

*Aarhus Convention* has been made in chapter five, relevant discussions in this chapter will be more concise in this chapter.

Further, it is prudent to compare the *EIA Directive* with the *Espoo Convention*. After several revisions, the current version of the *EIA Directive* is generally in line with the *Espoo Convention*, except that the Directive is formulated in a way that mainly focuses on international obligations to implement EIA at national level and then specifically addresses transboundary application in Article 7. In contrast, the structure of the *Espoo Convention* is based on the procedure of transboundary EIA, thus are more linked to general international law and having more specific provisions on notification, consultation and final decision-making. In addition, differences can be also identified in other aspects of EIA, such as screening, scoping, post-project analysis and dispute settlement, which will be addressed in detail later.

It should be noted that, even for EU countries which now embrace the most sophisticated transboundary EIA regimes, the process to achieve this level of international coercion has taken decades since the early 1980s. Moreover, as reflected in the EU Commission's 2009 Report, although the objectives of the Directive "has generally been achieved", its implementation in this region is still challenged by differences in national EIA procedures (especially the lack of harmonised practices for public participation), the risks of duplications, inconsistencies and administrative burdens, the necessity to improve formal and informal arrangements for consultation and language barriers, etc.[53] Meanwhile, the EU's unique circumstances should not be overlooked. Its combined supernational and intergovernmental feature obviously contributes to the process of transboundary EIA development. From a realistic perspective, numerous transboundary environmental issues in the EU region are also in need of greater cooperation among the EU countries. A well-designed transboundary EIA mechanism is not easy to pursue and it is unlikely to be any easier in other regions. To promote the development of transboundary EIA, the specific regional context needs to be better understood and priority issues should to be identified.

### B *Transboundary SEA*

As mentioned earlier, experience in transboundary application of SEA remains very limited across the globe. Therefore, it is still too early to discuss the "customary law" status of this mechanism. At best, it is now an emerging international mechanism to complement transboundary EIA and to encourage the public and other riparian states to become involved and to contribute

53 See European Commission, above n 48.

to settling regional disputes at a higher level and at an earlier stage. At the international level, SEA was first required by the EU's *SEA Directive* (*Directive 2001/42/EC*) in 2001. It is applicable to certain plans and programs, but SEA of policies are not mentioned at all. This is followed by the adoption of the *SEA Protocol* as a part of the *Espoo Convention* in 2003. This Protocol finally entered into force in July 2010. The *SEA Protocol* basically follows the structure and content of the *SEA Directive*, except that it (1) extends the jurisdictional area to the UNECE member states, (2) enlarges the scope to include policies on a voluntary basis, (3) equates health issues with environmental issues, (4) extends public participation to screening and scoping processes on a voluntary basis, (5) improves transparency during the monitoring process and (6) strengthens the requirements on final decision-making.[54] In contrast, some aspects of the *SEA Directive* are viewed to be more stringent than the Protocol itself, such as the issue of who can participate.[55] Similar to the *EIA Directive*, however, both of the SEA documents focus more on domestic rather than transboundary applications, each using one article to specifically address transboundary issues in terms of notification, public participation and consultation.[56] Since the structure or process of the SEA mechanism is akin to the EIA process, discussions on transboundary SEA will impact on the above identified key issues for the EIA process as well.

## III The Development of Transboundary SEA in the Context of the Mekong Region

### A *General Background*

Among all six Mekong countries, only China and Vietnam have legislated SEA as a compulsory legal mechanism for certain kinds of strategies and plans.[57]

---

54 Gernot Stoeglehner and Gerald Wegerer, 'The SEA Directive and the SEA Protocol Adopted to Spatial Planning: Similarities and Differences' in Simon Marsden and Timo Koivurova (eds), *Transboundary Environmental Impact Assessment in the European Union* (Earthscan, 2011) 243, 243, 249–51.

55 Ibid. 250.

56 *Directive 2001/42/EC of the European Parliament and of the Council of 27 June 2001 on the Assessment of the Effects of Certain Plans and Programmes on the Environment* [2001] OJ L 197/30, art 7; *Protocol on Strategic Environmental Assessment to the Convention on Environmental Impact Assessment in a Transboundary Context*, UN Doc ECE/MP.EIA/2003/2 (21 May 2003) art 10.

57 See《中华人民共和国环境影响评价法》[Environmental Impact Assessment Law of the People's Republic of China] (People's Republic of China) Standing Committee of the

It should be noted, however, that when China planned the lower Lancang dam cascade in the 1980s and 1990s, there was no domestic requirement for SEA. Even if there had been, as it does now, the situation would have been the same as the case of the Nu River hydropower planning, in which the Chinese government denied the public from having access to the SEA report due to the confidentiality of certain information regarding international rivers. Vietnam, on the other hand, does not have any Mekong mainstream dam plans. The domestic SEA procedure in the region does not have much impact on mainstream hydropower development on the Mekong River. With regard to Thailand, Cambodia and Laos, a few pilot SEAs has been done in the past.[58] But a lack of political will, relevant legislation and necessary capacity ultimately reduces the chances of effective implementation for domestic SEA pilot practices. The World Bank[59] and the Greater Mekong Subregion (GMS) program[60] have adopted the SEA as a method or as a part of environmental protection programs. To date, two SEAs have been completed for power development planning in Vietnam. Moreover, energy sector SEA capacity building is being undertaken in Laos, which aims to increase awareness and build capacity for the application of SEA to energy sector planning.[61] The GMS is also supporting the GMS Regional Power Trade Coordination Committee to apply SEA in regional power trade planning.[62] Therefore, they can, at least, play

National People's Congress, 28 October 2002, arts 7–15; 《规划环境影响评价条例》 [Regulations on Environmental Impact Assessment of Planning] (People's Republic of China) State Council, 12 August 2009; *Law on Environmental Protection* (Socialist Republic of Vietnam) National Assembly, 29 November 2005, arts 14–17.

58 See International Centre for Environmental Management, 'Strategic Environmental Assessment in the Greater Mekong Subregion—Status Report' (Report, Greater Mekong Subregion Environment Operations Centre, 2006).

59 See generally World Bank, *Strategic Environmental Assessment* (*SEA*) <http://go.worldbank.org/1RT0P09R80>; World Bank, 'Environmental Impact Assessment Regulations and Strategic Environmental Assessment Requirements: Practices and Lessons Learned in East and Southeast Asia' (Report, World Bank, 2006).

60 Greater Mekong Subregion Core Environmental Program, *Strategic Planning* <http://www.gms-eoc.org/strategic-planning>.

61 Greater Mekong Subregion Core Environmental Program, *Environmental Assessment of Economic Corridors and Sectors* <http://www.gms-eoc.org/uploads/resources/18/attachment/Environmental%20Assessment%20of%20Economic%20Corridors%20and%20Sectors%20-%20Status%20Report.pdf>.

62 Greater Mekong Subregion Environment Operations Centre, 'The Core Environment Program and Biodiversity Conservation Corridors Initiative Progress Report for the Period April–September 2011' (Report, Greater Mekong Subregion Economic Cooperation Program, 2011) 4.

an important role in promoting SEA practices in the lower Mekong countries through their projects and programs.[63]

At the regional level, however, there is no general commitment for transboundary SEA among Mekong countries and there is no specific arrangement or guideline document available for pilot practices in a transboundary context. This is further complicated by the fact that infrastructure developments which may have a transboundary impact or as a part of a regional development strategy (such as roads, railways, electricity transmissions lines, hydropower projects) are often initiated under different cooperation regimes and are funded by different international and domestic investors. Therefore, it is very difficult to apply unified standards at the regional level to cover development framework for the entire plan or program, not to mention developing regional SEA arrangements that are applicable for all development plans that may have significant environmental effects. In addition, the polycentric feature of regional water cooperation and the danger of Mekong River Commission (MRC) marginalisation add uncertainties to the future development in this aspect.

### B *Transboundary SEA Practice in the Lower Mekong Region*

Among all economic sectors, hydropower development has taken a leading role in stimulating regional responses from a perspective of transboundary EIA and SEA. Although SEA has not been formally introduced to most of the lower Mekong countries, the MRC Secretariat (with the approval from the Joint Committee) commissioned the International Centre for Environmental Management (ICEM)[64] in May 2009 to conduct a SEA report for all twelve proposed mainstream hydropower projects[65] in the lower Mekong region which took 16 months to finish.[66] Notably, most of the SEA process was done before the *SEA Protocol* came into force. On the positive side, except for the EU, this case in fact took the lead in attempting to apply SEA in a transboundary

---

63 See Greater Mekong Subregion Core Environmental Program, above n 60; Bruce Dunn et al., 'Vietnam: Strategic Environmental Assessment on the Quang Nam Hydropower Plan' in OECD (ed), *Strategic Environmental Assessment in Development Practice: A Review of Recent Experience* (OECD Publishing, 2012) 29.

64 ICEM is an Australian background independent technical service centre.

65 Ten of them are in Laos or on the Lao-Thailand reaches of the mainstream.

66 International Centre for Environmental Management, 'Strategic Environmental Assessment of Hydropower on the Mekong Mainstream: Final Report' (SEA Report, ICEM, 2010) 4. The SEA process also included the participation of China through the high level Ecosystem Study Commission for International Rivers.

context. On the negative side, there is certainly not much past experience to learn from.

No formal notification was made by the Lao government before the SEA process. Different from the provisions under the *SEA Directive* and *Protocol* which requires the state of origin to actively engage in transboundary consultation with the affected states and their public, the Lao government did not take a leading role in initiating and facilitating this process. Instead, this process was triggered by the MRC and draws extensively from the work of all MRC Programs. Technically, this is still a decision made by all member countries, given that it has to gain approval from the Joint Committee. But due to the fact that Laos has no legislation on domestic SEA and there are no regional arrangements on this issue, Laos indeed has very limited capacity, legal coercion or political will to conduct a transboundary SEA study, to facilitate effective governmental and public consultations, or to take due account of the SEA report. It was the MRC Secretariat and the ICEM that played a key role in conducting the research and organising dialogues. The Lao government was basically no more than a participant of the process. Most people argue that this arrangement is more neutral in a way that the evaluation is less interfered or manipulated by the Lao government, but it also raises concerns on whether this process may be over-controlled by the affected states and external forces outside this region. The SEA process illustrates the complicated relationship between science and politics. But considering the lack of democracy, rule of law and transparency of the Lao government, it has to admit that this arrangement has more credibility to deliver more reliable evaluations. Moreover, this SEA process and its conclusions are transparent and open to further reviews and criticisms, thus providing ample opportunities for the Lao government to defend its decisions.

The contents of the report cover all kinds of information that are required under the *SEA Protocol* and *Directive*. It identifies four strategic options. Other than giving permission to the proposed projects to be developed and constructed as fast as developers and regulators allow in response to market demand for electricity, there are three alternatives: (1) no development of mainstream dams, (2) deferred decision on all mainstream dams for a set period of time, (3) and gradual development that has to proceed in a cautious and planned manner (including consideration of alternative designs that will only partially block the mainstream flow). The report then considers issues regarding power systems, economic systems, hydrology and sediment regimes, terrestrial systems, aquatic systems, fisheries, social systems, navigation and climate change. Each of these key strategic issues are then analysed from the perspectives of past trends in those issues and their projection to 2030 without mainstream hydropower, and an impact assessment of the effects of mainstream hydropower on those trends. This is enhanced by research to identify ways of avoiding and mitigating the environmental impact and enhancing the benefits.[67]

According to the report, through all assessment phases of SEA, there has been intensive consultation "involving over 60 line agencies, 40 NGOs and civil society organizations and some 20 international development organizations in meetings and workshops".[68] The contents of the report and all documents from different SEA phases are available for public access on the MRC website and the summary of the final report and SEA media release are translated into lower Mekong county languages.[69] There is no detailed information, however, on whether the public has been provided with sufficient information early enough before the consultation. This aspect of public participation has been emphasised by the *SEA Protocol* and the relevant *Aarhus Convention*.[70] But in general, international consensus on access to information during the SEA process is not as specific as that of the EIA process.

The public, especially civil society organisations, does appear to be engaged throughout the SEA process. This process is combined with transboundary consultations with government agencies. The report lists all stakeholders consulted in Annex II, including civil society organisations in a country-specific manner.[71] According to the list, the numbers of civil society organisation participants located in Thailand and Vietnam are much more than those in Cambodia and Laos. In addition, there is a high percentage of representation from international NGOs rather than local NGOs. Other than round table meetings and workshops, NGOs and individuals have directly submitted their comments and petitions to the MRC via the MRC website.[72] In particular, the

67 Information in this paragraph is based on the SEA Final Report. Ibid. 6–7, 9, 23, 32–4.

68 Ibid. 9, 37.

69 Mekong River Commission, *Strategic Environmental Assessment of Mainstream Dams* <http://www.mrcmekong.org/about-the-mrc/programmes/initiative-on-sustainable-hydropower/strategic-environmental-assessment-of-mainstream-dams/>.

70 *Directive 2001/42/EC of the European Parliament and of the Council of 27 June 2001 on the Assessment of the Effects of Certain Plans and Programmes on the Environment* [2001] OJ L 197/30, art 7; *Protocol on Strategic Environmental Assessment to the Convention on Environmental Impact Assessment in a Transboundary Context*, UN Doc ECE/MP.EIA/2003/2 (21 May 2003) arts 8, 10(4), 15. In particular, the SEA Protocol requires the member states to apply the Protocol without prejudice to the *Aarhus Convention*.

71 International Centre for Environmental Management, above n 66, 152–6.

72 *SEA Stakeholder Submissions*, Mekong River Commission <http://www.mrcmekong.org/about-the-mrc/programmes/initiative-on-sustainable-hydropower/strategic-

petitions are all formally responded to by the MRC Secretariat. Although it is argued that the views and information of government experts, line agencies and the non-government community are analysed and reflected in the report,[73] there is no specific section of the report available to describe and respond to the comments gained from public participation. Instead, the opinions of the public are mainly analysed in a country-specific way together with other stakeholders like government agencies and developers.[74] But even the *SEA Directive* and *Protocol* does not require public opinion to be formally addressed and commented on in the SEA report.[75] Interestingly, this is a compulsory requirement for the SEA process in China.[76]

As mentioned in chapter four, notable information gaps and uncertainties were expressly stressed in the SEA findings and the report specifically recommends a 10-year deferral for mainstream hydropower development.[77]After the final report was released to the public in October 2011, the MRC has proposed consultations with the MRC Programs and member countries on the final SEA report findings and recommendations for next steps.[78] The release of the report was immediately followed by the MRC notification and consultation process for the Xayaburi Dam project and the content of the SEA report served as a technical input of this process. Details regarding this process have been discussed at length in chapter four, which identified many of the problems existing in the context of the MRC Procedures for Notification, Prior Consultation and Agreement, especially issues regarding public participation,

environmental-assessment-of-mainstream-dams/sea-stakeholder-submissions/>; *SEA Petitions and MRC Responses*, Mekong River Commission <http://www.mrcmekong.org/about-the-mrc/programmes/initiative-on-sustainable-hydropower/strategic-environmental-assessment-of-mainstream-dams/sea-petitions-and-mrc-responses/>.

73 International Centre for Environmental Management, above n 66, 9.

74 See ibid. 145.

75 The Protocol does require the SEA report to take public interests into account. *Protocol on Strategic Environmental Assessment to the Convention on Environmental Impact Assessment in a Transboundary Context*, UN Doc ECE/MP.EIA/2003/2 (21 May 2003) art 7(2).

76 Notably, only the SEA of sectoral plans is required to consult the public. See《规划环境影响评价条例》[Regulations on Environmental Impact Assessment of Planning] (People's Republic of China) State Council, 12 August 2009, art 13. This issue has been discussed in detailed in section III(B)(1) of chapter five.

77 See generally International Centre for Environmental Management, above n 66.

78 Mekong River Commission, *SEA Frequently Asked Questions: What are some of the Next Steps for the MRC on the SEA?* <http://www.mrcmekong.org/about-the-mrc/programmes/initiative-on-sustainable-hydropower/strategic-environmental-assessment-of-mainstream-dams/sea-frequently-asked-questions/>.

information availability and accessibility, time-frame and disputes on relevant international obligations in practice. It is argued, however, that the whole process may have been started too late considering the fact that the Xayaburi Dam was already close to its final stage of planning and preparation when the SEA process was initiated.

Another major problem underlying this SEA process is the huge disconnection between the attempt to consider these dam projects in an integrated way and the highly polycentric reality of hydropower policy-making and the increasingly marginalised status of the MRC itself. Despite the fact that the MRC intends to deal with these projects holistically, it in fact falls short of enough power or governmental support to do so. The technical inputs of the report are detached from the complicated decision-making structure. But there are in fact limited options for the MRC. Given most of the lower Mekong mainstream dams are planned by Laos and its government is very keen on pushing them forward under the national policy to boost hydropower development, it is almost certain that once one project was built, all the others will follow. Indeed, there is probably too much expectation on this SEA process, hoping it could lead to dispute settlement that could, at least, win enough time for more prudent consideration.

This SEA report and the relevant consultations have proved to be a prelude of intensifying regional debates on the lower Mekong mainstream hydropower development. It is therefore not surprising to see contradictions between this SEA report and other environmental assessment results commissioned by different authorities and conducted under different foreign and domestic influences. A typical example in this area is the Swiss company—Pöyry Energy AG's (Pöyry)'s review on the Xayaburi dam's social and environmental impact, which was commissioned by Laos. Its pro-dam conclusion was heavily criticised by the ICEM and World Wildlife Fund.[79]

79 The International Centre for Environmental Management concluded that the Pöyry review "presents a number of inconsistencies regarding the understanding of the Mekong River system" and its recommendations "represent a serious escalation of risk". Based on a review by fisheries and sediment experts, the World Wildlife Fund announced that:

> "the Pöyry review does identify uncertainties and weaknesses with the proposed fish passes and even acknowledges that the Xayaburi Dam fails to comply with at least a quarter of the MRC's guidance on this. This is completely at odds with their advice to green light the project..."

Even the Pöyry review itself acknowledges that an additional 40 studies are needed. See International Centre for Environmental Management, 'Comments on the Xayaburi HPP Compliance Report: With a Focus on the Mekong Delta' (Comments, ICEM, 2011) 16; World Wildlife Fund, *Make or Break Time for Mekong River as Xayaburi Dam Decision Looms*

In order to give a fair evaluation on this SEA process, it is important to differentiate the problems that are unique to the SEA process itself with other obstacles that are more deeply rooted in the domestic legal/political systems and the regional cooperative regimes. With regard to the latter, it is unrealistic to expect a fundamental change through a mere SEA process, but it is not completely impossible to trigger some changes towards a more sustainable decision-making via the SEA approach. This SEA process represents a major development in the lower Mekong region in terms of transboundary water management. As a region that basically has no domestic SEA legislation, this transboundary SEA effort was largely commendable, especially when there are still limited experiences elsewhere.

From a legal perspective, issues like access to information and public participation can be further improved. While the public are given wider opportunities to participate during all four stages of the transboundary SEA identified in the report, the depth of participation was more restrained. But many of the reasons can be attributed to the problematic domestic situation of information transparency and public participation which have been addressed in chapter five. Other than consultations during the preparation of the SEA report, there was no specific governmental consultation regarding the final conclusions of the report and the ensuing notification and consultation was too short to fully discuss both the general hydropower plans and the Xayaburi project.

As a mechanism that is supposed to engage the affected states and their public during decision-making process, the objective of a transboundary SEA process has not been fully achieved in this case. While it is probably true that there were intensive consultations during the preparation of the report, theses should not replace the consultations after the report was released. This problem can be also attributed to the late introduction of the transboundary SEA process. But better late than never is very much suitable to the current circumstances in the Mekong. It is doubtful though, to what extent the credit can be attributed to the MRC member countries, especially Laos. While it set a precedent for other plans in the region that may have a transboundary impact, so far it looks less likely that it will become a mechanism that can be sustained in future development practices of the lower Mekong countries.

---

(29 November 2011) <http://www.wwf.or.th/en/publications/?202579/Make-or-break-time-for-Mekong-river-as-Xayaburi-dam-decision-looms>; International Rivers, *Sidestepping Science: Review of the Pöyry Report on the Xayaburi Dam* (November 2011) <http://www.internationalrivers.org/files/attached-files/poyryreview_areasofnon-compliance.pdf>; Pöyry, 'Xayaburi Hydroelectric Power Project Run-of-River Plant' (Report, Pöyry, 2011).

## C *The Way Forward*

With regard to future development of SEA in the context of the Mekong region, it is argued that more attention should be paid at the domestic level. The most obvious task is to legislate on the SEA procedure in Thailand, Cambodia, Laos and Myanmar. While the situation in Myanmar remains difficult to predict and the SEA legislation is certainly not on top of their priority list for reforms, the other three Mekong countries are in relatively more enabling circumstances to promote legal reforms in this aspect. This process can be assisted and facilitated by the World Bank and the ADB via their respective funding programs. Increasing pilot programs are probably a necessary and more realistic approach to gain more experience before pursuing any institutionalised reforms.

Experiences and lessons in China and Vietnam can also provide some comparative insights. China has incorporated provisions on SEA of plans prepared at or above the municipal (cities with district setting) level into the *EIA Law* and further entrenched it through a specific regulation. Plans are further separated into two categories: comprehensive plans like those regarding river basin development and specific/sector-based plans like framework plans for energy sector or the development of hydraulic projects.[80] Both categories are subject to a SEA procedure, but reasonable alternatives are not required to be assessed in the context of the process. Moreover, public participation is only required for the SEA of specific/sector-based plans.[81] As mentioned in chapter five, public participation at this level still suffers from issues such as the late introduction of public participation, lack of information transparency, no requirement for active disclosure of responses to public opinion, no detailed arrangements on participation procedures and the broad interpretation of state secrets.

The SEA report should be reviewed by the environmental protection authority and should be considered as an important basis for decision-making on the adoption of plans by the government above the municipal level.[82] Only the specific or sector-based plans have to be reviewed by a review panel constituted by no less than 50 percent of experts.[83] The decision on not to adopt

80 《中华人民共和国环境影响评价法》[Environmental Impact Assessment Law of the People's Republic of China] (People's Republic of China) Standing Committee of the National People's Congress, 28 October 2002, arts 7, 8.

81 Ibid. art 11;《规划环境影响评价条例》[Regulations on Environmental Impact Assessment of Planning] (People's Republic of China) State Council, 12 August 2009, art 13.

82 《规划环境影响评价条例》[Regulations on Environmental Impact Assessment of Planning] (People's Republic of China) State Council, 12 August 2009, arts 17–8.

83 《中华人民共和国环境影响评价法》 [Environmental Impact Assessment Law of the People's Republic of China] (People's Republic of China) Standing Committee of the National People's Congress, 28 October 2002, art 17.

the conclusions of the SEA report or the opinions from the environmental protection authority should be further explained and documented.[84] This is followed by several provisions on monitoring. But a major problem at the decision-making stage is the weak status of environment protection authorities against the municipal or provincial government, since it is the latter that controls the budget and funding for environmental protection agencies at these levels.

In addition, in instances where the agency that prepares the SEA report or the decision-making authority violated the relevant legislation, the most common remedy is administrative punishment under the *Civil Servants Law*, unless the individual violates the *Criminal Law*.[85] There is no access to justice for the public on this matter and the government accountability system in China remains very immature due to obvious political and legal reasons. Another relevant issue is the relationship between government and private actors. In many developed countries, due to a more mature market economy and highly developed political and legal systems, the private sector can be vibrant in many areas that are traditionally state-controlled in China and can offer more to attract the most experienced experts. Therefore, the preparation of many government plans and the corresponding SEA research are usually outsourced to the private sector or independent agencies, which may provide more opportunities for serious environmental debate. Moreover, given the SEA procedure generally relies on the administrative system in China, its application suffers from other problems existing in the plan approval system and the restricted government budget for conducting SEAs.[86] Due to the above deficiencies, the implementation of China's SEA procedure remains far from effective.

The status quo of SEA in Vietnam does not encourage optimism. The *Law on Environmental Protection* addresses the basic issues regarding screening, scoping and reviewing.[87] Alternatives are not considered and no specific requirement is made for public participation during the SEA, except for the general right to send petitions and recommendations to government agencies. There

84 Ibid. art 14.

85 Ibid. arts 29, 30;《规划环境影响评价条例》[Regulations on Environmental Impact Assessment of Planning] (People's Republic of China) State Council, 12 August 2009, arts 31–4.

86 郄建荣 [Qie Jianrong],《艰难推进之中的"规划环评"》[Difficult Development of the SEA of Plans] (4 May 2008) 中国网 [China.com.cn] <http://www.china.com.cn/aboutchina/zhuanti/hjwj08/2008-05/04/content_15054585.htm>.

87 *Law on Environmental Protection* (Socialist Republic of Vietnam) National Assembly, 29 November 2005, arts 14–17.

is no requirement for monitoring the implementation of plans. In addition, no specific provision is made to address the violation of the SEA requirements and the general requirements regarding access to justice and punishment for violations are restrained.

In light of the above observations, it is clear that the SEA procedure remains very immature across the region. There are still enormous gaps between the domestic development of SEA and the transboundary practice of SEA on lower Mekong mainstream hydropower development. Although it is possible that the foreign donors and investors can continue to promote transboundary SEA practice at the regional level, this mechanism is too disconnected from most of the domestic political and legal systems and there is no domestic or regional requirement on states to duly consider any results flowing from the transboundary SEA process. It is suggested that more regional efforts at this stage should be devoted to the development of transboundary EIA in the region.

## IV The Development of Transboundary EIA in the Context of the Mekong Region

### A *General Background*

The development of transboundary EIA is comparatively less controversial than that of SEA. In light of increasing momentum of the Mekong hydropower development, there are urgent needs for regional arrangements on transboundary EIA in the area of Mekong water management. Domestically, except Myanmar, all Mekong countries have adopted some form of legislation on EIA. Thailand and Vietnam incorporated provisions on EIA into their overarching environmental protection law.[88] Currently, Vietnam is in the process of reviewing the *Law on Environmental Protection* and its provisions on EIA. China upgraded its 1998 Regulation on EIA into a specific EIA Law in 2002 and then developed more detailed interim measures of public participation in EIA.[89] Laos and Cambodia introduced EIA via a decree and a sub-decree

88 See *Enhancement and Conservation of National Environmental Quality Act* (Kingdom of Thailand) National Assembly, 29 March 1992, s 46–51; *Law on Environmental Protection* (Socialist Republic of Vietnam) National Assembly, 29 November 2005, arts 18–23.

89 See《中华人民共和国环境影响评价法》[Environmental Impact Assessment Law of the People's Republic of China] (People's Republic of China) Standing Committee of the National People's Congress, 28 October 2002;《环评公众参与暂行办法》[Interim Measures of Public Participation in EIA] (People's Republic of China) State Environmental

respectively.[90] Notably, Cambodia is drafting a new EIA law, the latest draft of which takes into account of the transboundary impact.[91] But even if the future Cambodian EIA Law did consider the transboundary impact, it is not applicable for most of the Mekong mainstream projects. It also raises issues on reciprocity: at this stage, none of the Mekong countries includes the transboundary impact under their domestic EIA legislation. Combined with the often criticised domestic EIA legislation and its implementation in the Mekong region, it will probably be less effective to rely on domestic legislation to address transboundary effects. Moreover, domestic legislation on EIA varies widely across the region and the capacity for proper implementation in Mekong countries is generally weak. Although similar problems are also faced by the member states of the *Espoo Convention*, there is at least a difference in terms of the degree of severity. At the regional level, there is no general commitment for transboundary EIA across the Mekong region, but international institutions like the World Bank[92] and ADB[93] have adopted the EIA as a methodology that should be applied to their projects.

As mentioned earlier, the increasing acceptance of the customary status of transboundary EIA can provide a strong argument for transboundary EIA practices. Even if this rule is unenforceable in the context of the Mekong region, there are growing pressures on the Mekong countries to adopt this procedure as an approach to avoid and resolve transboundary disputes. This is represented by the ongoing consultations on developing a MRC procedural document on transboundary EIA. With regard to China, this is reflected in its joint EIA practices with three other Mekong countries for the Mekong navigation channel improvement project and in the Greater Tumen region. The two examples can provide valuable insights for future development between China and the lower

---

Protection Administration, 22 February 2006. The development of EIA in China can be traced to the 1970s. But not until the 1980s did the real progress is made. In 1989, after a 10-year trial, the *Environmental Protection Law* was revised and formally enacted. Article 13 of the Law includes a general provision on EIA of construction projects.

90 See *Decree on Environmental Impact Assessment* (Lao People's Democratic Republic) Prime Minister's Office, 18 February 2010; *Sub-Decree on Environmental Impact Process* (Kingdom of Cambodia) Council of Ministers, 11 August 1999.

91 See Sok Phanna, 'Trans-boundary Aspect in the EIA Law of Cambodia' (Speech delivered at the Mekong Legal Network 4th Regional Meeting, Chiang Mai, 29 June 2012).

92 See generally World Bank, *Environmental Assessment in Operational Policy 4.01* <http://go.worldbank.org/9LF3YQWTP0>; World Bank, above n 59.

93 See generally Asian Development Bank, 'Environmental Assessment Guidelines' (Guidelines, Asian Development Bank, 2003).

Mekong countries on transboundary EIA. This will be followed by a detailed analysis on the key issues regarding transboundary EIA. In particular, this section will explore the common grounds in domestic EIA legislation across the region that can provide a foundation for regional consultation and will identify the gaps between international best practices and the status quo in the region.

### B *The Joint EIA Practice for the Mekong Navigation Channel Improvement Project*

With the aim of facilitating commercial navigation on the Mekong River, the governments of China, Myanmar, Laos and Thailand signed an agreement on 20 April 2000 and committed to opening the Mekong River for commercial navigation among the four countries within one year.[94] But the waterway from China-Myanmar Boundary Marker 243 to Ban Houei Sai of Laos is a natural waterway with the worst navigability from Simao in China to Luang Prabang in Laos.[95] In order to allow large ships to freely navigate from China to Laos, a Mekong Navigation Channel Improvement Project was necessary.[96] In March 2001, a joint EIA team, with the Chinese side as coordinator, was established to

94 *Agreement on Commercial Navigation on Lancang-Mekong River among the Governments of the People's Republic of China, the Lao People's Democratic Republic, the Union of Myanmar and the Kingdom of Thailand* (signed and entered into force 20 April 2000) art 2.

95 Joint Experts Group on EIA of China, Laos, Myanmar and Thailand, *Executive Summary of Environmental Impact Assessment on the Navigation Channel Improvement Project of the Lancang-Mekong River from China-Myanmar Boundary Maker 243 to Ban Houeisai of Laos* (2001) <http://portal.mrcmekong.org/master-catalogue/search?giai=9506000003825_00009784E01006q1>.

96 Under natural conditions, the Mekong River is navigable throughout the year for vessels of 60 tons only. The long term aim of the whole project is to enable larger shipping vessels (up to 500 tons) to navigate the River for most of the year. The project is divided into three phases: the first phase (2002–2004) removed 11 major rapids and 10 scattered reefs, mostly along the Burma-Lao stretch of the river. Under the second phase, it is planned to remove an additional 51 rapids and shoals and in the third phase, the waterway is to be further canalised. The first stage aimed to enable passage of vessels up to 150 tonnes while the second and third aimed to enable navigation by boats of 300 and 500 tonnes respectively. As observed in a 2006 report, the project was "declared finished after implementation of only the first two stages, following protests in Thailand by communities opposed to further rapids blasting". But according to the information provided by a Chinese official, negotiations are now underway among the four countries to move on to the next stage of the project. Philip Hirsch et al., 'National Interests and Transboundary Water Governance in the Mekong' (Report, University of Sydney, 2006) 155.

carry out a half-year study on the environmental impact of the project. At the time, China already adopted a Regulation on EIA (1998) and the Decree on EIA in Laos was only just promulgated in 2000 (later updated in 2010).

The report focuses on the hydrologic impact on discharge, flow velocity, water level, waterfront and thalweg after navigation channel improvement and the impact on aquatic lives during the construction period.[97] Mitigation measures are listed that reduce the impact on aquatic lives, water quality and manage solid waste during the construction. The report concludes that the environmental impact on hydrology is either minor or non-existing.[98] Monitoring arrangements are also included in the report. The content of the report, however, was heavily criticised by another study sponsored in December 2001 by the MRC as "substantively inadequate and in many places fundamentally flawed".[99] Unfortunately, no detailed information can be found regarding the basis of such an argument.

Other than the scientific controversies, several key issues should be noted from a procedural perspective. Different from the typical transboundary EIA where there is only one state of origin, the development project here involves four countries and the actual work starts from the China-Myanmar Border where the Lancang-Mekong River serves as a boundary river between the two countries. As a joint EIA study, the four formally involved Mekong countries were both the affected and originating states of this project. Cambodia and Vietnam, however, were neither excluded from the joint EIA, nor formally participated in the process. According to a Chinese official, their representatives have visited the project sites several times. The joint EIA report is unclear on what approaches are adopted to evaluate the impact and but the conclusions do mention that there will be no negative impact on them.[100] From this perspective, the consideration given to the impact on Cambodia and Vietnam is not prudent to say the least.

In addition, given the coordinator and the biggest promoter of the project (China) is not a member of the MRC, the whole project and the joint EIA study were carried out without any real engagement of the MRC, indicating a sense of alienation to this cooperative regime. Moreover, by signing the agreement on navigation, the navigation channel improvement project is almost unavoidable in order to achieve the commercial objective underlying the agreement. Inasmuch as the transboundary EIA occurred during the implementation

97 Joint Experts Group on EIA of China, Laos, Myanmar and Thailand, above n 95.

98 Ibid.

99 Hirsch et al., above n 96.

100 Joint Experts Group on EIA of China, Laos, Myanmar and Thailand, above n 95.

period of the agreement there was increased motivation to legitimise the decision already made.[101]

Moreover, this joint EIA process did not involve public participation as a formal component of the EIA. Some argue that most of the project sites are very remote and have very few people living along side of them. Therefore, public participation is somehow trivial and unrealistic, in view of the potential economic benefits for many people along the river that are still struggling under the poverty line. But from a procedural perspective, one should not draw conclusions only based on presumptions or allegations. No matter how obvious the public opinion on a particular issue may look like, the process of public participation should not be subverted or neglected. In addition, although there are disputes on the legitimacy of NGOs in representing the interests of the local community, opportunities for them to express their opinions should be provided. However, at the time, public participation was not mentioned in China's Regulation on EIA. The Lao Decree on EIA (2000) involves some relatively clear provisions on public involvement, but it is obvious that they were not really implemented in practice. Although public participation is required by the Thailand *1997 Constitution* and *Enhancement and Conservation of National Environmental Quality Act*, as discussed in chapter five, there are no provisions on how to incorporate this process into the EIA procedures. While there were some legal grounds for arguing that the lack of public participation violated domestic legislation in Laos and Thailand, the general awareness of the issue was probably extremely low.

Compared to China's decision-making process on the upper Mekong dam projects and its practices in most other transboundary water management cases, it is commendable that at least some form of joint EIA was conducted in this case. As the only joint EIA practice to date in the Mekong region, this case provides valuable lessons on the key issues regarding transboundary EIA, particularly from the aspects of timing, scoping and public participation. This government-led EIA practice is also in sharp contrast with the aforementioned SEA practice, which is mainly facilitated by the MRC and the ICEM. The latter is certainly a much more prudent example, but it is the former that reflects the real level of EIA in the Mekong region. From a technical point of view, the Chinese engineers and officials stressed the point that given the scale and the design of the project, there will be no significant damage to the downstream states. However, deficiencies can be identified from a legal perspective. Although the process itself may not violate any international agreement that is

101 In fact, plans for the Mekong navigation channel improvement project were conceived in the early 1990s.

applicable to the four countries at the time, this practice did not reflect international best practice. In fact, after the implementation of the improvement project, the navigability of this session of the Mekong remains fairly low. Talks are now underway to conduct further improvement projects in order to facilitate navigation. Another joint EIA process should thus be incorporated into the decision-making process. Answers regarding how to improve the future EIA practices in the region, or at least a major part of it, will be put forward at the end of this chapter. But before that, it is necessary to consider China's experience on developing transboundary EIA in the Greater Tumen region.

### C *China's Experience with Transboundary EIA in the Greater Tumen Region*

As a country that shares many international rivers with neighbouring countries and in most cases is located upstream of these rivers, China has been reluctant to disclose information regarding international rivers (such as the Nu River case)[102] and experiences on transboundary cooperation in water management are still very immature. But the situation is gradually changing. As mentioned before, China has established some rudimentary water management cooperation regimes with its neighbouring countries on the north, northeast and northwest of China. With regard to transboundary EIA, China's experience in the Greater Tumen region can provide some guidance on how to develop transboundary EIA in the context of the Mekong region.

The Tumen River is bordered by China, Russia and North Korea and is vital for biodiversity preservation in the delta, as well as agricultural and industrial development in the region. Water pollution from industrial sewage has now become one of the key priority environmental concerns.[103] In 1991, the United Nations Development Programme (UNDP) initiated a Tumen River Area Development Program and a formal agreement was signed in December 1995 to establish a Consultative Commission with membership of China, North Korea, Mongolia, South Korea and Russia.[104] The Agreement is further

102 For more information, see chapter three.

103 Simon Marsden, 'China's Experience with Transboundary Environmental Impact Assessment' (Speech delivered at 7th Colloquium of the IUCN Academy of Environmental Law, Wuhan, China, 4 November 2009).

104 Steve S. Sin, *Greater Tumen Area Economic Development Project: A Background* (27 January 2010) Scribd, 5 <http://www.scribd.com/doc/25888213/Greater-Tumen-Area-Economic-Development-Project-A-Background>. Another agreement was signed at the same time to establish a Coordination Committee with membership of China, Russia and North Korea.

supplemented by the 1995 Memorandum of Understanding (MOU) on Environmental Principles Governing the Tumen River Economic Development Area and Northeast Asia (the 1995 MOU). Then, at the Eighth Consultative Commission Meeting in 2005, a new Greater Tumen Initiative (GTI) was established.[105] Supported by the UNDP and Global Environmental Facility (GEF), it now serves as "an intergovernmental platform for economic cooperation and exchanges for Northeast Asia" and "a catalyst in expanding policy dialogue and strengthening fundamentals for improving the cooperation".[106]

The Ninth Meeting of Consultative Commission in 2007 reaffirmed member states' commitment to sustainable development and agreed on two concrete GTI projects. One of them is a Feasibility Study on Tumen River Water Protection, which aims to improve water quality and protect the Tumen River from environmental degradation through the promotion of regional cooperation and sustainable development in the Greater Tumen region.[107] Meanwhile, a Cooperation Framework on Environment (now called the GTI Environment Board) was established to coordinate environmental protection efforts, among which capacity building is considered to be a key aspect.[108]

In particular, some common understandings on transboundary EIA and even SEA were recorded in the 1995 MOU. Article 1.2 generally requires a joint "regional environmental assessment" for regional development plans for the region as a whole and a specific mitigation plan needs to be prepared accordingly.[109] It provides a basic provision on transboundary SEA, but no detailed arrangements are made on how to carry out such an assessment. More specific requirements are made for transboundary EIA. Article 1.5 states that an EIA and a mitigation plan should to be conducted and prepared for any proposed project in the region which may have a significant environmental impact. But no detailed list or criteria is elaborated to guide the screening or scoping process. The whole EIA process will be led by the member state where the project is located and with the participation of experts from affected

105 Ibid. 8.

106 United Nations, *Greater Tumen Initiative Breakfast Draws International Business Leaders* <http://www.un.org/partnerships/YNewsTumenBreakfast.htm>.

107 Rongxing Guo, *Cross-border Resource Management* (Elsevier, 2nd ed, 2012) 317.

108 Marsden, above n 103. In 10th Meeting of Consultative Commission in 2009, the composition of the GTI Environment Board was formally approved.

109 Information in this paragraph regarding the 1995 MoU is available at: http://www.law.go.kr/trtyInfoPWah.do?trtySeq=2111&chrClsCd=010203.

states. The affected public and the NGOs, however, are not expressly required to be included in the process. Instead, countries only agree on a broad basis to "consult with, give access to information to and provide opportunities for involvement by affected citizens and interested NGOs at *appropriate stages* of the development and environmental planning processes for the region".[110] In addition, there are no specific arrangements on how to notify or consult with the affected states.

Article 1.6 requires the results of both SEA and EIA to be "taken into account" in developing planning activities and the corresponding mitigation plans. Here, "due diligence" is not explicitly required. Furthermore, Articles 1.7 and 2.1 simply state that both the SEA and EIA will be conducted "in accordance of internationally accepted procedures and guidelines" and parties will strive to "meet the objectives of international environmental agreements and norms".[111] The language used here is very vague and impractical. Finally, parties are required to provide or seek necessary funding for the preparation of transboundary EIA and to carry out their other environmental responsibilities under this MOU.

From the above observations, it can be concluded that, although the MOU briefly covers some of the key issues regarding transboundary EIA, most of these provisions are very general and ambiguous, not to mention the fact that the MOU itself is not a legally binding document. Instead of making a normative commitment, the whole MOU resembles more of a political statement upon which further negotiations can be based and is less likely to provide necessary guidance to any transboundary EIA practices in reality. This document reflects the degree of difficulty for developing a transboundary EIA mechanism between China and other downstream states. Although what has been accomplished so far remains quite immature in many ways, it does at least provide some minimal commitments for China where previously there had been none.

Further cooperation and negotiation on relevant matters were facilitated through the TumenNet project and Strategic Action Programme. Since 2004, an annual transboundary EIA workshop has been held six times.[112] In 2000, based on Art 1.2 of the MOU, the Tumen Programme undertook a long-overdue EIA for the development of Hunchun Border Economic Cooperation Zone in China, which was established in 1992 without any form of EIA. Interestingly, although the establishment of an economic cooperation zone should be

110 Ibid. (emphasis added).

111 Ibid.

112 Marsden, above n 103.

categorised as a regional development plan instead of a specific project and be subject to a SEA rather than an EIA, this environmental assessment was in fact conducted based on standards and legislation on EIA. The confusion can be mainly attributed to both the misguided understanding of EIA and the fact that there was no requirement for SEA in China at the time. Since it is the EIA requirements that apply to "development plans", after some hesitation, this mix of SEA and EIA methodology will likely still to be used as an example regarding transboundary or joint EIA.

This EIA study was conducted by the Chinese Research Academy of Environmental Sciences with the participation of one specialist from South Korean Academy of Environmental Sciences. In the EIA report which is open to the public only in English, environmental analysis focused on water issues (including Tumen River), pollution control, solid waste disposal and ecological environment, while economic benefits were considered as well.[113] Given the after-the-fact nature of the EIA, alternatives were not mentioned, although it is not sure whether they will be considered in future. The outcomes of public participation were also included. As outlined in the report, individuals in and around the economic cooperation zone participated mainly through questionnaires, while the approach of spot visits were also used.[114] But the public from the affected states were not consulted at all. As a conclusion, the report stated that as long as the development of economic cooperation zone is subject to the relevant laws and fulfils the environmental protection measures proposed in the report, its construction is absolutely feasible in terms of environmental protection.[115] There is no information on whether countries entered into further consultation after the release of the EIA report.

The EIA methodology is based on the relevant Chinese legislation at the time and two documents from International Financial Organisation regarding EIA or environmental protection. The whole report makes no mention of the *Espoo Convention* or other oft-cited international documents on EIA. In addition, an environmental assessment conducted subsequent to the establishment of the economic cooperation zone does not really embody the essence of what constitutes a proper EIA and is more akin to a post-project analysis or monitoring effort. The timing of this EIA raises serious doubt on whether

113 See generally Chinese Research Academy of Environmental Sciences, *Environmental Impact Statement for Hunchun Border Economic Cooperation Zone* (2000) Greater Tumen Initiative, 106 <http://www.tumenprogram.org/news.php?id=375>.

114 Ibid. 98–9.

115 Ibid. 111.

the whole gesture was merely employed to justify the decision already made. In addition, this EIA falls short of active public participation and adequate information transparency. The approach used to collect public opinion was wholly inadequate and only 50 people were able to participate through questionnaires. Since the affected public is not actively engaged in the process, it is difficult for them to fully express their opinions and comments on the project through formal channels. The public also lacks necessary information on the environmental issues in the region and the government and media usually tend to focus on the possible economic benefits. A large number of the population is not even aware of the EIA being undertaken at all. Moreover, even though the preparation of the EIA report includes the participation of a South Korean expert, the governments of affected states and their citizens are not really involved in the process. In fact, the whole assessed area does not fall outside of Chinese territory.[116] In reality, this after-the-fact exercise can be characterised as a domestic EIA carried out under a regional development program with very limited participation from other states.

After this first attempt, the project of the GTI Environmental Cooperation (Focusing on Transboundary EIA in the Greater Tumen Region and Environmental Standardisation in North-East Asia) was approved in 2007 to promote further development of transboundary EIA. It recognised that since the general ability of member states to produce and distribute environmental information varies significantly, a transboundary EIA mechanism is necessary to evaluate the impact on environment of undergoing projects.[117] But with highly varied domestic legislation and capacity, the development of transboundary EIA mechanism at the regional level will be very difficult and the implementation of such regional arrangements will likely to be less effective. The project also seems to recognise the significance of information transparency and public participation. It stated that environmental information data should be available for public and private institutions. As well, standardised data collection procedures are promoted in this project. The main tasks of this project will be undertaken by the GTI Environmental Board in cooperation with local authorities. Since the Ninth Meeting of the Consultative Commission, some progress

116 Ibid. 4.

117 Greater Tumen Initiative, *GTI Environmental Cooperation (Focusing on Trans-boundary Environmental Impact Assessment (TEIA) in GTR and Environmental Standardization in North-East Asia (ESNA))* (7 April 2010) <http://www.tumenprogramme.org/news.php?id=1012>.

has been achieved, such as the annual transboundary EIA Workshop.[118] But there is no substantive progress in this area so far. In addition, transboundary EIA will be applied to other projects within the region. At the Ninth Meeting of the Consultative Commission, specific projects were identified, such as the Mongolia-China Railway Feasibility Study (this railway will link Mongolia with seaports) and the Road and Harbour Project on the China-North Korean Border, which includes reconstruction of the existing trans-border road into a new road and bridge.[119]

As illustrated in chapter five, since 2000, China's domestic legislation on EIA has undergone several important improvements. There are reasons to believe that EIA as conducted practices in China today is better than the situation a decade ago. But public participation and the relevant information transparency remains one of the major problems in China's contemporary EIA legislation and practice. While the transboundary EIA arrangements under the MOU and the ongoing workshops on transboundary EIA marks a milestone in China's cooperation with neighbouring countries, further progress in this area seems to be quite limited. It is very unlikely for countries in this region to agree on a more solid foundation regarding transboundary EIA in the near future. But it is possible that transboundary EIA will be increasingly applied to joint development projects in the region. Russia has signed but not yet ratified the *Espoo Convention*. This is a potential boost for the development of transboundary EIA in the Greater Tumen region. For China, at least the concept of transboundary EIA has begun to be introduced into economic and environmental cooperation initiatives with neighbouring countries. Due to different geopolitical considerations, China's compromise in the Greater Tumen region cooperation does not necessarily lead to the conclusion that China will likely to do the same in the context of the Mekong region. But it will certainly provide a more positive example for future domestic and regional discussions on whether and how to develop the transboundary EIA mechanism with the participation of China.

## D *Key Issues*

Based on the *Espoo Convention*, the main procedural steps for transboundary EIA are illustrated in the following flow chart:

118 Ibid.

119 Marsden, above n 103; *Feasibility Study on Tumen River Water Protection*, Tumen Programme <http://tumenprogramme.org/?info-612-1.html>.

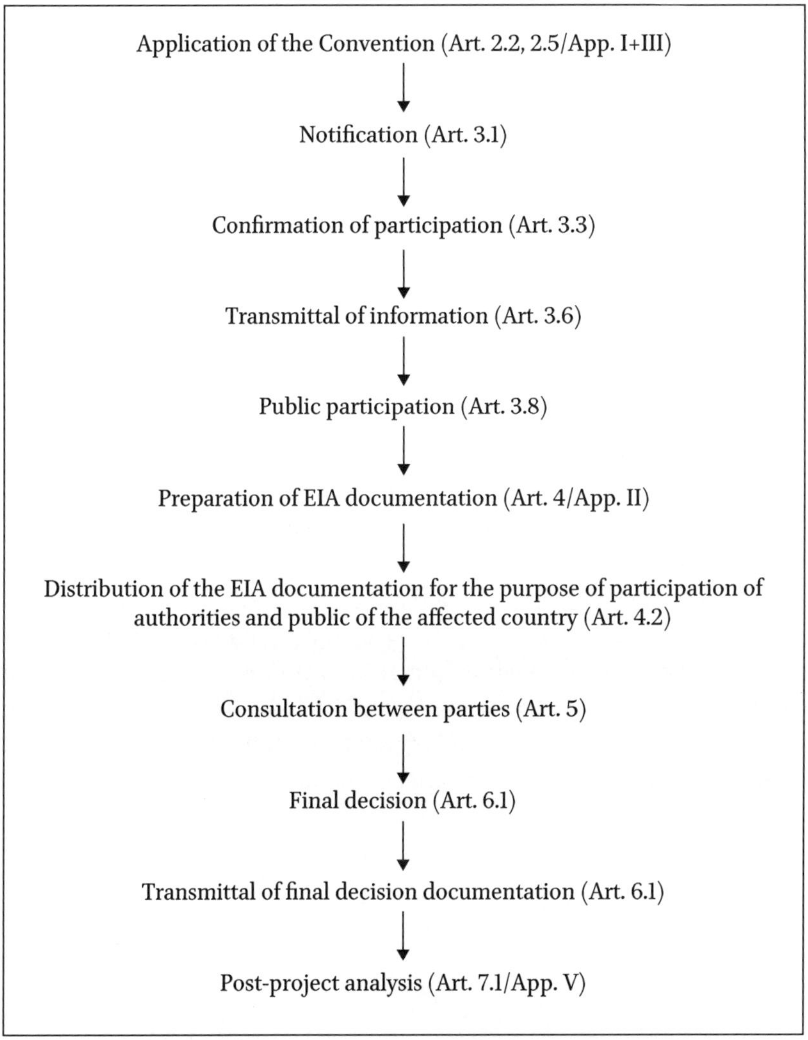


FIGURE 2 *Main procedural steps of transboundary* EIA *under the Espoo Convention*
SOURCE: WIEK SCHRAGE, 'THE CONVENTION ON ENVIRONMENTAL IMPACT ASSESSMENT IN A TRANSBOUNDARY CONTEXT' IN KEES BASTMEIJER AND TIMO KOIVUROVA (EDS), *THEORY AND PRACTICE OF TRANSBOUNDARY ENVIRONMENTAL IMPACT ASSESSMENT* (MARTINUS NIJHOFF PUBLISHERS, 2008) 29, 37.

In contrast to the process involved in carrying out any domestic EIA, how and when to engage the affected states and their public are the two questions that are unique to EIA in the transboundary context. As an institutionalised EIA regime, countries should develop some minimum standards for issues that are common for both domestic and transboundary EIA procedures, such as screening, scoping, public participation, final decision and, to a lesser extent, post-project analysis. As an international assessment mechanism, compliance also constitutes an important aspect of an international EIA regime. The following discussion on developing a transboundary EIA mechanism in the context of the Mekong region will be based on the representative international documents, existing regional arrangements and the domestic EIA legislation in the Mekong countries.

### 1 Screening

As previously mentioned, the screening process determines whether an EIA process will be required for certain projects.[120] The prevalent practice is that a transboundary EIA is only necessary when the proposed activity is likely to cause a "significant" adverse transboundary impact. This is in line with the criterion set for the obligation to prevent harm. Not much controversy exists regarding to the term "significant", especially considering the domestic EIA legislation in the Mekong region is generally in line with this threshold requirement. For example, in China there are three kinds of "EIA documents" required under the *EIA Law* according to the significance of the projects. Only when the potential environmental impact of a construction project is "significant" will an EIA report be required.[121] Thailand, as well as Laos and Cambodia, separates the initial environmental examination (IEE) with the full EIA, and projects with less environmental impact are only required to do an IEE.[122] Interestingly, in Cambodia, an IEE is an essential screening step for all listed projects, namely the list itself does not differentiate the significance of

120 European Commission, above n 48.

121 《中华人民共和国环境影响评价法》 [Environmental Impact Assessment Law of the People's Republic of China] (People's Republic of China) Standing Committee of the National People's Congress, 28 October 2002, art 16.

122 Pranee Pantumsinchai and Thongchai Panswad, *Improvement of EIA Process in Thailand*, Civil Engineering <http://www.civil.rtaf.mi.th/CivilInternet/05Knowledge/03RegulationLaw/%E0%B8%81%E0%B8%8E%E0%B8%AB%E0%B8%A1%E0%B8%B2%E0%B8%A2%E0%B8%AA%E0%B8%B4%E0%B9%88%E0%B8%87%E0%B9%81%E0%B8%A7%E0%B8%94%E0%B8%A5%E0%B9%89%E0%B8%AD%E0%B8%A1/ImprovementofEIA.pdf>; *Enhancement and Conservation of National Environmental Quality Act* (Kingdom of Thailand) National Assembly, 29 March 1992, s 48; *Sub-Decree on Environmental Impact Process* (Kingdom of Cambodia) Council of Ministers, 11 August 1999, art 8; *Decree on Environmental Impact Assessment* (Lao People's Democratic Republic) Prime Minister's Office, 18 February 2010, art 6.

projects.[123] Vietnam, however, does not expressly adopt the standard of "significant" or "serious". Instead, it briefly enumerates the kinds of activities that should be subject to EIA and the government should further provide a detailed list to guide the practice.[124]

In order to provide further guidance on the determination of environmental significance, the *Espoo Convention* clarifies the threshold requirement by enumerating certain types of activities which are subject to transboundary EIA when they are likely to have a significant adverse transboundary impact and further develop some general criteria to assist countries in the determination of the environmental significance of activities that are not included in the list.[125] A range of industrial activities, such as groundwater extraction activities, waste disposal and large dams and reservoirs are included in the list.[126] The selection criteria usually include the size and location of the project, and characteristics of the potential impact.[127] Disputes on whether a listed proposed activity is likely to have a significant transboundary impact will be addressed later in respect to the notification process.

---

123 *Sub-Decree on Environmental Impact Process* (Kingdom of Cambodia) Council of Ministers, 11 August 1999, arts 6, 8.

124 *Law on Environmental Protection* (Socialist Republic of Vietnam) National Assembly, 29 November 2005, art 18.

125 See *Convention on Environmental Impact Assessment in a Transboundary Context*, opened of signature 25 February 1991, 1989 UNTS 309 (entered into force 10 September 1997) art 2, apps I, III. In contrast, focusing on developing regional standards for domestic EIA, the *EIA Directive* first creates a detailed list of projects that are automatically subject to an EIA and then identifies another set of projects which are left for the member states to decide whether the EIA procedure should be applied. For projects enumerated in the second list, selection criteria are set out in the Annex III to be taken into account by member states. *Directive 2011/92/EU of the European Parliament and of the Council of 13 December 2011 on the Assessment of the Effects of Certain Public and Private Projects on the Environment (Codification) (Text with EEA Relevance)* [2011] OJ L 26/1, art 4, annexes I, II, III.

126 *Convention on Environmental Impact Assessment in a Transboundary Context*, opened of signature 25 February 1991, 1989 UNTS 309 (entered into force 10 September 1997) app I. Comparatively, the list under the *EIA Directive* is generally more stringent and specific. For example, while the *Espoo Convention* simply lists "large" dams and reservoirs, the *EIA Directive* clearly requires dams that will hold back or store more than 10 million cubic metres to be subject to an EIA. Moreover, the *EIA Directive* includes several kinds of projects that are not listed in the Convention, such as power transmission lines and works for the transfer of water resources between river basins.

127 Ibid. app III; *Directive 2011/92/EU of the European Parliament and of the Council of 13 December 2011 on the Assessment of the Effects of Certain Public and Private Projects on the Environment (Codification) (Text with EEA Relevance)* [2011] OJ L 26/1, annex III.

Similar approaches are adopted under the domestic EIA legislation as well. For example, China issued the Catalogue of Construction Projects for Classified Management of EIA in 2008, which specifies the kind of EIA documents needed for various activities in accordance to different types, sizes and locations. With respect to dam and reservoir construction, two criteria are applied to decide whether a full environmental impact report is needed. One is based on size, namely those with storage volumes of 10 million cubic metres or more.[128] The standard here is the same as the one set under the *EIA Directive*. The other criterion is by location, viz. the hydropower project located in certain environmental sensitivity areas will be subject to a full EIA.[129] China, however, does not include a flexible provision to allow projects that are not listed in the Catalogue to be subject to EIA according to a case-by-case decision, which is allowed in Laos.[130] But in cases like Thailand, where the environmental protection authority is required to categorise each type and size of project or activity either for an IEE or a full EIA,[131] the margin left for additional discretion can be seriously curtailed.

In Thailand, the activities subject to an EIA process are categorised into seven groups based on different type, size and location, among which the dams or reservoirs with storage volumes of 100 million cubic metres or more, or with storage surface areas of 15 square kilometres or more are subject to a full EIA.[132] Here, the criterion of storage volume is not as strict as the counterparts in China, but the size of storage surface area is taken into consideration. In addition, all types of projects located in the areas approved by the Cabinet as class 1B watershed area are also required to prepare a full EIA report.[133] Therefore, the dam projects which do not satisfy the size requirement may still have to go through an EIA process. According to the 2010 Directive on the List of Projects to Undertake IEE and EIA in Laos, dams and reservoirs with stor-

128 环境保护部 [Ministry of Environmental Protection of the People's Republic of China], 《建设项目环境影响评价分类管理名录》 [Classified Catalogue of Construction Projects Subject to Environmental Impact Assessment] (2008) 4 <http://www.mep.gov.cn/info/bgw/bl/200809/W020080905398664224537.pdf>.

129 Ibid.

130 *Decree on Environmental Impact Assessment* (Lao People's Democratic Republic) Prime Minister's Office, 18 February 2010, art 6.

131 *Enhancement and Conservation of National Environmental Quality Act* (Kingdom of Thailand) National Assembly, 29 March 1992, s 46.

132 Office of Natural Resources and Environmental Policy and Planning, *Environmental Impact Assessment in Thailand* (2012) 82 Asian Environmental Compliance and Enforcement Network <http://www.aecen.org/sites/default/files/environmental_impact_assessment_in_thailand.pdf>.

133 Ibid. 6.

age volume of 200 million cubic metres or more, or with installed capacity of 15 megawatts or more, or with a reservoir area of 1500 hectare or more are subject to a full EIA.[134] Although installed capacity is a new factor introduced into the threshold consideration, its standard based on the storage volume is much looser than that of China and Thailand, leaving ample room for its national agenda to become the "battery of Southeast Asia". What is even more surprising or bizarre is the threshold standard set according to the reservoir area: 1500 hectares is a huge area. But there is no other information available to further interpret this criterion. Despite the above domestic standards, the threshold standards adopted by the *1995 Mekong Agreement* and the MRC Procedures for Notification, Prior Consultation and Agreement are in fact very different from the domestic criteria.

In order to address the screening issue in the Mekong context, several questions need to be answered first. For one thing, which template will the future transboundary EIA document in the Mekong region follow? Is it the *Espoo Convention* which focuses on the application of EIA in a transboundary context, or the *EIA Directive* which focuses on the development of European standards for domestic EIA and only partially addresses the transboundary EIA? Considering the circumstances in the Mekong region, although the Association of Southeast Asian Nations (ASEAN) has attempted to standardise or harmonise member states' legislation on various issues, this job remains a very difficult task in Southeast Asia. Therefore, it is more likely that the future efforts on developing a regional EIA document will focuses on the transboundary application of EIA. The next issue is whether we should attempt to develop a transboundary EIA document that is applicable to various kinds of activities, or only target water management of the Mekong. It further relates to another question, namely under which platform should we develop this mechanism: the MRC, ASEAN, GMS or others?

Currently, the MRC is in the process of drafting a procedural document on transboundary EIA. But discussion under this platform excludes the participation of China or Myanmar. In addition, given the MRC Procedures for

134 ກະຊວງ ຊັບພະຍາກອນ ທຳມະຊາດ ແລະ ສິ່ງແວດລ້ອມ [Ministry of Natural Resources and Environment of the Lao People's Democratic Republic], ຂໍ້ຕົກລົງ ວ່າດ້ວຍການຮັບຮອງ ແລະ ປະກາດໃຊ້ບັນຊີໂຄງການລົງທຶນ ທີ່ຈະຕ້ອງດຳເນີນການ ສຶກສາສິ່ງແວດລ້ອມເບື້ອງຕົ້ນ ແລະ ດຳເນີນການ ປະເມີນຜົນກະທົບ ຕໍ່ສິ່ງແວດລ້ອມ ເລກທີ 697/ສນຍ.ອຊນສ, ລົງວັນທີ 12 ມີນາ 2010 [Directive on the List of Projects to Undertake IEE and EIA] (2010) <http://monre.gov.la/esia/images/download/type%20and%20size%20697%20pm%20wrea%2012%20mar%202010.pdf>. The relevant provision is translated by Manolinh Thepkhamvong and verified by Oulavanh Keovilignavong.

Notification, Prior Consultation and Agreement only applies to mainstream Mekong development, it is likely that the future transboundary EIA document will leave out tributary developments as well. It is certainly not the most reasonable screening arrangement, but it is probably the most feasible under the current MRC regime. Even this degree of consensus will not be easy. The GMS platform does involve all six Mekong countries and deals with numerous infrastructure development projects regarding hydropower, but the platform itself remains loosely structured, operates in an obvious "ASEAN Way" and does not have enough incentives to develop regional arrangements around this mechanism. Dialogue cooperation between ASEAN and China is another potential stage for transboundary EIA, but it involves too many countries and consensus would be difficult to achieve. Therefore, a more realistic approach is to pursue relevant development through the MRC. Meanwhile, it is important to try to engage China in the dialogues and negotiations via China's dialogue relationship with the MRC or through the GMS. Even if it is probably too late to conduct a transboundary EIA for China's hydropower projects on the upstream Mekong, arrangements could be made regarding post-project analysis or monitoring.

## 2 Scoping

The scoping process determines the "content and extent of the matters which should be covered" in the EIA report.[135] According to the *Espoo Convention*, the EIA report should at least contain the following information: a description of the proposed activity and its purpose; *where appropriate*, reasonable alternatives to the proposed activity and also the no-action or nil alternative; the aspects of environment that are likely to be significantly affected by the proposed activity and its alternatives; the potential environmental impact and an estimation of its significance; mitigation measures; predictive methods and underlying assumptions; gaps in knowledge and uncertainties encountered; an outline for monitoring and management programs (where appropriate) and any plans for post-project analysis; and a non-technical summary.[136]

The list provided by the *EIA Directive* is more specific in many of the above aspects and the *reasonable alternatives* are an obligatory requirement of EIA methodology. In addition, the *EIA Directive* is successful in expressly requiring the assessment of any indirect, secondary and/or cumulative impact of

135 European Commission, above n 48.

136 *Convention on Environmental Impact Assessment in a Transboundary Context*, opened of signature 25 February 1991, 1989 UNTS 309 (entered into force 10 September 1997) app II (emphasis added).

proposed activities, which is implicit in the *Espoo Convention*.[137] However, the EIA *Directive* makes no mention of plans for monitoring or post-project analysis at all, which is a voluntary measure expressly identified under the *Espoo Convention*. Another interpretation regarding the term "where appropriate" is provided by Craik, indicating that where alternatives or an outline of plans for post-project analysis are required under domestic legislation, it is appropriate to consider them in a transboundary context as well as in order to comply with the non-discrimination principle.[138]

With regard to the situation in the Mekong countries, the current EIA legislation in Cambodia and Thailand does not specify what information should be included in the full EIA report. In Thailand, this is compensated for by the General Guidelines in Preparing EIA Report issued by the Ministry of Natural Resources and Environment. These guidelines should be followed in conducting an EIA in Thailand. For Cambodia, this major deficiency may be addressed in developing Cambodia's EIA Law. Among the Mekong countries' legislation, only the recently updated Decree on EIA in Laos includes consideration for "appropriate alternatives".[139] Notably, alternatives including no-action should be considered, according to the Thailand EIA Guidelines.[140] The lack of requirements on alternatives in most of the domestic EIA legislation in the Mekong region indicates that it is less likely to be included in the future transboundary EIA document unless the domestic legislation in this area can be further improved. In addition, both China and Vietnam expressly require the EIA report to include the public opinion.[141] Public participation during the EIA process has been discussed in length in chapter five and will be briefly reviewed later.

Generally speaking, none of the domestic EIA legislation in the Mekong region is as specific as the *EIA Directive* in terms of the contents of the EIA

---

137 *Directive 2011/92/EU of the European Parliament and of the Council of 13 December 2011 on the Assessment of the Effects of Certain Public and Private Projects on the Environment (Codification) (Text with EEA Relevance)* [2011] OJ L 26/1, annex IV.

138 Craik, above n 6, 139.

139 *Decree on Environmental Impact Assessment* (Lao People's Democratic Republic) Prime Minister's Office, 18 February 2010, art 3(2).

140 Office of Natural Resources and Environmental Policy and Planning, above n 132, 22 <http://www.onep.go.th/eia/images/stories/inf/Environmental_Impact_Assessment_in_Thailand.pdf>.

141 《中华人民共和国环境影响评价法》 [Environmental Impact Assessment Law of the People's Republic of China] (People's Republic of China) Standing Committee of the National People's Congress, 28 October 2002, art 21; *Law on Environmental Protection* (Socialist Republic of Vietnam) National Assembly, 29 November 2005, art 20.

report. For example, except in Vietnam,[142] there is no express requirement under the Mekong countries' EIA legislation for a description of the forecasting methods used to assess the environmental impact. Moreover, except the Lao EIA Decree's explicit request for consideration of the short, long-term, direct and indirect impact and the similar instructions under the Thailand EIA Guidelines,[143] other EIA legislation includes no specific requirements with respect to the kinds of impact that should be examined. None of the EIA legislation in the Mekong region considers cumulative effects or requires an indication of any difficulties or knowledge gaps encountered in carrying out the EIA. But almost all Mekong countries do require the inclusion of an outline of or suggestions for ongoing monitoring and management plans.[144]

The above deficiencies in domestic requirements on scoping have a negative impact on the effectiveness of EIA in each country to varying degrees. And the differences in domestic legislation on this issue increase the difficulty for reaching specific regional consensus in this area. Notably, the Lao EIA Decree appears more favourable in several aspects of the scoping issue, but the effectiveness of these provisions in practice remains highly doubtful. With regard to several criteria that countries have not accepted under their domestic EIA legislation, it is difficult to adopt them at the regional level. Nevertheless, there remains a possibility that, similar to the aforementioned transboundary SEA practices, transboundary application of EIA may transcend domestic practice as a result of the influences and pressures mandated by foreign donors and investors. If this proves to be the case it may contribute to future review and revision of the domestic legislation on EIA and may facilitate more effective implementation according to more stringent international standards.

---

142 *Law on Environmental Protection* (Socialist Republic of Vietnam) National Assembly, 29 November 2005, art 20(9).

143 *Decree on Environmental Impact Assessment* (Lao People's Democratic Republic) Prime Minister's Office, 18 February 2010, arts 3(2), 12(4); Office of Natural Resources and Environmental Policy and Planning, above n 132, 22.

144 《中华人民共和国环境影响评价法》 [Environmental Impact Assessment Law of the People's Republic of China] (People's Republic of China) Standing Committee of the National People's Congress, 28 October 2002, art 17(6); *Decree on Environmental Impact Assessment* (Lao People's Democratic Republic) Prime Minister's Office, 18 February 2010, art 13; *Law on Environmental Protection* (Socialist Republic of Vietnam) National Assembly, 29 November 2005, art 20(6); Office of Natural Resources and Environmental Policy and Planning, above n 132, 23.

## 3 Notification

According to the *Espoo Convention* and the *EIA Directive*, in case a proposed activity may cause a significant transboundary impact, the state of origin shall notify any affected state "as early as possible and no later than when informing its own public".[145] This provision applies the non-discrimination principle to address the issue of who should receive notification and when. But, as mentioned in chapter four, in a region where public participation and information transparency is generally restrained, the linkage between the timing of notification and that of informing the domestic public can be much less reliable or realistic. In the MRC Procedures for Notification, Prior Consultation and Agreement, the only term used regarding this particular issue is "timely". There is no further explanation on what counts as "timely" notification and the public's right to know is not expressly mentioned. Although the application of the non-discrimination principle sets no minimum standard at the international level, its combination with the requirement on "as early as possible" under the *Espoo Convention* is more stringent than the broad term of "timely" used in the MRC procedural document. Meanwhile, it is only in the agreement with Russia that China briefly, but formally, agreed to notify each other on any hydraulic project that may cause significant transboundary effects.[146] No detailed arrangements have been made regarding the timing or the content of such notification.

In addition, it should be noted that the above provisions regarding the Mekong countries only refers to the general obligation to notify, instead of considering notification as a procedural issue during the transboundary EIA process. This is reflected in the different requirements on the content of notification. Similar to the *UN Watercourses Convention*, the MRC Procedures for Notification, Prior Consultation and Agreement requires the provision of feasibility study reports, implementation plans, schedules and all other available technical data and information on the proposed activity in order to enable

145 *Convention on Environmental Impact Assessment in a Transboundary Context*, opened of signature 25 February 1991, 1989 UNTS 309 (entered into force 10 September 1997) art 3(1); *Directive 2011/92/EU of the European Parliament and of the Council of 13 December 2011 on the Assessment of the Effects of Certain Public and Private Projects on the Environment (Codification) (Text with EEA Relevance)* [2011] OJ L 26/1, art 7(1).

146 《中华人民共和国政府和俄罗斯联邦政府关于合理利用和保护跨界水的协定》[Cooperation Agreement between China and Russia on the Reasonable Utilisation and Protection of Transboundary Waters] (2008) 外交部 [Ministry of Foreign Affairs of the People's Republic of China], art 2(8) <http://www.fmprc.gov.cn/mfa_chn/ziliao_611306/tytj_611312/tyfg_611314/t708160.shtml>.

the notified states to evaluate its impact.[147] The *summary* of required impact assessment documents is expressly mentioned in the guideline.[148] Since in most of the lower Mekong countries, the domestic EIA procedure is triggered at the same time when the feasibility study begins,[149] it is clear that the general obligation to notify actually occurs after any domestic EIA has been undertaken. The transboundary EIA procedure is supposed to be integrated with any domestic EIA process. Hence, notification as a part of the transboundary EIA procedure should in fact occur at a much earlier time. This illustrates the desirability of applying the non-discrimination principle. The obligation to notify the affected states should occur no later than when informing its own public serves as a link between the domestic EIA procedures and the transboundary EIA process.

Despite the connection between notification and public participation, it is less likely that the Mekong countries can agree to use the timing of informing its own public as the trigger for notification. This is due to the fact that information transparency and public participation in the region are far from satisfactory and there is as yet no formal regional consensus on public participation. Considering the necessity to differentiate two kinds of notification, it is recommended that, at the very least, the future transboundary EIA document should link the transboundary EIA process with the domestic EIA procedure and require the affected states and their public to be notified during the corresponding domestic EIA process. This approach is supported by the ICJ judgment in the *Pulp Mills Case*, which stated unequivocally that the duty to inform "become applicable at the stage when the relevant authority has had the project referred to it with the aim of obtaining initial environmental authorization

147 Mekong River Commission, *Procedures for Notification, Prior Consultation and Agreement* (30 November 2003), arts 4(2), 5(2) <http://www.mrcmekong.org/assets/Publications/policies/Procedures-Notification-Prior-Consultation-Agreement.pdf>.

148 Mekong River Commission, *Guidelines on Implementation of the Procedures for Notification, Prior Consultation and Agreement* (31 August 2005), 5 <http://www.mrcmekong.org/assets/Publications/policies/Guidelines-on-implementation-of-the-PNPCA.pdf> (emphasis added).

149 *Law on Environmental Protection* (Socialist Republic of Vietnam) National Assembly, 29 November 2005, art 19(2); *Enhancement and Conservation of National Environmental Quality Act* (Kingdom of Thailand) National Assembly, 29 March 1992, s 47; *Sub-Decree on Environmental Impact Process* (Kingdom of Cambodia) Council of Ministers, 11 August 1999, art 8.

and before the granting of that authorization".[150] Nevertheless, the application of the non-discrimination principle remains a more preferable option.

The *Espoo Convention*'s formulation with respect to the contents of notification has been updated by the *Aarhus Convention*. The *EIA Directive* now reflects a combination of the requirements under both conventions. According to the Directive, along with the notification, at least the following information should be provided: a description of the project, available information on its potential transboundary impact, information on the nature of the decision and providing reasonable time for the notified state to response.[151] In case the notified state indicated its desire to participate in the EIA procedure, the state of origin should, if it has not already done so, provide the affected state with the same information that is also required by the Directive to be disclosed or made available for the domestic public.[152] Again, it indicates a strong connection between the domestic requirement for public participation and the transboundary obligation to notify the affected states and their citizens. Hence, in order to ensure the information transparency for effective consultation with the affected states and their public, a certain degree of protection on the domestic public's right to know and participate is logically essential. However, there is also a possibility that the regional arrangements on transboundary EIA may transcend the relevant domestic stipulations. Given there is a lack of sufficient domestic requirements on access to information on specific activities in the Mekong region, it is recommended that at least some minimum standards should be established at the regional level.

In addition, for projects listed in Appendix I of the *Espoo Convention* (which will be subject to transboundary EIA if it may cause a significant transboundary impact), in case the state of origin failed to satisfy the obligation to notify, the concerned states shall, at the request of the affected state, exchange sufficient information to hold discussions on whether the proposed activity should be subject to a transboundary EIA.[153] Here, the Convention provides a cooperative way for countries to resolve the disputes regarding the issue of screening in

150 *Pulp Mills on the River Uruguay (Argentina v Uruguay) (Judgment)* [2010] ICJ Rep 14, paras 105, 121.

151 *Directive 2011/92/EU of the European Parliament and of the Council of 13 December 2011 on the Assessment of the Effects of Certain Public and Private Projects on the Environment (Codification) (Text with EEA Relevance)* [2011] OJ L 26/1, art 7 (1).

152 Ibid. arts 7, 6(2), 6(3).

153 *Convention on Environmental Impact Assessment in a Transboundary Context*, opened of signature 25 February 1991, 1989 UNTS 309 (entered into force 10 September 1997) art 3(7).

accordance with the criteria set forth by the Convention to assist the screening process. If countries cannot reach consensus on this issue after discussion, or agree on another method of settling this dispute, any member state can bring this question to an inquiry commission which makes decision on a majority basis and is constituted by two experts each appointed by one side of the concerning parties and a third expert designated by the two experts.[154] This is a prudent complement to the general requirements on the screening process and consensus building as a method of dispute settlement. Unless the future transboundary EIA document clearly identified certain kinds of Mekong mainstream water utilisation as projects that may cause a significant transboundary impact (like the MRC Procedures for Notification, Prior Consultation and Agreement), this approach of dispute settlement should at least be considered as a possible way to resolve disputes at this stage.

The affected state can request additional information, but the state of origin is only required to provide "*reasonably obtainable information* relating to the potentially affected environment under the jurisdiction of the affected party, where such information is *necessary* for the *preparation*" of the EIA report.[155] There is no further clarification on what counts as reasonably obtainable information. And information necessary for the preparation of the EIA report does not automatically mean the information necessary for effective evaluation. Disputes in this area have to be resolved by the states via cooperative consultation. For example, the *Espoo Convention* cannot provide an answer for the dispute regarding the additional information provision that occurred during the prior notification and consultation process for the Xayaburi Dam. This is more of a substantive issue concerning the quality of the EIA report rather than a procedural one regarding the transboundary EIA process.

The above discussion covers the pivotal issues regarding notification. It is important to separate notification during the transboundary EIA process with the more general obligation to notify as a direct extension of the obligation to prevent harm. Meanwhile, the connection between notification and the obligation to inform the public should be highlighted. The above two points are crucial in determining who should be notified, when to notify and what information should be provided with the notification. In addition, the *Espoo*

154 The third expert should "not be a national of one of the parties to the inquiry procedure, nor have his or her usual place of residence in the territory of one of these parties, nor be employed by any of them, nor have dealt with the matter in any other capacity". Ibid. app IV.

155 Ibid. art 3(6) (emphasis added).

*Convention* provides a discreet approach to resolving disputes at this stage of transboundary EIA.

## 4 Public Participation

Public participation in decisions on specific activities, as an important aspect of a systematic environmental deliberative democracy, has been discussed in considerable length in chapter five. The earlier analysis has focused more on the *Aarhus Convention* and country-specific discussions within the Mekong region. This chapter pays more attention on how to integrate the *Aarhus Convention* with the *Espoo Convention*. A typical example in this area is the revised *EIA Directive*. Moreover, a comprehensive analysis will be undertaken in this chapter based on chapter five to identify the major problems of public participation during the domestic EIA process in the context of the Mekong region.

The *Espoo Convention* only requires the member states to provide an *opportunity* to the affected public (equal treatment for domestic public and the public of the affected states) to participate and to ensure relevant information transparency.[156] The current version of the *EIA Directive* is much more advanced in this area since it incorporates the contents of the *Aarhus Convention*.[157] In particular, most of the relevant provisions focus on addressing the issue of informing the public. This obligation is reflected in different stages of the EIA procedure: during the screening process (Article 4), (in a transboundary context) during notification (Article 7), before and after the preparation of the EIA documentation (Articles 5 and 6) and after the final decision is made (Article 9). In addition, information relating to the decision granting any exemption of the Directive and the reasons for granting it should be made available to the public (Article 2).

Other than the broad coverage of information disclosure requirements throughout the EIA process, minimum standards are set for the kinds of information that should be made available to the public. This includes information regarding the nature of the possible decisions, the fact that the project is subject to EIA and public participation, information that should be revealed

---

156 Ibid. arts 2(6), 3(8), 4(2).

157 As observed by Craik, the relationship between the *Aarhus Convention* and the *Espoo Convention* is not explicit. But since the *Aarhus Convention* addresses environmental decision-making more generally instead of focusing on transboundary environmental issues, the member states will be required to apply the *Aarhus Convention* for "any activity subject to a national EIA process regardless of whether it is otherwise enumerated in Appendix I to the *Espoo Convention*". Craik, above n 6, 148.

in the EIA report, details of the arrangements for public participation and the relevant information disclosure process, and the content and reasons of the final decision.[158] Two criteria are set for the timing of information disclosure: (1) early in the decision-making procedures and, at the latest, as soon as information can reasonably be provided; (2) within reasonable time-frames.[159] Details for informing the public are left for the discretion of the member states. The provisions under the *EIA Directive* on the obligation to inform the public are largely derived from the *Aarhus Convention*, but are better integrated with the domestic and transboundary EIA procedure.

Compared to the requirements on informing the public, the provisions on public participation are much more general. The public should be provided with early and effective opportunities to participate and express their opinions when all options are open before the decision is taken.[160] Considering the diversity of domestic legislation on this issue, detailed arrangements with respect to public participation shall be determined by member states, including reasonable time-frames for the different phases to allow sufficient time for informing the public and for the public concerned to prepare and participate effectively. The information and comments gathered through the participation process should be taken into account during the decision-making.[161] Technically speaking, the *Aarhus Convention* is more stringent by requiring the member state to take *due* account of public opinions.[162] Another issue only addressed by the *Aarhus Convention* is that, where appropriate, in case a specific activity is reconsidered or updated in terms of the operating conditions, the public participation requirements should also be applied *mutatis mutandis*.[163] Therefore, post-project analysis can be also subject to public participation. Further, both the *EIA Directive* and the *Aarhus Convention* require the member states to ensure the public's right of access to justice regarding the public participation provisions.[164]

---

158 *Directive 2011/92/EU of the European Parliament and of the Council of 13 December 2011 on the Assessment of the Effects of Certain Public and Private Projects on the Environment (Codification) (Text with EEA Relevance)* [2011] OJ L 26/1, arts 5, 6, 7, 9.

159 Ibid. art 6.

160 Ibid. art 6(4).

161 Ibid. art 8.

162 *Convention on Access to Information, Public Participation in Decision-making and Access to Justice in Environmental Matters*, opened for signature 25 June 1998, 2161 UNTS 447 (entered into force 10 October 2001) art 6(8).

163 Ibid. art 6(10).

164 *Directive 2011/92/EU of the European Parliament and of the Council of 13 December 2011 on the Assessment of the Effects of Certain Public and Private Projects on the Environment*

Based on the above provisions, it is clear that while there are relatively more international standards on the obligation to inform the public, details regarding the obligation to consult with the public during the EIA procedure remain largely left to the discretion of the member states. Therefore, the domestic development of public participation, both in general and specifically on proposed activities, still plays a dominate role in ensuring effective participation in each member state. But the increasing recognition of the procedural rights at the international level is also valuable in setting international benchmarks and principles. As mentioned in chapter five, there are no regional arrangements among the Mekong countries on the obligation to inform and consult the public, except some stakeholder participation policies and communication strategies regarding the operation of the MRC (not the member states) and the relevant policies under the World Bank and the ADB and other multilateral funding institutions.

Despite the relatively better status of transparency and public engagement during the operation of the MRC than most of its member states, problems with the MRC policies regarding access to information and public participation have been previously identified in chapter five. For example, the current major approach of information disclosure (electronic databases) under the MRC remains distant from local communities and accessibility information for them still needs to be improved; the misunderstanding in the usage of the term "public participation" when it actually refers to more broad stakeholder participation which also involves the governments and business sectors; no differentiation of specific activities between the more general plans, programs and policies when applying the public participation strategies; the participation agenda is very much disconnected to the situation in the field; limited attention given to the directly affected people (compared to NGOs); and lower degrees of participation according to Arnstein's ladder. In addition, the lack of real influence on water development decision-making by the MRC creates a more fundamental challenge to the effectiveness of public participation under the MRC regime. Whilst there are merits in continuing to promote public participation and information transparency under the MRC platform, especially with regard to the drafting of the transboundary EIA document, more fundamental challenges lie in the relevant political and legal reforms at the domestic level.

---

(*Codification*) (*Text with EEA Relevance*) [2011] OJ L 26/1, art 11; *Convention on Access to Information, Public Participation in Decision-making and Access to Justice in Environmental Matters*, opened for signature 25 June 1998, 2161 UNTS 447 (entered into force 10 October 2001) art 9.

As detailed in chapter five, the major deficiencies of public participation in the Mekong countries include, but are not limited to:

The Mekong countries tend to interpret and apply exemption clauses in a broad sense, especially with regard to national security and even the so-called national stability (represented by the status quo in China). Public participation across the region is challenged by diversified, often problematic domestic legislation, restricted political freedom and civil society development. With an exception of Thailand, other Mekong countries fall short of formal recognition of access to information and public participation as rights under the existing legislation.

Thailand has not yet expressly incorporated public participation into its EIA provisions, but has the most vibrant civil society and enjoys more political tolerance for implementing public participation. China probably has the most specific arrangements in this aspect among all the Mekong countries, but they are heavily criticised for not enough information transparency,[165] late involvement by the public and a short time-frame allowed for participation. The recently updated Lao EIA Decree (under the influence of foreign donors and investors) adopts some strong provisions on public participation, but the political reform towards effective implementation is very restricted. Vietnam has some minimal requirements on information disclosure and the requirement that the public opinion should be included in the EIA report, but still falls short of more specific legislation and more open political tolerance. Cambodia only has some hortatory provisions on public participation during the EIA process, but is likely to develop more specific provisions on public participation in future EIA legislation.

Civil society development in most Mekong countries is constrained or underdeveloped to varying degrees, reflected in the fact that "civil society" is still a relatively new concept and theory to these countries; the lack of awareness of the general public on their participation rights; unclear separation of civil society organisations with the government and business sectors; various restrictions on the formation, registration, management and operation of NGOs; and the lack of free media.

The public also has a relatively weak ability to participate and the governments or developers fall short of the necessary capacity and willingness to facilitate participation. This includes the lack of confidence, training and education (basic education and professional knowledge), necessary infrastructure and economic resources, etc.

165 In particular, only the summary, instead of the full EIA report, is required to be disclosed and the public do not have access to the responses of their comments.

There is a prevalent feature of formality in existing participation practices and notable gaps still exist between the legislation and the situation in the field. The tokenism of implementation is very detrimental for the confidence and activeness of the public to participate via this newly emerging mechanism. Since the concept of access to justice is not very well developed or entrenched, public opinion is either restricted or more likely to be expressed though more violent and non-conventional methods. Further, the development of public participation on proposed activities often falls short of necessary support from other levels of participation (i.e. plans and legislation) and the status of information transparency in most of the Mekong countries remains far from satisfactory, in part a result of varying degrees of immature representative democracy and the establishment of rule of law across the region.

Nevertheless, it should be recognised that public participation during the EIA process is taking a leading role in promoting legal reforms towards deliberative democracy. The growth of environmental NGOs is the most vibrant aspect of civil society development and their operation is relatively less sensitive compared to other areas involving advocacy. For most Mekong countries, public participation during the EIA process is a breakthrough point for a wider or expanded application of this mechanism at different levels of decision-making in the future. Major historical impediments created by the political and legal environment cannot be overcome overnight and it is important to fully utilise the existing opportunities to raise awareness, to gain more experience in the field and to continue with political reform. While top-down processes remains vital to encourage future reforms, bottom-up approaches should attract at least equal attention. In addition to efforts in promoting public participation at the national level, it is argued that at least some general principles regarding public participation should be included in the regional arrangements on transboundary EIA. Considering the fact that Laos is likely to be the state of origin for most projects that may be subject to a transboundary EIA, its recently updated provisions on public participation for domestic EIAs can provide a necessary foundation for future negotiations. Although the relevant legislation in Vietnam and Cambodia is much less strong or specific, their downstream status can create incentives for them to apply more stringent requirements on public participation to strengthen transboundary EIA methodology. But as mentioned in chapter five, disincentives like other geopolitical concerns (such as Vietnam's intention to win support from Laos on its territorial disputes with China in the South China Sea) and domestic obstacles impeding relevant reforms should not be overlooked. With regard to China, its past transboundary cooperation has not yet included public participation, except a very general and opaque reference in the case of Greater Tumen region.

## 5 Consultation

The *Espoo Convention* requires the state of origin to enter into consultations with the affected state without undue delay after the completion of the EIA report.[166] The *EIA Directive*, however, does not specify on when the consultation should be held, implying that it can occur prior to the completion of the EIA report. Different from the consultation process stipulated under the *UN Watercourses Convention*, it is the potential transboundary effects of the proposed activity and the corresponding mitigation measures that are the major focus of this consultation process. In addition, since the consultation with the public of the affected state often occurs at the same time in conjunction with the consultation process among states, it is clear that the *Espoo Convention* does not provide an opportunity for the public to participate during the scoping or report preparation stages of the EIA.[167] The *Aarhus Convention* and the *EIA Directive* is not explicit on this issue. Compared to the Directive, the *Espoo Convention* further sets out several issues that may be included in the consultation, such as possible alternatives and measures to monitor the effects of preventive measure. Although it is commendable for mentioning these issues, it is not, however, obligatory to consider them during consultation. Moreover, countries are required to agree on a reasonable time-frame for the duration of the consultation period. But there is no further explanation on what counts as reasonable and no minimum standard is set. This is in contrast with the provisions under the *UN Watercourses Convention*, which stipulates six months as a minimum period for consultation and this period can be extended by unanimous decision.

As discussed in chapter four, the MRC Procedures for Notification, Prior Consultation and Agreement is not directly applicable to transboundary EIA. It is argued that future consultation requirements for transboundary EIA in the Mekong region, particularly the document prepared under the MRC platform, should be coordinated with the more general consultation process under the international watercourse law. Transboundary EIA process represents an attempt to de-politicise disputes by causing parties to focus on the technical issues. The general obligation to notify and consult, however, attempts to seek political resolution. The different focus of these two mechanisms leads to different consultation agendas. The former targets at s consideration of the factual findings of the transboundary EIA report, while the latter entails a broader agenda to reach agreement on a particular project. The

166 *Convention on Environmental Impact Assessment in a Transboundary Context*, opened of signature 25 February 1991, 1989 UNTS 309 (entered into force 10 September 1997) art 5.

167 Craik, above n 6, 143.

above difference should not be neglected in the designing of transboundary EIA procedure in the Mekong region. Due to the deficiencies of the existing MRC procedural requirements on consultation, especially with respect to the time-frame and the provision of information, future provisions on consultation during the transboundary EIA process does not necessarily have to mirror the existing document. It is suggested that consultation should be encouraged and welcomed even prior to the completion of the EIA report. With respect to China, consultation in a general sense is also an oft-used approach during transboundary cooperation on water management with countries like Russia and Kazakhstan. If China was able to agree on any form of transboundary EIA commitment, the introduction of a consultation process is less likely to be a highly disputed issue. But at this stage, it may be difficult to agree on specific or relatively detailed provisions.

## 6 Final Decision and Post-Project Analysis

The right to make a final decision on whether to approve a proposed activity belongs to the state of origin. The authority is not required to follow the recommendation of a transboundary EIA report, but should take due account of the report, as well as opinions gained through consultation with the public and the affected states.[168] The *EIA Directive*, however, does not expressly require the above information to be considered "duly", or does the MoU document signed by China in the case of Greater Tumen region. But countries are still bound by the general obligation to prevent harm and to cooperate. As mentioned before, consultation should be introduced into the final decision-making process and provide an opportunity for countries to reach agreement on the proposed activity before, not after, any final decision is made.

In addition, countries often vary on domestic arrangements for the EIA approval process and the ensuing permitting process for a proposed activity. For example, the Province of Ontario, Canada, introduced as far back as 1975 an independent and quasi-judicial tribunal, the Environmental Board of Ontario, during the EIA process as the ultimate decision-making authority which can depoliticise the process and provide a more rigorous testing of scientific evidence via an adversarial hearing procedure.[169] This approval

168 *Convention on Environmental Impact Assessment in a Transboundary Context*, opened of signature 25 February 1991, 1989 UNTS 309 (entered into force 10 September 1997) art 6.

169 See Michael I. Jeffery, QC, 'The New Canadian Environmental Assessment Act–Bill C-78: A Disappointing Response to Promised Reform' (1991) 36(3) *McGill Law Journal* 1070, 1081, 1085. Another interesting and controversial innovation in the Canadian EIA approval process triggered by the work of the Ontario Environmental Assessment Board in the

design certainly has a better chance to enhance the effectiveness of the EIA process, but how to introduce this decision-making process more indicative to a British common law jurisdiction into the continental legal system is a huge challenge. It also needs the judges to acquire both the legal knowledge and a certain level of scientific understanding, which is generally not the case for the Mekong countries, since their court systems are usually unfamiliar with dealing environmental disputes. Some Mekong countries require the environmental protection agency to appoint a panel of experts (Thailand), or an appraisal council constituted by both experts and representatives of government officials or other organisations and individuals (Vietnam) to decide whether the EIA report should be approved or rejected.[170] But other countries in this region are not specific on this issue in their EIA legislation. In addition, the time-frame set for the review process varies across the region, normally ranging from 15 days (Vietnam and Laos) to 60 days (China).[171] Further, issues such as whether the public is allowed to participate in the approval process and the actual power of the environmental protection agency compared to other government departments also have an important influence on the design of the final decision-making process. However, the above issues are too difficult and complex to be addressed by international law at this stage. For the Mekong

---

1980s is the issue of the *Ontario's Intervenor Funding Project Act* which basically embraces the concept of a "proponent of the project funding its own opposition in cases involving significant public interest" to enhance the citizen's ability to participate effectively in the environmental decision-making process. The relevant decision is made through a special hearing process before a joint board, the Ontario Energy Board or the Environmental Assessment Board. Although this Act expired in 1996, it represents a meaningful legal innovation in exploring solutions to enhance the capacity for effective public participation. See generally Michael I. Jeffery, QC., 'Intervenor Funding as the Key to Effective Citizen Participation in Environmental Decision-making: Putting the People back into the Picture' (2002) 19(2) *Arizona Journal of International and Comparative Law* 643; Susan J. McWilliams, 'The Costs of Intervenor Funding and Their Control: The Experience of the Ontario Energy Board' (1991) 11 *Windsor Yearbook of Access to Justice* 217; Richard D. Lindgren and Burgandy Dunn, 'Environmental Assessment in Ontario: Rhetoric vs. Reality' (2010) 21 *Journal of Environmental Law and Practice* 279; David McRobert and Paula Boutis, *Proposal for a New Ontario Participant and Intervenor Funding Act Filed with the Environmental Commissioner of Ontario* (2012) Ontario Bar Association <http://www.oba.org/en/pdf/sec_news_env_mar12_Proposal_Boutis.pdf>.

170 See *Enhancement and Conservation of National Environmental Quality Act* (Kingdom of Thailand) National Assembly, 29 March 1992, s 48; *Law on Environmental Protection* (Socialist Republic of Vietnam) National Assembly, 29 November 2005, art 21.

171 In Thailand, the time-frame is 45 days. In case the proposed project is "complex", the time-frame set by the Lao Decree on EIA is 120 working days.

countries, it is unlikely they can address the above detailed issues in the future transboundary EIA document, but it is beneficial to bear them in mind in practice and they can be raised during the consultation process at this stage the development of EIA.

The final decision should be notified to the affected states and their public along with accompanying reasons for the decision. If additional information on any significant transboundary impact of a proposed activity that was not available at the time of decision-making becomes available before the actual implementation of the project, this information should be immediately notified to other concerned member states and consultations should be held upon request of any of the affected countries on whether the decision needs to be revised.[172] But the post-project analysis or monitoring during or after the implementation phase is not compulsory under the *Espoo Convention*[173] and is not even mentioned in the *EIA Directive*. However, in case there are reasonable grounds for concluding that there is a potential or existing significant adverse transboundary impact of the project, countries are still bound by the obligation to prevent harm and timely notification and consultation is necessary to respond to emergencies and to reduce or eliminate the negative impact. As a valuable feedback mechanism, post-project analysis and monitoring is included in the EIA legislation in China, Vietnam and Laos.[174] In particular, the EIA provisions in Vietnam require the owner of the project to disclose certain information during construction and the local communities have the right to supervise.[175] Although there are some features of extending public participation to the post-project analysis process, the effectiveness of this process in Vietnam is in doubt considering the lack of sufficient legal protection and political opportunities for the public to exercise their rights.

Post-project analysis is an important mechanism for future cooperation between China and other Mekong countries regarding its mainstream hydropower projects. China does have relatively detailed provisions on this issue,

---

172 *Convention on Environmental Impact Assessment in a Transboundary Context*, opened of signature 25 February 1991, 1989 UNTS 309 (entered into force 10 September 1997) art 6.

173 Ibid. art 7.

174 《中华人民共和国环境影响评价法》 [Environmental Impact Assessment Law of the People's Republic of China] (People's Republic of China) Standing Committee of the National People's Congress, 28 October 2002, arts 24–8; *Law on Environmental Protection* (Socialist Republic of Vietnam) National Assembly, 29 November 2005, art 23; *Decree on Environmental Impact Assessment* (Lao People's Democratic Republic) Prime Minister's Office, 18 February 2010, arts 22–5.

175 *Law on Environmental Protection* (Socialist Republic of Vietnam) National Assembly, 29 November 2005, art 23.

although the public has not yet been involved in this process. Even if countries may not agree on post-project analysis to be included as a part of the transboundary EIA document, joint monitoring and study between China and the other Mekong countries is a promising approach to deepen the cooperation on transboundary water management.

## 7 Compliance

Compliance, in a nutshell, is an ongoing process which refers to "a state of conformity or identity between an actor's behavior and specified rule".[176] As an international regime for transboundary EIA, the *Espoo Convention* addresses the issue by requiring regular meetings of parties, information exchange, self-reporting evaluation, encouraging implementation via new bilateral and multilateral cooperation, developing research programs, seeking methodological and technical support from competent third parties and establishing dispute settlement mechanisms.[177] While member states can voluntarily accept the jurisdiction of ICJ or agree to resolve disputes via arbitration, they have further adopted a non-adversarial and assistance-oriented compliance monitoring mechanism which allows states to bring issues of non-compliance before an Implementation Committee to seek its recommendations.[178] Compared to the non-compliance mechanism established under the *Aarhus Convention*, non-state actors have not yet been able to be directly involved under this mechanism.[179]

With regard to the MRC regime, however, there is no self-reporting system introduced and information exchange focuses more on scientific data rather than relevant domestic legislation and policies. In addition, considering the contents of the MRC Procedures for Notification, Prior Consultation and Agreement, it is likely that the future transboundary EIA document will pay more attention to technical issues regarding how to carry out this process via the MRC institutions instead of dealing with non-compliance situations. Other than the lack of necessary information exchange on domestic implementation, the MRC regime also suffers from the ambiguity of the *Mekong Agreement* itself and the sole reliance on consensus building (underpinned by the "ASEAN

176 Kal Raustiala, 'Compliance & Effectiveness in International Regulatory Cooperation' (2000) 32 *Case Western Reserve Journal of International Law* 387, 391.

177 *Convention on Environmental Impact Assessment in a Transboundary Context*, opened of signature 25 February 1991, 1989 UNTS 309 (entered into force 10 September 1997) arts 8, 9, 11, 15.

178 Craik, above n 6, 160.

179 Ibid.

Way") or mediation to settle disputes. These problems also widely exist in other cooperative regimes in the region. Dialogue relationships between China and the MRC and ASEAN are even less systematic and the structure of the GMS program remains very loose.

Further, a major difficulty in addressing the above issues also lies in the donor-driven feature of the MRC and its increasingly marginalised situation, resulting in the passive involvement of the lower Mekong countries (particularly Laos) and the MRC's limited impact on hydropower decision-making. Introducing transboundary EIA as a mechanism or a tool under the MRC regime is different from developing a new regional regime to address this issue and the pre-existing deficiencies of the general compliance system of the MRC will be very difficult to overcome. Therefore, future discussions on the non-compliance mechanism for transboundary EIA in the context of the Mekong region probably will not lead to a breakthrough in this aspect. Another fundamental challenge is that none of the MRC procedural documents are legally-binding documents. Therefore, unfortunately, there is no hard law foundation for any kind of non-compliance mechanism if transboundary EIA mechanisms were introduced in this way.

Nonetheless, it is argued that at least more active information exchange on relevant domestic policy and experiences and a self-reporting evaluation system are relatively less-controversial compared to others. In addition, scientific services and research is another approach to assist the EIA implementation of the Mekong countries. A direct approach of implementing international commitments on transboundary EIA is to incorporate the international requirements into domestic EIA procedures. For example, the domestic EIA legislation can include the transboundary impact. As discussed earlier, this is now being considered by the experts in drafting the Cambodian new EIA Law. Aside from this, administrative or other measures should be taken to incorporate transboundary EIA commitments into national policies, programs or strategies. But the degree of implementation via domestic measures also depends on the influences of the MRC on domestic policies and legislation in general.

Moreover, domestic EIA legislation itself should be improved to better secure its implementation. As illustrated by the Huangdeng Dam (the sixth of the first half of the Lancang dam cascade),[180] developers in China may overtly violates the EIA Law by implementing the project without getting approval from the environmental protection authorities. According to the EIA Law in China, in case the developer did not submit EIA report for approval, the environmental protection agency shall order the construction to be halted and the

180 See section I(2)(a) of chapter two.

corresponding EIA procedure should be done within the period designated by the authority.[181] If the developer failed to conduct EIA within the deadline, only a fine between 50,000 or 200,000 yuan can be applied and administrative discipline can be given to officials that are directly responsible.[182] While this provision aims to improve the implementation of the EIA Law, in reality its impact are mostly negative. Given the above punishment for not conducting EIA *prior to* the implementation of the project is not comparable to the economic benefits generated by the proposed project, developers are more prone to violate the EIA requirements. Even they are later ordered to halt the project and conduct EIA, the economic interests and investment involved often made it impossible to conduct a proper EIA. The relatively weak status of environmental protection authority compared to many other government sectors and the lack of effective approaches to access to justice in China further deteriorated the situation. As revealed by the case of Huangdeng dam, it is clear that the existing domestic EIA Law is not good enough to offer the coercion needed for law enforcement.

Relevant to the issue of compliance, a more fundamental question is how to ensure the effectiveness of the transboundary EIA mechanism. Once a transboundary EIA document is incorporated under the MRC regime, it is less likely that there will be obvious violations of these requirements, especially when the provisions are ambiguous. Even if countries complied with the procedural document, the effectiveness of a transboundary EIA in avoiding and addressing environmental disputes should not be over-exaggerated. But it certainly provides another valuable opportunity to engage with the affected states and their citizens. It remains the most feasible and reliable approach to evaluate the potential transboundary environmental impact of a proposed project. But in light of the difficulties for international law to dictate the precise form of transboundary EIA,[183] domestic EIA legislation is important due to the great state discretion on details of EIA procedures.

## E *The Way Forward*

Transboundary EIA is not a purely legal issue. Instead, political and scientific factors have strong influences on a transboundary EIA in practice. From the

181 《中华人民共和国环境影响评价法》 [Environmental Impact Assessment Law of the People's Republic of China] (People's Republic of China) Standing Committee of the National People's Congress, 28 October 2002, art 31.

182 Ibid.

183 See *Pulp Mills on the River Uruguay* (*Argentina v Uruguay*) (*Judgment*) [2010] ICJ Rep 14, para 205.

legal perspective, the major task is to provide suitable arrangements for such factors to work properly towards a more cooperative decision-making process and a more benign environmental outcome. Having discussed the major international developments regarding transboundary EIA, its emerging customary law status, the existing transboundary and joint EIA practices of the Mekong countries and key issues of the transboundary EIA procedure, some conclusions on how to best promote the establishment of an effective transboundary EIA mechanism in the context of the Mekong region can be drawn as follows:

Although a lot of attention in this chapter has been paid to international and regional arrangements on transboundary EIA, the foundation provided by the domestic EIA arrangements and practices cannot be overlooked. While the existence of some forms of EIA legislation in most of the Mekong countries can at least provide a basic foundation for regional negotiations on transboundary EIA, the general effectiveness of domestic EIA in this region remains far from satisfactory and the deficiencies of relevant legislation still needs to be improved. This is particularly true with regard to issues like consideration of alternatives, the public's right to be notified and to participate, the approval of the EIA report and the penalties applicable for violation of domestic EIA legislation. Notably, the confidentiality of information regarding international rivers and the corresponding rejection for public participation during the relevant EIA process is a major legal obstacle for China to engage in any transboundary or domestic public consultation regarding hydropower development on international rivers. In addition, whoever prepares the EIA report is highly relevant to the quality of the EIA report. According to the *EIA Law*, the developer in China has to commission the preparation of the EIA report from a competent institution approved by environmental protection agency.[184] But it is not expressly required by the legislation in Thailand, Laos and Cambodia. In Vietnam, the report can be prepared by the developer themselves or consultancy service organisations.[185] Moreover, threshold settings for projects that should be subject to EIA vary across the region. The diversity and deficiencies of the domestic EIA arrangements in the region increase the difficulties for the Mekong countries to reach consensus on a better-designed transboundary EIA document or to promote extraterritorial application of their domestic legislation with expectation of reciprocity. Although this chapter focuses on

184 《中华人民共和国环境影响评价法》 [Environmental Impact Assessment Law of the People's Republic of China] (People's Republic of China) Standing Committee of the National People's Congress, 28 October 2002, art 20.

185 *Law on Environmental Protection* (Socialist Republic of Vietnam) National Assembly, 29 November 2005, art 19.

transboundary EIA, it is argued that the enhancement of domestic legislation and implementation is vital for the effectiveness of transboundary EIA mechanism at the regional level. Another relevant issue is that the EIA procedure should be further combined with other social, cultural and economic impact assessment procedures as well. At this stage, relevant procedures often only partly exist at the domestic level. Multilateral development banks can contribute to this process by better complying with its own EIA policies or funding programs in each country to promote relevant domestic reforms. This, however, is a long process and no comprehensive remedy is available.

At the regional level, an initial question is: which existing cooperative mechanism should be used as the platform for transboundary EIA development? Under the current circumstances, the MRC is the most likely cooperative regime to adopt the transboundary EIA procedures in the near future. Similar to notification and consultation, it will probably be introduced via a non-binding procedural document. As mentioned before, the non-binding nature will add another level of uncertainty to its compliance, let alone other problems like potential ambiguity of the document and the difficulties of introducing a functional non-compliance mechanism. In addition, the lack of China's participation and the marginalisation of the donor-driven MRC increase the necessity for developing transboundary EIA procedure under other regional platforms, such as the GMS and ASEAN. Nevertheless, in light of the dominant need for economic development and the problematic domestic EIA legislation and implementation, the Mekong countries have insufficient incentives to actively introduce transboundary EIA procedures that are applicable to a wider range of environmental issues beyond only water management issues. Even if they did, it is very doubtful on whether the relevant practice would meet international standards. Currently, the promotion of transboundary EIA under the MRC should certainly be considered as a priority, especially given the urgent situation of Mekong mainstream hydropower development. But over the longer term it is the riparian states' domestic reform and political will that is going to play a fundamental role in ensuring the stable progress regarding transboundary EIA.

As discussed before, transboundary EIA can be established at two levels: namely as a basic notion and framework, or as an institution with more detailed arrangements. The former is a more realistic target for relevant negotiations under other regional platforms, while the latter may be pursued, at least partly, under the MRC regime. By arguing that the transboundary EIA has already obtained a customary status under the international environmental law can provide a powerful persuasion to urge the Mekong countries to engage in transboundary EIA practices or discussions on introducing it via regional soft law or hard law document. But there are disputes on whether its customary status has already been established or is still emerging. And this general legal status itself often only has limited impact on the effectiveness of transboundary EIA in the field.

In order to pursue more specific arrangements under the MRC regime, it is necessary to integrate transboundary EIA with the existing mechanism of notification and consultation. In addition, during the negotiations on transboundary EIA, policy makers should endeavour to put in place provisions on public participation and an improved non-compliance mechanism. Moreover, whether the future procedural document on transboundary EIA will develop any minimum standards for domestic EIA should be viewed as an important question during the formulation of the document. Although the domestic EIA legislation serves as a basic foundation for international discussions on transboundary EIA, it does not necessarily mean that countries will not make any commitment on transboundary EIA that is more stringent than the domestic counterparts. Therefore, bolder proposals on future transboundary EIA agreements should not be completely rejected. Other than enhancing the cooperation among the Mekong countries, it is beneficial to cooperate with other international organisations, regions and countries on the issue. The MRC certainly has more advantages in facilitating such broader cooperation. Last, but not least, it is important to encourage more joint research programs and piloting practices in this area.

CHAPTER 7

# Conclusions and Recommendations

## I Summary: A Procedural Framework

As a problem-oriented study, the propositions and recommendations made in this book are built upon the foundation of several mainstream or prevalent international environmental law concepts and theories. While this research derives theoretical support from sustainable development, integrated water resources management (IWRM) and existing international environmental law (particularly in terms of water law), it also identifies some of the notable gaps between theory and reality and between what is accepted international best practice and the current situation prevalent in the Mekong region. Some regional geopolitical concerns have been incorporated as well.

The study set out to identify and analyse the major environmental challenges in the Mekong region and the corresponding cooperative measures that have already been taken by countries in the Mekong region to avoid or mitigate any potential or existing negative environmental impact and to resolve transboundary dispute among riparian states. It gave most of its attention on the rapid hydropower expansion on both the mainstream and tributaries of Mekong, mainly as it is now subject to the most controversial environmental debates in the region. Other related issues include climate change, conservation of biodiversity, flooding and drought. The relatively less prominent water pollution concerns are not overlooked as well. Having examined water management regimes at both the domestic and regional levels and from the perspectives of different stakeholders such as governments, intergovernmental organisations, business investors and civil society, it is difficult to avoid the conclusion that water management in the Mekong region is largely polycentric despite efforts to promote IWRM in the region. Civil society (especially the public directly affected by water management) in these countries enjoys limited political opportunities and legal rights to significantly influence the decision-making process.

In light of the top-down decision-making traditions in the region, the one-sided emphasis on more centralised institutional structures for water management often fails to incorporate the decentralised aspects of IWRM, which are characterised by more negotiated, cooperative, coordinated and bottom-up approaches. This is especially important in the case of international rivers, for integration under such circumstances often relies on horizontal cooperation

 | DOI 10.1163/9789004266797_008

and coercion among riparian states rather than being achieved in a hierarchical manner.

Considering the difficulties and opportunities created by the polycentric features of current Mekong water governance regimes, what is urgently needed is to improve existing decision-making processes by promoting cross-boundary and cross-sectoral cooperation and coordination. Legal mechanisms to institutionalise sustainability concepts at both program and policy levels, as well as in relation to specific cases, through strategic environmental assessment (SEA) and environmental impact assessment (EIA) respectively, could offer a more realistic and constructive approach to promote IWRM in the Mekong region.

Data collection and information exchange on a regular basis are addressed in chapter three. Countries often do not explicitly claim absolute sovereignty over shared water resources located in their own territories. Rather, the reluctance to adhere to fundamental principles is often disguised by the creation of information barriers. With respect to the Mekong region, developing a basin-wide (at least in the lower Mekong basin) river monitoring network has been the focus of the information and knowledge production agenda under the Mekong River Commission (MRC).

In fact, compared to its regulatory role, the MRC does a much better job at providing technical support and information services. However, the lack of necessary technical, financial, infrastructure and human resources support from the Mekong countries remains a major problem in the Mekong region. Knowledge concerning ecosystem impact scenarios and assessments also illustrates the blurring of boundaries between politics and science. Power structures, diverging interests among stakeholders and different policy motivations all have a negative impact on the modelling and assessment process.[1]

Another major deficiency of information exchange under the MRC is the lack of formal arrangements for information sharing on domestic water management, particularly the relevant legislation, administrative arrangements and the domestic implementation of the *Mekong Agreement*. It is argued that the MRC should improve the information exchange on more localised water governance experiences and lessons, at least via a regular self-reporting system. In addition, the cooperation between the MRC, GMS and ASEAN on sharing information should be improved. Further, public participation in this mechanism can contribute to redressing the power imbalances that shape the

1 See Mira Käkönen and Philip Hirsch, 'The Anti-Politics of Mekong Knowledge Production' in François Molle, Tira Foran and Mira Käkönen (eds), *Contested Waterscapes in the Mekong Region: Hydropower, Livelihoods and Governance* (Earthscan, 2009) 333, 350.

production of knowledge.[2] However, even if the quality of information in this area can be improved, in order to really influence the decision-making process, the mechanism of information exchange and data collection needs to be further combined with other procedural mechanisms and reforms.

Compared to the information system established among four member states of the MRC (Thailand, Laos, Cambodia and Vietnam), relevant cooperation between the MRC and China is still at an initial stage. The biggest legal obstacle for China to share flow information of the Mekong River actually comes from the confidential status of many kinds of information concerning international rivers. This reflects an overly broad interpretation of protecting information for state security reasons. While the increasing domestic demand for transparency has put more pressure on the Chinese government and the current legislation for the lower Mekong countries, the only possible way to overcome this legal barrier is to achieve further agreements with China on sharing relevant information.

Prior notification and consultation on planned activities is addressed at length in chapter four. Tributary developments are completely left out of the existing mechanism under the MRC, but they may also have a significant adverse impact on other countries. The Xayaburi case illustrates the tension between the attempt to resolve the issue in a timely manner and the need for necessary information to make an informed decision. It is argued that future reforms with respect to this mechanism should focus on the issues of threshold setting, timing and time-frames, provision of information, public participation and appropriate ways to interface with the proposed EIA process. Compared to the provisions under the *UN Watercourses Convention* (allowing a maximum of one year for the notified country to reply with a minimum of six months set for consultation), the time-frame under the MRC procedural document for the whole process is indeed a very short period: notification of certain mainstream activities will automatically trigger the consultation process which should last for six months at a minimum. Existing state practice undoubtedly suggests that the consultation process is often much more protracted than the initial agreement envisages.[3]

Since international law is very ambiguous on collecting and providing information that is not yet available at the time of notification and consultation, relevant disputes are largely left to the discretion of countries themselves and can only be resolved via negotiation. Although the notified country is still

2 Ibid.

3 Patricia Birnie, Alan Boyle and Catherine Redgwell, *International Law and the Environment* (Oxford University Press, 3rd ed, 2009) 570.

subject to the general obligation to prevent harm and utilise water resources equitably and reasonably, without the support of other procedural mechanisms, such as EIA or SEA, there is ample evidence that the sole reliance on the prior notification and consultation process is often not enough to avoid or to resolve disputes in advance. The best way to evaluate adverse effects on the notified state, as argued by McCaffrey, is through a transboundary EIA or SEA, with participation of the affected public and other stakeholders.[4]

China has not formally notified or consulted with the other Mekong countries regarding its existing dams on the upper Mekong. Given notification and consultation is yet to be recognised as a customary international law and there is no pre-existing agreement between China and other Mekong countries regarding this mechanism, it is hard to argue that China violates international law by not engaging in notification and consultation with downstream states. But it is reasonable to criticise that China's behaviour does not comply with international best practice in this area and risks violating the general obligation to prevent harm and the principle of equitable utilisation.

In addition, early notification/warning is viewed as an important initial response to natural disasters and other emergencies that might cause transboundary harm. Problems regarding the effectiveness of this mechanism under the MRC mainly include: the lack of sufficient funding and training; insufficient compatibility of monitoring and modelling systems and varying risk and impact assessment technologies.[5] Further issues involve difficulties for remote communities to gain accessibility of relevant information; the lack of public participation on the operation of the warning system; insufficient consideration of the impact of tributary dam construction and operation; emerging, but immature sub-basins flood forecasting; excessive bureaucracy at the domestic level; and the lack of coordination of national flood mitigation plans. Future efforts should be made to address all of these issues.

With regard to China, support for this mechanism can be identified in China's *2007 Emergency Response Law*, which requires the Chinese government to cooperate and communicate with foreign governments and relevant international organisations regarding emergency incidents and accidents on

4 Stephen C. McCaffrey, *The Law of International Watercourses* (Oxford University Press, 2007) 474–5.

5 See Erich J. Plate and Thanongdeth Insisiengmay, *Early Warning System for the Mekong River* (2002) 9 <http://www.cws.net.cn/cwsnet/meeting-fanghong/v10101.pdf>; Guillaume Lacombe, *Effectiveness of Early Warning Systems and Monitoring Tools in the Mekong Basin* (2009) 2 <http://www.adbi.org/files/2009.06.09.cpp.day2.sess3.2.lacombe.paper.early.warning.systems.mekong.pdf>.

relevant prevention, monitoring, warning, response and aid, ex post recovery and reconstruction.[6] This domestic requirement can open a door for the development of an effective emergency notification system between China and the other Mekong countries.

Recent decades have witnessed a proliferation of non-state actors in international affairs. It has occurred against the background of the emergence of environmental human rights from a procedural perspective under both international and domestic environmental law and the growing popularity surrounding environmental deliberative democracy. Having analysed the *Aarhus Convention*, the relevant arrangements under different regional cooperative platforms in the area and the domestic circumstances in all six Mekong countries, chapter five concluded that a huge chasm still exists between what is currently occurring in the Mekong region and international best practice. In particular, the polycentric feature of water governance in the region is reflected in the piecemeal development of access to information and public participation at the regional level. The lack of homogeneity with respect to domestic legislation and the uneven pace of development among the Mekong countries provide additional challenges to address many of these issues in a regional context. Almost all of the Mekong countries are at different stages of political, social and economic reforms in their journey towards representative democracy and establishing market economies. Deliberative democracy, as a relatively new concept, remains unfamiliar to many of the Mekong countries and their citizens.

The interaction and contradictions between western and eastern cultures set the general background for the introduction of these primarily western discourses in the context of the Mekong region. Although the prevalent political theories in countries like China and Vietnam are different from that in the west, the will of the people is recognised as a major source of government legitimacy. This recognition can provide a foundation for the reformists from within the regime to promote progressive changes towards more democracy decision-making and better protection of human rights. Areas for reform include restricting or clarifying exemptions for access to information, the accessibility of information, public participation at different levels of decision-making (especially in the EIA process), the regulations on association and media and the corresponding judicial and quasi-judicial remedies.

6 《中华人民共和国突发事件应对法》 [Emergency Response Law of the People's Republic of China] National People's Congress Standing Committee, Order No 69, 30 August 2007, art 15.

Although the ultimate transformation has to be made at the domestic level, it should be noted that regional arrangements are not a mere crystallisation of domestic measures. Instead, regional efforts can be made to stimulate this process as well. The current MRC Policy on Information Disclosure only has real impact on the organisation itself rather than on member states and its current major approach of information disclosure remains inadequate from the perspective of local communities. However, the increasing transparency of the MRC itself does have some positive influences on the current restrained political space and the information available from the MRC is quite beneficial for the work of local media, academics and advocates, who can serve as bridges to link the MRC and local communities.

With regard to public participation, the so-called MRC policies on public participation in fact focus more on the participation of other stakeholders like riparian governments and business sectors. It is therefore strongly recommended that the MRC should clarify the existing confusion and ambiguity concerning public participation and institute more specific policies accordingly, or at least develop a specific section for public participation in the context of general stakeholder policy. In addition, the MRC mainly addresses participation on plans, programs and policy, but largely ignores public participation on specific development activities, thus providing very limited guidance on the decision-making involving the mainstream hydropower projects. How to link the transboundary EIA process with public participation should also be a major concern of the MRC in future.

Despite the fact that the main responsibility for transparency and public participation lies with the governmental and business sectors, the Asian Development Bank (ADB) and the World Bank should adopt more stringent measures to promote the implementations of its relevant policies by member states. The accountability of the ADB and the World Bank in ensuring its projects follow international standards for transparency and public participation should not, however, be shifted to the member states or developers. It is therefore recommended they increase lobbying and support for domestic legal reforms in this area and to initiate programs designed to specifically focus on relevant awareness raising and capacity building, including measures to facilitate the implementation of information disclosure and public participation. In addition, transparency and public participation should be incorporated into the GMS environmental protection agenda.

The application of EIA and SEA in a transboundary context can provide a valuable opportunity to involve the public and other riparian states in evaluating and discussing the likely transboundary impact of a proposed activity, plan or program. With regard to future development of SEA in the region, chapter six argues that more attention should be paid at the domestic level. The most obvious task is to legislate on SEA procedures in Thailand, Cambodia, Laos and Myanmar. However, considering the problematic history of SEA legislation and practices in China and Vietnam, even if the SEA procedure became a compulsory legal procedure in the other Mekong countries, the effectiveness of the SEA procedure will be unlikely to improve significantly in the near future. In view of the current development of hydropower projects on the lower Mekong mainstream river, a more urgent matter is to introduce a transboundary EIA procedure.

Although the existence of some forms of EIA legislation in most of the Mekong countries can at least provide a basic foundation for regional negotiations on transboundary EIA, the general effectiveness of domestic EIA in this region remains far from satisfactory and the deficiencies identified with the relevant legislation still needs to be improved. This is particularly true with regard to issues concerning the consideration of alternatives, the public's right to be notified and to participate, the approval of the EIA report and measures to secure law enforcement.

At the regional level, the promotion of transboundary EIA under the MRC should certainly be considered as a priority, especially given the urgency of Mekong mainstream hydropower development. The diversity and deficiencies of the domestic EIA arrangements in the region increase the difficulties for the Mekong countries to reach consensus on a better-designed transboundary EIA document or to promote extraterritorial application of their domestic legislation with expectation of reciprocity. It is argued that regional cooperation remains the better passway for the development of transboundary EIA in the region. Transboundary EIA can be established at two levels: namely as a basic concept framework, or as an institutionalised process with more detailed arrangements. The former is a more realistic target for relevant negotiations under other regional platforms, while the latter may be pursued, at least partly, under the MRC regime. In particular, it is necessary to integrate transboundary EIA with the mechanisms of information exchange, notification and consultation, access to information and public participation. Bolder proposals on future transboundary EIA agreements should not be completely rejected and the cooperation with other international organisations, regions and countries should be welcomed.

Post-project analysis is an important mechanism for future cooperation between China and the other Mekong countries regarding the existing upper Mekong hydropower projects. China does have relatively detailed provisions on this issue, although the public has not yet been involved in this process. Even if countries may not agree on post-project analysis, at least joint monitoring and study between China and the other Mekong countries is a possible direction to deepen the cooperation on transboundary water management. It is also prudent to combine the negotiation on post-project analysis and monitoring of these dams with the need for more accurate basin-wide flood warning and mitigation system.

## II The Effectiveness of Procedural Mechanisms

Having describe and analysed the above procedural framework, the final question one may ask is how effective these mechanisms can be in having a real and positive impact on water management in the Mekong region. The first issue to address is how to improve the implementation of these procedural arrangements. Attention in this section will first be given to the roles of hard law and soft law in managing transboundary water resources. The concepts of hard law and soft law will be reconsidered, followed by a specific analysis on how these procedural mechanisms should be introduced or improved via different documents with soft law and/or hard law features. With regard to legally-binding documents, the possibility and design of a non-compliance mechanism will be discussed as well. Then, the issue of proceduralism will be analysed, taking into account of the substantive aspects of IWRM and international environmental law.

### A *The Soft Law and Hard Law Spectrum*

As mentioned several times in earlier chapters, the strong preference for soft law approaches rather than hard law in the region raises concerns on how to secure the implementation of substantive procedural requirements. The so-called "ASEAN Way" which was analysed at length in chapter two is not a legal concept. The attempt to interpret and evaluate the "ASEAN Way" from a legal perspective using western concepts can be oversimplified and risk overlooking some of its pragmatic merits in the context of societies where the rule of law is generally weak. Some scholars have argued that the traditional "ASEAN Way" is largely ineffective in dealing with problems where members have opposing interests.[7] Meanwhile, rule-based legal reforms at the domestic and regional

7 Koh Kheng-Lian and Nicholas A. Robinson, 'Regional Environmental Governance: Examining the Association of Southeast Asian Nations (ASEAN) Model' in Daniel C. Esty and Maria H. Ivanova (eds), *Global Environmental Governance: Options and Opportunities* (Yale School of Forestry and Environmental Studies, 2002) 1, 15; Amitav Acharya, 'Ideas, Identity, and Institution-building: From the "ASEAN Way" to the "Asia-Pacific" Way' (1997) 10(3) *Pacific Review* 319, 332.

levels are stagnant in many cases.[8] Even if more stringent requirements were put in place, their implementation in reality is often unsatisfactory, as illustrated by legal reforms in Laos. Without a rule-based society and culture, even the most stringent legislation may not be able to deliver an effective outcome. However, since the overall tendency is still moving towards rule of law and democracy, taking a legal perspective in analysing how to improve the implementation of procedural mechanisms is nevertheless necessary.

Soft law and hard law are often referred to in terms of international law which interact with each other and shape international governance. As identified by Shaffer and Pollack, their definitions are fiercely debated in the existing literature.[9] A typical standard applied to differentiate them is a simple binary binding/non-binding divide.[10] According to this standard, the only hard law concerning Mekong water management is the *1995 Mekong Agreement* and the data sharing agreement between China and the MRC. Other forms of consensus are all categorised as "soft law", such as the MRC procedural documents, policies and guidelines adopted under the MRC, the GMS and other cooperative platforms. However, as mentioned in chapter two, the *Mekong Agreement* has been criticised for the fact that most parts of the document is drafted in "hortatory" language and are unable to be enforced.[11]

It is thus argued that "hard and soft law are best seen not as binary categories but rather as choices arrayed along a continuum".[12] The "hardness" of non-binding rules (the impact of pressures to conform and discursive transformations) and the "softness" of legally-binding rules (its indeterminacy and the pervasiveness of prerogative power) should not be underestimated.[13] Some scholars hold the view that "the vagueness of the terms 'hard' and 'soft' obscures a wide range of different normative characteristics of particular legal instruments, sources or materials".[14] In order to avoid the confusion, the follow-

8 See chapter two.

9 Gregory C. Shaffer and Mark A. Pollack, 'Hard vs. Soft Law: Alternatives, Complements and Antagonists in International Governance' (2010) 94 *Minnesota Law Review* 706, 712.

10 Ibid.

11 Philip Hirsch et al., 'National Interests and Transboundary Water Governance in the Mekong' (Report, University of Sydney, 2006) 26–7.

12 Shaffer and Pollack, above n 9, 716.

13 David M. Trubek and Louise G. Trubek, 'Hard and Soft Law in the Construction of Social Europe: the Role of the Open Method of Co-ordination' (2005) 11 *European Law Journal* 343, 355–61.

14 Fleur Johns et al., 'Law and the Mekong River Basin: A Socio-Legal Research Agenda on the Role of Hard and Soft Law in Regulating Transboundary Water Resources' (2010) 11(1)

ing discussion will be based on the categorisation of binding and non-binding rules. It should be noted, however, that non-binding documents can include legally-binding requirements, namely international customary rules that have acquired a "binding" status through continued usage and application by a large number of countries. However, other than the general obligation to prevent harm, the principle of equitable and reasonable utilisation and the obligation to cooperate, it is still difficult to claim that any of the specific procedural rules has obtained the similar degree of state acceptance across the world.[15]

How to integrate the considerations of both the realistic need to adapt the entrenched political and legal system and the constructive objective to improve and reshape the existing regime is a fundamental challenge facing the development of procedural arrangements in this region. Indeed, it is the "characteristics of the issue and the negotiating and institutional context in question" that should be considered as the key factor while choosing between binding and non-binding instruments.[16] In the context of the Mekong countries, the general reluctance to frame their interests in legal terms is obvious. While there is still merit in continuing to urge countries to enter into formal binding agreements with each other, it is probably more realistic and constructive to focus on the aspect of the "hardness" of non-binding documents.

In particular, some scholars have pointed out that, in the field of transboundary water management, "informal, non-binding norms may come to shape practice more effectively" than legally-binding norms.[17] This is represented by the remarkable achievement of the 1987 Rhine Action Programme compared

---

*Melbourne Journal of International Law* 154, 163; Arnold N Pronto, 'Some Thoughts on the Making of International Law' (2008) 19 *European Journal of International Law* 601, 613–4.

15 Some supporting arguments for the customary status of prior notification and consultation, notification in emergency situations or transboundary EIA are available at: Alistair Rieu-Clarke, *International Law and Sustainable Development: Lessons from the Law of International Watercourses* (International Water Association Publishing, 2006) 138; Phoebe N. Okowa, 'Procedural Obligations in International Environmental Agreements' (1996) 67 *British Yearbook of International Law* 317; David Hunter, James Salzman and Durwood Zaelke, *International Environmental Law and Policy* (Foundation Press, 3rd ed, 2007) 532; *Pulp Mills on the River Uruguay (Argentina v Uruguay) (Judgment)* [2010] ICJ Rep 14, para 101. In particular, relevant discussion concerning transboundary EIA is available in chapter six.

16 Shaffer and Pollack, above n 9, 721.

17 Stephen J. Toope, 'Formality and Informality' in Daniel Bodansky, Jutta Brunnée and Ellen Hay (eds), *The Oxford Handbook of International Environmental Law* (Oxford University Press, 2007) 107, 119.

to the less effective *1976 Rhine Chlorides Convention* and *1976 Chemical Pollution Convention*. It set out clearly defined objectives to be reached by 2000 and the ambitious political goals have been successfully translated into concrete measures and activities at the regional and local levels.[18] The success of this non-binding approach led to the adoption of the Rhine 2020 Programme in 2001. Although transboundary cooperation on the governance of the Rhine River has also benefited from the supernational governance of the European Community/Union and the more mature domestic legal and political systems, the effectiveness of the Rhine Action Programme should not be underestimated. In addition, the merits of informal communication and personal relationships are noted in the transboundary water management cooperation between the United States and Mexico.[19]

Based on some general provisions under the *Mekong Agreement*, the information exchange and data collection system and the emergency warning system under the MRC have been mainly characterised by non-binding rules, programs and policies. The progress made in the above areas is largely commendable, although certain major deficiencies are identified in chapters three and four. It should be noted, however, that the lower Mekong countries do not have major conflicts of interest in these aspects of water governance. But even in areas where countries have more diverse interests, such as hydropower development, countries have generally complied with the MRC procedural rules on notification and consultation. Difficulties and controversies surrounding the Xayaburi consultation process can be mainly attributed to the deficiencies of the MRC Procedures for Notification, Prior Consultation and Agreement itself and the sole reliance on notification and consultation to resolve transboundary disputes.

The hardness of non-binding rules could refer to the more action-oriented targets and measures; more detailed and clearer stipulations which often hard to be achieved through the legally-binding treaties; and the possibility of transforming into hard law based on its implementation. The softness of legally-binding rules often involves the ambiguity and incertitude of the provisions ("consensus often being attainable only at the price of constructive ambiguity");[20] the lack of participation of important countries (such as the

---

18 See Koos Wieriks and Anne Schulte-Wulwer-Leidig, 'Integrated Water Management for the Rhine River Basin, from Pollution Prevention to Ecosystem Improvement' (1997) 21(2) *Natural Resources Form* 151–3.

19 See chapter three, section I(B)(2).

20 Peter H. Hand, 'Institution-building to Assist Compliance with International Environmental Law: Perspectives' (1996) 56(3) *Zeitschrift für ausländisches öffentliches Recht und Völkerrecht* (*Heidelberg Journal of International Law*) 774, 776.

cases of the *1995 Mekong Agreement*; the ASEAN *Agreement on Transboundary Haze Pollution* and the *Kyoto Protocol*);[21] and the lack of a proper non-compliance mechanism to secure its implementation.

With regard to the development of procedural mechanisms in the Mekong region, it is argued that non-binding procedural rules can have very practical effects on transboundary water governance. Compared to the need to update the existing guidelines, policies and non-binding rules concerning information exchange, notification and consultation into legally-binding rules, it is probably more beneficial to deepen mutual understanding on many specific issues regarding their application in practice, review and revise them according to the recommendations provided in earlier chapters. The MRC has a comparatively better foundation in this area compared to ASEAN and the GMS.

In addition, among the procedural mechanisms that have not yet been addressed by the MRC procedural documents, there is an urgent need for a specific transboundary EIA procedure. The non-binding nature of this form of consensus is certainly one feature of softness, but the degree of ambiguity can be significantly reduced than that which can be achieved through a legally-binding treaty. The "ASEAN Way" also means that there is a good chance that countries will not commit to an obvious violation of the established procedural rules. Among the various key issues regarding transboundary EIA, it is argued that public participation and the relevant information transparency should be highlighted. Efforts on public participation at this level will likely to take a lead in promoting regional arrangements on access to information and public participation at different levels of decision-making. Meanwhile, multilateral development banks, foreign investors and other international organisations can develop action-oriented programs and policies to promote the improvement of domestic EIA and increase practice of transboundary EIA in the region. Experiences gained from this process have the potential to be crystallised into legally-binding documents.

Public participation and access to information are by far the most challenging procedural elements to be introduced into the Mekong water governance. Except for relevant developments in the transboundary EIA process, regional consensus on their application at other levels of decision-making in the Mekong countries may only be achieved via softer and more hortatory non-binding documents. As a region that is still new to environmental deliberative democracy, this kind of consensus at least represents a first step towards increasing recognition and practice of government transparency and public involvement. While it is certainly more difficult to develop regional arrangements to directly

21 China, Indonesia and the United States have not bounded by these agreements respectively.

regulate the behaviour of the riparian governments, more detailed and better designed policies should be adopted to improve the operation of regional cooperative organisations and multilateral development banks. Due to the different stages of institutional building, the MRC has more chance than the GMS in embracing further changes in this area. The loose structure of the GMS itself poses challenges for adopting specific transparency and public participation policies. But since the ADB funds many projects through the GMS, the relevant policies of the ADB can be partly applied to the GMS operation.

Considering the fact that the GMS is becoming less ADB-driven and more owned by the Mekong countries, relevant policy-making should be borne in mind in future institutional building. In addition, although the ASEAN Human Rights Commission has been criticised for a lack of real influence, its existence and operation has the potential to provide some additional political opportunities on relevant discussions and practices. It is important for the commission to consider the right to know and to participate as a priority issue among various human rights agendas.

With regard to cooperation between China and the other Mekong countries, it is more likely that China will continue to engage with the lower Mekong countries on the governance of the Mekong mainly via non-binding approaches and mechanisms. In particular, increasing pilot practices and research concerning these procedural mechanisms should be highlighted in future efforts to enhance cooperation. For example, opportunities like the ongoing negotiations on information exchange and conducting further improvement projects in order to facilitate navigation should be noted.

The *Mekong Agreement* provides a vivid example concerning the softness of legally-binding rules. In addition to the need to revise the Agreement and involve China in the future, a relatively less controversial approach that can be applied to enhance its implementation is the establishment of a self-reporting system among the member states. China and Myanmar can prepare reports as the dialogue partners of the MRC. Further, along with the ongoing legal reforms among the existing members of the MRC, the provisions of the *Mekong Agreement* should be further incorporated into its domestic legislation. The proliferation of procedural non-binding rules, guidelines and action plans can also contribute to the implementation and have the potential to eventually evolve into concrete legal obligations.

Consultation remains the primary method used in the Mekong region to resolve disputes.[22] A similar approach was also adopted by China when deal-

22 *Agreement on the Cooperation for the Sustainable Development of the Mekong River Basin*, opened for signature 5 April 1995, 2069 UNTS I-35844 (entered into force 5 April 1995) arts 18(c), 24(f), 34, 35.

ing with transboundary water issues with Russia and Kazakhstan. In an area where the non-interference principle has dominated diplomatic relations and foreign policy, it is extremely difficult for the Mekong countries to relinquish their sovereignty to any expert-based compliance monitoring mechanisms or international judicial system. Behind this "soft" *Mekong Agreement*, resides the hard politics that ultimately influences the decision-making. The fact that law is largely subordinate to politics at both the domestic and regional levels in the region demonstrates that there is still a long way to go to establish a proper non-compliance mechanism according to the mainstream theory under international law.[23]

Nevertheless, it is suggested that the immature domestic judicial systems may provide some coercive influence on the implementation of the *Mekong Agreement* and relevant domestic legislation at the domestic level. An attempt to challenge the Thai government's involvement in the Xayaburi Dam in a Thai court is discussed in chapters four and five. China recently revised its *Civil Procedure Act*, which added a few provisions on public interest litigation and recognised the right of civil society organisations to participate.[24] Due to the unresolved political and legal reforms in the region, the right to access to justice remains very constrained. But future developments in this respect can provide more opportunities to challenge the behaviour of both the business sector and governments on the utilisation and management of the Mekong water resources.

Compared to the period where no specific law existed in the region on how to resolve disputes and cultivate cooperation, the existence and proliferation of non-binding documents and procedural mechanisms across the Mekong region can certainly be considered constructive progress. Simply calling for more legally-binding rules in this area, however, is more easily said than done. Along with the gradual, but not necessarily sequential process of transformation, from the status of no existing laws to non-binding rules and legally-binding obligations, a more fundamental and challenging question should be how to interpret the "ASEAN Way" from a more pragmatic legal perspective.

---

23 See generally Durwood Zaelke, Donald Kaniaru and Eva Kružíková (eds), *Making Law Work: Environmental Compliance and Sustainable Development* (Cameron May Ltd, International Law Publishers, 2005) vols 1, 2.

24 《全国人民代表大会常务委员会关于修改〈中华人民共和国民事诉讼法〉的决定》[Decision of the Standing Committee of the National People's Congress to Revise the Civil Procedure Act] (31 August 2012) 中国政府网 [The Official Web Portal of the Central People's Government of the PRC] <http://www.gov.cn/flfg/2012-09/01/content_2214662.htm>.

There are different degrees of softness and hardness in the diverse approaches generally characterised as the "ASEAN Way". Among all of the informal rules in the region, some of them are in a written form, while others may remain unspoken or not known to the majority. Many of them have not been subject to serious studies. Therefore, this study calls for more focus and attention from legal and social researchers on the legal implications of the so-called phenomenon of the "ASEAN Way", bearing in mind the proposition that hard law and soft law can be considered as a continuum rather than binary categories as well as the very complicated political, economic and social norms endemic to the countries of this region. Currently, one innovative research project has been initiated in this aspect.[25]

### B *The Process and Substance of International Environmental Law*

Another issue concerning the effectiveness of procedural aspects of problem-solving is to what extent these procedures can have a real impact on resolving the substantive dispute among riparian states and lead to a sustainable outcome of water governance. This study is largely derived from a procedural point of view. The valuable regulatory implications of procedures are analysed in detail in chapter one. In addition to inherent procedural values, these mechanisms are also directed towards substantive aspects of IWRM. However, more research concerning these aspects of IWRM is needed in order to develop appropriate legal criteria to reconcile the often competing objectives of promoting both environmental protection and economic development in specific circumstances.

To date, existing standards applied to evaluate the decision-making outcomes remain less specific to provide sufficient guidance and regulation. Procedural rules may be unable to guarantee that a fair and environmental-friendly outcome can be achieved, but the interpretation of IWRM and international environmental obligations from a procedural perspective can provide a series of institutional arrangements that are applicable to different circumstances. In general, increasing development of procedural rules in the Mekong region can enhance commitments to promote equitable and reasonable utilisation of the Mekong water resources and avoid any major transboundary impact on other states.

It should be noted that relevant substantive obligations at the domestic level can have significant influences on government decision-making as well. While the substantive rules concerning international water law is still controversial, domestic obligations on governments and the business sector

25 See Johns et al., above n 14, 154–74.

to achieve certain environmental protection objectives can be used to partly supplement the failure to adopt and apply international environmental principles. As demonstrated in the earlier chapters, the uncoordinated development of different procedures will have a negative impact on the effectiveness of a single mechanism. However, the downside of expanding the procedural framework is not without risk and may lead to excessive rigidity, ritualism and increasing bureaucracy.

## III Possible Perspectives for Future Research

It was impossible to deal with all of the legal, political and economic issues related to governance of the water resources in the Mekong region due to restrictions on the length of this book and many issues will have to be left for future research.

There are several broader and more fundamental theoretical challenges underlying the Mekong water governance debate. Issues such as environmental human rights, environmental justice, general environmental principles, sustainable development, IWRM, international water law theory and domestic and international compliance theories will have a profound impact on the future development of environmental law and can provide new dimensions and discourses to shape and influence water governance in the Mekong region.

Questions remain such as: how to introduce, promote and understand environmental justice in the Mekong region; how to resolve the existing lack of reciprocity in the region's water governance policy-making and practice; what is the relationship between state sovereignty and environmental human rights; how to reach the balance and reconciliation required by the concept of sustainable development and the inviolability of human right, to name a few.

Given its inherent complexity, a comprehensive study of Mekong water governance requires further research and analysis from geopolitical, social, economic, scientific and technological perspectives. Questions that spring to mind include, but not limited to, are: how do geopolitical concerns influence water-related decision-making in the region? What other options are available to reduce poverty in the region other than hydropower expansion? How to reduce and respond to scientific uncertainty concerning the hydropower development and climate change in the Mekong region?

While legal scholars often tend to consider the impact of laws on different stakeholders, an interesting reverse perspective is to consider the different influences of governments, of business and of civil society stakeholders in shaping the rules on the Mekong water governance. In particular, little attention has historically has been paid to the influence of civil society. Some researchers have recently begun to frame new research topics from this perspective,[26] but more studies await to be conducted.

The resolution of environmental issues in the region also depends on future developments with respect to representative and deliberative democracy, the rule of law (particularly with respect to access to justice) and the transition to market economies. The profound differences in cultures between the east and west will undoubtedly play a significant role in this process.

This study relies more on doctrinal legal research and comparative analysis approaches rather than empirical research methodology. More country-specific and mechanism-specific case studies should be done in the future to validate the conclusions made in this book and provide a deeper understanding on how to promote and implement procedural reforms in practice.

This study begins with an attempt to provide some solutions to the complicated Mekong water governance issues. While many recommendations have been made from a procedural perspective, this research also reveals many other questions that cannot yet be resolved or answered. Therefore, it does not mark the end of my efforts to understand and contribute to the resolution of the problems identified and reflected in the current Mekong water governance. Rather, this book marks only the beginning of my increasing interest in someday witnessing sustainable governance of the Mekong River basin and the people living along this beautiful and generous river.

---

26 See Yumiko Yasuda, 'Institutional Influence on NGO Advocacy: Comparative Case Studies of Xayaburi Dam Advocacy' (Speech delivered at the Southeast Asia Seminar Series, University of Sydney, 7 September 2012).

# Bibliography


Acharya, Amitav, 'Ideas, Identity, and Institution-building: From the "ASEAN Way" to the "Asia-Pacific" Way' (1997) 10(3) *Pacific Review* 319.

*Act on Establishment of Administrative Courts and Administrative Court Procedure* (Kingdom of Thailand) National Assembly, 10 October 1999.

Agarwal, Anil et al., 'Integrated Water Resources Management' (TAC Background Papers No. 4, Global Water Partnership Technical Advisory Committee, 2000).

《中华人民共和国政府和俄罗斯联邦政府关于预防和消除紧急情况合作协定》 [Agreement between China and Russia regarding Cooperation on Prevention and Elimination of Emergency Situations] (21 March 2006) <http://www.fsou.com/redirect/index.asp?url=http://vip.chinalawinfo.com/newlaw2002/slc/slc.asp?db=eag&gid=100669464>.

*Agreement between the United States of America and the United Mexican States on Cooperation for the Protection and Improvement of the Environment in the Border Area*, signed 14 August 1983, 1352 UNTS 67 (entered into force 16 February 1984).

*Agreement on Commercial Navigation on Lancang-Mekong River among the Governments of the People's Republic of China, the Lao People's Democratic Republic, the Union of Myanmar and the Kingdom of Thailand* (signed and entered into force 20 April 2000).

*Agreement on the Cooperation for the Sustainable Development of the Mekong River Basin*, opened for signature 5 April 1995, 2069 UNTS I-35844 (entered into force 5 April 1995).

《中华人民共和国环境保护法修正案（草案二次审议稿）》 [Amendment of Environmental Protection Law (Draft for Second Reading)] (17 July 2013) 中国人大网 [National People's Congress of the PRC] <http://www.npc.gov.cn/npc/xinwen/lfgz/flca/2013-07/17/content_1801189.htm>.

Anstis, Siena, *Cambodia's Troubling NGO & Associations Law* (11 May 2011) <http://siena-anstis.com/wp-content/uploads/2011/05/11/cambodias-troubling-ngo-associations-law/>.

Antara News, *Indonesia to Ratify ASEAN Agreement on Trans-boundary Haze Pollution* (7 March 2011) <http://www.antaranews.com/en/news/68888/indonesia-to-ratify-asean-agreement-on-trans-boundary-haze-pollution>.

Apirumanekul, Chusit, 'Flood Forecasting and Early Warning System in Mekong River Commission' (Speech delivered at the 4th Annual Flood Forum, Siem Reap, 18–19 May 2006) <http://ns1.mrcmekong.org/download/free_download/AFF-4/session4/4-Flood_Forecasting_and_Warning_in_MRC.pdf>.

Arnstein, Sherry R., 'A Ladder of Citizen Participation' (1969) 35(4) *AIP Journal* 216.

Article 19, *Vietnam: Article 19 Assists with Drafting Freedom of Information Law* (11 May 2009) <http://www.article19.org/data/files/pdfs/press/vietnam-article-19-assists-with-drafting-freedom-of-information-law.pdf>.

ASEAN, *ASEAN Charter Enters into Force Next Month* (15 November 2008) <http://www.asean.org/news/item/asean-charter-enters-into-force-next-month-bangkok-15-november-2008>.

———, *Basic Framework of ASEAN-Mekong Basin Development Cooperation* (17 June 1996) <http://www.asean.org/communities/asean-economic-community/category/overview-16>.

———, *Joint Media Statement of the 11th Ministerial Meeting of the ASEAN-Mekong Basin Development Cooperation* (16 August 2009) <http://www.asean.org/news/asean-statement-communiques/item/joint-media-statement-of-the-11th-ministerial-meeting-of-the-asean-mekong-basin-development-cooperation-ambdc-bangkok-16-august-2009>.

ASEAN Environment, *An Overview on ASEAN Environmental Cooperation* <http://environment.asean.org/about-us-2/>.

Asia Development Bank, 'Lao People's Democratic Republic: Environment and Social Program' (Progress Report, Asian Development Bank, 2006).

———, 'Civil Society Briefs: Cambodia' (Briefs, Asian Development Bank, 2011).

———, 'Civil Society Briefs: Lao People's Democratic Republic' (Briefs, Asian Development Bank, 2011).

———, 'Civil Society Briefs: Thailand' (Briefs, Asian Development Bank, 2011).

———, 'Civil Society Briefs: Vietnam' (Briefs, Asian Development Bank, 2011).

———, 'Environmental Assessment Guidelines' (Guidelines, Asian Development Bank, 2003).

———, 'Midterm Review of the Greater Mekong Subregion Strategic Framework (2002–2012)' (Report, Asian Development Bank, 2007).

———, 'Public Communications Policy 2011: Disclosure and Exchange of Information' (Policy Document, 2011).

———, 'Safeguard Policy Statement' (Policy Paper, Asian Development Bank, 2009).

———, 'Strengthening Participation for Development Results: An Asian Development Bank Guide to Participation' (Guidelines, Asian Development Bank, 2012).

———, *ADB and Civil Society: Overview* <http://www.adb.org/site/ngos/overview>.

———, *ADB Public Communications Policy Review 2010: PCP Consultation Workshop Summary* (*PRC Resident Mission, ADB*) (6 July 2010) <http://www.adb.org/sites/default/files/prc-consultation-pcp.pdf>.

———, *Civil Society Participation* <http://www.adb.org/site/ngos/civil-society-participation>.

———, *Consultation Workshops* <http://www.adb.org/site/disclosure/policy-background-history/consultation-workshops>.

———, *Consultations on ADB's Public Communications Policy: PCP Consultation Workshop Summary (Nongovernment Organizations) (Cambodia Resident Mission)* (5 July 2010) <http://www.adb.org/sites/default/files/cam-consultation-cso-pcp.pdf>.

———, *Environmental Assessment Guidelines* (2003) <http://www.adb.org/sites/default/files/pub/2003/Environmental_Assessment_Guidelines.pdf>.

———, *External Comments and ADB Response* <http://www.adb.org/site/disclosure/policy-background-history/comments-external-stakeholders>.

———, *Greater Mekong Subregion* (22 July 2011) <http://www.adb.org/gms/>.

———, *Greater Mekong Subregion: Overview* <http://beta.adb.org/countries/gms/overview>.

———, *Key Recommendations from External Stakeholders on the Second Consultation Draft (November 2010) of the Public Communications Policy (PCP) and ADB's Response* (16 February 2011) <http://www.adb.org/sites/default/files/external-comments-2nd-draft_0.pdf>.

———, *Key Recommendations from External Stakeholders on the First Consultation Draft (June 2010) of the Public Communications Policy (PCP) and ADB's Response* (26 November 2010) <http://www.adb.org/sites/default/files/external-comments-1st-draft.pdf>.

———, *Project Database* <http://www.adb.org/Projects/summaries.asp?query=&browse=1&mode=1&ctry=LAO&sctr=3200&sctr=3800&year=ALL>.

———, *Song Bung 4 Hydropower Project* <http://www.adb.org/projects/36352-013/main>.

Aung, Hia Tun, *Myanmar Shelves $3.6 Billion Mega Dam, Officials Say* (30 September 2011) <http://www.reuters.com/article/2011/09/30/us-myanmar-dam-idUSTRE78T10H20110930>.

Australia and New Zealand Banking Group Limited, *ANZ Outlines New Regional Growth Focus in Vietnam, Cambodia and Laos* (2 March 2010) <http://media.corporate-ir.net/media_files/irol/24/248677/mediareleases/2010/100302-ANZ-outlines-new-regional-growth-focus-in-Vietnam-+Cambodia-and-Laos.pdf>.

Australian Government Aid Program, *GMS Ministerial Conference Statement—Australia—20 August 2010* (2010) <http://www.adb.org/documents/events/2010/16th-gms-ministerial-conference/16th-MC-statement-AusAID.pdf>.

Badenoch, Nathan, 'Transboundary Environmental Governance: Principles and Practice in Mainland Southeast Asia' (Report, World Resources Institute, 2002).

Baird, Ian G., 'Best Practices in Compensation and Resettlement for Large Dams: The Case of the Planned Lower Sesan 2 Hydropower Project in Northeastern Cambodia' (Report, River Coalition in Cambodia, 2009).

Bangkok Post, *China to Provide Water Data on Dams* (2010) <http://www.bangkokpost.com/news/asia/34970/china-to-provide-water-data-on-dams>.

Banisar, David, 'Freedom of Information around the World 2006' (Report, Privacy International, 2006).

Baran, Eric et al., 'Review of the Fish and Fisheries Aspects in the Feasibility Study and the Environmental Impact Assessment of the Proposed Xayaburi Dam' (Report, World Wildlife Fund, 2011).

BBC News, *'Text Protest' Blocks China Plant* (30 May 2007) <http://news.bbc.co.uk/2/hi/asia-pacific/6704359.stm>.

———, *Burma Abolishes Media Censorship* (20 August 2012) <http://www.bbc.co.uk/news/world-asia-19315806>.

———, *Burma Sets up Human Rights Commission* (6 September 2011) <http://www.bbc.co.uk/news/world-asia-pacific-14807362>.

———, *Burma's Aung San Suu Kyi Wins By-election: NLD Party* (1 April 2012) <http://www.bbc.co.uk/news/world-asia-17577620>.

———, *China Morning Round-Up: Shifang Protest* (4 July 2012) <http://www.bbc.co.uk/news/world-asia-china-18700819>.

Birnie, Patricia, Boyle, Alan and Redgwell, Catherine, *International Law and the Environment* (Oxford University Press, 3rd ed, 2009).

Biswas, Asit K., 'Integrated Water Resources Management: A Reassessment' (2004) 29(2) *Water International* 248.

Bonzon, Yves, 'Institutionalizing Public Participation in WTO Decision Making: Some Conceptual Hurdles and Avenues' (2008) 11(4) *Journal of International Economic Law* 751.

Both ENDS, *The ADB-GMS Support for Hydropower Dams and Power Grid: ADB and the Greater Mekong Subregion Program* <http://www.bothends.org/uploaded_files/hydropower-FINAL-1.pdf>.

Boulapha, Chanthanet and Lyle, Clive, 'Forming the Nam Ngum River Basin Committee' (Paper No. 35, Centre for River Basin Organizations and Management Small Publications Series, 2011).

Bourne, Charles B., 'Procedure in the Development of International Drainage Basins' (1972) 22 *University of Toronto Law Journal* 172.

Boyle, Alan, 'Developments in the International Law of Environmental Impact Assessments and their Relation to the Espoo Convention' (2011) 20(3) *Review of European Community & International Environmental Law* 227.

———, 'The Gabcikovo-Nagymaros Case: New Law in Old Bottles' (1997) 8 *Yearbook of International Environmental Law* 13.

Browder, Greg, 'An Analysis of the Negotiations for the 1995 Mekong Agreement' (2000) 5 *International Negotiations* 237.

Bunthan, Ngo, *The Review of Current Situation of Water Resources Management and the Role of Agricultural Education in Cambodia* (2005) University of Tsukuba <http://www.nourin.tsukuba.ac.jp/~tasae/2005/Cambodia.pdf>.

水利部综合事业局 [Bureau of Comprehensive Development of the Ministry of Water Resources],《中哈利用和保护跨界河流联合委员会第四次会议在阿拉木图召开》[Fourth Conference of the Joint Committee between China and Kazakhstan on Utilisation and Protection of Transboundary Rivers Held in Alma-Ata] (7 November 2006) <http://www.zhsyj.org.cn/zwgk/ywdt/19893.html>.

Bureekul, Thawilwadee, 'Access to Environmental Justice and Public Participation in Thailand' in Andrew Harding (ed), *Access to Environmental Justice: A Comparative Study* (Martinus Nijhoff Publishers, 2007) 271.

蔡定剑主编 [Cai, Dingjian (ed)],《公众参与：风险社会的制度建设》[Public Participation: Constructing a Framework for the 'Risk Society'] (法律出版社 [Law Press · China], 2009).

Cambodian Centre for Human Rights, 'Freedom of Information in Cambodia: A Right to Know or a Culture of Secrecy?' (Report, Cambodian Centre for Human Rights, 2012).

Cambodian League for the Promotion and Defense of Human Rights, 'Draft Law on Association & NGOs Cambodian Civil Society under Threat' (Briefing Paper, Cambodian League for the Promotion and Defense of Human Rights, 2010).

公众参与研究与支持中心 [Centre for Public Participation Studies and Supports],《中国行政透明度报告·2009（摘要）》[The 2009 Report on Chinese Administration Transparency (Abstract)] (2010) <http://www.cppss.cn/news_body.asp?id=808>.

长江水利委员会 [Changjiang Water Resources Commission],《单位简介》[Introduction of CWRC] <http://node.cjw.com.cn/cjwintro/cjw.asp>.

陈丽晖，何大明 [Chen, Lihui and He, Daming],《澜沧江-湄公河水电梯级开发的生态影响》[The Ecological Impact of Lancang-Mekong Cascade Hydropower Development] (2009) 55(5) 地理学报 *ACTA Grographica Sinica* 576.

陈义龙 [Chen, Yilong],《纪实：中俄跨界河流污染事件处置》[Report: China and Russia Respond to Transboundary Water Pollution Accidents] (20 June 2009) 中国价值 [China Value] <http://www.chinavalue.net/Finance/Article/2009-6-20/181849.html>.

Chenoweth, Jonathan L. and Feitelson, Eran, 'Analysis of Factors Influencing Data and Information Exchange in International River Basins' (2001) 26(4) *Water International* 499.

《中国-东盟注重云南生态，搭建环保合作平台》[China and ASEAN Set up Platform for Environmental Cooperation: Attention Paid to the Ecosystem in Yunnan Province], 新华社 [Xinhua News Agency] (11 June 2010) <http://www.yn.xinhuanet.com/newscenter/2010-06/11/content_20043796.htm>.

China Briefing, *China's Borders* <http://www.china-briefing.com/news/specialreport/chinas-borders>.

《中国在湄公河的水电开发将承受更大国际压力》 [China's Dam Construction on the Upper Mekong Faces Increasing International Pressure], 中国经营网 [China Business] (21 April 2011) <http://www.cb.com.cn/economy/2011_0421/201694.html>.

华能集团 [China Huaneng Group], 《华能澜沧江上游水电有限公司》 [Huaneng Upstream Lancang River Hydropower Co., LTD] (17 October 2010) <http://www.chng.com.cn/n93521/n93834/c95347/content.html>.

中国河流网 [China River], 《水电地图》 [Hydropower Map] <http://www.river.org.cn/map.aspx>.

China-ASEAN Environmental Cooperation Centre, *China-ASEAN Strategy on International Environmental Cooperation* <http://www.chinaaseanenv.org/english/events/271416.shtml>.

Chinese Research Academy of Environmental Sciences, *Environmental Impact Statement for Hunchun Border Economic Cooperation Zone* (2000) <http://www.tumenprogram.org/news.php?id=375>.

Chompunth, Chutarat, *An Evaluation of the Public Participation Practice in Environmental Development Projects in Thailand: A Case Study of the Hin Krut Power Plant Project* (PhD Thesis, University of East Anglia, 2011).

Civil Society International, *What is Civil Society* <http://www.civilsocietyinternational.org/whatisCS.htm>.

Cohen, Joshua, 'Deliberation and Democratic Legitimacy' in James Bohman and William Rehg (eds) *Deliberative Democracy: Essays on Reason and Politics* (MIT Press, 1997).

Commission for Environmental Cooperation, *Full-Text of Proposed North American Transboundary Environmental Impact Assessment Agreement Now On-Line* (1997) <http://www.cec.org/Page.asp?PageID=122&ContentID=1906&SiteNodeID=366>.

Conference of Rhine Ministers, *Living and Linking Rhine—Common Challenge of a Watershed* (18 October 2007) International Commission for the Protection of the Rhine <http://www.iksr.org/fileadmin/user_upload/Dokumente_en/MIN07-02e.pdf>.

*Constitution of the Kingdom of Cambodia* (Kingdom of Cambodia) Constitutional Assembly, 21 September 1993.

*Constitution of the Kingdom of Thailand 1997* (Kingdom of Thailand).

*Constitution of the Kingdom of Thailand 2007* (Kingdom of Thailand).

*Constitution of the Lao People's Democratic Republic* (Lao People's Democratic Republic) National Assembly, 6 May 2003.

《中华人民共和国宪法》 [Constitution of the People's Republic of China] (People's Republic of China) National People's Congress, 4 December 1982.

Constitutional Court of the Kingdom of Thailand, *Powers and Duties of the Constitutional Court* <http://www.constitutionalcourt.or.th/dmdocuments/Powers%20and%20Duties%20of%20the%20Constitutional%20Court.pdf>.

*Convention on Access to Information, Public Participation in Decision-making and Access to Justice in Environmental Matters*, opened for signature 25 June 1998, 2161 UNTS 447 (entered into force 10 September 1997).

*Convention on Cooperation for the Protection and Sustainable Use of the Danube River*, signed 29 June 1994, ROD 21997A1212(03) (31997D0825) (entered into force in 22 October 1998).

*Convention on Environmental Impact Assessment in a Transboundary Context*, opened for signature 25 February 1991, 1989 UNTS 309 (entered into force 10 September 1997).

*Convention on the Law of the Non-navigational Uses of International Watercourses*, UN GAOR 51/229, 51st sess, Supp No 49, UN Doc A/51/869 (21 May 1997).

*Convention on the Protection and Use of Transboundary Watercourses and International Lakes*, opened for signature 17 March 1992, 1936 UNTS 269 (entered into force 6 October 1996).

*Convention on the Protection of the Rhine* [2000] OJ L 289/31.

*Convention on the Transboundary Effects of Industrial Accidents*, opened for signature 17 March 1992, 2105 UNTS 457 (entered into force 19 April 2000).

《中华人民共和国政府和哈萨克斯坦共和国政府关于利用和保护跨界河流的合作协定》[Cooperation Agreement between China and Kazakhstan on the Utilisation and Protection of Transboundary Rivers], signed 12 September 2001 (entered into force 23 September 2002).

《中华人民共和国政府和俄罗斯联邦政府关于合理利用和保护跨界水的协定》[Cooperation Agreement between China and Russia on the Reasonable Utilisation and Protection of Transboundary Waters] (2008) 外交部 [Ministry of Foreign Affairs of the People's Republic of China] <http://www.fmprc.gov.cn/mfa_chn/ziliao_611306/tytj_611312/tyfg_611314/t708160.shtml>.

Cooperation Committee for Cambodia, 'NGO Contributions to Cambodia's Development 2004–2009' (Report, Cooperation Committee for Cambodia, 2010).

*Council Decision of 12 December 1977 Establishing a Common Procedure for the Exchange of Information on the Quality of Surface Fresh Water in the Community* [1977] OJ L 334/29.

*Council Directive 79/869/EEC of 9 October 1979 concerning the Methods of Measurement and Frequencies of Sampling and Analysis of Surface Water Intended for the Abstraction of Drinking Water in the Member States* [1979] OJ L 271/44.

*Council Directive 85/337/EEC of 27 June 1985 on the Assessment of the Effects of Certain Public and Private Projects on the Environment* [1985] OJ L 175/40.

*Council Directive 96/82/EC of 9 December 1996 on the Control of Major-Accident Hazards Involving Dangerous Substances* [1996] OJ L 10/13.

*Council Directive 97/11/EC of 3 March 1997 Amending Directive 85/337/EEC on the Assessment of the Effects of Certain Public and Private Projects on the Environment* [1997] OJ L 73/5.

Craik, Neil, 'Transboundary Environmental Impact Assessment in North America: Obstacles and Opportunities' in Kees Bastmeijer and Timo Koivurova (eds), *Theory and Practice of Transboundary Environmental Impact Assessment* (Martinus Nijhoff Publishers, 2008) 93.

———, *The International Law of Environmental Impact Assessment* (Cambridge University Press, 2008).

Cronin, Richard P. and Hamlin, Timothy, 'Mekong Tipping Point: Hydropower Dams, Human Security and Regional Stability' (Report, Henry L. Stimson Centre, 2010).

Davidsen, Pål Arne, 'Between Rhetoric and Reality—A Critical Account of Stakeholder Participation in Decision Making in the Mekong River Basin' in Anton Earle and Daniel Malzbender (eds), *Stakeholder Participation in Transboundary Water Management—Selected Case Studies* (InWEnt—Capacity Building International, 2006) 131.

Davis, L. Waldron, 'Reversing the Flow: International Law and Chinese Hydropower Development on the Headwaters of the Mekong River' (2006) 19 *New York International Law Review* 1.

《全国人大法律委员会关于<中华人民共和国水法（修订草案）>修改情况的汇报》[Debriefing of National People's Congress Standing Committee on the Revision of Water Law of the People's Republic of China] (26 April 2002) 中华人民共和国全国人民代表大会常务委员会公报 [Gazette of the Standing Committee of the National People's Congress of the People's Republic of China] <http://www.npc.gov.cn/wxzl/gongbao/2002-10/22/content_5301025.htm>.

《全国人民代表大会常务委员会关于修改〈中华人民共和国民事诉讼法〉的决定》[Decision of the Standing Committee of the National People's Congress to Revise the Civil Procedure Act] (31 August 2012) 中国政府网 [The Official Web Portal of the Central People's Government of the PRC] <http://www.gov.cn/flfg/2012-09/01/content_2214662.htm>.

*Decree on Associations* (Lao People's Democratic Republic) Prime Minister's Office, 29 April 2009.

*Decree on Environmental Impact Assessment* (Lao People's Democratic Republic) Prime Minister's Office, 18 February 2010.

Department of Energy Business, *19th November 2012—Statement of the Government of Lao PDR on Xayaburi Hydropower Project* (2012) <http://www.poweringprogress.org/index.php?option=com_content&view=article&id=947:19th-november-2012-statement-of-the-government-of-lao-pdr-on-xayaburi-hydropower-project&catid=85:press-releases&Itemid=50>.

Department of Natural Resources Assessment and Environmental Data Management, 'Cambodia Environment Outlook' (Report, Ministry of Environment, Kingdom of Cambodia, 2009).

Dictionary.com's 21st Century Lexicon, *Civil Society* <http://dictionary.reference.com/browse/civil+society>.

*Directive 2001/42/EC of the European Parliament and of the Council of 27 June 2001 on the Assessment of the Effects of Certain Plans and Programmes on the Environment* [2001] OJ L 197/30.

*Directive 2003/35/EC of the European Parliament and of the Council of 26 May 2003 Providing for Public Participation in Respect of the Drawing up of Certain Plans and Programmes relating to the Environment and Amending with Regard to Public Participation and Access to Justice Council Directives 85/337/EEC and 96/61/EC* [2003] OJ L 156/17.

*Directive 2007/60/EC of the European Parliament and of the Council of 23 October 2007 on the Assessment and Management of Flood Risks* [2007] OJ L 288/27.

*Directive 2009/31/EC of the European Parliament and of the Council of 23 April 2009 on the Geological Storage of Carbon Dioxide and Amending Council Directive 85/337/EEC, European Parliament and Council Directives 2000/60/EC, 2001/80/EC, 2004/35/EC, 2006/12/EC, 2008/1/EC and Regulation (EC) No 1013/2006 (Text with EEA Relevance)* [2009] OJ L 140/114.

*Directive 2011/92/EU of the European Parliament and of the Council of 13 December 2011 on the Assessment of the Effects of Certain Public and Private Projects on the Environment (Codification) (Text with EEA Relevance)* [2011] OJ L 26/1.

Dore, John and Yu, Xiaogang, 'Yunnan Hydropower Expansion: Update on China's Energy Industry Reforms & the Nu, Lancang & Jinsha Hydropower Dams' (Working Paper, Chiang Mai University's Unit for Social and Environmental Research and Green Watershed, 2004).

Dore, John, Yu, Xiaogang and Li, Kevin Yuk-shing, 'China's Energy Reforms and Hydropower Expansion in Yunnan' in Louis Lebel et al. (eds), *Democratizing Water Governance in the Mekong* (Mekong Press, 2007) 55.

Dunn, Bruce et al., 'Vietnam: Strategic Environmental Assessment on the Quang Nam Hydropower Plan' in OECD (ed), *Strategic Environmental Assessment in Development Practice: A Review of Recent Experience* (OECD Publishing, 2012) 29.

Dunoff, Jeffrey L., 'Public Participation in the Trade Regime: of Litigation, Frustration, Agitation and Legitimation' (2004) 56 *Rutgers Law Review* 961.

Durbach, Andrea, Renshaw, Catherine and Byrnes, Andrew, "'A Tongue but No Teeth?': The Emergence of a Regional Human Rights Mechanism in the Asia Pacific Region" (2009) 31 *Sydney Law Review* 211.

Elliott, Lorraine, 'ASEAN and Environmental Cooperation: Norms, Interests and Identity' (2003) 16(1) *Pacific Review* 29.

Email from Daniel King to Qi Gao, 21 February 2011.

《中华人民共和国突发事件应对法》 [Emergency Response Law of the People's Republic of China] National People's Congress Standing Committee, Order No 69, 30 August 2007.

*Enhancement and Conservation of National Environmental Quality Act* (Kingdom of Thailand) National Assembly, 29 March 1992.

《中华人民共和国环境影响评价法》[Environmental Impact Assessment Law of the People's Republic of China] (People's Republic of China) Standing Committee of the National People's Congress, 28 October 2002.

*Environmental Law Guidelines and Principles on Shared Natural Resources*, UN Doc A/33/25 (May 19, 1978).

*Environmental Protection Law* (Lao People's Democratic Republic) National Assembly, 3 April 1999.

Environmental Resources Management, 'Guidance on EIA Scoping' (Guiding Document, European Commission, 2001).

European Commission, 'Report from the Commission on the application and effectiveness of the EIA Directive (Directive 85/337/EEC, as Amended by Directives 97/11/EC and 2003/35/EC)' (Report, European Commission, 2009).

———, 'Report from the Commission to the European Parliament and the Council on the Application and Effectiveness of the EIA Directive (Directive 85/337/EEC as amended by Directive 97/11/EC): How Successful are the Member States in Implementing the EIA Directive' (Report, European Commission, 2003).

———, *Interesting Links concerning the Water Framework Directive* <http://ec.europa.eu/environment/water/water-framework/links/index_en.htm>.

Fall, Aboubacar and Cassar, Angela, 'Improving Governance and Public Participation in International Watercourse Management: Experience of the African Development Bank in the Senegal River Basin' in Carl Bruch et al. (eds), *Public Participation in the Governance of International Freshwater Resources* (United Nations University, 2005) 216.

*Feasibility Study on Tumen River Water Protection*, Tumen Programme <http://tumenprogramme.org/?info-612-1.html>.

Fernandez, Linda, 'Transboundary Water Management along the U.S.-Mexico Border' in Renan-Ulrich Goetz and Dolors Berga (eds), *Frontiers in Water Resource Economics* (Springer, 2006) 153.

Findley, Roger W. and Farber, Daniel A., *Environmental Law in a Nutshell* (West Publishing, 2000).

Fitzmaurice, Malgosia, 'Some Reflections on Public Participation in Environmental Matters as a Human Right in International Law' (2002) 2 *Non-state Actors and International Law* 1.

Foran, Tira and Manorom, Kanokwan, 'Pak Mun Dam: Perpetually Contested?' in François Molle, Tira Foran and Mira Käkönen (eds), *Contested Waterscapes in the Mekong Region: Hydropower, Livelihoods and Governance* (Earthscan, 2009) 55.

*Framework Convention for the Protection of the Marine Environment of the Caspian Sea*, signed 4 November 2003, [2005] 44 ILM 1 (entered into force 12 August 2006).

Frijters, Ine D. and Leentvaar, Jan, 'Rhine Case Study' (PCCP Series 17, UNESCO-IHP, 2003).

*Gabčíkovo-Nagymaros Project (Hungary/Slovakia) (Judgment)* [1997] ICJ Rep 7.

Ganjanakhundee, Supalak, *Laos: No Work on Xayaburi Dam until Green Concerns Solved* (4 May 2012) The Nation <http://www.nationmultimedia.com/politics/Laos-no-work-on-Xayaburi-dam-until-green-concerns--30181251.html>.

高丙中，袁瑞军主编 [Gao, Bingzhong and Yuan, Ruijun (eds)],《中国公民社会发展蓝皮书》[Blue Book on Civil Society Development in China] (北京大学出版社 [Peking University Press], 2008).

Gillespie, John, 'Localizing Global Rules: Public Participation in Lawmaking in Vietnam' (2008) 33(3) *Law and Social Inquiry* 673.

Global Times, *Shifang Protest Needs Law-Based Conclusion* (5 July 2012) <http://www.globaltimes.cn/content/719095.shtml>.

Global Water Partnership and International Network of Basin Organizations, *Handbook for IWRM in Basins* (Handbook, Global Water Partnership, 2009).

Global Water Partnership Technical Advisory Committee, 'Integrated Water Resources Management' (Background Paper No. 4, Global Water Partnership, 2000).

Global Water Partnership, 'Evaluation of the Status of IWRM Implementation in Southeast Asia 2000–2010 in Respect to Policy, Legal and Institutional Aspects' (Report, Global Water Partnership, 2011).

*Goals and Principles of Environmental Impact Assessment*, UN Doc UNEP/WG.152/4 Annex (1987).

Goh, Evelyn, 'China in the Mekong River Basin: The Regional Security Implications of Resource Development on the Lancang Jiang' (Working Paper, Institute of Defense and Strategic Studies, 2004).

Good Neighbor Environmental Board, 'Water Resources Management on the United States-Mexico Border' (Eighth Report to the President and the Congress of the United States, Good Neighbor Environmental Board, 2005).

Grant, M., 'Implementation of the EC Directive on Environmental Impact Assessment' (1989) 4 *Connecticut Journal of International Law* 463.

Greacen, Chris and Palettu, Apsara, 'Electricity Sector Planning and Hydropower' in Louis Lebel et al. (eds), *Democratizing Water Governance in the Mekong* (Mekong Press, 2007) 93.

Greater Mekong Subregion Economic Cooperation Program, *17th GMS Ministerial Conference Meeting Summary* (4 August 2011) <http://beta.adb.org/sites/default/files/17th-MC-SOP-Ministerial-Meeting.pdf>.

Greater Mekong Subregion Environment Operations Centre, 'The Core Environment Program and Biodiversity Conservation Corridors Initiative Progress Report for the Period April–September 2011' (Report, Greater Mekong Subregion Economic Cooperation Program, 2011).

Greater Mekong Subregion Environment Operations Centre, *3rd GMS Environment Ministers Meeting, 27–28 July 2011* (18 November 2011) <http://www.gms-eoc.org/events/3rd-gms-environment-ministers-meeting-phnom-penh-cambodia->.

Greater Mekong Subregion Core Environmental Program, *Strategic Planning* <http://www.gms-eoc.org/strategic-planning>.

Greater Mekong Subregion Core Environmental Program, *Environmental Assessment of Economic Corridors and Sectors* <http://www.gms-eoc.org/uploads/resources/18/attachment/Environmental%20Assessment%20of%20Economic%20Corridors%20and%20Sectors%20-%20Status%20Report.pdf>.

关俏俏，刁甜甜 [Guan, Qiaoqiao and Diao, Tiantian],《中哈两国共同建霍尔果斯河友谊联合引水枢纽工程》[China and Kazakhstan Jointly Construct Huoerguos Water Division Project] (16 April 2011) 新华网 [Xinhua News Agency] <http://www.xj.xinhuanet.com/2011-04/16/content_22539842.htm>.

*Guidance on Public Participation in Environmental Impact Assessment in a Transboundary Context*, UN ECE/MP.EIA/7 (2006).

Gunning, Marie J., 'The Projected Impact of the North American Free Trade Agreement on Transboundary Water Management between Mexico and the USA' in J. Ganoulis et al. (eds), *Transboundary Water Resources Management: Institutional and Engineering Approaches* (Springer, 1996) 71.

韩啸 [Han, Xiao],《水资源挑战迫近中国》[Challenge of Water Resources Approaching China] (26 April 2011) 人民论坛 [People's Tribune] <http://paper.people.com.cn/rmlt/html/2011-04/11/content_804553.htm?div=-1>.

Hand, Peter H., 'Institution-building to Assist Compliance with International Environmental Law: Perspectives' (1996) 56(3) *Zeitschrift für ausländisches öffentliches Recht und Völkerrecht* (*Heidelberg Journal of International Law*) 774.

Handl, Gunther, 'Environmental Security and Global Change: The Challenge to International Law' (1990) 1 *Yearbook of International Environmental Law* 3.

Hermawanto, Bambang, *Report of the 8th Mekong of APGCC* (23 June 2011) <http://www.hapuasecretariat.org/doc2011/Report%208_APGCC.pdf>.

Hirsch, Philip and Sciortino, Rosalia, 'Climate Change and the Resource Politics of the Greater Mekong Subregion' in Kobkun Rayanakorn (ed), *Climate Change Challenges in the Mekong Region* (Chiang Mai University Press, 2011) 223.

Hirsch, Philip et al., 'National Interests and Transboundary Water Governance in the Mekong' (Report, University of Sydney, 2006).

———, 'Beyond the Nation State: Natural Resource Conflict and National Interest in Mekong Hydropower Development' (1999) 29 *Golden Gate University Law Review* 399.

———, 'Globalisation, Regionalisation and Local Voices: The Asian Development Bank and Re-scaled Politics of Environment in the Mekong Region' (2001) 22(3) *Singapore Journal of Tropical Geography* 237.

———, 'The Changing Political Dynamics of Dam Building on the Mekong' (2010) 3(2) *Water Alternatives* 312.

———, *Cascade Effect* (8 February 2011) China Dialogue <http://www.chinadialogue.net/article/show/single/en/4093-Cascade-effect>.

———, 'Water Governance Reform and Catchment Management in the Mekong Region' (2006) 15(2) *Journal of Environment and Development* 184.

Hostovsky, Charles, Maclaren, Virginia and McGrath, Geoffrey, 'The Role of Public Involvement in Environmental Impact Assessment in Vietnam: Towards a More Culturally Sensitive Approach' (2010) 53(3) *Journal of Environmental Planning and Management* 405.

Human Rights Watch, *Cambodia: Withdraw Flawed Draft NGO and Association Law* (7 April 2011) <http://www.hrw.org/en/news/2011/04/07/cambodia-withdraw-flawed-draft-ngo-and-association-law>.

Hunter, David, Salzman, James and Zaelke, Durwood, *International Environmental Law and Policy* (West Publishing, 3rd ed, 2007).

Imamura, Masao, 'Introduction: Water Governance in the Mekong Region' in Louis Lebel et al. (eds), *Democratizing Water Governance in the Mekong* (Mekong Press, 2007) 1.

Integrated Regional Information Networks, *Laos: Government Boost for Local NGOs* (12 May 2009) <http://www.irinnews.org/Report/84347/LAOS-Government-boost-for-local-NGOs>.

《环评公众参与暂行办法》 [Interim Measures of Public Participation in EIA] (People's Republic of China) State Environmental Protection Administration, 22 February 2006.

International Boundary and Water Commission, *Joint Report of the Principle Engineers relative to Determination of Presence of Toxic Substances in the Waters of the Rio Grande in its International Boundary Reach* (11 November 1992) <http://www.ibwc.gov/Files/Minutes/JR289.pdf>.

International Boundary and Water Commission, *Minutes between the United States and Mexican Sections of the IBWC* <http://www.ibwc.state.gov/Treaties_Minutes/Minutes.html>.

International Centre for Environmental Management, 'Comments on the Xayaburi HPP Compliance Report: With a Focus on the Mekong Delta' (Comments, ICEM, 2011).

———, 'Mekong River Commission Strategic Environmental Assessment of Hydropower on the Mekong Mainstream' (Report, ICEM, 2010).

———, 'Strategic Environmental Assessment in the Greater Mekong Subregion—Status Report' (Report, Greater Mekong Subregion Environment Operations Centre, 2006).

International Commission for the Protection of the Rhine, 'Warning and Alarm Plan Rhine Reported Incidents 2010' (Report No. 191, ICPR, 2010).

———, *Action Plan on Floods* <http://www.iksr.org/index.php?id=123&L=3>.

———, *Flood Warning and Forecasting Centres* <http://www.iksr.org/index.php?id=140&L=3>.

———, *Prevention of Accidents and Security of Industrial Plants* <http://www.iksr.org/index.php?id=87&L=3>.

*International Covenant on Civil and Political Rights*, opened for signature 16 December 1966, 999 UNTS 1057 (entered into force 23 March 1976).

International Energy Agency, '$CO_2$ Emissions from Fuel Combustion: Highlights (2011 edition)' (Report, IEA, 2011).

International Freedom of Expression Exchange, 'Law Classification Series: Law on Freedom of Information' (Factsheet, International Freedom of Expression Exchange, 2012).

International Law Association, 'Helsinki Rules on the Uses of the Waters of International Rivers' (Report of the Committee on the Uses of the Waters of International Rivers, International Law Association, 1967).

———, 'Draft articles on the Law of the Non-navigational Uses of International Watercourses and Commentaries thereto and Resolution on Transboundary Confined Groundwater' (1994) 2(2) *Yearbook of the International Law Commission* 89.

———, *Prevention of Transboundary Harm from Hazardous Activities*, UN GAOR, 56th sess, UN Doc A/56/10.

International Rivers and BankTrack, *Western Banks Violate Rights, Law in Lao Dam Deal*, International Rivers (17 November 2009) <http://www.internationalrivers.org/resources/western-banks-violate-rights-law-in-lao-dam-deal-3779>.

International Rivers, 'Mekong under Threat: New Strategy Promotes Dams and Diversions' (Fact Sheet, International Rivers, 2006).

———, *Dirty Hydro: Dams and Greenhouse Gas Emissions* (November 2008) <http://www.internationalrivers.org/resources/dirty-hydro-dams-and-greenhouse-gas-emissions-2648>.

———, *Sidestepping Science: Review of the Pöyry Report on the Xayaburi Dam* (November 2011) <http://www.internationalrivers.org/files/attached-files/poyry review_areasofnon-compliance.pdf>.

———, *Spreadsheet of Major Dams in China* (23 May 2013) <http://www.internationalrivers.org/resources/spreadsheet-of-major-dams-in-china-7743>.

———, *Xayaburi Dam* <http://www.internationalrivers.org/campaigns/xayaburi-dam>.

International Tribunal for the Law of the Sea, *The MOX Plant Case (Ireland v. United Kingdom), Provisional Measures* <http://www.itlos.org/index.php?id=102>.

*Iron Rhine Arbitration* (*Belgium v. Netherlands*) (*Award*) (2005), 27 RIAA 35.

Ismail, Saifulbahri, *ASEAN Summit Fails to Agree on Concluding Joint Statement* (13 July 2012) Channelnewsasia.com <http://www.channelnewsasia.com/stories/southeastasia/view/1213369/1/.html>.

Jackson, John, 'Citizens Working Across National Borders: The Experience in the North American Great Lakes' in Carl Bruch et al. (eds), *Public Participation in the Governance of International Freshwater Resources* (United Nations University, 2005) 118.

Jacobs, Jeffrey W., 'Mekong Committee History and Lessons for River Basin Development' (1995) 161(2) *Geographical Journal* 135.

———, 'The United States and the Mekong Project' (2000) 1(6) *Water Policy* 587.

Jeffery, Michael I., QC., 'Intervenor Funding as the Key to Effective Citizen Participation in Environmental Decision-making: Putting the People back into the Picture' (2002) 19(2) *Arizona Journal of International and Comparative Law* 643.

———, 'The New Canadian Environmental Assessment Act—Bill C-78: A Disappointing Response to Promised Reform' (1991) 36(3) *McGill Law Journal* 1070.

纪逗 [Ji, Dou],《水资源市场配置管理体制障碍的法律分析》[A Legal Analysis of the Institutional Obstacles on Market Allocation of Water Resources] (16 September 2003) 武汉大学环境法研究所 [Research Institute of Environmental Law of Wuhan University] <http://www.riel.whu.edu.cn/article.asp?id=25668>.

Johns, Fleur et al., 'Law and the Mekong River Basin: A Socio-Legal Research Agenda on the Role of Hard and Soft Law in Regulating Transboundary Water Resources' (2010) 11(1) *Melbourne Journal of International Law* 154.

Joint Committee of Mekong River Commission, 'Guidelines on Custodianship and Management of the MRC Information System' (Guidelines, Mekong River Commission, 2002).

Joint Experts Group on EIA of China, Laos, Myanmar and Thailand, *Executive Summary of Environmental Impact Assessment on the Navigation Channel Improvement Project of the Lancang-Mekong River from China-Myanmar Boundary Maker 243 to Ban Houeisai of Laos* (2001) <http://portal.mrcmekong.org/master-catalogue/search?giai=9506000003825_00009784E01006ql>.

Käkönen, Mira and Hirsch, Philip, 'The Anti-Politics of Mekong Knowledge Production' in François Molle, Tira Foran and Mira Käkönen (eds), *Contested Waterscapes in the Mekong Region: Hydropower, Livelihoods and Governance* (Earthscan, 2009) 333.

Kelly, Mary and Székely, Alberto, 'Modernizing the International Boundary and Water Commission' (Policy Paper 1, Center for Latin American Studies, 2004).

Kersten, Charles M., 'Rethinking Transboundary Environmental Impact Assessment' (2009) 34 *Yale Journal of International Law* 173.

Keskinen, Marko, *Bring Back the Common Sense? Integrated Approaches in Water Management: Lessons Learnt from the Mekong* (PhD Thesis, Aalto University, 2010).

Kimeong, Kay, *Cambodian Media Struggles through Hard Time*, ASEAN Mass Communication Studies and Research Centre <http://utcc2.utcc.ac.th/localuser/amsar/about/document18.htm>.

Kirgis, Frederic L., Jr., *Prior Consultation in International Law* (University Press of Virginia, 1983).

Knox, John H., 'The Myth and Reality of Transboundary Environmental Impact Assessment' (2002) 96 *American Journal of International Law* 291.

———, 'The North American Commission for Environmental Cooperation and Transboundary Pollution' (2004) 34 *Environmental Law Reporter: News and Analysis* 10142.

Koivurova, Timo, 'Transboundary Environmental Impact Assessment in International Law' in Simon Marsden and Timo Koivurova (eds), *Transboundary Environmental Impact Assessment in the European Union* (Earthscan, 2011) 15.

Koh, Kheng-Lian (ed), *ASEAN Environmental Law, Policy and Governance: Selected Documents (Volume I)* (World Scientific, 2009).

Koh, Kheng-Lian and Robinson, Nicholas A., 'Regional Environmental Governance: Examining the Association of Southeast Asian Nations (ASEAN) Model' in Daniel C. Esty and Maria H. Ivanova (eds), *Global Environmental Governance: Options and Opportunities* (Yale School of Forestry and Environmental Studies, 2002) 1.

Koh, Kheng-Lian, 'ASEAN Environmental Protection in Natural Resources and Sustainable Development: Convergence versus Divergence' (2007) 4 *Macquarie Journal of International and Comparative Environmental Law* 43.

Koskenniemi, Martti, 'Peaceful Settlement of Environmental Disputes' (1991) 60 *Nordic Journal of International Law* 73.

Kravchenko, Svitlana, 'Strengthening Implementation of MEAs: The Innovative Aarhus Compliance Mechanism' in Durwood Zaelke, Donald Kaniaru and Eva Kružíková (eds), *Making Law Work: Environmental Compliance and Sustainable Development* (Cameron May Ltd, International Law Publishers, 2005) vol 1, 245.

Kummu, Matti et al., 'Sediment: Curse or Blessing for Tonle Sap Lake?' (2008) 37 *Ambio* 158.

Kunze, Gretchen A., *New Decree Opens Way for Civil Society in Laos* (2 June 2010) In Asia: the Asia Foundation Blog <http://asiafoundation.org/in-asia/2010/06/02/new-decree-opens-way-for-civil-society-in-laos/>.

Lacombe, Guillaume, *Effectiveness of Early Warning Systems and Monitoring Tools in the Mekong Basin* (2009) <http://www.adbi.org/files/2009.06.09.cpp.day2.sess3.2.lacombe.paper.early.warning.systems.mekong.pdf>.

*Lake Lanoux Arbitration (France v. Spain) (Decision)* (1957) 24 ILR 101.

Lammers, J. G., *Pollution of International Watercourses* (Martinus Nijhoff, 1984).

'Lao PDR: Water Resources Coordinating Committee' (Paper presented at the Regional Meeting of National Water Sector Apex Bodies, Hanoi, 18–21 May 2004).

《中华人民共和国水污染防治法》 [Law of the People's Republic of China on the Prevention and Control of Water Pollution] (People's Republic of China) National People's Congress Standing Committee, Order No 87, 2 February 2008.

*Law on Archives* (Kingdom of Cambodia) National Assembly, October 2005.

*Law on Environmental Protection* (Socialist Republic of Vietnam) National Assembly, 29 November 2005.

*Law on Environmental Protection and Natural Resource Management* (Kingdom of Cambodia) National Assembly, 24 December 1996.

*Law on the Regime of the Press* (Kingdom of Cambodia) National Assembly, 18 July 1995.

*Law on Water and Water Resources* (Lao People's Democratic Republic) National Assembly, 11 October 1996.

*Law on Water Resources Management* (Kingdom of Cambodia) National Assembly, 29 June 2007.

Lawrence, Shannon, 'The Nam Theun 2 Controversy and Its Lessons for Laos' in François Molle, Tira Foran and Mira Käkönen (eds), *Contested Waterscapes in the Mekong Region: Hydropower, Livelihoods and Governance* (Earthscan, 2009) 81.

《中华人民共和国立法法》[Legislation Law of the People's Republic of China] (People's Republic of China) National People's Congress, 15 March 2000.

Letter from the MRC Secretariat to Save the Mekong Coalition, 14 May 2012 <http://www.savethemekong.org/admin_controls/js/tiny_mce/plugins/imagemanager/files/May142012.pdf>.

Leviter, Lee, 'The ASEAN Charter: ASEAN Failure or Member Failure?' (2010) 43 *International Law and Politics* 159.

李晓莹 [Li, Xiaoying],《黄委携手流域8省（区）建立突发水污染事件信息沟通与协作机制》[The Yellow River Conservancy Commission, together with Eight Riparian Provinces, Developed Information Exchange and Collaboration Mechanisms for Water Pollution Accidents] (14 July 2011) 中国水利 [China Water Resources News] <http://www.chinawater.com.cn/newscenter/ly/huangh/201107/t20110714_154665.html>.

Lindgren, Richard D. and Dunn, Burgandy, 'Environmental Assessment in Ontario: Rhetoric vs. Reality' (2010) 21 *Journal of Environmental Law and Practice* 279.

Liu, Yuqiong, 'Monitoring Chinese-Russian Transboundary Waters' (2006) 5 (3) *Southwest Hydrology* 38.

Magee, Darrin, 'The Dragon Upstream: China's Role in Lancang-Mekong Development' in Joakim Öjendal, Stina Hansson and Sofie Hellberg (eds), *Politics and Development in a Transboundary Watershed* (Springer, 2012) 171.

Marsden, Simon, 'China's Experience with Transboundary Environmental Impact Assessment' (Speech delivered at 7th Colloquium of the IUCN Academy of Environmental Law, Wuhan, China, 4 November 2009).

———, 'MOX Plant and the Espoo Convention: Can Member State Disputes concerning Mixed Environmental Agreements be Resolved outside EC Law?' (2009) 18(3) *Review of European Community and International Environmental Law* 312.

Maurel, Pierre, 'Public Participation and the European Water Framework Directive: Role of Information and Communication Tools' (WorkPackage 3 Report, HarmoniCoP Project, 2003).

McCaffrey, Stephen C., 'The Harmon Doctrine One Hundred Years Later: Buried, not Praised' (1996) 36 *Natural Resources Journal* 549.

———, *The Law of International Watercourses* (Oxford University Press, 2007).

McIntyre, Owen, *Environmental Protection of International Watercourses under International Law* (Ashgate Publishing Group, 2007).

McRobert, David and Boutis, Paula, *Proposal for a New Ontario Participant and Intervenor Funding Act Filed with the Environmental Commissioner of Ontario* (2012) Ontario Bar Association <http://www.oba.org/en/pdf/sec_news_env_mar12_Proposal_Boutis.pdf>.

McWilliams, Susan J., 'The Costs of Intervenor Funding and Their Control: The Experience of the Ontario Energy Board' (1991) 11 *Windsor Yearbook of Access to Justice* 217.

*Meeting of the GMS Environment Ministers: Joint Ministerial Statement* (25 May 2005) <http://www.wwfchina.org/english/downloads/GMSstatement.pdf>.

Mehtonen, Katri, Keskinen, Marko and Varis, Olli, 'The Mekong: IWRM and Institutions' in Olli Varis, Cecilia Tortajada and Asit K. Biswas (eds), *Management of Transboundary Rivers and Lakes* (Springer, 2008) 207.

Mekong River Commission Secretariat, 'Prior Consultation Project Review Report Volume 2: Stakeholder Consultations related to the Proposed Xayaburi Dam Project' (Report, Mekong River Commission, 2011).

———, 'Proposed Xayaburi Dam Project: MRCS Prior Consultation Project Review Report' (Report, Mekong River Commission, 2011).

———, 'Public Participation in the Context of the MRC' (Report, Mekong River Commission, 1999).

Mekong River Commission, 'An Assessment of Water Quality in the Lower Mekong Basin' (Technical Paper No. 19, Mekong River Commission, 2008).

———, 'Stakeholder Analysis for the MRC Basin Development Plan Programme Phase 2 (BDP2)' (Report, Mekong River Commission, 2010).

———, 'Stakeholder Participation and Communication Plan for Basin Development Planning in the Lower Mekong Basin' (Programme Document, Mekong River Commission, 2009).

———, 'The Flood Management and Mitigation Programme 2011–2015' (Programme Document, Mekong River Commission, 2011).

———, 'The Information and Knowledge Management Programme 2011–2015' (Programme Document, Mekong River Commission, 2010).

———, 'The MRC Basin Development Plan: Stakeholder Participation' (Programme Document, Mekong River Commission, 2005).

———, *About Mekong—the Land & its Resources* <http://nsl.mrcmekong.org/about_mekong/about_mekong.htm>.

———, *Agreement on Provision of Hydrological Information Renewed by China and MRC* (2008) <http://www.mrcmekong.org/news-and-events/news/agreement-on-provision-of-hydrological-information-renewed-by-china-and-mrc/>.

———, *Climate Change* <http://www.mrcmekong.org/topics/climate-change/>.

———, *Climate Change and Adaptation Initiative* <http://www.mrcmekong.org/about-the-mrc/programmes/climate-change-and-adaptation-initiative/>.

———, *Communication Strategy and Disclosure Policy* (2009) <http://www.mrcmekong.org/assets/Publications/policies/Communication-Strategy-n-Disclosure-Policy.pdf>.

———, *Flood & Drought* <http://www.mrcmekong.org/topics/flood-and-drought/>.

———, *Flood Management & Mitigation Programme* <http://www.mrcmekong.org/about-the-mrc/programmes/flood-management-and-mitigation-programme/>.

———, *Guidelines on Implementation of the Procedures for Notification, Prior Consultation and Agreement* (31 August 2005) <http://www.mrcmekong.org/assets/Publications/policies/Guidelines-on-implementation-of-the-PNPCA.pdf>.

———, *Information and Knowledge Management Programme* <http://www.mrcmekong.org/about-the-mrc/programmes/information-and-knowledge-management-programme/>.

———, *Information Services*, Mekong River Commission Data and Information Services <http://portal.mrcmekong.org/cms/information-services>.

———, *Lao PDR Submits Notification on Don Sahong Hydropower Project* (3 October 2013) <http://www.mrcmekong.org/news-and-events/news/lao-pdr-submits-notification-on-don-sahong-hydropower-project/>.

———, *Lower Mekong Countries Take Prior Consultation on Xayaburi Project to Ministerial Level* (19 April 2011) <http://www.mrcmekong.org/news-and-events/news/lower-mekong-countries-take-prior-consultation-on-xayaburi-project-to-ministerial-level/>.

———, *Mekong River Commission and China Boost Water Data Exchange* (30 August 2013) <http://www.mrcmekong.org/news-and-events/news/mekong-river-commission-and-china-boost-water-data-exchange/>.

———, *Modelling Toolbox*, Mekong River Commission Data and Information Services <http://portal.mrcmekong.org/cms/models-and-scenarios>.

———, *Procedures for Data and Information Exchange and Sharing* (1 November 2001) <http://www.mrcmekong.org/assets/Publications/policies/Procedures-Data-Info-Exchange-n-Sharing.pdf>.

———, *Procedures for Notification, Prior Consultation and Agreement* (30 November 2003) <http://www.mrcmekong.org/assets/Publications/policies/Procedures-Notification-Prior-Consultation-Agreement.pdf>.

———, *Proposed Xayaburi Hydropower Project Prior Consultation Process* <http://www.mrcmekong.org/news-and-events/consultations/proposed-xayaburi-hydropower-project-prior-consultation-process/>.

———, *Public Participation in the Lower Mekong Basin* (2005) <http://www.mrcmekong.org/assets/Publications/governance/Public-Participation.pdf>.

———, *SEA Frequently Asked Questions: What are some of the Next Steps for the MRC on the SEA?* <http://www.mrcmekong.org/about-the-mrc/programmes/initiative-on-sustainable-hydropower/strategic-environmental-assessment-of-mainstream-dams/sea-frequently-asked-questions/>.

———, *Statement to the GMS Ministerial Conference by the Mekong River Commission* (2011) <http://www.scribd.com/doc/63622096/17th-GMS-MC-MRC-Secretariat-Statement>.

———, *Strategic Environmental Assessment of Mainstream Dams* <http://www.mrcmekong.org/about-the-mrc/programmes/initiative-on-sustainable-hydropower/strategic-environmental-assessment-of-mainstream-dams/>.

———, *The 17th Meeting of the MRC Council, Joint Meeting with the MRC Donor Consultative Group* (2011) <http://www.mrcmekong.org/news-and-events/speeches/the-17th-meeting-of-the-mrc-council-joint-meeting-with-the-mrc-donor-consultative-group-2/>.

———, *The Four 'R's for Mekong Cooperation Ministers and Diplomats Welcome New MRC CEO* (2008) <http://www.mrcmekong.org/news-and-events/news/the-four-r-s-for-mekong-cooperation-ministers-and-diplomats-welcome-new-mrc-ceo/>.

———, *Upstream Partners* <http://www.mrcmekong.org/about-the-mrc/upstream-partners-2/>.

———, *Water Quality Monitoring Map*, Mekong River Commission Data and Information Services <http://portal.mrcmekong.org/cms/water-quality-monitoring-map>.

Middelkoop, H. et al., 'Impact of Climate Change on Hydrological Regimes and Water Resources Management in the Rhine Basin' (2001) 49 *Climate Change* 105.

Middleton, Carl and Lee, Gary, 'Mekong Water Resources Assistance Strategy: Justifying Large Water Infrastructure with Transboundary Impacts' (2006) 12(1) *Watershed* 10.

Middleton, Carl, Garcia, Jelson and Foran, Tira, 'Old and New Hydropower Players in the Mekong Region: Agendas and Strategies' in François Molle, Tira Foran and Mira Käkönen (eds), *Contested Waterscapes in the Mekong Region* (Earthscan, 2009) 23.

Miller, Fiona and Hirsch, Philip, 'Civil Society and Internationalized River Basin Management' (Working Paper No. 7, Australian Mekong Resource Centre, 2003).

环境保护部 [Ministry of Environmental Protection of the People's Republic of China], 《建设项目环境影响评价分类管理名录》 [Classified Catalogue of Construction Projects Subject to Environmental Impact Assessment] (2008) <http://www.mep.gov.cn/info/bgw/bl/200809/W020080905398664224537.pdf>.

Ministry of Environmental Protection of People's Republic of China, *Major Responsibilities of the Department of Pollution Prevention and Control* <http://english.mep.gov.cn/About_SEPA/Internal_Departments/200910/t20091015_162419.htm>.

环境保护部 [Ministry of Environmental Protection of the People's Republic of China],《环境影响评价技术导则：公众参与（征求意见稿）》[Technical Guideline for Public Participation in Environmental Impact Assessment (Draft for Comments)] (30 January 2011) <http://www.es.org.cn/download/2011/1-6/2135-1.pdf>.

ກະຊວງ ຊັບພະຍາກອນ ທຳມະຊາດ ແລະ ສິ່ງແວດລ້ອມ [Ministry of Natural Resources and Environment of the Lao People's Democratic Republic], ຂໍ້ຕົກລົງ ວ່າດ້ວຍການຮັບຮອງ ແລະ ປະກາດໃຊ້ບັນຊີໂຄງການລົງທຶນ ທີ່ຈະຕ້ອງດຳເນີນການ ສຶກສາສິ່ງແວດລ້ອມເບື້ອງຕົ້ນ ແລະ ດຳເນີນການ ປະເມີນຜົນກະທົບ ຕໍ່ສິ່ງແວດລ້ອມ ເລກທີ 697/ສນຍ.ອຊນສ, ລົງວັນທີ 12 ມີນາ 2010 [Directive on the List of Projects to Undertake IEE and EIA] (2010) <http://monre.gov.la/esia/images/download/type%20and%20size%20697%20pm%20wrea%2012%20mar%202010.pdf>.

Ministry of Water Resources of the People's Republic of China, *About the Ministry of Water Resources* <http://www.mwr.gov.cn/english/aboutmwr.html>.

Moench, Marcus et al., 'The Fluid Mosaic: Water Governance in the Context of Variability, Uncertainty and Change' (Paper, Nepal Water Conservation Foundation, 2003).

Molle, François and Hoanh, Chu Thai, 'Implementing Integrated River Basin Management: Lessons from the Red River Basin, Vietnam' (Report, International Water Management Institute, 2009).

Molle, François, 'Irrigation and Water Policies: Trends and Challenges' in Louis Lebel et al. (eds), *Democratizing Water Governance in the Mekong* (Mekong Press, 2007) 9.

Molle, François, Foran, Tira and Floch, Philippe, 'Introduction: Changing Waterscapes in the Mekong Region-Historical Background and Context' in François Molle, Tira Foran and Mira Käkönen (eds), *Contested Waterscapes in the Mekong Region* (Earthscan, 2009) 1.

Moreno, Ignacia S. et al., 'Free Trade and the Environment: The NAFTA, the NAAEC and Implications for the Future' (1999) 12 *Tulane Environmental Law Journal* 405 .

MRC Summit 2010, *ASEAN, MRC to Boost Cooperation on Mekong Issues* (2010) <http://www.mrcsummit2010.org/ASEAN-MRC-to-Boost-Cooperation-4-apr-10.htm>.

Nakayama, Mikiyasu, 'International Collaboration on Water Systems in Asia and the Pacific: A Case of Transition' (2002) 3(2) *International Review for Environmental Strategies* 274.

中华人民共和国审计署 [National Audit Office of the People's Republic of China],《2013年第3号公告：中国华能集团公司2011年度财务收支审计结果》[No. 3 Notification in 2013: The Audit Result of Financial Revenue and Expenditure of the China Huaneng Group in 2011] (10 May 2013) <http://www.audit.gov.cn/n1992130/n1992150/n1992500/3277991.html>.

*National Environmental Policy Act*, 42 USC (1969).

《国家人权行动计划（2012–2015）》[National Human Rights Action Plan] (11 June 2012) 中华人民共和国中央人民政府 [Central People's Government of the PRC] <http://www.gov.cn/jrzg/2012-06/11/content_2158166.htm>.

NGO Forum on ADB, *Forum's Campaign on the Public Communications Policy* <http://www.forum-adb.org/inner.php?sec=13&ref=extras&id=8>.

NGO Forum on CAMBODIA, *Down River: The Consequences of Vietnam's Se San River Dams on Life in Cambodia and Their Meaning in International Law* (NGO Forum on Cambodia, 2005).

Nguitragool, Paruedee, 'Negotiating the Haze Treaty' (2011) 3(51) *Asian Survey* 356.

———, *Environmental Cooperation in Southeast Asia: ASEAN's Regime for Transboundary Haze Pollution* (Routledge, 2011).

Nguyen, Thai Lai, 'Viet Nam: National Water Resources Council' (Paper presented at the Regional Meeting of National Water Sector Apex Bodies, Hanoi, 18–21 May 2004).

Nguyen, Thanh Thao, *Water Resources Management in Vietnam* (2011) UBM Asia <http://news.ubmthailand.com/newsletter/2011/EPA/conference/ASEAN-Water-Conference/W-06-Vietnam-BKK-May2011-WRM-Vietnam-NTThao.pdf>.

Nguyen, Thi Dieu, *The Mekong River and the Struggle for Indochina: Water, War and Peace* (Praeger Publishers, 1999).

Nonthaxay, Phonechaleun, *Water Resources Management in Lao PDR* (2004) Network of Asian River Basin Organizations <http://www.narbo.jp/data/01_events/materials/tc01_cr_laopdr01.pdf>.

Nørlund, Irene, *Civil Society in Vietnam: Social Organisations and Approaches to New Concepts* (2007) <http://www.asienkunde.de/content/zeitschrift_asien/archiv/pdf/a105_ref_art_norlund.pdf>.

*North American Agreement on Environmental Cooperation*, signed 14 September 1993, 32 ILM 1480 (entered into force 1 January 1994).

东北网 [Northeast.com],《中俄联合跨界监测界江水质，黑龙江水质趋于好转》[China and Russia Jointly Monitor the Water Quality of Their Transboundary Waters: Water Quality of the Heilong River has Improved] (16 March 2012) <http://heilongjiang.dbw.cn/system/2012/03/16/053748868.shtml>.

Office of Natural Resources and Environmental Policy and Planning, *Environmental Impact Assessment in Thailand* (2012) Asian Environmental Compliance and Enforcement Network <http://www.aecen.org/sites/default/files/environmental_impact_assessment_in_thailand.pdf>.

Office of the Official Information Commission, *Committee* <http://www.oic.go.th/content_eng/committee.htm>.

———, *Diagram of Appeal and Complaint by Ministry* <http://www.oic.go.th/iwebstat/istatministry.asp?language=En>.

*Official Information Act* (Kingdom of Thailand) National Assembly, 2 September 1997.

Okowa, Phoebe N., 'Procedural Obligations in International Environmental Agreements' (1996) 67 *British Yearbook of International Law* 317.

Opassiriwit, Chungtong, *Thailand: A Case Study in the Interrelationship between Freedom of Information (FOI) and Privacy*, Official Information Commission <http://www.oic.go.th/content_eng/privacy.html>.

Osborne, Milton, 'River at Risk: The Mekong and the Water Politics of China and Southeast Asia' (Working Paper No 2, Lowy Institute, 2004).

———, 'The Mekong: River under Threat' (Working Paper No. 27, Lowy Institute, 2009).

Oxfam Australia, *Yali Fall Dam* <https://www.oxfam.org.au/explore/infrastructure-people-and-environment/save-the-mekong/3s-critical-environmental-zone/yali-falls-dam/>.

Pantumsinchai, Pranee and Panswad, Thongchai, *Improvement of EIA Process in Thailand*, Civil Engineering <http://www.civil.rtaf.mi.th/CivilInternet/05Knowledge/03RegulationLaw/%E0%B8%81%E0%B8%8E%E0%B8%AB%E0%B8%A1%E0%B8%B2%E0%B8%A2%E0%B8%AA%E0%B8%B4%E0%B9%88%E0%B8%87%E0%B9%81%E0%B8%A7%E0%B8%94%E0%B8%A5%E0%B9%89%E0%B8%AD%E0%B8%A1/ImprovementofEIA.pdf>.

Parry, M.L. et al. (eds), 'Climate Change 2007: Impacts, Adaptation and Vulnerability. Contribution of Working Group II to the Fourth Assessment Report of the Intergovernmental Panel on Climate Change' (Fourth Assessment Report, IPCC, 2007).

Patel, Mita and Stel, Jan H. (eds), 'Public Participation in River Basin Management in Europe: A National Approach and Background Study Synthesising Experiences of 9 European Countries' (Workpackage 4, HarmoniCOP Project, 2004).

People's Daily Online, *Yuanmingyuan Lakebed Project Questioned* (30 March 2005) <http://english.peopledaily.com.cn/200503/30/eng20050330_178760.html>.

Phalla, Chem et al., 'Framing Research on Water Resources Management and Governance in Cambodia: A Literature Review' (Working Paper 37, Cambodia Development Resource Institute, 2008).

Phanna, Sok, 'Trans-boundary Aspect in the EIA Law of Cambodia' (Speech delivered at the Mekong Legal Network 4th Regional Meeting, Chiang Mai, 29 June 2012).

Phnom Penh Post, *Xayaburi Study Locks in Funding* (23 April 2012) Eco-Business <http://www.eco-business.com/news/xayaburi-study-locks-in-funding/>.

Phomsoupha, Xaypaseuth, 'Hydropower Development Plans and Progress in Lao PDR' (2009) 4 *Hydro Nepal* 15.

Plate, Erich J. and Insisiengmay, Thanongdeth, *Early Warning System for the Mekong River* (2002) <http://www.cws.net.cn/cwsnet/meeting-fanghong/v10101.pdf>.

北极星电力网 [Polestar Electricity Website],《华能澜沧江水电一个月2项目获批》[Two Huaneng Projects Approved within one Month] (20 March 2013) <http://news.bjx.com.cn/html/20130320/423733.shtml>.

Pöyry, 'Xayaburi Hydroelectric Power Project Run-of-River Plant' (Report, Pöyry, 2011) Probe International, *Heavy Water Release from Vietnam's Yali Falls Dam Floods Communities in Northeastern Cambodia* (29 July 2008) <http://eprf.probeinternational.org/node/4179>.

Pronto, Arnold N., 'Some Thoughts on the Making of International Law' (2008) 19 *European Journal of International Law* 601.

*Protocol on Strategic Environmental Assessment to the Convention on Environmental Impact Assessment in a Transboundary Context*, UN Doc ECE/MP.EIA/2003/2 (21 May 2003).

《民办非企业单位登记管理暂行条例》[Provisional Regulation on the Registration of People-run Non-enterprise Unit] (People's Republic of China) State Council, 25 October 1998.

*Pulp Mills on the River Uruguay* (*Argentina v Uruguay*) (*Judgment*) [2010] ICJ Rep 14.

郄建荣 [Qie, Jianrong], 《艰难推进之中的"规划环评"》 [Difficult Development of the SEA of Plans] (4 May 2008) 中国网 [China.com.cn] <http://www.china.com.cn/aboutchina/zhuanti/hjwj08/2008-05/04/content_15054585.htm>.

青海新闻网 [Qinghai News],《龙青峡水电站试运行发电 杂多县将结束无电历史》[Test Run of the Longqingxia Dam has begun and the History of No Electricity in Zadoi will Come to an End] (23 November 2006) <http://www.qhnews.com/newscenter/system/2006/11/23/000025460.shtml>.

Raadgever, Tom, 'Transboundary River Basin Management Regimes: The Rhine Basin Case Study' (Background Report of the NeWater Project, Centre for River Basin Management, Delft University of Technology, August 2005).

Radio Free Asia, *Cambodia Warns Laos over Mekong Dam* (19 April 2011) <http://www.rfa.org/english/news/cambodia/dam-04192012143244.html>.

Ratner, Blake D., 'The Politics of Regional Governance in the Mekong River Basin' (2003) 15(1) *Global Change, Peace and Security* 59.

Raustiala, Kal, 'Compliance & Effectiveness in International Regulatory Cooperation' (2000) 32 *Case Western Reserve Journal of International Law* 387.

Rayanakorn, Kobkun (ed), *Climate Change Challenges in the Mekong Region* (Chiang Mai University Press, 2011).

《规划环境影响评价条例》[Regulations on Environmental Impact Assessment of Planning] (People's Republic of China) State Council, 12 August 2009.

《中华人民共和国政府信息公开条例》[Regulations on Government Information Disclosure of the People's Republic of China] (People's Republic of China) State Council, 17 January 2007.

《社会团体登记管理条例》[Regulations on Social Groups Registration Management] (People's Republic of China) State Council, 25 October 1998.

《水利工作中国家秘密及其密级具体范围的规定》[Regulations on State Confidentiality in Water Resources Management and its Specific Scope and Security Classification] (People's Republic of China) 水利部及国家保密局 [Ministry of Water Resources and State Secrets Bureau], 29 December 2000.

《基金会管理条例》[Regulation on the Administration of Foundations of the People's Republic of China] (People's Republic of China) State Council, 11 February 2004.

任景明 [Ren, Jingming],《公众参与何时成为润滑剂》[When can Public Participation actually Become the Lubricant during Decision-making Process] (19 September 2012) 湖北省环境保护厅 [Hubei Environmental Protection Bureau] <http://www.hbepb.gov.cn/hbdt/hjzl/201209/t20120919_55903.html>.

*Report of the United Nations Conference on Environment and Development*, UN Doc. A/CONF.151/26 (vol. I) (28 September 1992).

Reporters Without Borders, *Press Freedom Index 2011–2012* <http://en.rsf.org/press-freedom-index-2011-2012,1043.html>.

Reuters, *Laos Holds Groundbreaking Ceremony for Contentious Mekong Dam* (7 November 2012) <http://www.reuters.com/article/2012/11/07/us-laos-dam-idUSBRE8A618I20121107>.

Rieu-Clarke, Alistair, *International Law and Sustainable Development: Lessons from the Law of International Watercourses* (International Water Association Publishing, 2006).

Rigg, Jonathan, 'Thailand's Nam Choan Dam Project: A Case Study in the "Greening" of South-East Asia' (1991) 1(2) *Global Ecology and Biogeography Letters* 42.

Robertson, Scott and Tran, Thi Hai, 'NGO/Civil Society Development in Vietnam' (Working Reference, Vietnam Assistance for the Handicapped, 2004).

*Rule on Maintenance of Official Secrets* (Kingdom of Thailand) Council of Ministers, 5 February 2001.

Sands, Philippe, *Principles of International Environmental Law* (Cambridge University Press, 2nd ed, 2003).

Schrage, Wiek, 'The Convention on Environmental Impact Assessment in a Transboundary Context' in Kees Bastmeijer and Timo Koivurova (eds), *Theory and Practice of Transboundary Environmental Impact Assessment* (Martinus Nijhoff Publishers, 2008) 29.

*SEA Petitions and MRC Responses*, Mekong River Commission <http://www.mrcmekong.org/about-the-mrc/programmes/initiative-on-sustainable-hydropower/strategic-environmental-assessment-of-mainstream-dams/sea-petitions-and-mrc-responses/>.

SEA *Stakeholder Submissions*, Mekong River Commission <http://www.mrcmekong.org/about-the-mrc/programmes/initiative-on-sustainable-hydropower/strategic-environmental-assessment-of-mainstream-dams/sea-stakeholder-submissions/>.

Serirak, Nakorn, *Challenges of Thailand's Freedom of Information* <http://www.worldlii.org/int/journals/PLBIN/2000/29.html>.

Sethaputra, Sacha et al., 'Thailand's Water Vision: A Case Study' in Le Huu Ti and Thierry Facon (eds), *A Synthesis of Experiences in Southeast Asia* (RAP Publication, 2001) 71.

Shaffer, Gregory C. and Pollack, Mark A., 'Hard vs. Soft Law: Alternatives, Complements and Antagonists in International Governance' (2010) 94 *Minnesota Law Review* 706.

Shen, Dajun, 'River Basin Water Resources Management in China: A Legal and Institutional Assessment' (2009) 34(4) *Water International* 484.

Sida Advisory Team, 'Civil Society and Democracy in Cambodia: Changing Roles and Trends' (Report, Sida Advisory Team, 2003).

Sinh, Bach Tan, 'Civil Society and NGOs in Vietnam: Some Initial Thoughts on Developments and Obstacles' (Paper presented at the Meeting with the Delegation of the Swedish Parliamentary Commission on Swedish Policy for Global Development to Vietnam, 2 March 2001).

Smidt, Pieter M., 'Creating Synergy and ADB's Water Policy' (Paper presented at the International Water Conference, Hanoi, 14–16 October).

Sokhna, Ain, 'International Conflict Management in the Basin of the Rhine' (Report, Egyptian-Dutch Advisory Panel on Water Management, 2010).

Somchanmavong, Sengmanichanh, 'The Challenge of Water Resources Management in Laos' (Speech delivered at the Commonwealth Scientific and Industrial Research Organisation Land and Water Seminar, Perth, 28 June 2007) <http://www.clw.csiro.au/division/perth/seminars/2007/documents/Somchanmavong_July2007.pdf>.

Soutar, Lindsay, 'Asian Development Bank: NGO Encounters and the Theun-Hinboun Dam, Laos' in Barbara Rugendyke (ed), *NGOs as Advocates for Development in a Globalising World* (Routledge, 2007) 200.

Southeast Asian Water Utilities Network, *Water Links Regional* <http://seawun.org/index.php?page=water-links-regional-and-local>.

State Council Information Office of the People's Republic of China, *China's Policies and Actions for Addressing Climate Change* (22 November 2011) Xinhua News Agency <http://news.xinhuanet.com/english2010/china/2011-11/22/c_131262368.htm>.

国家环境保护总局 [State Environmental Protection Administration of the People's Republic of China],《关于公众申请公开建设项目环评文件有关问题的复函》[Response Concerning the Issues of Public's Request for the Disclosure of the EIA Document] (30 January 2008) <http://www.zhb.gov.cn/info/gw/huanhan/200802/t20080202_117941.htm>.

《中华人民共和国保守国家秘密法》[State Secret Protection Law of the People's Republic of China] (People's Republic of China) Standing Committee of the National Congress, 5 September 1988, revised at 29 April 2010.

*Statute of the International Court of Justice*, opened for signature 26 June 1945, 3 Bevans 1179 (entered into force 24 October 1945).

Stoeglehner, Gernot and Wegerer, Gerald, 'The SEA Directive and the SEA Protocol Adopted to Spatial Planning: Similarities and Differences' in Simon Marsden and Timo Koivurova (eds), *Transboundary Environmental Impact Assessment in the European Union* (Earthscan, 2011) 243.

Stone, Richard, 'Severe Drought Puts Spotlight on Chinese Dams' (2010) 327(5971) *Science* 1311.

Strategic Environmental Assessment Course Module, *Timing of the SEA* (3 September 2006) <http://sea.unu.edu/course/index.html%3Fpage_id=110.html>.

*Sub-Decree on Environmental Impact Process* (Kingdom of Cambodia) Council of Ministers, 11 August 1999.

Suhardiman, Diana, Giordano, Mark and Molle, François, 'Scalar Disconnect: The Logic of Transboundary Water Governance in the Mekong' (2011) 0 *Society & Natural Resources: An International Journal* 1 <http://www.tandfonline.com/doi/abs/10.1080/08941920.2011.604398>.

最高人民法院 [Supreme People's Court],《最高人民法院关于审理政府信息公开行政案件若干问题的规定》[Provisions of the Supreme People's Court about Several Issues Concerning the Trail of Administrative Cases on Government Information Disclosure] (15 August 2011) 新华网 [Xinhua News Agency] <http://news.xinhuanet.com/legal/2011-08/15/c_121860879.htm>.

Tan, Alan Khee-Jin, 'The ASEAN Agreement on Transboundary Haze Pollution: Prospects for Compliance and Effectiveness in Post-Suharto Indonesia' (2005) 13 *New York University Environmental Law Journal* 647.

*Terms of Reference of the ASEAN Intergovernmental Commission on Human Rights*, ASEAN <http://www.asean.org/communities/asean-political-security-community/category/asean-intergovernmental-commission-on-human-rights-aichr>.

*The Aarhus Convention: An Implementation Guide*, UN Doc ECE/CEP/72 (2000).

*The Charter of the Association of South East Asian Nations*, opened for signature 20 November 2007 (entered into force 15 December 2008).

*The Dublin Statement on Water and Sustainable Development* (1992) Global Development Research Center <http://www.gdrc.org/uem/water/dublin-statement.html>.

《中国-东盟环保合作中心组建》[The Establishment of the ASEAN-China Environmental Cooperation Centre], 中华人民共和国环境保护部 [Ministry of Environmental Protection of the People's Republic of China] (19 March 2010) <http://www.zhb.gov.cn/zhxx/hjyw/201003/t20100319_187059.htm>.

*The Water Information System for Europe* <http://water.europa.eu/>.

Thorne, Colin et al., 'Review of Sediment Transport, Morphology, and Nutrient Balance' (Sediment Experts Group Report, Mekong River Commission, 2011).

Toope, Stephen J., 'Formality and Informality' in Daniel Bodansky, Jutta Brunnée and Ellen Hay (eds), *The Oxford Handbook of International Environmental Law* (Oxford University Press, 2007) 107.

*Transport, Health and Environment Pan-European Programme* (*THE PEP*) *and Environmental Aspects of Transport: Strengthening of Environmental and Health Aspects of Transportation*, UN ESCOR, ITC, 70th sess, UN Doc ECE/TRANS/2008/4 (2007).

*Treaty regarding Utilization of Waters of Colorado and Tijuana Rivers and of the Rio Grande*, signed 3 February 1944, 3 UNTS 313 (entered into force 8 November 1945).

《环境信息公开办法（试行）》 [Trial Regulation on Environmental Information Disclosure] (People's Republic of China) State Environmental Protection Administration, 8 February 2007.

Trubek, David M. and Trubek, Louise G., 'Hard and Soft Law in the Construction of Social Europe: the Role of the Open Method of Co-ordination' (2005) 11 *European Law Journal* 343.

Tsutsumi, Rie and Robinson, Kristy, 'Environmental Impact Assessment and the Framework Convention for the Protection of the Marine Environment of the Caspian Sea' in Kees Bastmeijer and Timo Koivurova (eds), *Theory and Practice of Transboundary Environmental Impact Assessment* (Martinus Nijhoff Publishers, 2008) 53.

Tumen Programme, *GTI Environmental Cooperation* (*Focusing on Trans-boundary Environmental Impact Assessment* (*TEIA*) *in GTR and Environmental Standardization in North-East Asia* (*ESNA*)) <http://www.tumenprogramme.org/news.php?id=1012>.

United Nations, *Greater Tumen Initiative Breakfast Draws International Business Leaders* <http://www.un.org/partnerships/YNewsTumenBreakfast.htm>.

United Nations Economic Commission for Europe, *Report of the First Meeting of the Parties* (*Addendum*)*: Decision 1/7 Review of Compliance* (*Adopted at the First Meeting of the Parties Held in Lucca, Italy, on 21–23 October 2002*), UN Doc ECE/MP.PP/2/Add.8 (2 April 2004).

United Nations Environment Programme, 'The Songhua River Spill' (Field Mission Report, United Nations Environment Programme, 2005).

United Nations Treaty Collection, *Convention on Environmental Impact Assessment in a Transboundary Context* <http://treaties.un.org/Pages/ViewDetails.aspx?src=TREATY&mtdsg_no=XXVII-4&chapter=27&lang=en>.

United States Department of Justice, *Official Opinions of the Attorneys General of the United States: Advising the President and Heads of Departments in Relation to their Official Duties Volume 21* (Government Printing Office, 1985).

United States Environmental Protection Agency and Mexico's Secretariat of Urban Development and Ecology, *Integrated Environmental Plan for the Mexican-U.S. Border Area (First Stage, 1992–1994)* (1992) <http://pdf.usaid.gov/pdf_docs/PNABM228.pdf>.

Vaagan, Robert W., 'Media Systems, Access to Information and Human Rights in China and Vietnam' (2011) 29(4) *Nordic Journal of Human Rights* 302.

Varis, Olli, Stucki, Virpi and Fraboulet-Jussila, Sylvie, *The Senegal River Case* (2006) United Nations Development Programme <http://hdr.undp.org/en/content/senegal-river-case>.

Verweij, Marco, 'A Watershed on the Rhine: Changing Approaches to International Environmental Cooperation' (1999) 47 *GeoJournal* 453.

Voice of America, *Thai Company Says Work on Disputed Dam Has Started* (19 April 2012) <http://blogs.voanews.com/breaking-news/2012/04/19/thai-company-says-work-on-disputed-dam-has-started/>.

Volbeda, M. Bruce, 'The MOX Plant Case: The Question of "Supplemental Jurisdiction" for International Environmental Claims under UNCLOS' (2006) 42 *Texas International Law Journal* 211.

王静怡 [Wang, Jingyi], 《垃圾焚烧厂急上马，二恶英信息难公开》 [Rush for the Waste Incineration Plant: Difficulties to Gain Access to Information on Dioxin] (22 April 2012) 南方周末 [Southern Weekly] <http://www.infzm.com/content/74373>.

Wang, Xiangwei, 'Mainland's Environmental Chief Sacked over Toxic Chemical Spill', *South China Morning Post* (Hong Kong), 3 December 2005, 1.

《中华人民共和国水法》 [Water Law of the People's Republic of China] (People's Republic of China) National People's Congress Standing Committee, Order No. 74, 29 August 2002 .

Weatherbee, Donald E., 'Cooperation and Conflict in the Mekong River Basin' (1997) 20(2) *Studies in Conflict and Terrorism* 167.

Wende, Wolfgang et al., 'Climate Change Mitigation and Adaptation in Strategic Environmental Assessment' (2012) 32(1) *Environmental Impact Assessment Review* 88.

Wieriks, Koos and Schulte-Wulwer-Leidig, Anne, 'Integrated Water Management for the Rhine River Basin, from Pollution Prevention to Ecosystem Improvement' (1997) 21(2) *Natural Resources Form* 147.

World Bank, 'Environmental Impact Assessment Regulations and Strategic Environmental Assessment Requirements: Practices and Lessons Learned in East and Southeast Asia' (Report, World Bank, 2006).

———, 'Thailand Environment Monitor: Integrated Water Resources Management—A Way Forward' (Report, World Bank, 2011).

———, *Environmental Assessment in Operational Policy* <http://web.worldbank.org/WBSITE/EXTERNAL/TOPICS/ENVIRONMENT/EXTENVASS/0,,contentMDK:20482652~menuPK:1182600~pagePK:148956~piPK:216618~theSitePK:407988,00.html>.

———, *Environmental Assessment in Operational Policy 4.01* <http://go.worldbank.org/9LF3YQWTP0>.

———, *Strategic Environmental Assessment* (SEA) <http://go.worldbank.org/1RT0P09R80>.

World Bank and Asian Development Bank, 'WB/ADB Joint Working Paper on Future Directions for Water Resources Management in the Mekong River Basin: Mekong Water Resources Assistance Strategy' (Working Paper, World Bank and Asian Development Bank, 2006).

*World Charter for Nature*, GA Res 37/7, UN GAOR, 48th plen mtg, UN Doc A/RES/37/7 (28 October 1982).

World Meteorological Organization and Mekong River Commission, 'Establishment of a Hydrological Information System in the Mekong River Basin' (Project Document, World Meteorological Organization and Mekong River Commission, 2006).

World Wildlife Fund Cambodia, *Xayaburi Dam Delay Pending Further Studies is a Positive Step* (8 December 2012) <http://m.cambodia.panda.org/news_cambodia/?202755/Xayaburi-dam-delay-pending-further-studies-is-a-positive-step>.

World Wildlife Fund, *Greater Mekong* <http://wwf.panda.org/what_we_do/where_we_work/ greatermekong/>.

World Wildlife Fund, *Make or Break Time for Mekong River as Xayaburi Dam Decision Looms* (29 November 2011) <http://www.wwf.or.th/en/publications/?202579/Make-or-break-time-for-Mekong-river-as-Xayaburi-dam-decision-looms> .

Worrell, Shane, *Dam Firm Violated Law* (05 June 2013) <http://www.phnompenhpost.com/2013060566083/National/dam-firm-violated-law.html>.

*Xiaowan Hydropower Station Easing Electricity Demand in YN* (16 March 2010) In Kunming <http://en.kunming.cn/index/content/2011-03/16/content_2448960.htm>.

新华社 [Xinhua News Agency],《中国俄罗斯开展跨界水体水质联合检测》[China and Russia Agreed to Jointly Monitor the Water Quality of their Transboundary Waters] (29 June 2007) <http://news.xinhuanet.com/society/2007-06/29/content_6306824.htm>.

新华社 [Xinhua News Agency],《中俄界河水环境联合监测2005年启动》[China and Russia Decided to Deepen Cooperation on Joint Monitoring in 2005] (25 September 2004) <http://news.xinhuanet.com/newscenter/2004-09/25/content_2019525.htm>.

Xinhua News Agency, *China Assigns Mandatory Emission Reduction Tasks to Local Gov'ts, State-owned Enterprises* (20 December 2011) <http://news.xinhuanet.com/english/china/2011-12/20/c_131317697.htm>.

杨洁篪 [Yang, Jiechi],《维护世界和平，促进共同发展：纪念新中国外交60周年》[Maintaining World Peace and Promoting Common Development: Commemoration of the 60th Anniversary of the New China's Diplomacy] (13 October 2009) <http://www.china-embassy.org/chn/zmgx/t619945.htm>.

Yasuda, Yumiko, 'Institutional Influence on NGO Advocacy: Comparative Case Studies of Xayaburi Dam Advocacy' (Speech delivered at the Southeast Asia Seminar Series, University of Sydney, 7 September 2012).

Yu, Xiaojiang, 'Regional Cooperation and Energy Development in the Greater Mekong Sub-region' (2003) 31 *Energy Policy* 1221.

Zaelke, Durwood, Kaniaru, Donald and Kružíková, Eva (eds), *Making Law Work: Environmental Compliance & Sustainable Development* (Cameron May Ltd, International Law Publishers, 2005) vols 1, 2.

Zaelke, Durwood, Stilwell, Matthew and Young, Oran, 'What Reason Demands: Making Law Work for Sustainable Development' in Durwood Zaelke, Donald Kaniaru and Eva Kružíková (eds), *Making Law Work: Environmental Compliance and Sustainable Development* (Cameron May Ltd, International Law Publishers, 2005) vol 1, 29.

Zou, Keyuan, 'Transnational Cooperation for Managing the Control of Environmental Disputes in East Asia' (2004) 16 *Journal of Environmental Law* 341.

# Index